MARCHING HOME

MARCHING HOME

HOME

~Union Veterans~
and Their Unending
Civil War

BRIAN MATTHEW JORDAN

LIVERIGHT PUBLISHING CORPORATION

A Division of W. W. Norton & Company ✢ New York ✢ London

For information about special discounts for bulk purchases, please contact
W. W. Norton Special Sales at specialsales@wwnorton.com or 800-233-4830

Manufacturing by Quad Graphics Fairfield
Book design by Dana Sloan
Production manager: Julia Druskin

ISBN 978-0-87140-781-8

Liveright Publishing Corporation
500 Fifth Avenue, New York, N.Y. 10110
www.wwnorton.com

W. W. Norton & Company Ltd.
Castle House, 75/76 Wells Street, London W1T 3QT

1 2 3 4 5 6 7 8 9 0

FOR MY MOM

CONTENTS

———◦———

MARCHING HOME

WHEN THIS CRUEL WAR WAS "OVER"

The living remain'd and suffer'd, the mother suffer'd,
And the wife and the child and the musing comrade suffer'd,
And the armies that remain'd suffer'd.

—WALT WHITMAN,
"WHEN LILACS LAST IN THE DOORYARD BLOOM'D"

O N A HUMID July afternoon in 1913, a knot of Union veterans gathered near the spot where the low stone fence that rambled down Gettysburg's Cemetery Ridge pointed sharply east. Here, a half century before, the men of the Union army had repulsed nine stubborn brigades of gray-clad troops during the cataclysmic battle's final act. Now, the bewhiskered men who had worn the blue waited for their enemy once more, supporting their wobbly, seventy-year old frames with gold-tipped hickory canes. The bronze Grand Army of the Republic badges proudly affixed to their lapels (they were cast from melted rebel cannon tubes) glinted as they caught the blistering sun of a Pennsylvania summer.

From just behind the stone wall, the Union veterans watched as the ex-Confederates crested the ridge. The passing of five decades had audibly diminished the ferocity of the old "rebel yell," now just a coarse snarl. When the southerners reached the wall, the blue-coated men extended

their wrinkled hands and doffed their campaign hats in a gesture of conciliation. With only blissful memories of the war, Union veterans absolved
their former enemies and basked in the glow of a nation reunited. Later
that evening, huddled around the sparks of a summer campfire, Lincoln's
hale troops swapped nostalgic tales of the old army days. As they puffed
on pungent cigars, wreaths of white smoke curling into the air, it was difficult—indeed, it was nearly impossible—to imagine that these jolly old
men had shouldered muskets in a bloody civil war.

⋯═◉═⋯

Americans are very familiar with romanticized scenes like this one,
mounted in dusty old scrapbooks and captured on dozens of creaky news-
reels. For generations, the presumption has been that the survivors of the
Union armies beat a hasty retreat from the Civil War; that victory, unlike
defeat, was essentially painless; and that time mended, like most things, the
war's most horrible injuries. Popular notions persist that Union veterans
returned to northern society awed, not beguiled, by the past. To be sure,
many scholars have enthusiastically embraced historian Gerald F. Linderman's contention that Union soldiers paid "as little heed as possible to the
memories of war." According to Linderman, Union veterans permitted
their "martial past" to simply fade away. They "hibernated" for decades after
the war, only to reemerge in the late nineteenth century as nostalgic
heroes—cherished heirlooms who willingly relinquished to their former
enemies the war's meaning and legacy. Working from this premise, many
observers have derided Union veterans as little more than effete old men
who, after returning home and putting their hands to the plow, abandoned
the fledgling promise of "a new birth of freedom." One leading historian
writes that by the 1890s, it was "easy for Northern veterans to accept
Southern claims that the war was really about arcane constitutional issues."[1]

Indeed, despite all that has been written about the American Civil
War, Union veterans remain eccentric caricatures lurking in the unwar-

ranted shadows of historical obscurity—as distant and unfamiliar to us as they were to those who lived in post–Civil War America. Although a few historians have trailed the blue-coated armies home from Appomattox (most often by analyzing their fraternal rituals, their infamous pension lobbying, and their reunions, parades, and monuments), none have penetrated the most intimate human details of their lives.[2]

Much of what we know—or think we know—about Union veterans is informed by a sprawling literature on common soldiers. For generations, historians have revered Billy Yank, marveling at his uncommon sense of duty, his fearsome patriotism, and his principled devotion to the Union cause. Historian Chandra Manning has even suggested that the blue-coated armies were "abolitionized" by their experiences in battle. Encountering firsthand the cruel landscape of slavery, she insists, helped to sustain the fighting spirit of the rank and file—even the resolve of those troops billeted in the sun-baked Virginia trenches of the war's final year. Esteeming the men who, with clenched jaw and burnished bayonet, triumphed over their rebel enemies, historians have supposed that the Union soldier was undoubtedly prepared for the peace. Consummate citizen-soldiers steeped in the classical republicanism of their fathers and grandfathers—taught to be upright, virtuous, and self-sacrificing—they returned to their homes demanding no reward.[3]

Yet yellowed veterans' newspapers, soldiers' home records, disability pension files, and personal manuscripts chillingly demonstrate that even victory had a price—that the terror of this unprecedented war long outlived the stacking of arms at Appomattox. As the West Point military scientist Lieutenant Colonel Dave Grossman has argued so persuasively, abandoning the precepts of peace for the rigors of war—learning how to kill and maim—is psychologically demanding even for soldiers who emerge from battle victorious and unscathed. Afflicted with guilt, sorrow, and purposelessness, Union soldiers considered homecoming a task as onerous and demanding as any military campaign. Billy Yank often stumbled home after guzzling gallons of rum in dodgy grogshops. Many thousands returned north hopelessly addicted to the laudanum they had first sampled in the Civil War field hospital. Especially for those sporting empty sleeves or staggering along with irksome and ill-fitting wooden legs, joblessness, vagrancy, and penury loomed. Vivid nightmares of the picket post and the prison pen mocked any proclamation of peace—no matter how fiercely coveted. And, worst of all, the contemptuous sneers of northern civilians, combined as they were with mounting evidence that the southern rebellion was not yet snuffed out, urged these men to ask what their war had achieved after all. Postwar society could reach no compromise about how—or even if—the massive human costs of the war should be handled, and the federal government proved both ideologically and infrastructurally ill equipped to mitigate the challenges of homecoming. The stage was set for the veterans' decades-long struggle to ensure that the scope and significance of their sacrifices would not be forgotten.[4]

After the shock of Shiloh, the carnage of Antietam, and the horrors of the Wilderness, hundreds of thousands of ordinary men would never be the same again. They peopled a living "republic of suffering." The twinge of a "phantom limb," the decades-old gunshot wound that wept pus, and the gaunt faces of Andersonville survivors ensured that the war's costs could not be counted in crowded cemeteries alone. Union veterans endured the tragedy of the American Civil War until they, too, answered the final roll call. Suspended between the dead and the living, the rest of their days were disturbed by memories of the war. "The dead come back and live with us," Oliver Wendell Holmes once declared. "I see them now, more than I can number, as once I saw them on earth."[5]

⋆⟞◉⟝⋆

Most Civil War histories end where this one begins—in the harried and uncertain weeks after Appomattox. During the final year of the conflict, coiled in a maze of crude trenches, the Union armies waged grueling military campaigns in Virginia, Georgia, and the Carolinas—inflicting crushing losses. Unable to replenish the thousands of men he lost to battle, disease, and desertion, on April 9, 1865—Palm Sunday—Robert E. Lee met a begrimed Ulysses S. Grant in Wilmer McLean's front parlor and surrendered the tattered remnants of his Army of Northern Virginia. Northerners indulged in an hour of jubilation as church steeples announced everywhere the long-awaited news. "Gloria in Excelcis Deo!" the New York lawyer George Templeton Strong triumphantly scrawled in his diary. A little more than two weeks later, Joseph Eggleston Johnston, commanding the now forlorn rebel forces in North Carolina, capitulated to his federal counterpart, the rough-hewn William Tecumseh Sherman, near Durham Station. Within the month, victorious brigades of blue-coated soldiers were tramping toward Washington City, where they would parade down Pennsylvania Avenue in the final performance of the war.[6]

All knew that Confederate defeat ensured the death of chattel slavery, but the implications of Union victory were—despite the euphoria in the streets—not nearly as transparent. Although Billy Yank had repeatedly professed his allegiance to liberty, freedom, and self-government, wartime northerners ultimately achieved little consensus about the meaning of such lofty ideas. Cleaved by intense social and political divisions, the North hardly maintained a united front during the war. Draft dodging, backbiting, and partisan sniping divided communities frazzled by an increasingly unpopular conflict. At the same time, the South offered little reassurance that it would acquiesce to any brokered peace. The unprecedented assassination of a president, cruel race riots in Memphis and New Orleans, and reports of hooded terror throughout the states of the former Confederacy left Union ex-soldiers rather unconvinced that the war's noble work had been finished. Fears that these flickers of violence would ignite a new rebellion were all too real. In May 1865, one Illinoisan, observing the "sin, crime, wrong, injustice & demoralization" all around him, concluded that he could not "see any light ahead to give me hopes of the continuance of republican institutions, such as we once enjoyed." From the fighting ranks, the future loomed dim, undecided. Unable, then, to "look somewhat com-placently on the war," Union veterans resolved to define the peace and to remind the nation of their unprecedented sacrifices.[7]

But beginning almost immediately after Appomattox, northern civil-ians sought to put the war behind them. By 1865, many northerners could do little more than declare victory if they sought broad agreement. Wearied of news from the front and eager to embrace the defeated South, they became stagehands for the "romance of reunion," peddling a sani-tized and depoliticized narrative of the war. To be sure, northerners were cognizant of the conflict's horrors; after all, lengthy casualty lists bearing the names of fathers, husbands, and sons consumed newspaper columns, and Mathew Brady's glass plates brought home the grisly realities of the battlefield. Yet, unlike their southern counterparts, northerners did not endure the war's "democracy of devastation"; they experienced the rebel-lion at great physical distance. The only significant battle fought in the North occurred fewer than a dozen miles above the Mason-Dixon Line, and the threat of invasion was rarely made in earnest. Battle remained something imagined and—more often than not—idealized. There existed "no significant conveyer of information about the nature of combat." Indeed, some angst-ridden contemporaries wondered if immoderate and profiteering northern civilians were even "worthy" of victory.[8]

To be sure, while the Confederate troops had quite literally defended their hearths and homes, Union soldiers had waged a war of ideas that seemed especially removed from the immediate needs of the northern homefront. Having privileged national integrity over self-interest throughout the war, and feeling no particular sympathy for the legions of newly freed African-American slaves, northern civilians ambled into the postwar ready to let bygones be bygones. Even the most enlightened abo-litionists and progressive reformers, after decades of labor-intensive agita-tion, staggered away from the war rather breathless. Moreover, by vindicating "free labor" and oiling the engine of commerce, the war had—

however incongruously—encouraged northern civilians to subordinate the past to the dazzling promises of future prosperity. Almost overnight, sectionalism yielded to the hum of industry—to violent labor disputes, seething class conflict, and the growing pains of empire.[9]

Thus while southern civilians marinated in the backward-looking mythology of the Lost Cause, northerners deemed Union veterans impossible nuisances who, by obsessing over their past, merely threatened the future and all of its possibilities. Although Johnny Reb faced the humiliation of defeat, the personal affront of emancipation, and the shame of financial ruin, he could at least rest assured that most white southerners eulogized his sacrifices and perpetuated his memory. While not easily explained, defeat was nonetheless effortlessly defined. Billy Yank, on the other hand, had to live within the redeeming narrative that northern civilians wanted to believe in—a narrative that often denied the tough realities and lingering consequences of Civil War soldiering. In short, Union veterans won the Civil War only to return home to another one.[10]

By the time they met their former enemies on Cemetery Ridge that sweltering summer of 1913 then, Grand Army men were losing not only that war, but also their battle with mortality. Thousands died as the wards of county poorhouses, state insane asylums, and squalid soldiers' homes. The "unpayable debt" that the republic owed its veterans went literally unpaid—or was paid grudgingly amid a storm of withering skepticism. And an endless parade of cultural and literary productions had so erased the differences between the contending armies that the Civil War could masquerade as a valiant struggle with only fortunate results. Still, so long as Union veterans lived, there remained some compelling reminder of the war—some undeniable challenge to the public's self-imposed amnesia.

⊷⇒◉⇐⊷

In his autobiography, Bruce Catton, the most widely read Civil War historian of the mid twentieth century, recalled the stooped and furrowed company of Union veterans who lived in Benzonia, the remote Michigan village of his boyhood. Most belonged to the Edward Case Post of the Grand Army of the Republic, the nation's largest fraternal order for northern soldiers. "On formal occasions they wore blue uniforms with brass buttons and black campaign hats," he wrote admiringly. "They had an unassuming natural dignity in old age." In 1916, the Case Post hosted Robert Henry Hendershot, an enterprising Michigan veteran who, with son J.C. in tow, crisscrossed the country to perform his "carefully rehearsed" and "highly specialized" stage routine, "The Drummer Boy of the Rappahannock." Young Catton was one of the few nonveterans in the crowd. "He and his partner ran through their regular line of jokes, anecdotes and reminiscences, and they came at last to the big set piece of the performance—the reproduction, on a taut drumhead, by a drummer boy grown gray with years, of the mighty sound and tumult of a Civil War battle."[11]

With machine guns "stuttering" on the Western Front, it was difficult not to conclude, as Catton did, that his "gallant old Civil War veterans had been left behind by time." Shiloh was a world away from the Somme. On the other hand, those bearded old soldiers had never really belonged to the present. After Appomattox, they lived on "completely in the past." "There was something faintly pathetic about these lonely old men," Catton later reflected, adding a lament that as a youngster, he "never saw the pathos."[12]

But even today, as soldiers return home from new and more complex wars farther away and more difficult to imagine, we still have trouble seeing the pathos of American veteranhood. More than 26,000 veterans of the wars in Iraq and Afghanistan dwell in homeless shelters; thousands suffering from posttraumatic stress and traumatic brain injuries have yielded to drugs and alcohol; divorce and suicide rates among recent veterans have reached record highs; and bureaucratic delays have kept some veterans waiting impatiently for promised benefits. These veterans, too, are fighting an unending war. And like their forerunners in blue, they will ensure that debates over the meaning of war will be long, difficult, and complex.[13]

CHAPTER 1

A DAY FOR SONGS AND CONTESTS

Rousing their zeal,
their curiosity, each and every man, and soon enough
the assembly seats were filled with people thronging,
gazing in wonder at the seasoned man of war.

—HOMER, *THE ODYSSEY*[1]

THE VOLLEYS OF thunder continued well into the evening, but with sunrise the clouds broke, leaving behind an unbroken canvas of blue. The puddles slowly vanished, though many of Washington's wagon-rutted streets and narrow alleys were now porridge. It was before seven o'clock in the morning and, already, thousands of "well clad" spectators, many gripping green wreaths and sweet-smelling bouquets, were collecting along Pennsylvania Avenue's freshly paved footways. A "seething mass of humanity" huddled in garret windows, stood on rooftops, and leaned over balconies attempting to get a view of the street. Even "lamp posts, trees, and telegraph poles," one bemused Michigander recalled, had spectators "clinging to them." Congressmen and cabinet members, of course, did not contend with the crowds; they took advantage of a sturdy, timber platform erected on the lawn of the President's House. The private homes and public buildings nearby were adorned with aromatic "ribbons of evergreen," and proudly unfurled flags snapped sprightly in the humid May breeze. Burly and bewhiskered Benjamin Brown French, the commissioner of public buildings, festooned his East Capitol Street home with an American flag and affixed a golden eagle to his front door. He selected a verse from Isaiah ("Speak ye comfortably to Jerusalem, and cry unto her that her warfare is accomplished, that her inquiry is pardoned") and placed it on a placard facing the street.[2]

To honor the returning soldiers, the Board of Trustees of the Public Schools granted the pupils of the capital city a welcome reprieve from their studies on Tuesday, May 23, and Wednesday, May 24, insisting that the children "appropriately testify their gratitude to the soldiers, devotion to their country, and joy at the return of peace." And so minutes before nine o'clock, several thousand local grammar- and intermediate-school students—the boys donning hemmed white pants and navy blue jackets, the girls attired in their white calico dresses—assembled on the north end of the Capitol beneath a carefully lettered canvas banner welcoming THE HEROES OF THE REPUBLIC. They, too, toted bouquets, which they would soon distribute to the parading columns. Students from the Wallach School hoisted an American flag. More "adventurous and foolhardy," other school-age boys, white and black, scaled the shade trees to steal more commanding views. From the groaning maple limbs, they caught glimpses of Maryland Avenue, where blue-coated soldiers impatiently stirred as they formed for one, final time a single marching column behind the purple silk headquarters flag of Major General George Gordon Meade's Army of the Potomac.[3]

Other banners proudly spanned Pennsylvania Avenue. It was a dazzling display. For the first time in four, long years, Washington was at peace; the cloud of war had been lifted. Every spectator, it seemed, stood ready to extol the "unfaltering courage" and "steady resolution" of the hale warriors who had, at long last, suppressed the stubborn southern rebellion. WELCOME, BRAVE SOLDIERS! one placard read. UNION AND FREEDOM FOR-

EVER, boasted another. ALL HONOR TO THE BRAVE AND GALLANT DEFEND-
ERS OF OUR COUNTRY. Perhaps the most impressive ensign was the panel
adorning the thick marble walls of the stately columned Treasury Build-
ing. Adorned with flowers, it announced in oversized gold lettering: THE
ONLY NATIONAL DEBT WE CAN NEVER REPAY IS THE DEBT WE OWE OUR
VICTORIOUS UNION SOLDIERS.[4]

The troops breakfasted on hardtack and weak coffee in the wee hours of
the morning (even victory could not improve army rations), stowed their
knapsacks in camp, and then moved out for Washington City. They gathered along Maryland Avenue, where large barrels brimming with fresh
drinking water were placed between Seventh and Third Streets to relieve
thirsty soldiers before the more than two-mile procession. The parade
would take them around the Capitol Building and down Pennsylvania
Avenue to the canopied dais at the President's House where, by now,
President Andrew Johnson and his pin-striped cabinet, Generals Grant
and Sherman, a dozen senators, and seven northern governors were in
place. At nine o'clock, the soldiers received orders to step off. General
Meade, his headquarters staff, and their escort, a squadron of the First
Massachusetts Cavalry, stepped off first—followed by the cavalry corps,
the provost marshal's brigade, the engineers, and then three divisions of
the Ninth Corps. The crowds filled the air with their wild applause. Many
of the spectators had traveled several days to witness the review, and they
delighted in the festive atmosphere—a glittering display of war's supposed
splendor. To be sure, none of the onlookers had ever seen so many uni-
formed soldiers congregated in one place. "What a magnificent pageant
was presented to the world by those brave heroes," wrote a professor from
the Theological Seminary in Lancaster, Pennsylvania, who had traveled
down to Washington for what he called the "inestimable privilege" of
"beholding the entire grand display." "The sight," wrote a Granite State

veteran named Thomas Leonard Livermore, "was worth coming from the ends of the world to see."[5]

For six hours each day, the hardened ranks of blue-coated regiments strode down the nation's avenue. For six hours each day advanced the men whose wearied steps, anguished sighs, and frayed regimental standards testified eloquently to the unprecedented horror through which they had passed. "Two divisions marching and returning to march past again would have created *almost* as grand an exhibition as ours of to-day," a Maine veteran named John Mead Gould jotted in his diary. "But to see the particular troops that had fought here and there, and to see the famous generals, these were worthwhile to be sure." "It was a splendid scene, such as never will be seen in our land again," commented Lyman Jackman, the lanky, long-faced, twenty-seven-year-old New Hampshire native who had marked time in three hellish southern prisons during the war.[6]

Benjamin French might have had the best view of all. He took two houseguests visiting from Columbus, Ohio, up to the gleaming new dome crowning the Capitol, from which they could inspect the length of Pennsylvania Avenue, "literally filled with troops." French supposed that there were "more than 50,000 [men] in sight at one time." It was this panorama of the army "swarming like bees everywhere" that John Gould yearned for from the ranks; the marchers were unable to see much beyond the row of troops immediately ahead. "The grand evil was that no one could see the combined army," he grumbled. "At no point could the eye take in more than eight or ten thousand troops and this only by standing at the head or foot of the column in view." "I did not see a fiftieth part of the show myself," he concluded.[7]

As the blue columns tramped up Maryland Avenue toward the Capitol, the school children, led by Professor Daniel, greeted the troops with a stirring rendition of "The Battle Cry of Freedom." Then, the veterans curled down the subtle slopes of Capitol Hill, and as they went on, "rolling like a mighty river," the spectators laughed, cheered, and applauded. With innocent delight, the crowds waved handkerchiefs and miniature flags, offered passing soldiers pitchers of cold water, and adorned generals' horses and their riders with floral garlands. As the blue lines bent around the curve at Fifteenth Street, a platform of nearly five hundred middle-aged spectators took up the strains of Julia Ward Howe's "The Battle Hymn of the Republic." "I could not keep back my tears," Gould remembered.[8]

Just beyond the serenade, the troops filed past the reviewing stand, which was adorned with pots of azaleas in full bloom and wooden slats emblazoned with the names of the great victories of Union armies: Shiloh, South Mountain, Antietam, Gettysburg, Vicksburg, Atlanta, and Richmond. General Meade, the victor of Gettysburg, dismounted upon reaching the platform so that he might offer one last salute to his men. Soon, the ranks and files would reach Seventeenth Street, where veteran-hood awaited. As one Vermont volunteer observed, these men who had experienced many a hard-fought campaign, leaving behind a litany of dead to contend with the record of their deeds, were citizens once more.[9]

⁕⟞◉⟝⁕

The size of the crowd ballooned overnight as Washington-bound trains delivered another 10,000 civilians anxiously yearning to witness the Grand Review. Most of the fresh arrivals could not find a vacant hotel room or boardinghouse for miles. But these men and women were hardly disheartened, hoping only to catch a parting glimpse of those "brave veterans"—the fortunate survivors who had fought "to preserve the liberties for which their fathers fought so well." The crowds were especially electrified, for the second day of the review would be devoted to the victorious western armies—those strapping and unrefined men who had marched from Atlanta to the sea. The revelry prevailed throughout the evening as amateur bands spontaneously took up patriotic airs, including at least one rendition of "Dixie."[10]

The next morning, the first sight of "Uncle Billy" Sherman prompted prolonged applause. "It was such a shout of unalloyed joy," one Ohio infantry captain remembered. Sherman, whose square jaw was forested by his trademark reddish stubble, removed his campaign hat, waving it in response to the crowds. Major General Oliver Otis Howard, who had been tapped to be the commissioner of the Freedmen's Bureau, rode at his side, prominently displaying his memento of the battle of Fair Oaks—an empty right coat sleeve. Not far behind, at the head of the Fifteenth Corps, rode General John Alexander Logan from Illinois. "For six hours and a half," Sherman remembered, "that strong tread of the Army of the West resounded along Pennsylvania Avenue." Moving "with the regularity of a pendulum," division after division of the Fifteenth, Seventeenth, Twentieth, and Fourteenth corps passed, their muskets resembling "a solid mass of steel." "It looked like a rolling river of steel glinting, glistening, and glittering till the dazzled eye was forced to seek relief by turning from the scene," one awed Pennsylvanian wrote. At least six ambulances trailed each division, as did a "very amusing and quite mirth provoking" mélange of horses, army mules, milch cows, goats, pigs, dogs, roosters, and even opossums. As though they were performers in a pageant, newly freed men, women, and children also followed along in their "pitiable" garb, generating spiteful commentary from many observers. In front of Willard's Hotel, as bands fittingly took up "Marching Through Georgia," an "especially jubilant" contingent of Iowans presented Brigadier General William Worth Belknap, riding at the head of his Iowa Brigade veterans, with a fresh bouquet.[11]

And then, almost as swiftly as it began, the splendid procession was over. Sixty-five thousand of Sherman's exhausted, foot-sore veterans (in sweltering temperatures, they had marched some 2,000 miles through Georgia and the Carolinas before their arrival in Washington), crossed the Long Bridge and pitched their well-worn Sibleys on the heights above the capital city. Now began the impatient wait for mustering out, for the long journey home.[12]

◦━◉◉━◦

Both days of the review, the cheers of the crowds were punctuated by the staccato of telegraphs feverishly clicking away colorful descriptions of the review to newspapers across the country. "The Grand Review of the armies at Washington City yesterday was, undoubtedly, the most magnificent military demonstration that ever took place in this country, and, perhaps, the largest that ever took place in any country," crowed the *Daily Ohio Statesman*. The *Hartford Daily Courant* reported that the day was "beautiful beyond description" and that "everything" was "in most perfect order." It was a "grand affair," the "greatest which has ever taken place on this continent," the *Albany Evening Journal* concurred. A handsome engraving of the troops rounding the corner at Fifteenth Street as they made "their triumphant return" consumed the *Philadelphia Inquirer*'s front page, above the fold. The *Daily National Intelligencer* concluded confidently that, "with the grand review of the great armies of the republic, it may be assumed that the curtain has fallen on the tragedy of our civil war." Only one newspaper correspondent, Lois Bryan Adams, a shrewd reporter and Washington clerk who filed her columns with the *Detroit Advertiser*, seemed troubled that the rejoicing crowds did not earnestly reflect on the war's meaning. "[The soldiers] were cheered, as they deserved to be," she explained, "but oh, how poor, how empty does all this pageantry and cheering seem." "Shouts and songs and fading flowers," she continued, "seem almost like mockery when offered to such men who have accomplished a work so grand." Yet even someone as thoughtful and perceptive as Adams was helpless to recommend "what else" these crowds might have offered.[13]

Now that the fighting appeared to be over, most enlisted men could discern no good reason for a formal military review. They were "little impressed" by the pomp and circumstance. "The nerves of the soldiery had not yet recovered from their tremor of the battle charge," one Wisconsin veteran insisted. He recalled that on the second day of the review, as Sherman's armies passed between "two rows of admiring humanity stretched for a mile on either side," the veterans of New Hope Church and Bentonville marched "in perfunctory silence." "They heard with indifference the cheers at their automatic maneuvers," he explained. "To them this magnificent display which so impressed the thousands who had not been in the war, was merely the last ordered duty in a long, arduous and deadly struggle in which they had triumphed and from which they were only too glad to get away." "As for the soldiers themselves, grand pageantry in the line of reviews had 'played out,'" veteran John Ritchey Kinnear observed candidly. "What was charming to the assembled multitude was no joyous affair [for us]." Corporal William B. Westervelt of the 27th New York Volunteers, for example, thought the entire parade "border[ed] strongly on the ridiculous."[14]

For the veterans, the Grand Review stirred a cauldron of conflicting emotions. "These were, indeed, days of joy and gladness," one ex-soldier maintained, "but under all ran a current of sadness." For one, the blue-coated columns had made a most sobering march to Washington, necessarily tramping over old battlefields still littered with the detritus of war. The experience haunted them. The week before the review, William Barron, a New Hampshire soldier, "spent the night at a Negros Shanty" on the Seven Pines battleground still strewn with bleached bones. The next day, he visited "the field of Coal Harbor, where many Thousands of our Brave Boys were murdered in cold blood." "Nothing remains to be seen," he remarked, "but bones and the ruins of a Grand Army." When the men of the 129th Illinois halted for dinner near Spotsylvania Court House on May 15, Joshua Rilea roamed into the eerie trenches and stumbled over the stiffened bodies of three Union soldiers. Later that night, when Rilea and his comrades pitched their tents just up the road on the old Chancellorsville battleground, they happened upon "several more" unburied soldiers. On the march to the review, Edmund Spencer Packard of the 31st Wisconsin was equally astounded by the spectacle of Chancellorsville. "Our men lay on top o[f] the ground by the hundred, and most of those that were buried are in sight now, for the dirt which merely covered them has washed off," he confided to his diary. Packard, like many of his fellow veterans, combed the battlefields for relics that would attest to the horrors unspeakably etched into the folds of their memories. The immediate and easily overlooked context of the Grand Review for the rank and file, then, was a visceral encounter with the grim consequences of the war—and with the harassing guilt of survival. One soldier recalled that as he marched down Pennsylvania Avenue, "memories of comrades slain, of messmates torn and maimed, of friends gone hence through war's sad privations," flooded his mind and "chilled" his heart. "The last passing," one Pennsylvania lieutenant wrote, "evoked sad memories—the defeats at First and Second Manassas, the strip of wall at Fredericksburg, the crimson Wheatfield at Gettysburg, the bloody fields of Spotsylvania, and the dead line at Cold Harbor, which has claimed far more gallant warriors than those who marched before the reviewing stands."[15]

The procession was also painful because the soldiers realized that they would soon be parting with cherished comrades—men who had cheered and inspired them, who had tended to their bodies and souls in camp and battle. According to one Massachusetts veteran, bidding farewell to wartime companions rendered the review an assignment in which there was "no little bitter mingled with the sweet." The sudden storm of emotion was bewildering. "My head is fuddled yet from all I seen and felt yesterday in Washington," Corporal Patrick Sloan of the 90th Illinois Volunteers wrote. "Don't misunderstand that I was drunk," he advised his wife. "I tasted nothing Stronger than water but it was my feelings . . . like many others I could not control them." One veteran, lost in thought, irritated at the cheering crowds, and profoundly disenchanted upon his first glimpse of the nation's adolescent capital, resolved that "a great many lives had been foolishly sacrificed to keep Washington out of the hands of the rebels."[16]

To be sure, for so many soldiers, the absence of the dead was particularly palpable as they strode down Pennsylvania Avenue, reaping laurels for battles won with the blood of their dead comrades. "Look up!" Henry N. Evans implored. "*There* is a grander review! Look up! See the hosts assembling upon the parade ground of the heavens. What mighty army is above!" While marveling at the endless rows of blue coats, Lieutenant Colonel Theodore Lyman, who served as General Meade's chief of staff during the war, perhaps inevitably visualized how much grander the demonstration might have appeared if only the organizers could have resurrected the dead. "Where, on the day of the great review, were Reynolds and Reno, Kearny and Rodman, Whipple and Berry, Stevens and Bayard, Rice and Wadsworth, Zook and Alexander Hays, Weed and Vincent, Taylor and Rodman, Stevenson and Smythe?" demanded General Francis Amasa Walker years later at an army reunion near Orange, New Jersey. "Had the eye of the spirit been opened upon that 23rd of May, the spectator would have seen by the side of each man who moved firmly and proudly in the victorious column three wounded and crippled men, limping and stumbling in their eager desire to keep up with their more fortunate comrades, while with the four stalked one pale ghost."[17]

For others, it was the absence of President Lincoln that was most upsetting. The parade route was only blocks away from Ford's Theater, where Booth's bullet had martyred the president just forty days before, and many public buildings were still swaddled in black mourning crepe. "The thought of the martyred President obtruded itself in every mind," Albion Tourgée recalled in the regimental history that he penned for the 105th Ohio Volunteers. "The fact that he would not enjoy their triumph robbed it of no little of its sweetness." To be sure, many of the parading soldiers were the very men who only weeks before had sworn "violent retribution" on the perpetrators of the unprecedented crime. "The feeling in the Army among the soldiers is intense in the extreme," Hervey Eaton reported in the days after the assassination. "I have heard men say, that if they ever got into battle again, they never would *take any more prisoners.*" With each step down Pennsylvania Avenue, their indignation swelled. "Oh, that our beloved President, our 'Father Abraham' might have been spared to see his boys come marching home," one Wisconsin volunteer lamented.[18]

Shortly after the review, the poet Bret Harte captured these haunting sentiments in his poignant verse, imagining a "second review" of the miraculously restored armies of the republic. The marching columns not only included the dead, but also, quite tellingly, the many brigades of African-American soldiers excluded from the first review: "And there came the nameless dead,—the men / Who perished in the fever-swamp and fen / The slowly-starved of the prison pen; / And marching beside the others, / Came the dusky martyrs of Pillow's fight, / With limbs enfranchised and bearing bright; / I thought—perhaps 'twas the pale moonlight— / They looked as white as their brothers!" In the coming decades, in a multitude of ways, Union veterans would continue to negotiate the mysterious shadow world between the living and the dead.[19]

⟶⊶◉⊷⟵

For still other veterans, the review was nothing more than an irksome delay on the way home. When rumors of the procession began circling in the federal camps in early May, Private Oscar Cram of the 11th Massachusetts wrote to his wife, Ellen, that he hoped the impending parade would be over rather quickly. "I expect there will be a big time reviewing [the troops] in Washington in a few days and the sooner they do it the sooner we shall get home." Tourgée noted that the review's only charm for many homesick soldiers was the admittedly faint prospect of detecting a "familiar face" or "some loved eye" in the crowd. New York heavy artillerist Charles Edgar Abbey, his face disfigured by his Spotsylvania wound, passed hurriedly over the Grand Review in his diary, barely affording it a mention, as did an acutely demoralized ex-soldier named Stephen P. Chase. "My mind is on home," he wrote, indifferent to the triumphant mood encircling him. "My mind is on home and I am real discontented." Unlike the admiring civilian masses, Chase sensed that the pious proclamations of Union "victory" were imprudent. "I used to think I would be perfectly happy when the war was over, but I am not," he confessed rather incredulously to his pocket diary. He was so anxious to return home to his loved ones that he threatened on one occasion to leave the army without his discharge papers—something "hundreds" of his fellow soldiers would do in the coming weeks. The surgeon of a Connecticut regiment marking time in Goldsboro, North Carolina, noted that "home on the brain" was, among his troopers, the latest "epidemic of a most violent form."[20]

Much unlike the satisfaction and immodesty that filled the hearts of the crowds in Washington, it was a chastening sense of loss and uncertainty that seized Chase and his comrades—and would not let them go. "I find I cannot sit still as I could before the war," John Gould observed. George Shuman confessed to his young bride, Fannie, that he did not know "what to do" with himself now that the constant marching and maneuvering had ended, but assured her that he would try to avoid demon rum. "I have not got into the habit of *ruming* through the County as some others & I will try to keep out of the habit as I think it is verry demoralizing." The tempo of peacetime was odd and unfamiliar. "All was stilled," drummer boy Delavan Miller observed years later as he contemplated the "aural history" of the rebellion. "No more lying behind the hastily thrown up breastworks, listening to the booming cannon, screaming shells and waiting for the command 'forward!' No more rumbling of the artillery along the roads. No clanking of sabers as the cavalry dashed by. No bugle calls. No noise of fife and drum." According to Miller, the piercing "still-ness" after four years of war was enough to "almost startle one."[21]

However incongruously, many soldiers were discomfited by the peace and desperate to reproduce the familiar "zip, zip, zip" of musketry. Some decided to take matters into their own hands and made "a great game" of placing spare percussion caps on active railroad tracks. Former artillerists outwitted their comrades by deploying friction primers along the rails; they sounded "almost as loud as a pistol" when crushed beneath the weight of a passing locomotive. Lyman Jackman remembered that one afternoon, shortly after the Grand Review, the boys of his 6th New Hampshire Regiment determined to "make a stir in camp." Discovering several unexploded shells lying around, the veterans buried one in the ground. After concealing the mortar with loose earth, the men laid "a train of powder to it," ensuring the anxiously anticipated discharge. When the powder train was fired, the shell detonated, "with a noise that roused the whole camp." A horse grazing nearby went tumbling to the ground, and an adjacent stack of muskets exploded. "All rushed out," Jackman recalled, "but all that could be seen was a smoking hole in the ground about large enough to take in a small cottage."[22]

For other veterans, even emulating the sounds of battle was altogether insufficient. Jacob Harrison Allspaugh, an Ohio private, recalled that one June afternoon in 1865, the boys of his brigade—Colonel Morton Hunter's—decided to feign a battle charge and began firing their muskets "all over" camp. "Our boys formed a line of battle when on came the 17th [Ohio] and our boys opened on them," he remembered. "A terrible fight ensued and for an hour the noise and yells . . . were kept up." The skirmish was "fun" and great "sport" until an enlisted man from the 82nd Indiana was shot in the leg and very seriously injured.[23]

Regimental and company officers devoted little serious attention to these and similar shenanigans, explaining them away as the work of physically and mentally exhausted soldiers exhaling at the end of a trying war.

Yet these excuses—and the genuine yearning of many soldiers to return home—masked profound reservations among veterans about their aptitude for life beyond the battlefield. In a letter mailed home to Maine, tucked in a black-rimmed envelope mourning President Lincoln, a soldier named W. Frank Cox captured this tension perfectly. "I had rather go home then to go any wh[e]re else from here," he began, "but I don't for I am to[o] leazy to work." Cox estimated that "half of the boys want to stay [in the army] very bad." Expressing fear of and contempt for civilian life, these men candidly registered their preference for "the sound of Cannons and rifles."[24]

Gould, for instance, despite bouts of homesickness, noted that nothing was "so demoralizing . . . as the prospect of going home." "The prospect of soon being a citizen," he noted, "discouraged both the officers and men." "Shall not we all grow lazy as drones and throw away the manliness that hard service has forced upon us?" he asked. Gould explained that he was "hungering for some hard work to do, yet I have not the slightest desire to work, to read, or talk." "These are the hardest days I have ever lived . . . I feel very stupid and all worn out." "Four years of fighting, of defeat and victory, had hardened many of them into warriors," the muckraking journalist Ida M. Tarbell remarked, "and many of them loved their trade." Between battles, soldiers notoriously thirsted for the adrenaline of the firing line. "No man who has once learned to love war," she continued, "steps back to a civilian's life with a whole heart." And so it was that when he arrived at the moment of discharge in his military memoir, Francis T. Moore, the captain of an Illinois cavalry squadron, could not determine if he had been "reduced, or elevated to the rank of citizenship."[25]

For one, the prospect of resuming intimate relationships back home was startling. William Henry Church, a handsome Wisconsin lieutenant who fought and was wounded in the storied ranks of the Iron Brigade, wondered if he could ever be a desirable man again. In a June letter to his wife, Ella, the soldier readied her for his return, and for the "despondency, which will creep over me at times." "Don't you almost wish you had not married?" Church queried in another letter. "Then, you know, you could have some gay young beau to wait upon you, and escort you around to all the places of amusement, and you would be free."[26]

Sometimes the seemingly inexplicable desire to remain in the ranks was fueled by the harassing feeling that the war's work was unfinished. "I am not in good humor with Rebles yet," Ohioan Sam Evans explained to his father, Andrew, from camp in Memphis, Tennessee, in May 1865. "They have caused too many [losses of] valuable life to be easily forgotten . . . I have something more to do yet. Then I can come home and stay in peace." Henry Weldo Hart insisted that the former rebels were "yet desirous of and willing to fight for independence." "I have believed and do now firmly believe that they will fight again as soon as they can get strength," he warned his wife. "I see no indications of true allegiance." For his part, the New Hampshire volunteer Arlon S. Atherton wished only that he could "get hold of some of [the rebel] leaders" so as to "make an example [out] of them."[27]

But there would be no opportunities for the kind of justice that these soldiers hoped to exact; the knots of blue-coated men marooned in dozens of squalid army camps made that palpably, painfully evident. "Time does not fly as fast now as it did when I was in active service," William Barron sighed. "There is not that excitement to keep a soldier awake." Boredom was a most dreadful affliction. "I can't keep still long enough to eat my dinner," one Pennsylvania cavalryman demurred. "I am afraid some of us will get nearly crazy if our officers don't sober up a little and send us home." Chronic rumors of discharge day did little for morale and even less for discipline. "The boys grumble considerably over 'drill,' and say they 'can't see the point,'" the uneasy and impatient quartermaster of the 117th Illinois Volunteers, Henry Clay Fike, wrote to his wife from the regiment's camp near Montgomery, Alabama. Nor were rations any reward. "They don't feed us half as well as they did at Petersburg," one soldier carped. "We thought then that the rations were small enough, but here they don't even give us vinegar to kill the taste of their stinking meat."[28]

Significantly, some restless volunteers began to equate their military experiences with confinement. Without rebels to fight, they thought themselves captives, foolishly detained by a domineering government. "I am tired of wearing strait jackets since the war is over, and I much prefer to choose my own path and companions in life," explained Ohio volunteer Edmund Burritt Wakefield. From camp one evening in early July, a Wisconsin soldier wrote that he was afflicted by "fatigue." "But it is not the kind of fatigue which affects you," he clarified. "*My* fatigue arises from confinement." So incensed was this soldier that he resolved to "disown the country altogether and leave it" as soon as he was released from the service. Nettled by waterlogged marches in the weeks after the Grand Review, Edmund Spencer Packard likewise raised his voice in spirited protest. "They [the regimental commanders] can't dog us around forever to suit their idle whims," he railed. A first lieutenant from Iowa went so far as to compare his service to human bondage, labeling himself "a soldier slave."[29]

But soon enough, those "thousand rumors" that "set our hearts to fluttering" became realities. When the officers in the field received word that they could disband their regiments, only the labor-intensive preparation of muster-out rolls and receipt of their final pay kept the rank and file from starting for their homes. "We have a task to perform which is very fatiguing and disagreeable though agreeable," William Henry Church explained, "and that is making out our final Rolls and accounts with the Govt." The task was enormous (there were seven lengthy rolls to complete for each company) and even for a tiny regiment, it took four or five days to bring the work of accounting to a close. "We worked on them until late last night and are at them again this morning," one New York cavalryman complained.[30]

At least on paper, the war was over. "I felt sad as I took each by the hand and thought perhaps I should never behold them again," Lyman Jackman recollected. "I love those that I have suffered with." When the time to disband finally came, "there were struggles with the emotions which showed themselves," though not in words. "No language," one Illinois private wrote, "can express the feelings of sorrow at parting between comrades whose regard for each other has grown from long companionship amid the scenes of a bloody war." "Many a tear trickled down the bronzed cheeks of old comrades when the time came to bid each other goodbye," one Pennsylvania soldier remembered. "The thing was over," Irving Bronson mused. "We had said goodbye and shaken hands, some of us for the last time. It was like breaking up a family, and about as cheerful as a funeral."[31]

—⊷⊚⊶—

Vincent Colyer always seemed to be a lonely voice in the wilderness. Unlike most men and women on the northern homefront, he prophesied that demobilization would demand much from both soldiers and civilians. Warm, jovial, and genteel, he was nonetheless a crusader whose zeal for humanitarian reform could hardly be quenched. In the spring of 1865, the forty year old wore a long, unkempt beard which, when placed alongside his high forehead and prominent nose, gave him the appearance of a pious gnome.[32]

Colyer was born in a sycamore-lined Manhattan neighborhood in September 1824, two years after his father, George, and mother, Cordelia Webb, emigrated from Kent County in England. When Vincent was eight years old, tragedy arrived in the form of cholera, which ravaged the squalid streets of New York and claimed several thousand lives—including George Colyer's. Vincent matured overnight, determined to wrest his family from the abject poverty they now faced. He trained with the prolific printmaker John Rubens Smith at the National Academy of Design and then rented a studio on Bleecker Street, supporting his insolvent kin with crayon portraits and oil landscapes. By the time the war came, Colyer's work was profitable and, like his John Brown portrait, *Freedom's Martyr*, well known.[33]

But the war compelled Colyer to fold up his easel. Emancipation and the cause of the Union stirred deep within him. Slavery, he said, "was a crime against both God and man." In New York City throughout the spring of 1861, he greeted enlistees en route to Washington, ensuring that before these men reached the front, they were armed with a Bible. In late July, fearing for the spiritual health of federal soldiers after their devastating rout at Bull Run, Colyer hurried south on a consolation mission with Frank Ballard, a fellow member of the New York Young Men's Christian Association. "Our duty led us at an early hour to the hospitals," Colyer remembered. "The wounded men stretched upon neat and tidy single cots were glad to see visitors." Colyer encountered ward upon ward of bullet-riddled men, but not a single chaplain. Incensed, he returned home determined to rally a national organization devoted to "the spiritual wants of the young men of our army." The resulting United States Christian Commission met for the first time in November 1861 and aided soldiers for the balance of the war.[34]

Colyer spent the winter months supplying Bibles to troops huddled in the army camps around Washington. Then, in February 1862, he made his way to North Carolina, where the federal troops had scored a string of impressive victories along the coast. Fugitive slaves began collecting in massive numbers on Roanoke Island, now occupied by the federal army. Ambrose Burnside, the general commanding the operations in North Carolina, charged Colyer with oversight of the "contraband" slave population. Cheerfully and efficiently, he fed and clothed thousands of African-American refugees—many of whom would, in due course, shoulder Springfield muskets and don Union blue.[35]

Increasingly at odds with officials on the ground, Colyer left Roanoke Island and returned home. Nonetheless, indefatigable, he promptly accepted one more humanitarian assignment, replacing Colonel John S. Neville as superintendent of the New York State Soldiers'

Depot. Housed in two spacious five-story buildings at the corner of Mercer and Howard streets in Manhattan, the Soldiers' Depot opened its doors in May 1863 as "a temporary home, or free hotel, for all sick, wounded, furloughed, and discharged soldiers passing through" New York. Here men could find a warm meal, comfortable beds, a well-stocked library, evening entertainment, and, if needed, skilled doctors and nurses.[36]

By the spring of 1865, then, Colyer had amassed valuable experience in demobilizing soldiers. Union veterans making their way to the Soldiers' Depot were very often robbed, deceived, and swindled by enterprising sharps. Colyer decided to do something about it. He traveled to Washington City for the Grand Review, not to celebrate the end of the war—nor to shower the parading troops with floral garlands—but to alert the victors to the dangers lurking ahead. He hooked his way through the crowds until he reached the edge of Pennsylvania Avenue and there he distributed to the passing companies pocket-sized cards lined with earnest warnings: "Sharpers abound in the vicinity of all railroad depots and steamboat landings, on the lookout for discharged soldiers who have their pay with them. Bogus ambulances tempt the bewildered veteran, and he is cheated into going to places that he would fain avoid, and persuaded into making purchases that prove worthless bargains." Colyer supplied on the reverse side the address of the Soldiers' Depot. "None are turned away," he assured. Within the month, hundreds of soldiers gripping these cards lined up along Howard Street to take advantage of his compassionate offer.[37]

Colyer's reservations were hardly unfounded. During the Grand Review, the War Department opted to post sentinels along Maryland Avenue, seeking to prevent anyone from spiking the soldiers' barrels of drinking water with "deleterious substances." Less than a week later, one Washington newspaper announced that "unprincipled persons" were serving former soldiers "drugged or poisonous drinks, that a better opportunity may be afforded to rob them of their money and valuables." "There is undoubtedly a gang of thieves and gamblers following in the wake of returning soldiers," the *Milwaukee Sentinel* reported, "and they should be watched." "Scarcely a day passes but we hear of some soldier having been robbed by the sharpers, gamblers, and thieves who invest our city," one Iowa newspaper echoed. Especially at war's end, veterans were ready-made prey for "swarms of rum-selling harpies." Many ex-soldiers were deceived by pickpockets who served beer and whiskey spiked with "knock-out drops"; the "thugs" loitered in the shadowy corners of every last doggery and dive. Sergeant James Henry Avery, who rode with Custer's Michigan Brigade, held that the reason for "so many robberies of soldiers on their way home" was alcohol. "Through drink, some were boldly attacked and robbed in the streets," he lamented. Avery also observed that cunning decoys had successfully defrauded many victims. Thieves sometimes "appeared in the guise of lame soldiers" and quickly earned the trust of their "comrade." One disabled soldier, who fell asleep on the long train ride home to Utica, New York, woke only to discover that his pockets had been emptied of bounty money. "The heartless scoundrel who would rob a discharged and crippled soldier deserves to be branded with a hot iron," one veteran scowled. After a flurry of similar incidents in Chicago, the editors of the *Tribune* unsuccessfully proposed a "Soldier Protective Society," intended to safeguard returning veterans' assets.[38]

Rascals and quick charlatans began offering ex-soldiers up to $300 in exchange for army discharge papers, with which they could pretend to be Union veterans and petition for government employment, bounty equalization, disability pensions, or homestead lands. One perplexed veteran who was approached by such a swindler on his way home wrote to the editor of the *New York Evening Post*, asking for information regarding the value of his discharge. "Boys, keep your discharges," the editor cautioned. "Keep them as an evidence for the cause for which you imperiled your life." Perry Oliver Nixon from the 10th Illinois might have read this newspaper column, for the brown haired, hazel-eyed sergeant remembered reaching into his pocket "several times" on his way back to Chicago "to be sure if I had my discharge yet." Even more intrepid than the discharge thieves, however, were the swindlers who instructed returning veterans that they were entitled to and would receive 160-acre plots upon forwarding a thirty-dollar fee for "professional services." Only realizing months later that they had been duped, some veterans struggled for years to retrieve their embezzled funds.[39]

⊷⊷◉◎⊷

During the months of May and June, brigades of men began lumbering north, traveling by iron horse, paddle-wheel steamer, or, in some rare cases, on foot. "The brave heroes of our Army are being sent home by thousands every day," one Massachusetts captain reported. Desiring a swift demobilization, the ever-resourceful Quartermaster General Montgomery Cunningham Meigs devised detailed itineraries for returning soldiers—charting routes, contacting rail lines, and scheduling river transportation. "Every thing," Meigs maintained, "should be done to enable those soldiers who have survived the dangers of four years of warfare to reach their homes with the least inconvenience, fatigue, suffering, and danger." With a squall of circulars, he issued the men of the Union armies their final marching orders. Troops headed to New England were advised to march to Baltimore, board a Philadelphia-bound locomotive, and from there mount another train for New Haven, Hartford, or Springfield. Men bound for Iowa would rail through Harrisburg, Pittsburgh, Fort Wayne, and Chicago before reaching Dubuque, Fulton, Burlington, or Keokuk; troops returning to central Pennsylvania or upstate New York would ride the North Central Railway to Harrisburg or Elmira. Those headed to the far west would use the Baltimore & Ohio Railroad as far as the Ohio River, and then board a steamer in either Parkersburg or Cincinnati. Meigs advised railroad companies to make frequent stops, ensuring that the soldiers could "attend to the calls of nature." As a result, most northern cities received almost daily shipments of returning veterans, which served only to reinforce the idea of Union victory in the minds of civilians.[40]

Despite Meigs's best efforts, rail transportation grew so congested in June and July that many regiments—hoping to circumvent the inevitable delays—agreed to make taxing marches to less congested depots. After learning that Chicago-bound trains from Louisville were hopelessly behind schedule, the men of the 96th Illinois marched across the Ohio River to New Albany, Indiana, where, they were informed, there were "no delays." Upon their arrival at the depot, however, the veterans discovered that there were no passenger trains available to convey them farther north. Reluctantly, and with no little "outrage," the soldiers piled into frigid freight cars reeking of "cattle offal" and "wet sawdust."[41]

The day after he received his discharge from a mustering officer in Vicksburg, Francis Moore and the "colored servant" who had shadowed him through the war took passage on a St. Louis–bound steamer teeming with over 1,000 discharged soldiers. They "watched with much interest" as Memphis, New Madrid, Island Number Ten, Columbus, Belmont, and other places made famous by the Union armies and navies passed the windows of their tiny stateroom. Every mile, in the words of one veteran, seemed to "lengthen intolerably" as home drew nearer. A steamer weighted down with recently discharged Iowa infantrymen navigated the driftwood-choked Mississippi at such a slothful pace that the veterans began making "piteous appeals" to the boat's exasperated engineer. "Making eight hours a mile!" they jeered.[42]

At first glance, demobilization was a stunning success, accomplished at breakneck speed. But the striking fact that over 800,000 men were released from military service in the space of six months should not mislead us—the demobilization of the Union armies was a protracted process, punctuated with delay, discomfort, and even disaster. On April 27, 1865, half a dozen miles or so beyond Memphis, some 1,500 newly liberated inmates of Andersonville, Cahaba, and other Confederate prisoner-of-war camps perished in the mud of the Mississippi when a boiler erupted on the wooden-hulled steamer *Sultana*. When the boiler exploded, it ignited the cabins and decks, sending hundreds of emaciated bodies plunging into the frigid water to "[drown] in huge squads, those who could swim being unable to get away from those who could not and consequently perishing with them." "Oh God, what a sight to behold," remembered survivor William N. Fast of the 102nd Ohio decades later, the piteous pleas for help and "groans of suffering" yet ringing in his ears. For those who had survived the ravages and exposure of southern prison hells, the sight of singed bodies jumping to their graves was at once spiteful and surreal.[43]

From the ranks, demobilization made little sense. There was no discernible logic when it came to discharging regiments. Because the armies were much too large to disband at once, many restless brigades were obliged to wait for their muster-out papers. Many lamented that legions of sick and disabled comrades convalescing in hospital wards throughout the north were unceremoniously overlooked at mustering out. And although many outfits were mustered out together, a significant number were dissolved company by company. "I think if I had been at Newbern I would [have] been on my way home before this time, [for] there has been some of our company discharged already," Connecticut soldier Hiram Blaisdell wrote to his wife. After having shared such trying experiences, Charles Addison Partridge expressed great "regret" that not all members of his 96th Illinois Volunteers were to be sent home together. One soldier explained his frustration that by June, his was the last unit awaiting discharge from the brigade he fought with throughout the war. Most galling, some companies awaiting discharge were "tacked as an unnecessary tail" onto other regiments, a situation that New Jersey soldier Harvey Hyde regarded as "a disgrace." "Under the impulse of such feelings," he noted, "scores of men are going home without leave who would not have left their standards [during] the war."[44]

Sometimes the delays of demobilization mixed a seething cocktail of resentment and conspiracy. Troops from New Jersey, for example, witnessing a stream of soldiers from other states being discharged daily, determined that they were the objects of a "venomous Copperhead scheme" intended to stop them from returning home to possible political power. The men were deeply suspicious of Governor Joel Parker, a mouthpiece for the antiwar arm of the Democratic Party. Throughout the war, Republicans had scorned men like Parker as insidious snakes, eager to poison the republic. As a measure of their insolence, the so-called Copperheads embraced the slur, affixing Liberty cents to their lapels as a token of their opposition to emancipation and the Union war effort. "The Democratic party in the North is essentially a pro slavery party with little or no sympathy for 'the freedmen,'" one Illinois soldier conceded in the waning days of his service. Copperhead ranks swelled over the course of the war. So frequently had these politicians and their followers straddled the line between loyalty and treachery that it became inevitable for soldiers to perceive an intentional snub. Thus when New Jersey regiments were among the last troops left in the Second Army Corps, James O. Sherman asked candidly, "Why are we thus excluded? Have we not fought as faithfully as any other state troops?" "We hear Every Day of soldier[s] going home but not a word is said about the cavalry of New Jersey," complained a riled Amos Featherolf, who saw heavy combat in Virginia at Todd's Tavern, Hatcher's Run, and Sailor's Creek. "[W]e have freely bourn the hardship [and] Risk[ed] Life as Long as there was any fighting and I think that we deserve Better Treatment from our government than we are getting."[45]

Western troops, who felt personally injured by their notorious reputation as the agents of "hard war," were likewise convinced that they were deliberately detained longer than those soldiers who had fought in the war's eastern theater. Many veterans of the Georgia and Tennessee campaigns, for example, were assigned to seemingly interminable garrison duties across the occupied South and along the frontier. Following the battles of Spanish Fort and Fort Blakely, the men of the 2nd Illinois Artillery were shuttled off to Montgomery. In early August, "desirous of returning to their homes," the animated troops, "likely to remain here for some time yet," petitioned Illinois Governor Richard Oglesby to intervene on their behalf. Reports that his regiment was to be placed on garrison duty similarly stirred Wisconsin infantryman William Henry Church. "They are discharging Eastern troops every day ... with their banners flying, with music and cheers," he fumed, "and still no gladsome tidings comes to us, the war-worn Veterans of the West." He had done his duty, faithfully, and now only wanted to go home. Political leaders who did nothing to expedite demobilization, Church insisted, deserved the "everlasting enmity" of "each and every man thus retained." "If they don't muster us out after we get to Louisville, and give us our rights," he began, "I'll *never* take up arms in defense of the U.S. government again, so help me God!"[46]

These soldiers drew from a deep well of distrust about those civilian "stay-at-homes." But men, women, and children back north were even more suspicious of the returning warriors. "They are coming back to us, these brave, disbanded soldiers," one New York newspaper editor announced, "scarred and mutilated, crippled in body, crippled in mind." He was certain that veterans would carry with them "long trains" of disease and—"worse" still—moral maladies. Elizabeth Caleff Bowler shared the same concerns from the small Mississippi River town of Nininger, Minnesota, stewing about the moral consequences of "the trials, hardships, and horrors" of army service in a letter to her husband, James, who subsequently attempted to reassure his new bride. All the same, the *Cleveland Plain Dealer* wondered about the "constitutions" of the discharged. "No doubt considerable apprehension is felt," one Wisconsin newspaper editor explained, "of suddenly disbanding and sending home the many thousands employed for the past few years in the avocation of war."[47]

Yet in the next breath, recounting the historian Thomas Babington Macaulay's sanguine appraisal of the disbanding of Cromwell's army, the Wisconsin writer willed away the notion that homecoming would pose any significant trial for battle-tested ex-soldiers. "This host of returned veterans will be speedily absorbed into the constituents of society, without suffering or disturbance on any hand." After all, these men had defeated an "invincible" enemy on the battlefield; surely they would make an "effortless" return to their homes and families. Presuming that Union soldiers were decent and hearty "citizen soldiers," northern civilians foreclosed the opportunity to acknowledge the unprecedented needs of men who fought an unprecedented war. At least one newspaper editor assured his readers that "the returning soldiers of the Union" would live up to the "character" that they had displayed on the battlefield. "These are only dutiful American *citizens,* coming home to disband after a long successful work in behalf of their country," noted one newspaper in the nation's capital. The *Trenton State Gazette* similarly concluded that there could be "no better vindication of the theory of republican government" than the rapidity with which ex-soldiers desired to return to the pursuits of peaceful life.[48]

Moreover, many of the same civilians determined that as the "victors," Union soldiers would never endure the "trauma of defeat." In one of the many speeches that he delivered to returning regiments that passed through Indianapolis, Governor Oliver Perry Morton gave thanks to the "conquerors" whose herculean efforts preserved the Union, but noted "how different" the homecoming of their vanquished foes must have been. "These men had gone back without banners, without triumph, without hope," he explained. The satisfaction of victory, it seemed to Morton, would conquer and prevail over any hardships of homecoming. In a poem that she prepared for a soldiers' welcome-home reception held in the small village of Damascoville, Ohio, on July 4, 1865, a young Mattie Morrison concurred: "Well we know *we ne'er can pay* you / For the service you have

done / But, perhaps, *you all may have it* / In the *priceless triumph* won /
And again we bid you, truly / All a joyous welcome home."[49]

⟶━◉━⟵

The question of precisely *how* civilians would bid "a joyous welcome home"
to the returning soldiers triggered some angst. Demobilization demanded
some expression of "gratitude and veneration" for the Union soldiery. To
explore the matter fully, Yale College assembled an ad hoc committee that
ultimately resolved to host a commemorative celebration on July 26, 1865,
in honor of the nearly 450 alumni who had served in the Union armies
and navies. Organizers invited the leading Connecticut theologian, Rev.
Horace Bushnell, to deliver an after-dinner oration on "The Results of the
War" and announced plans for a permanent memorial dedicated to the
memory of the Yalies who had taken a part in suppressing the rebellion.
Although a number of veterans, "ready to lay aside the panoply of carnal
warfare," responded enthusiastically to the committee's printed invitation,
many more declined. "I should doubtless meet many of the class of '60
who with myself have battled with the enemy under the scorching rays of
a Louisiana sun, and I would with them shed tears to the memory of
those who have fully given their lives for their country's cause," noted a
discharged Massachusetts cavalryman in a letter conveying his regrets to
the organizers. A few of the ex-soldiers cautioned that a celebration of
victory was yet premature. "The rebellious south is subdued," explained
veteran Horace James, "but [it] retain[s] a degree of spiteful bitter feeling
which it dares not vent upon the Yankee, and so expends upon the negro."
More generally, these veterans were "far more thankful for a good supper,
a good lodging, and a good breakfast" than for "an empty municipal pageant." "These soldiers care little for mere parade," one New Jersey newspaper observed, "and less for flattering speeches." A Fifteenth Corps veteran
explained to his wife that he wanted no "great ado," only his "children well

clad . . . in good natured smiles." "By no means kill a fatted calf," he admonished.[50]

Nevertheless, in the months following the surrender at Appomattox, "mere parade" and "flattering speeches" became the standard regimen. Victory arches celebrated war's end across the land. New York City, draped in "an almost continuous canopy of bunting," hailed the war's end with the uninterrupted "booming" of howitzers. In Madison, Wisconsin, church belfries melodiously announced the return of each regiment. Springfield, Massachusetts, hosted a celebration at city hall, which was, of course, perfectly appointed with the national colors and banners emblazoned with "appropriate mottoes." Twenty-one year old Private William Royal Oake of the 26th Iowa Volunteers remembered being "banqueted most royally" in Pittsburgh and again in Chicago while waiting for the train that would convey him to Deep Creek Township after three long years of service. And Philadelphia officials, hoping to "afford the public a glimpse" of its hearty veterans, organized its own Grand Review on June 10, 1865. Even driving showers did not prevent the parade from stepping off at Camp Cadwalader.[51]

Not surprisingly, Vincent Colyer was one of the few civilians who dismissed these efforts out of hand, concentrating instead on providing for the returning veterans' most immediate needs. Aided by generous donations from Manhattan philanthropists like Theodore Roosevelt, Sr., he endeavored to provide discharged men with the fresh fruit and vegetables that had been replaced during the war by stale hardtack and rancid salt pork. He routinely accosted arriving steamers conveying ex-soldiers, hoisting up hundreds of baskets brimming with strawberries, cherries, radishes, beets, cabbage, and lettuce that he had purchased from local street vendors. "To see these gallant and sunburn[ed] boys in the army blue eagerly rush for strawberries, and enthusiastically eat the same, was a sight indeed," Colyer remembered. The veterans, remembering the effort as the so-called Strawberry Movement, later thanked Colyer for his "many acts of kindness" and the "bountiful refreshments," which, "after four years of hard service in the field was most gratifying."[52]

Throughout the summer, Colyer provided free meals, lodging, and medical attention for some 60,000 "war stained" veterans at the Howard Street Soldiers' Depot. One night, needy troops arrived in such large numbers that "no less than three regiments" slept on the sidewalks and in the streets surrounding the agency, forcing Colyer to secure additional space in nearby armories. The men often approached the building "in a state of complete destitution," hobbling on crutches and evincing "traces of the perils and dangers of the battlefield." One veteran of Sherman's campaigns arrived cradled by two comrades; his legs had been severed by a rebel solid shot lobbed somewhere in Georgia. Recently released prisoners of war fresh from Andersonville, Millen, and Libby, however, were the most haunting sights of all. Many of the skeletal survivors were unable to walk. "The cruelties to which they had been subject were plainly to be seen in their emaciated forms and hollow cheeks," Colyer observed.[53]

⟶❖⟵

Still other veterans experienced neither welcome-home celebrations nor Colyer's charity. More than a few soldiers who passed through Chicago on their journey home recalled the shrugs they received upon their arrival in the city. "We met with a very cold reception in the city of Chicago," Joshua Rilea recalled. "We passed out of the city as we entered it, none to recognize us, not one to waive [sic] a handkerchief or bid us, 'God speed,'" carped the surgeon of the 30th Iowa Volunteers. Lieutenant Colonel Allen Fahnestock noted that the men of his Illinois regiment, veterans of hard fighting at Perryville, Chickamauga, and Kennesaw Mountain, were "received [so] coolly" when they arrived in Chicago on the afternoon of June 11 that they proceeded to their camp at once to remedy the slight with whiskey.[54]

The *Boston Daily Advertiser* reported that returning warriors were "allowed to pass through" the streets of Massachusetts's capital in "as chilly a silence as if they came home humbled with defeat." Without a crowd to trumpet their arrival, the soldiers marched "hungry through careless, bustling streets," meeting their most hearty greeting in the liquor shops. When twenty-four-year-old William Haines returned to his hometown of Mullica Hill, New Jersey, a well-shaded settlement anchored by the lazy Raccoon Creek, he and his "subdued" Gettysburg comrades unassumingly "shed the names and clothes of soldiers," having met with "no reception committee, no fuss, no brass band." Leander Stillwell's late-September return home was about as unremarkable as his tiny settlement of Otter Creek, Illinois, perched opposite St. Louis on the Mississippi River. Hoping to attract some attention, Stillwell paraded down the village's only street, clutching his sword as though ready to lead a charge. "I looked eagerly around as I passed along, hoping to see some old friend," he recalled. "As I went by the store, a man who was seated therein on the counter leaned forward and looked at me, but said nothing." Stillwell unavoidably resolved that discharged soldiers were already "old news," no longer worthy of fanfare. He pled indifference to this reception, although within a year he had relocated to Neosho County, Kansas, in search of a new life. Twenty-seven-year-old carriage-maker Francis Moore, another Illinois veteran, also felt like a back number when he finally returned home. Although he encountered "familiar faces on the wharf and in the streets" of his native Quincy, Illinois, "no one recognized" him, and he "spoke to no one." Moore instead "rode directly to [his] father's office, determined that he should be the first person I would speak to."[55]

It was a long way from the pomp and pageantry of the Grand Review to these soldiers' modest homecomings. Yet, in another sense, the "greeting" received by veterans like Haines, Stillwell, and Moore share much in common with our iconic image of soldiers parading proudly down Pennsylvania Avenue. The denizens of places like Mullica Hill, Otter Creek, and Quincy were as unprepared to receive Uncle Sam's demobilized

armies as the thousands who had lined Washington's streets, unaware—
and contentedly so—of the burdens of war and the looming trials of
homecoming. In the absence of any social-welfare policy, and clinging to
strident, laissez-faire individualism, civilians hardly knew what to do with
so many needy veterans. Even Vincent Colyer soon found himself at the
mercy of the masses. On August 31, 1865, "in view of the fact that the war
has been successfully terminated and the necessities growing out of the
same have become greatly lessened," he received a letter of termination
from Governor Reuben Fenton, who, seeking to trim the state's nonessen-
tial expenditures, decided to close up the Soldier's Depot.[56]

⤞⟴⤝

When they have written about it, historians have considered the Grand
Review as either a stirring epilogue to four years of conflict or as an omen
of white supremacy's "strange" postwar career. But it was also the first of
many struggles between veterans, who would forever peer over their
shoulders and into the past, and civilians, who, having missed the distinctive experience of the war, were stubbornly unwilling to remember. For
that reason, Colonel Charles Wainwright, a celebrated artillery officer in
the Army of the Potomac, was disturbed by the patriotic banners and
affected speechifying at the review. Wainwright "could not help wondering whether, having made up their minds that they *can never* pay the debt,"
northern civilians might "think it useless to try." When the blue-coated
armies strode down Pennsylvania Avenue, they were not marching confidently into the future. Instead, they tramped toward an unsettled peace.
That week, in fact, ten veterans, nine of them in their twenties and thirties,
were admitted to St. Elizabeth's in Washington—the government hospital
for the insane.[57]

Those who returned to their homes could not help but reflect that "so
much of history" had been crammed into the last four years; for many, it
seemed as though "a century" had elapsed since they had marched off to

war. Upon his release from Andersonville and return home to Massachusetts, infantryman George Hitchcock noted that he felt "like Rip Van
Winkle awakening from a long sleep." "A lifetime of experience has been
crowded into this fierce term of war," Private Wilbur Fisk mused upon
returning to his small town, nestled in the Green Mountains of Vermont.
Reflecting on "the school of the soldier," a young volunteer from the
hearty stock of Ohio's Western Reserve marveled, "Do you think any
other year of my life will be crowded so full of such great and strange
events?" "So many changes have been made," observed another veteran,
and so "greatly altered is the condition of our country." Likewise, in a letter to his father, one Iowa sergeant reflected that he did "not feel like the
same person I was a year ago." Already, Union veterans were realizing that
they, much like the nation, would never be the same again.[58]

CHAPTER 2

STRANGER AT THE GATES

So damn those lords and captains,
Those Phaeacians! Not entirely honest or upright, were they?
Sweeping me off to this, this no-man's-land, and they,
they swore they'd sail me home to sunny Ithaca—well,
they never kept their word.

—HOMER, *THE ODYSSEY*

ON MAY 20, 1865, a few months before it was shuttered, Vincent Colyer's New York State Soldier's Depot saw a tiny army of veterans huddled outside its doors. A few of the soldiers depended on crutches, but "all evinced upon their persons some traces of the perils and dangers of the battlefield." They applauded wildly when the governor, Reuben Fenton, took his place on the platform. "We have followed you beyond the Mississippi, from Chattanooga to the Gulf, through the swamps of Florida to the very gates of Richmond, from Virginia to Georgia," Fenton began, assuring the crowd that New York had not been "unmindful" of her sons. "You have," he declared, reveling in the hour of victory, "perpetuated the free institutions of the country, and your noble deeds in the cause of liberty will live in fiery letters in the page of history. You are going to your homes, and no longer will you be called upon to fight the good fight or suffer for the right." But near the end of his address, the newly inaugurated Republican, trimmed in thick whiskers, posed one of the many questions that bedeviled northern civilians that strange summer after Appomattox. Flushed with victory, would victorious Union soldiers "abandon the weapons of dreadful war" and once again yield to the "peaceful ways of civil life"?[1]

This question was nothing new. By the mid-nineteenth century, American armies had returned home from quarrels with Barbary pirates, British regulars, Mexican soldiers, and scores of native tribes—each time prompting civilians (who, despite their periodic taste for war, lacked an appetite for most things martial) to wilt in fear. Indeed, for a people reared on republicanism, an army was not a collection of virtuous warriors, but a looming menace to personal liberty—a gathering coup d'état. In peace, after all, soldiers were no longer subject to the self-effacing demands of war. One only needed to recall those irate Revolutionary War veterans who, when their promised pensions and service bonuses went unpaid, began whispering threats against the government from their chilly tents in Newburgh.[2]

But the return of northern soldiers after the Civil War was even more alarming because an American war had never been waged on such an immense scale. During the American Revolution, the Continental Army was "rarely larger than about thirty-thousand men," and throughout the early decades of the nineteenth century, the army was an unimposing, ill-prepared, and poorly equipped outfit of only 16,000 men, most stowed away in dingy frontier garrisons. Even the Mexican War had mobilized only 115,000 men, the approximate size of the Army of the Potomac at the battle of Gettysburg. By the time Robert E. Lee met Ulysses S. Grant in Wilmer McLean's parlor at Appomattox Court House, more than 2 million men had shouldered muskets in defense of the Union. Never before were there so many men who called themselves veterans.[3]

It was not merely the size of the returning armies, but also the sort of men who fought in their ranks that troubled many northerners. According to the estimate of one historian, nearly three-quarters of the men who donned Union blue were under the age of thirty. Young and impulsive roughs suddenly unmoored from the drudgeries of war could hardly be expected to behave in a restrained way. After all, they had confiscated acres of cotton and thousands of slaves, torched southern cities, maimed enemies, and waged a more devastating kind of war from Virginia to Georgia to the Carolinas. "Human life," one typical northern newspaper editorialized, "cannot but seem cheaper to him who has seen men shot down and thrown in a ditch like cattle."[4]

Few Union veterans, moreover, owned property before the war or had any compelling reason to settle into quiet routine. Thus the writer Nathaniel Hawthorne, who expressed his opposition to the war with an unrivaled rancor, predicted that New Englanders would surrender their bucolic towns to crude, drunken, and sinister men after Appomattox. After all, many soldiers—especially the conscripts and bounty jumpers of the war's final years—emanated "from a lower grade of society, from the slums of the cities and towns, and even from the jails and penitentiaries." How would they behave without goading officers and army discipline? Nativist observers, convinced that immigrants were foul degenerates, likewise shuddered that by the end of the war, foreign-born men constituted at least a quarter of all enlistees. Most chilling, some would even return armed, thanks to a recently inked general order that permitted volunteers to purchase their weapons and sidearms from the Ordnance Department for a nominal fee.[5]

"There is no disguising it, boys, *the people are afraid of us,*" insisted Phineas Whitehouse, a New Hampshire veteran who was learning to write with his left hand after a rebel bullet fractured his right at Spotsylvania Court House. "They heard many strange and bad stories about some of us while we were in the army, which have done us no good." Public officials in several cities, including Baltimore, Harrisburg, and Jackson, Michigan, "took every precaution" by criminalizing the sale of intoxicating liquors to returning troops. "It is earnestly hoped," Harrisburg's Democratic Mayor Augustus Roumfort declared, "that upon the occasion of the return of our brave volunteers from the war, and during their sojourn in this city, every good citizen will use his best endeavors to make their stay in our midst agreeable, and to warn them on all proper occasions of any impositions to which they may be exposed." The authors of an 1865 pocket almanac published expressly for Union soldiers not only warned the soon-to-be veterans about the hazards of "ardent spirits," but invited them to ask the Lord for salvation from "the sins and vices" of a soldier's life: "Let me not join any wickedness going on around me. Give me courage to say No, when asked to do wrong. Make me strong against the enemies of my soul." Another publication aimed at the newly discharged men of the Union armies counseled moderation, urging them to become respectable and "good citizens." "It is a dangerous period to a young man," one writer advised, "when he is just released from army service."[6]

But nowhere in this blizzard of alarm and advice was there any serious consideration of the duties and obligations of northern civilians. Lacking any notion of social-welfare policy, and absent any ideology of veterans' rights, even the most stubbornly loyal and patriotic citizens were inept when it came to recommending "appropriate" expressions of sympathy and appreciation. As one newspaper editor aptly pointed out, gratitude was the "rarest of human virtues." In the immediate aftermath of the war, then, northern celebration and triumphalism were routinely mistaken for a genuine acknowledgment of wartime sacrifice. Worst of all, beyond staging superficial victory celebrations, the only role that many postwar civilians could imagine for themselves was profiteering. One Boston apothecary shop, for instance, hawked bottles of Dr. Richardson's Blood Root Elixir, a miracle tonic that claimed to cure chronic diarrhea, dysentery, and render invisible any vestiges of the war.[7]

Major General John Alexander Logan was one who predicted that demobilizing the Union armies would be no simple task. In his final address to
the Fifteenth Army Corps, the memorably mustached Illinoisan cautioned his troops, then about to return to their homes scattered throughout the Midwest. "Let not the luster of that bright name you have won as
soldiers," he entreated, "be dimmed by any improper acts as citizens." Yet
"exasperated by long restraint" and imagining themselves "going into a
land flowing with milk and honey, and drinks," some returning soldiers
"felt impelled to burst into unrestrained joy" the moment they stepped
foot on northern soil. Each maddening delay on the way home rendered
the new veterans more irascible, volatile, and unpredictable. When the
20th Maine halted temporarily in Providence, Rhode Island, one afternoon in late July, a nagging dread of drunken brawling and misbehavior
prompted Brigadier General Ellis Spear to post a guard at the door of
"every saloon and grocery." "That was," he wrote, "my last picket line." A
few days later, the ranks of the regiment that immortalized Little Round
Top and saved the Union left at Gettysburg arrived safely in Portland,
their sterling war record intact.[8]

Many regimental commanders were less fortunate. As Sergeant William Henry Jones of the 114th Ohio Volunteers noted in July 1865, some
officers were "as afraid as death" of their "stubborn" enlisted men—especially those who binged on whiskey and demon rum. Just days before his
discharge, Edwin Coles landed in the lockup at New York's Fort Columbus for a year after hurling drunken insults at one of his superior officers.
"My wife and family are the sufferers for my guilt," he wrote from his
dank cell, full of remorse. "I wish I was Dead and out of Misery." Captain
Daniel Eldredge recalled that when the ranks of his 3rd New Hampshire
reached their mustering-out camp in New Haven, Connecticut, "drunk-
enness and rioting was the order of the day." To make matters worse, sev-

eral of the muskets stacked in the camp by the recently returned 6th Connecticut had been filched. Fearing the worst, officers posted sentinels throughout the garrison, declaring that anyone attempting to make off with a gun would be summarily arrested. A few evenings later, frantically attempting to retrieve his old Springfield, an enlisted man assaulted a guard manning the makeshift armory. Startled, and possessing orders to "defend himself" if necessary, the sentinel fired at the hysterical soldier, who slumped to the ground in a pool of blood—a Minié ball having lodged in one of his lungs. Bedlam ensued as men gathered around their fallen comrade, swearing with whiskey-tainted breath that his shooting was "a damned shame" and cursing the "son of a bitch" who shot him. By morning, order was restored in camp, but the soldier, after twelve, anguished hours, succumbed to his wound. He was the regiment's last recorded casualty.[9]

Even once they reached their homes, the veterans' campaign of debauchery continued. "Maddened by liquor," the soldiers who returned to Davenport, Iowa, mutinied in the streets. They smashed windows, ransacked houses, and "destroyed everything generally." One squad of soldiers even plundered Charles Chamberlain's dairy and vegetable wagon, emptying every last milk jug in the street as the startled vendor looked on. By August, local citizens were so rattled by veteran misdeeds that they collected on the docks as the next regiment to arrive—the 33rd Iowa Volunteers—chugged into the city. " 'Don't let a man get off!' " they beseeched. " 'Don't let a man get off!' " Hoping to avoid an altercation, the colonel opted to discharge his men on nearby Rock Island, where they were quarantined for an entire week. "Even the negro children in the South," recalled one of the regiment's enlisted men, "had many times been more glad to see us than our own fellow-citizens here."[10]

Returning soldiers angered by perceived slights or improper welcome-home receptions were especially prone to violence. Following a particularly inconsiderate greeting delivered by Governor Joel Parker, the veterans of the 12th New Jersey "verged on mutiny"—pillaging, marauding, and "cutting up all kind of shines." Brimming with frustration and slightly intoxicated, two New York soldiers, veterans of hard fighting at Antietam and Fredericksburg, fixed tarnished bayonets to the ends of their muskets and made "a headlong rush" for several taunting civilians gathered at a welcome reception on the Tompkinsville green.[11]

Perhaps no regiment made more of a scene than the hard-edged 105th Illinois, still protesting their breakneck march to the Grand Review. When these western theater veterans arrived in Chicago, they "found neither quarters nor rations," and "camped without any supper." "We had no money and could not buy anything to eat," complained the boyish Private Robert Hale Strong. The slights did not end there. The following day, municipal police scolded the men for parading down city sidewalks. Refusing to heed civilian instructions to "leave the walk for gentlemen," the troops reflexively "fixed bayonets and constituted ourselves a rear guard." "It was fun to see them [civilians] run from those bayonets," Strong chortled.[12]

Even Strong was rather embarrassed about what happened next. Still waiting for their discharge papers, a few boys hoping to remedy boredom visited a dodgy saloon located near the regimental camp. One of the soldiers offered a toast to "Uncle Billy," which caught the attention of the crowd. "Damn Sherman!" one civilian provocatively hissed. The men in blue stirred with righteous indignation. "Sherman's Bummers to the rescue!" one shouted. For the next two hours, the soldiers fought their last battle in the streets of Chicago—assailing incredulous patrons and policemen armed with clubs. "The saloon keeper had not a bottle or keg or box of cigars un-smashed," Strong remembered, "and he himself lay senseless on the ground." Only the unlikely intervention of rumpled, whiskey-guzzling Joseph Hooker, the one-time commander of the Army of the Potomac, brought an end to the mayhem. Hooker assured the police that the veterans would go quietly if permitted, but nevertheless urged extreme caution. "They have faced cannon and musketry for three years, and do not know what fear is," he began. "Let them alone, or they will burn down your city."[13]

By midsummer, gasping editors declared that the nation was fatally afflicted by an "epidemic" of veteran misdeeds. "From day to day, and week to week, in every direction, the terrible circle seems to spread," one Connecticut paper explained. "Records of murders, garrotings, burglaries, and rapes are laid on every breakfast table." "The summer of 1865," the *Philadelphia Inquirer* predicted, "will be long remembered as a season when crimes of fearful character were unusually abundant."[14]

The real epidemic, of course, was alcoholism. Despite the earnest efforts of teetotal officers, Union soldiers binged on untold gallons of whiskey during the war—mitigating tedium in camp, cowardice on the battlefield, and anguish in the field hospital. Such pervasive imbibing had posed significant challenges to the discipline, cohesion, and fighting effectiveness of individual regiments. Now, the "deadly" drink habit stalked veterans staggering their way back home. "Only yesterday we saw a man who had fought on many a bloody field, and who had been discharged on account of wounds received in battle, lying at the back end of one of our respectable doggeries in a dirty, filthy corner, dead drunk," one Ohio newspaper reported a few weeks after Appomattox. "This man was a hero on the battlefield, but now we see him beneath the level of the brute."[15]

Inebriated veterans seemed to surface everywhere that summer. Shortly after his return to Philadelphia, an honorably discharged second lieutenant who crowed about the cache of captured "Rebel fire-arms" that he stockpiled in his room at the Continental Hotel was arrested for public intoxication. When the police discovered him, he was behaving "like a mad dog"—loudly baying, repeatedly biting himself, and "tearing the clothes from off his back." In July, several New York City pedestrians discovered the body of twenty-six-year-old Charles Murphy, who had manned the guns of the 15th New York Heavy Artillery along the siege lines of Petersburg, keeled over on the sandstone stoop of a Mercer Street townhouse. He had finally succumbed to alcohol poisoning. Weeks later, the decapitated body of a veteran was discovered near New Albany, Indiana, on the track of the Illinois Central with a crushed, empty whiskey flask pitched to his side.[16]

For northern civilians, these discoveries were particularly alarming. As early as the 1830s, a significant number of Americans had begun to denounce liquor as a menace to both self and society. Alcohol consumption rates, which had reached stratospheric levels in the first decades of the new republic, plunged to record lows as medical journals, religious tracts, stump speakers, circuit riders, and political parties all deplored the tyranny of the bottle. Throughout the 1840s and 1850s, teetotal organizations secured pledges from those who promised to abstain from intoxicating beverages, while legislatures belted the northern states with new temperance laws. Those who could not quench a thirst for whiskey, it was assumed, lacked respectability or self-control.[17]

By supplying such devastatingly vivid examples of alcohol's consequences, the return of Union veterans lent a new and certain urgency to the cause of temperance. Methodist Episcopal minister J. B. Merwin, a temperance reformer who had served as a chaplain in many army hospitals, lamented in a speech on Boston Common that ex-soldiers were "left to seek sympathy and companionship in the grogshops." "The liquor sellers are on the alert, watching for them," he bemoaned, "for they know that [the returning soldiers] have money, and that they have time on their hands." Merwin made a desperate appeal to his audience: we "owe it to our returning soldiers," he declared, to save the country and to "shut up the grogshop." For his part, William Oland Bourne, a New York social reformer and fellow former army chaplain, appealed to the "patriotism" and "humanity" of the New York State Liquor Dealers' Association. The "spectacle of a one armed or a one legged soldier, more or less intoxicated," had become so routine in New York City that Bourne urged consideration of the "disabled man, his comparative helplessness, the necessities of his family, and the insufficiency of his pension to provide for his wants." "Under these circumstances, it seems to me that the want and receipt of any of his means of payment for strong drink rises almost to the dignity of a crime on the part of a dealer," he insisted, demanding that the association agree to revoke permanently the vendor's licenses of any members known to hawk "ardent spirits" to disabled soldiers. But no action was taken, and veterans continued tipping the bottle.[18]

⊷═◉═⊶

Among the many difficulties that drove veterans to the bottle was the onerous task of attempting to reestablish life at home. "One cannot tell how the loss of home influence affects him," John Mead Gould insisted, "till he is thrown in contact with his own or another's home and learns how awkward he has become."[19] When Private Frederick Walster of the 153rd New York Volunteers returned to his hometown of Fort Plain, he reported that he was "miserable" and "very lonesome." "Things are so different now," Walster, whose brother succumbed to disease in an Alexandria hospital in December 1862, told his pocket diary one afternoon.[20] Even the climate was "different." "The weather is uncommonly cool for the latitude," explained W. B. Emmons from the 34th Illinois, "and we that have spent the last four years in the sunny south feel the chill of these cool northern nights."[21] "We appeared to be living in a new world," wrote Henry Wood of the 121st New York.[22]

All too frequently, ex-soldiers hardly recognized the people and the places of their youth—and vice versa.[23] When John Dulebohn, his chin now sporting untamed whiskers, returned to his home in rural Franklin County, Pennsylvania, his mother did not recognize him. "Who are you?" she demanded. Eric Paul, who spent many months in rebel captivity, noted that he was "so changed in appearance that nobody knew me, not even my mother. She said positively that I was not her Eric, and that broke me all up."[24] When the weathered Illinois infantryman William Wallace Hensley returned home earlier than anticipated, his wife, Nancy, "stared at me like she was scared." "I guess it was because I looked so different to what I did when she saw me last," he reasoned.[25]

"We felt kind of lost," one Pennsylvania soldier candidly confessed. "Settling down to routine daily employment in slow shop and store was not favorable to our habits of life."[26] When his stagecoach finally arrived in Wayland, Michigan, Sergeant James Henry Avery was "surprised to find quite a nice thriving business town, where, when I went away three years before, there were but a few buildings."[27] Jacob Roemer thought himself marooned on some distant island when he returned to Flushing with the members of his 34th New York Battery, a sea of conflicting emotions eddying around him. "I know we marched down Main Street to the hotel where a splendid dinner was waiting for us, but how I reached the place I hardly know," he recalled in his memoir. "When I beheld that table bountifully laden with all the delicacies of the season, my feelings quite overcame me . . . it did not seem to be real."[28] "It hardly seems as though it could be so," veteran Arlon Atherton echoed on the day he received his discharge papers in the small southern New Hampshire town of Richmond. "I am once more a Freeman."[29]

War's end was anything but "joyous" for Samuel Cormany, the twenty-seven-year-old college-educated son of a Pennsylvania farmer whose wife, Rachel, anxiously awaited his return to the lush Cumberland Valley. With the rebels defeated and "soldiering" now a "dead service," the whiskered cavalryman began contemplating if he was even "worthy" of his beloved sweetheart and their daughters. In a blizzard of letters home, Samuel admonished that in the service, he had lost all self-control; that after four years of pounding combat, he was "inclined to be short, quick-tempered," and generally intolerant. Cataloging his behavioral "irregularities"—which included succumbing, on more than one occasion, to the temptations of whiskey—he begged Rachel for a forgiveness that he denied himself, wondering how they would "over-come all evil" to "attain to our ideals as Husband and Wife."

Once Samuel returned, he and Rachel prayed, imploring God to hide the "gloomy spots" of the past. But Samuel continued his descent into the dark oblivion of despair. "He seems almost heartbroken over his missteps," Rachel commented in September. The two eventually left their Pennsylvania home and attempted to start anew in Missouri. Though they remained married and never separated, they never again experienced the bliss they had known before the war.[30]

While Samuel's candor was exceptional, his apprehensions were not. In the weeks leading up to his discharge, the augustly named Isaac Newton Carr, who fought at Shiloh and marched to the sea with Sherman, restlessly contemplated how he and his wife would relate to one another once he returned to their home in rural Wellman, Iowa. Other veterans left behind indirect but compelling evidence of these anxieties when they "frequented" so-called "dark places of resort." Ensembles of recently discharged Iowa infantrymen visited "houses of ill-fame" in an effort "to see some of the lewd females therein." In July 1865, a "grand raid" by the Philadelphia police at Catharine Lewis's squalid brothel near Broad and Cherry Streets resulted in the arrest of several "half drunken soldiers." The following month, two discharged soldiers arrived in the Michigan town of Grass Lake, escorting "two women of disreputable character."[31]

⇢⟐⇠

While chilling tales of violent crime and descriptions of inebriated veterans visiting prostitutes made for great copy, civilians took no satisfaction in having their worst fears so quickly realized. "We must wait, impatiently, for the awful scourge to pass by," one New England newspaper editor remarked, betraying in his dull resignation popular notions that the war could be forgotten at will, and that the grief of readjustment would be short-lived.[32]

Much like Vincent Colyer, gregarious William Oland Bourne was one of the few civilians who knew otherwise. He was the son of Rev. George Bourne, the British-born abolitionist whose blistering treatise *The Book and Slavery Irreconcilable* (1816) stirred a generation of antislavery reformers. Following in the path blazed by his father, William became an outspoken antislavery activist and social reformer. He began his career in journalism, editing the *Northern Journal* in New York's Black River Valley before relocating to Manhattan in 1850. There he met Horace Greeley, the reform-minded newspaperman who routinely published Bourne's poetry in the columns of his *New York Tribune*. Syndicated in dozens of antebellum newspapers, Bourne's stanzas chastised slaveholders, advocated temperance, and urged reforms on behalf of careworn wage laborers.[33]

Yet as one contemporary observed after his death, Bourne was "a philanthropist rather than a poet." His verse tended to be stilted—even stale—and he much preferred deeds to words. When the war came, he unconditionally supported the Union war effort. At forty-two, he was too old to rush off to the front lines, so instead spent countless hours pacing the sobering wards of Central Park Hospital, designed exclusively for amputees being fitted with prosthetic limbs. "There is none in this hospital but cripples and men with rheumatism," one patient explained to his sister. "In one ward there is nearly a hundred men with one leg off."[34]

The heaps of dismembered arms and legs made a lasting impression on Bourne, who collected in three leather-bound books the wobbly signatures of the soldiers he assisted. The enlisted men showered him with affection. "You cannot fully understand how a 'blue coat' feels to be taken by the hand," one soldier explained, how meaningful it was to "know that some one is actually interested in his welfare." Daily access to these veterans conveyed to him in the most compelling way the war's human consequences. While Vincent Colyer anticipated the dangers of demobilization, Bourne foresaw the obstacles these men would face after they returned. For one, he predicted that thousands of disabled and dismembered veterans would struggle to secure work. Not only did these soldiers have significant physical limitations, they were returning to a feeble economy—one yet making the wrenching transition from the self-sufficiency of the antebellum years to the mechanized industry of the Gilded Age. War-related manufacturing had sputtered to a halt, shuttering factories throughout the North that had once hummed with activity. Inflation soared and, with thousands of newly arrived immigrants jockeying for wages, unemployment rates reached stratospheric levels. Labor unions began organizing, plotting strikes and positing an unbridgeable chasm between workers and capital. The wartime promise of free labor seemed imperiled.[35]

Worse still, supposing that returning soldiers could "do nothing hereafter for a living but fight," many employers refused to hire veterans. "They are actually afraid to employ us," a New Hampshire soldier concluded months into his wearying job search. "Why is it," he asked, "that when a vacancy occurs in their stores and offices, it is so frequently filled by the stay-at-home citizen, while the discharged soldier is turned away without as much as a hearing?" Even fathers had difficulty lending career advice, unable to think of their sons as anything but hardened soldiers. "I am not now prepared to say what sort of employment would be best for you," Connecticut clergyman Leonard Bacon told his son, Edward, who abandoned his studies at Yale when the war broke out.[36]

Bourne was determined to remedy the situation. He began rolling the presses on the *Soldier's Friend*, a handsomely typeset newspaper designed to lend aid and a measure of solace to Union veterans. From his cluttered office at No. 12 Centre Street in New York, he published two editions of the paper—a weekly, printed each Saturday, and a monthly, released on the first of every month. Editorials offered returning soldiers tips about seeking employment and encouraged them not to despair. "It is a paper that every soldier and sailor needs to strengthen him," explained one soldier-reader from Rutland, Vermont. By 1869, more than 60,000 veterans were taking the monthly edition of the *Soldiers' Friend*.[37]

While the paper buoyed the flagging spirits of veterans throughout the North, ex-soldiers who lived in New York found Bourne's office a most welcome respite from the demands of civilian life. Each day, one-armed and one-legged veterans collected in the reception area seeking employment, advice, and sympathy. Bourne hired many of these boys to sell subscriptions and individual issues of the *Soldier's Friend*. While the veterans were no doubt thankful for the tiny measure of dignity such work provided, they found the hours long and the task wearisome. Exasperated civilians routinely rebuffed veterans hawking papers on ferryboats and streetcars. One New Yorker even registered his objection with a letter to Bourne. "They thrust the paper in [our] faces, lay them on [our] laps, and throw them on other papers which passengers are reading." This was nothing if not "veteran impoliteness" and a "crime committed in the name of patriotism," he explained.[38]

Few others labored on behalf of unemployed veterans with the determination of William Oland Bourne. The United States Sanitary Commission, for example—the well-oiled humanitarian organization that during the war established supply depots, disbursed extra rations, raised funds for army relief, and dispatched agents to inspect squalid army camps and disease-ridden hospitals—nodded rather complacently at the problem. In several northern cities, a select number of commissioners redirected their labors to so-called Bureaus of Information and Employment. The bureau invited returned soldiers to register their names, work experience, and medical histories at its branch offices. After processing this information, agents hunted for vacancies and worked to reassure potential employers that veteran applicants did "not desire to be soldiers in time of peace." With these efforts, the Sanitary Commission hoped "to prevent, as far as possible, the necessity for costly charitable institutions" and "to lessen the pauperism and crime, necessarily more or less a consequence of the war, which surely attend on large numbers of unoccupied men left to themselves without employment or means of subsistence."[39]

In September 1865 alone, 84 veterans (including 59 able-bodied men and 25 disabled soldiers) appealed to the bureau's Detroit office for work. By November, there were more than 200 veterans with résumés on file. The bureau no doubt secured positions for many of their hopefuls, but its overall success rate—perhaps owing to its less than altruistic motives— was rather uninspiring. In Detroit, the bureau was unable to place nearly half of the veterans who appealed for assistance. Men who hoped to secure work on farms, as police officers, in button factories and cabinet shops, left the city; even those whose applications were successful found only the most menial employment, taking up work as book peddlers, woodcutters, and fruit vendors.[40]

Unable to rely on either government aid or civic philanthropy, out-of-luck comrades turned to each other and readied one more campaign. On the morning of August 11, 1865, some 250 jobless soldiers stirred on Canal Street before Pythagoras Hall, ready to rally for work and a decent wage in the streets of New York City. By choreographing this "grand public demonstration"—the first major veterans' parade since the Grand Review—they hoped to persuade civilians once and for all of their virtue as citizens. At one o'clock in the afternoon, the fifes of the United States Army Band began whistling their "lively air." The veterans tramped down the Bowery to Broadway, lapping City Hall and the offices of the *New York Herald* before filing past the well-heeled on Wall Street. The humid summer breeze revealed the mottoes emblazoned on the canvas banners that punctuated the ranks:

GIVE US EMPLOYMENT TO SUPPORT
OUR FAMILIES
We represent thousands of discharged soldiers and
sailors now asking for bread

Our last employers were Grant, Sherman,
Sheridan, Meade, Hancock, and Hooker
WE ARE NOW THE SOLDIER CITIZENS.[41]

However predictably, little relief followed. In September, a soldier from Frankfort, New York, who lost his right arm at Petersburg protested that he and his comrades continued to endure "many rebuffs and insults" from the "empty-headed, heartless, and soulless votaries of fashion." Many veterans made a last resort to the public purse. Destitute soldiers unable to subsist solely on trifling $4 or $8-per-month pensions (by way of comparison, the average laborer earned $44 per month in 1865, while those in skilled trades took home as much as $80) filed a majority of the applications for assistance received by the overseer of the poor in Charlestown, Massachusetts. Among the claimants were men like twenty-nine year old Philip McGuire, an Irish immigrant who lost a leg at Gettysburg in the repulse of Pickett's Charge, and William Quinn, whose Malvern Hill wound resulted in his disability discharge from the army. While McGuire was unable to heat the home where he lived with his wife and three young children, thirty-six year old Quinn could not afford to feed his family.[42]

Poverty among veterans was especially pronounced in urban areas. In New York City, pensioners settled into tiny, dank, and foul-smelling tenements. Edward Crapsey, a crack reporter who rummaged the city for stories about crime and pauperism, prepared an investigative report that paid particular attention to something he christened the "Pensioner's apartment." Insolvent veterans, he wrote, very often lived in "the contracted space" of two "doleful" rooms, furnished only with "three broken wooden chairs, a few dishes and cooking utensils, and two 'shakedowns,' as the piles of straw stuffed into bed-ticks are called."[43]

While prowling around a Cherry Street tenement, carefully avoiding the fetid pools of "stagnant" water that collected "at the foot of the stairs,"

Crapsey met a thirty-five-year-old ex-soldier who, at Spotsylvania Court House, lost his right arm in the ranks of the 39th New York Volunteers. The man was living with his wife, their three children, and four boarders who helped them meet the rent. Assuming that true citizen-soldiers returned from war without needs or demands, Crapsey found it altogether implausible that a victorious and "honorably scarred" ex-soldier would permit himself to live in such abject conditions. He even posed "test questions" to the veteran in an effort to confirm his identity. To which brigade, division, and army corps was his regiment attached at Spotsylvania? How much did he receive per month from the Pension Bureau? Much to the journalist's surprise, the old soldier responded satisfactorily. "Here was a hero!" Crapsey incredulously exclaimed, recalling the "lurid pageantry" of that "stubborn fight" where Major General John Sedgwick fell. "This man," he continued, "crammed with his family into twelve feet square at the top of Sweeney's Shambles, was once part of that glorious scene."[44]

Many more veterans—including some even less fortunate than Crapsey's one-armed tenant—took to the streets, leading one observer to note that "the blue coat made glorious by the heroism of a hundred battlefields" was being "degraded into the badge of pauperism." "It is a sad sight to see so many disabled soldiers begging for the necessities of life," one Massachusetts soldier wrote. "In too many cases," another echoed, "the poor victim of the war . . . must either force himself to beg, or be compelled to starve." From Boston to New York to Chicago, Union veterans turned the cranks of hand organs as pedestrians either looked the other way or "quiet[ed] their consciences with dropping five or ten cents in the soldier's box."[45]

Each month for several years after the war, the *Soldier's Friend* bemoaned an "apparent forgetfulness" and "noticeable indifference" to the "sufferings of the 'mustered out.'" "Too often," one disturbed Des Moines man wrote, the "wandering mendicant" and "insolent beggar . . . those whom the nation should delight to honor, are compelled to beg for their daily bread" on highways and street corners. One Wisconsin newspaper described with pronounced disinterest the veterans compelled to sit "on door steps, and in alley ways, eating crackers, cheese, raw pork, and hard bread." In Hartford, Connecticut, the local veterans' newspaper reported that the public dismissed as "obnoxious" the rings of disabled Union soldiers begging for dimes on the street corners. Frederick Lee Allen, the mayor of New London, Connecticut, deemed "an intolerable nuisance" the two crippled soldiers who made such a living on the town green. He ordered them to leave town at once. Most civilians wanted the "piteous" sight of the one-armed soldier begging in the streets, like the memory of the war, to just go away. "Very few care for the 'veteran soldier' now," one New Yorker explained. "This is the sad truth." The "good people of this country," one veteran echoed, "are tired of giving, and disgusted at the sight of the crippled relic of the war." "The returning wounded, with powerless arms, shattered legs, or bloody and fearfully disfigured faces," Phineas Whitehouse concluded, "were objects too dreadful to look upon."[46]

Some veterans were simply incapable of weathering rejection. Loath to beg, lacking any semblance of purpose, and uncertain of their station in life, they opted to take some rash steps. In August, a twenty-seven-year-old first lieutenant named Henry Erdman, who had been wounded in the shoulder at Chancellorsville, committed suicide by pitching himself under a freight train near Philadelphia. Then, in October, within Dyckman's Woods near old Fort George, two New York City policemen discovered in a pool of blood the corpse of forty-four-year-old Henry Van Nierop who, as a corporal in the 46th New York Volunteers, spent a fatiguing year settled into the siege lines that encircled Petersburg, Virginia. Strewn beside his five-foot four-inch frame was the razor that he had used to slice his throat—as well as an empty whiskey bottle. Instead of a suicide letter, Van

Nierop left behind a simple and chilling indication of his motive, resting on his chest the army discharge papers that he had been issued at the Delancey House in Washington the last week of July.[47]

The following month, Philadelphia policemen discovered the body of Herman Powell, who rode with a regiment of lancers during the war, "writhing in mortal agony" in the dank Walnut Street basement where he boarded. The carbine Powell had pointed at his chest a few minutes before rested on the floor astride his body. A neighbor informed that Powell was "destitute" and "had no money to buy food." The 15 cents found in his pocket and a suicide note confirmed this report. "I tride my best to make an honest living," Powell scrawled, "but I could not do it." Described only as "insane," one Massachusetts veteran guzzled a lethal dose of rat poison, while a similarly disturbed ex-soldier in New York donned his "soldier clothes" one last time and tarried on the tracks of the Hudson River Railroad, waiting for the whistle of the locomotive that would end his misery.[48]

⊶≡◉⊫⊷

Even as the challenges of returning home from war were made agonizingly apparent, northern civilians remained stubbornly indifferent to the plight of Union veterans. Soldiers' aid societies and ladies' sewing circles determined that their work on behalf of the Union was "substantially accomplished and ended." In June 1865, the ladies of the Marion, Iowa, Soldiers' Aid Society effectively ceased their work on behalf of the enlisted men, voting to change the name of their organization to the "Soldiers' Orphan Aid Society." Likewise, the United States Sanitary Commission ended its philanthropic undertakings almost immediately after the cessation of hostilities. By October 1865, only "skeleton crews" were on hand in three northern cities.[49]

The war had, in the words of the Sanitary Commission's President Henry Whitney Bellows, "drained [volunteers] of strength." "I think I crammed ten years into the four," he wrote. Recalling an endless parade of appeals on behalf of soldiers—of sanitary fairs, fast days, and broadsides demanding ever more—Bellows predicted that he would "never recover the vigour I then squandered." During the war, the spirit of individualism increasingly yielded to the melancholy of bureaucracy. After Cold Harbor and Spotsylvania, the quest for utopia became a sobering search for order. Religious faith and sentimentality faded into a distressed skepticism. Countless reformers buried their millennial hopes and prewar optimism in the war's crowded graveyards. All the same, a deepening economic depression and mounting class-consciousness led many to fear "that relief was turning into a right." With some intellectuals positing that empathy actually "encouraged" dependence, private charities grew hesitant to dispense relief, offering aid in only the most "urgent cases."[50]

For his part, Bellows concluded that relief for Union veterans was "a wicked waste of money and time, and wisdom." "We don't want a vast network of soldiers' poor houses scattered through the land, in which these brave fellows will languish away dull and wretched lives," he insisted. "We want to economize our battered heroes, and take care of them in such a way as to maintain the military spirit and the national pride; to nurse the memories of the war, and to keep in the eye of the Nation the price of its liberties." For the president of the Sanitary Commission, Union veterans were not objects of legitimate sympathy, but rather priceless commodities—baubles to be peddled in the name of patriotism. Bellows, known to tilt his large, dome-shaped head for a cameraman, recommended a "law of local sympathy" in the place of a well-articulated national policy—dismissing out of hand the advice of his subordinate, Frederick Knapp, who predicted a "vast amount of suffering, & poverty & toil" among the Boys in Blue. The very communities that had raised these regiments, Bellows argued, were now entirely responsible for providing any "employment and sympathetic aid."[51]

If new ideas about charity and the roots of poverty recommended indifference to the plight of veterans, though, so too did the redemptive stories that civilians preferred to tell about the war. A glut of narrative histories, popular broadsides, steel engravings, arresting lithographs, and patriotic prints cheerfully interpreted the war as a noble crusade, insisting that brave volunteer soldiers had died "good deaths" and collected "honorable scars" in the name of the republic. Of course, at crucial moments—when they cowered in anticipation of Billy Yank's return, for example—civilians betrayed their ignorance of the "real war." Indeed, whenever northern men and women rehearsed an ennobling war story, they revealed their brooding yet unspeakable suspicion that the war was nothing more than nonsensical butchery. Yet few Civil War Americans could resist romance—and even fewer were willing to confront reality. "[Civilians] would all the sooner listen to a description of a grand battle where all the bravery and dash of trained soldiers in assault and defense is portrayed in the most vivid and glowing colors than a tale which has little in it but that which is revolting, sickening, and sorrowful," one Andersonville survivor concluded. Charles Dodge, an Ohio veteran who lost his right arm in battle, railed against the civilian who, "secure in his home, and far from the scene of danger," was "prone to regard the mingled horrors of a battlefield much as he would some brilliant spectacular drama."[52]

Most northern civilians began to blissfully amble down the "road to reunion" almost immediately after Appomattox. Historians often write as though sectional reconciliation was an achievement of the late nineteenth century—that only after America went off to its "splendid little war" with Spain, fielding an army of former Union and Confederate troops, did northerners extend their hands across the bloody chasm. Yet in April 1865, one cantankerous Michigan soldier was "already" objecting that Rev. Henry Ward Beecher had "commenced to preach 'forgiveness and forgetfulness' of the past." That very month, following the stirring ceremony in which the national colors were once again hoisted above the rubble of Fort Sumter, one northern woman observed that the time had arrived to "lay aside the sins of the past." Never mind the questions of Reconstruction. Confederate President Jefferson Davis—following his humiliating capture by a federal cavalry contingent in the piney woods of northern Georgia—was safely detained in a whitewashed cell at Fortress Monroe; Lincoln's assassin, John Wilkes Booth, was dead, and his misanthropic co-conspirators had been tried, convicted, and cut down from the gallows; and the military commission headed by Major General Lew Wallace had returned its guilty verdict in the war crimes tribunal of Captain Henry Wirz, the Swiss-born commandant of the Confederacy's infamous prison hell at Andersonville. The war's loose ends, it seemed, had all been tied up.[53]

Within the year, national reconciliation—aided and abetted by an ugly racism, gendered metaphors, fictional stories, heartfelt sermons, and the stern dictates of commerce—had become a cultural and political force without peer. As early as 1867, intersectional healing was so pervasive it could be parodied in verse:

> You may sing of the Blue and the Gray
> And mingle their hues in your rhyme, but the Blue that
> > we wore in the fray
> Is covered with glory sublime
> Let the traitors all go if you may
> But never confound with Gray The Blue, whether living or dead.[54]

In an obstinate editorial published that same year, one ex-soldier noted that "if it were not for the evidences of war—such as the dead and dying, the wounded, and the many sad and sickening sights of the battlefield, seen with our own eyes, I should almost be inclined to admit that it was a vain delusion of a disordered brain." "Jefferson Davis is today a hero, and more care is taken of him, than the soldiers who fought to preserve the Union," he continued. "He, Davis, would today be feted and toasted while the man who has periled life and limb would be thrust aside as of no consequence whatsoever."[55]

Union veterans looked on with genuine astonishment as northern civilians "nourish[ed]" the "spirit of rebellion into life again," truckling to the former rebels at the expense of the victors. "Have you no sympathy for the heroes of 1865, who fought to perpetuate that which their fathers fought to inaugurate—liberty and self-government?" queried one Connecticut veteran. William Henry Church, an Iron Brigade lieutenant from Leeds, Wisconsin, was even more incensed. "Their tongues were very smooth and their promises fair, when they needed men to save the Union," he began in a letter to his wife, Ella. "But now that the crisis is past, and danger no longer to be apprehended, they think not of us," he continued. "It makes my blood fairly boil, when I recall the risks we have seen."[56]

Believing himself "forever ruined" by the rogue rebel round that severed his right arm at Shiloh, Robert Rothwell insisted that Union veterans were nearly indistinguishable from African-Americans—who, of course, in the postwar years, continued to meet with inequity, discrimination, and hostility. "I lived like a white man," he wrote of the years before his enlistment in the 70th Ohio Volunteer Infantry in November of 1861, "[but] now [I live] a little like a nigger." Unable to wear the Marvin Lincoln prosthetic arm manufactured for him in Boston and helpless to return to his blacksmithing anvil, he was instead consigned to a life of pleading for pension increases.[57]

Still trembling from "battle shock," able to sense "the bullets whistling" and tearing away his limbs, Rothwell's fellow Ohioan James McCormick Dalzell likewise lived on in misery after the war. The glib dismissal of civilians did little to remedy his suffering. "O God! Can this be so?" he asked. "The soldier wounded *by his friends*, as well as by the foe!" The long-faced soldier who, for the remainder of his life, demanded to be addressed as "Private," fancied a day in the not so distant future when "the surviving veterans of the war against *treason* and *rebellion*" would be "held in higher esteem than at present." The eccentric veteran of "the slavery war" resolved that he would win the hearts and minds of civilians himself, dashing off hundreds of acerbic letters and poems to northern newspaper editors from his home in Caldwell, a tiny village of 100 nestled on the banks of Duck Creek in southeastern Ohio. With his ideas coming "down from God like the rain," "Private Dalzell" became a regular contributor to papers like the *Daily Inter Ocean*, the Republican alternative to the *Chicago Tribune*. "He paid more postage to the United States government than any other citizen," one comrade taunted. Often hunched over his desk well into the wee hours of the morning, his wife, Hettie, and their seven children hardly knew him.[58]

But Dalzell's fervent hopes went unrealized. Like so many of his comrades, the "Private" had to confront the hard truth that he was part of a past Americans preferred only to forget.

⊷═◉◓═⊷

Only awkwardly, then—if indeed at all—did Union veterans return to their homes and families. Neither veterans nor civilians were equipped for the challenges of the postwar years. Either unable or unwilling to exorcise the demons of the past, they could imagine no future together. "Four years of one's life, during youth or early manhood, devoted to a particular calling, however monotonous, cannot fail to leave their trace upon the character," one veteran resolved. "In the army, as elsewhere, habits are acquired which are not readily shaken off, and lessons learned never afterward to be forgotten." "The army," echoed the Illinois veteran Henry Baltzell, "was a poor school to keep on the right track." "[I] was like a balky horse, I kept pulling back."[59]

In a poem that undoubtedly touched the thousands of veterans who encountered its stanzas on the front page of the *Soldier's Friend*, William Oland Bourne captured the realities of the postwar period for some Union veterans:

Suffering and sad
Knowing not where to go,
Wandering the city through
Having no work to do
Wishing he had!
Wishing all day in vain
With a heart filled with pain,
And a hard, bitter strain,
Driving him mad!
What shall he do for bread?
Where shall he lay his head?
Suffering and sad!"[60]

CHAPTER 3

⟦※⟧

ITHACA AT LAST

Well I know when you leave this lodging of the dead
That you and your ship will put ashore again
At the island of Aeaea—then and there,
My lord, remember me, I beg you! Don't sail off
And desert me, left behind unwept, unburied, don't,
Or my curse may draw god's fury on your head.
No, burn me in full armor, all my harness,
Heap my mound by the churning gray surf—
A man whose luck ran out—
So even men to come will learn my story.

—HOMER, *THE ODYSSEY*

Twenty-eight-year-old Ohio-born Major Augustus Vignos planted his troops on the loamy heights above the river, so as to afford them a commanding view of the valley below. He had some 1,500 men in all—hard-edged veterans who were ready for anything. These were soldiers, mostly Iowa troops, who had "seen the elephant" at Pea Ridge, survived the horrors of Shiloh, and besieged Vicksburg and Port Hudson on the Mississippi. Their bronzed faces told their grisly stories, as did the empty right sleeve that Vignos pinned to his bullet-riddled blue coat.

When the brass tubes of the 12-pound Napoleons began to grumble, that familiar rush of adrenaline animated them for impending battle. But the rebel forces were nowhere to be found on this balmy spring afternoon. For the date was May 31, 1867, and these soldiers were staging a "sham battle" in Marengo, Iowa, where they had assembled to hold a colossal veterans' reunion.[1]

The soldiers had two reasons for organizing the event. First, they sought "to renew the acquaintance of those who had together shared the hardships of the camp, the march and the field." Veterans from four Iowa counties—from ten infantry and three cavalry regiments—arrived in the quaint, steepled town perched on the Iowa River (it was named for Napoleon's great victory against the Austrians) to swap stories, hear speeches, and share dinner. The men also sought to raise much-needed funds to build a state home for the children of comrades slain in battle. The whole affair was deemed "productive" and "a happy success." "The sympathy between men who together fought against treason is not less lasting than the principles for which they fought," one observer wrote, predicting that "so long as a dozen Iowa soldiers live," the old days would not be forgotten.[2]

The thought of Union veterans waging pretend warfare scarcely two years after Appomattox strains credulity—especially if one embraces the orthodox view of the Boys in Blue. According to historian Gerald Linderman, "once at home," veterans "became subject to an acceleration of selective memory, that strong psychological propensity to suppress the painful." "On all counts," he wrote, "returned soldiers felt impelled to turn rapidly from the war." Not until the mid-1880s, Linderman concluded, did veterans probe their wartime memories. "The mood of the country reinforced the veteran inclination to pay as little heed as possible to the memories of the war." Only after the decades cooled passions did Union veterans slink out of their preferred state of "hibernation," deploying "positive memories of the war" in the drive for sectional reconciliation.[3]

Yet upon closer inspection it is the very notion of "hibernation" that is implausible, for the many obstacles that Union veterans encountered returning to civilian life could only be surmounted together. In July 1865, Frederick Walster returned to his tiny village of Fort Plain, nestled in the shadow of the Adirondacks, finding the place much changed. The veteran of many sweltering marches through Louisiana's swamps and bayous plunged into a deep melancholy, wondering in the leaves of his diary if his life was even worth living. He wondered if the war was not just some terrible dream. "Shall I never see the time when I shall be happy again as I had been four years ago?" he asked. The soldier's lone reprieve from anguish came in October, when his beloved messmate, Horatio Gilbert, paid him a visit. "It seems real good to be together once more," Walster wrote after an evening of reminiscing about stale hardtack and weak coffee.

Ironically enough, the determination of northern civilians to leave the war behind ensured that Union veterans could not. Left without aid, charity, or sympathy, veterans went to work for themselves. In June 1865, a collection of veterans from Scott County, Iowa, organized the Old Soldiers' Society, while in New Hampshire, seeking to "keep alive the military associations of the last four years," ex-soldiers framed a constitution and by-laws for their Grand Veteran League. In April of 1866, the Grand Army of the Republic—soon to be the nation's largest fraternal organization for northern veterans—was founded by a former regimental surgeon in Decatur, Illinois, on the principles of "fraternity, charity, and loyalty." These organizations got to work quickly, planning scores of reunions and doling out much-needed spiritual, emotional, and financial relief.[4]

While the nation sought release from her worrisome past, then, Union veterans marinated in their memories. Some had no choice. Take, for example, the "one poor Soldier" that Sarah McLean of Shipman, Illinois, described in a July 1865 letter to her veteran son, Edgar. "[He] has come home crazy," she wrote. "He thinks there is going to be another campaign . . . that seems to be the impression he is laboring under." Take Patrick Cleary, the ex-soldier who was living on his brother-in-law John Spain's farm in Hollandtown, Wisconsin, in the fall of 1871. Cleary "talked in a rambling, incoherent way," often standing uninterestedly by the threshing machine, muttering to himself about George McClellan, General Grant, and "a certain Captain Chase." William Cunningham, who boarded with Spain and was himself a veteran, remembered on more than one occasion being roused from his sleep by his agitated former comrade. Into the ground behind Spain's barn, Cleary had pounded a row of wooden stakes to represent "an imaginary enemy." By moonlight, he would drill a white bulldog, commanding him in perfect military parlance to "charge the stakes" and to fight the "supposed rebels."[5]

Or take Oliver Perry Newberry, the enlisted Missouri infantryman with a painful gunshot wound to his left leg who, upon his return home, attempted to replace the sights, sounds, and smells of the war fixed in his mind with the mischievous memories of childhood. But the war—a war he had grown "sick and tired of" in its final year—kept coming back like a nagging cough. "Cool reason runs dethroned and anarchy and confusion reigns supreme, where common sense should be chief ruler," he wrote of his unfriendly mind. "*Strange thoughts* run my head crazy." He passed the entire summer after Appomattox "laying around at the Grocery and drinking whiskey" and had become "so cross" and so cussed by January 1866 that he was "impossible" to live with any longer. "He has become so dissipated since he left the army," Newberry's wife, Lydia, explained in a letter to her brother-in-law. "He has done nothing for himself or his family.[6]

For these and for countless other veterans, the war was not something that could be quickly put away. It was something that they lived with every day. "The momentous events of less than ten years ago are too fresh in memory to be forgotten at the command of any party that may be benefited by ignoring them," one veteran wrote. "That sickly sentiment which would have us believe that the soldiers on either side can ever forget the privations they have endured, the painful marches, the dreadful battle fields, their suffering in field, camp and prison," concluded another ex-soldier, "is more than foolish."[7]

One significant obstacle that prevented Union veterans from leaving the rebellion behind was their unwavering conviction that its achievements, like the nation, remained in peril. Though they frequently and emphatically announced that they had "subdued and conquered" the rebellion, many ex-soldiers were wracked by niggling fears that the war's results were tentative at best. Throughout the South, reports of street battles, white vigilantes, torched buildings, raped women, and freedmen slaughtered in cold blood prompted one Pennsylvania veteran to ask if his labors were in vain. "There are still enemies to face and overcome," he declared. The "fighting part of the rebellion," Samuel Dickson insisted in a letter to a comrade, had only lapsed momentarily. "Does it ever occur to you that we may again be driven to arms?" echoed one Illinois ex-soldier. All but convinced that "the intensity of the hatred of the southern whites" would inevitably result in "another civil war," Eugene B. Payne told the men of his Illinois regiment that the nation "must put the ballot into the hands of the colored man." Achieving black suffrage would do justice to his "wooly headed battle field companions," and prevent white southerners from assuming power too soon after the thorough "crushing out" of their insidious rebellion. "We see, everyday, the old hostility cropping out in continued acts of antagonism to the reconstruction laws of Congress," another veteran dolefully observed. "The animus of treason and rebellion is as vindictive and deadly now," he continued, "as in 1861 and during the late war."[8]

Especially as a nation hungover on military combat staggered its way into Reconstruction, many Union veterans grew apprehensive about the future. The Civil War, as historian Mark Wahlgren Summers has written, had not only "not cleared the miasma in the political air," but had "intensified it." "After five years of fierce and destructive war, in which our arms were gloriously triumphant," fumed an assembly of Union ex-soldiers and ex-sailors gathered at Cleveland, Ohio, "the Union for which we fought is still practically un-restored." "We might have well hoped when the last Rebel surrendered, and when our arms were victorious everywhere, that peace and concord and unity should prevail," Major General Benjamin Franklin Butler roared, but, "unfortunately for the country," such optimism had been misplaced. Throughout the South, guerrilla bands murdered Union veterans and freed slaves in cold blood. "There are perplexing questions to be solved," conceded James J. Creigh of Pennsylvania. "We were equal to all the necessities of the war," he began, but "are we equal to the necessities of the country in time of peace?"⁹

⋄━◉━⋄

In addition to lingering suspicions about victory, there was another, more compelling barrier to veterans' solace. Upon their return, ex-soldiers found themselves living in the shadow of the dead. "The war and all connected with it was a stern reality," one veteran explained. "Are the survivors expected to forget their dead comrades?" he asked. As survivors, veterans felt a genuine sense of "duty," both to remember their fallen comrades and to find some enduring meaning in their demise. "Who can forget the days of mad frenzy of battle, when bullets whizzed and screamed, and shells burst, taking the life of one and the limb of another comrade at our side?" While storming the rebel earthworks in the opening federal assaults around Petersburg, Virginia, on June 16, 1864, Stephen Chase looked on in horror as a rebel shell hurtled unexpectedly in his direction and disemboweled his company commander, standing immediately to his right. "I can see my old comrade lying there in his own gore and being carried to his last resting place under the wild apple tree," he wrote years later. First Lieutenant Wilson Hopkins, who fought with the 16th New York, wrote that the memories of the first time he collected the stiffened, bullet-riddled bodies from a battlefield—at South Mountain in Maryland—would "remain with me to the end."[10]

To be a veteran, then, was to live with these disturbing memories. "With our own eyes, with our own ears, we have seen and heard something of the great conflict," Creigh declared. "Its reminiscences are interwoven with the lives of every one of us." To be a veteran also meant untangling those memories. "*My* bruises are inward," explained Private John Haley of the 17th Maine Volunteers. Without civilian understanding and lacking what historian Stuart McConnell has called "an explanatory myth" about his place in postwar society, the Union veteran turned instead to his beloved comrades. As Susan-Mary Grant argues, the veteran—neither admitted to the "cult of the fallen" nor constituents of their antebellum communities—created his own world. Together, they devised their own rituals, created their own spaces, and even developed their own lexicon and sense of time.[11]

Civilians unavoidably took notice of their bizarre guild, though most often with some blend of confusion, spite, and dread. These "cranks"—or, as some observers put it, "tiresome back numbers" hobbling around on crutches and cork legs—simply posed too much of a threat to the nation's "romance of reunion." "No one of even common observation can have failed to notice in the faces of returned veteran regiments, as they have marched along our streets, a stereotyped cast of countenance," one writer observed in the spring of 1865. Beyond the "tattered garments" soiled with the dust and sweat of long marches, he wrote, there was an "imprint of sternness" on each ex-soldier's brow. Union veterans got up with the war in the morning, and went to bed with it at night.[12]

--•-=—◦ ◦—=-•--

It was not only their countenance and physical appearance, however, that marked them as exceptional; the manner in which Union veterans ordered their lives betrayed just how fundamentally the war had changed them. For one, the war had imposed a new calendar. Quite literally "marching to the beat of a different drummer," veterans marked time on a calendar now solemnized by enlistment dates ("My Soldier Birthday," as one Iowa veteran coined it), discharge dates, and the anniversaries of wounds, imprisonment, and battles—both great and small. Diary pages once crowded with frenetic entries were now blank, except to announce important war anniversaries. (Indeed, rather than record new life events, one lieutenant proceeded to copy his entire war diary day by day after he returned home.) "Just one year ago today I was taken prisoner by the Rebels at Poplar Grove Church, Va.," Lyman Jackman scrawled in his otherwise frozen diary on September 30, 1865. Nearly a decade later, only remembrances of stubbornly fought battles prompted any disruption in Jackman's monotonous record of the weather. "10 years ago today we fought the Big Battle of the Wilderness. It was a *Hard Hat* day ... to be remembered," he observed on May 6, 1874. The very next week, he recollected the "all day" fighting at "Spottselvania," where the beloved major of his company had been killed. To aid their reminiscing, many veterans purchased and tattered half-dime copies of the Soldiers' & Sailors' Publishing Company's *Almanac and History of the Late Rebellion*, which offered readers a "reliable" calendar of the war's most significant events. Those without a copy of the almanac could, on the other hand, purchase the *Souvenir, Principal Events and Battles of the Rebellion*, a handy timeline extending "from the election of Abraham Lincoln, 1860, to the execution of Wirz, 1865."[13]

For some regiments, the memory of a particular battle was so affecting that its anniversary assumed the attributes of a "feast day." The battle of South Mountain, Maryland, a pitched rendezvous with the rebels along the rugged spine of the Blue Ridge three days before Antietam, was such an engagement for the men of the 23rd Ohio Volunteers. "Our little squad remembered to talk over the battle at South Mountain, fought on such a day as this twenty-two years ago today," Rutherford B. Hayes, the regiment's lieutenant colonel, noted in his diary. Hayes had been very seriously wounded in the battle's opening brawl. Soon after he left the presidency, the old colonel commemorated "the anniversary of South Mountain" by removing "the old coat which I wore when wounded" from its "anti-moth box." "This is South Mountain Day," Hayes recorded in his diary in 1891, two years before his death. "Twenty-nine years ago this morning we marched up the old National Road.... We had gained the victory!"[14]

Just as civilian calendars were no longer adequate for ex-soldiers, neither were civilian newspapers. Beginning with Bourne's the *Soldier's Friend* immediately after the war, more than forty veterans' newspapers began competing for subscribers. In the early years, Bourne's leading rival was the *Great Republic*, which became the "official organ" of the Grand Army of the Republic. In brazenly conspiratorial tones, the *Republic* cautioned uneasy veterans that the old rebels "continued to plot." In 1868, the New York City–based Soldiers' & Sailors' Publishing Company began issuing a weekly illustrated magazine, *Half Dime Tales of the Late Rebellion*, which offered its readers personal anecdotes of camp life, "stories of the army and navy," a "chronological record" of important wartime events, and "authentic sketches" of life in rebel prisons. Two years later, William T. Collins, the blunt adjutant general of the Grand Army of the Republic who lost his left leg at the battle of Rappahannock Station, began publishing the weekly *Grand Army Journal* ("a paper for the surviving soldiers and sailors who united to suppress the rebellion") from the Woodward Building at Tenth and D streets in Washington. "A soldier's paper was felt to be wanted," Collins explained, "that is, such a paper as soldiers would understand to be identical in interest with themselves." "Bold enough to speak the truth," the *Grand Army Journal* advocated hiring preferences for veterans and promoted the claims of soldiers disabled by the war. For two dollars per year, subscribers could read articles celebrating the heroes who had "periled life to save the Republic," review full reports of army and corps reunions, and even peruse Grand Army personals.[15]

Within a decade of Appomattox, nearly every major northern city boasted a veterans' newspaper. Ex-soldiers from Madison, Wisconsin, touted the *Soldiers' Record*, with its elegant masthead depicting a nurse affectionately bandaging a wounded soldier, as the most comprehensive bulletin serving the Boys in Blue. Minnesota ex-soldiers, resolving to "stand together" in the face of unemployment and destitution ("if we must starve together let us starve together"), turned to the pages of the *St. Paul Relief Guard*, while Kansas veterans eagerly awaited issues of the *Weekly Knight and Soldier*, published in Topeka. In the Granite State, comrades gleefully consumed the *Veteran's Advocate*, an eight-page, half-dime weekly published by Ira Evans, the drummer boy of the 12th New Hampshire. "I have been much pleased with each number of the *Advocate*, and I have heard many a comrade express a similar satisfaction," one subscriber wrote. "It is *the* journal that the veterans of New Hampshire have long needed." Evans invited veterans to submit their appalling tales and remembrances of "queer incidents" for publication—something that offered the old comrades the validation, respect, and understanding that civilians too often denied. Each issue became a conversation among the "living wrecks" of the army. "Let us fill up the pipe," Evans urged his comrades, "and while engaged in a good, solid smoke, we will chat of the days that are gone."[16]

Veterans everywhere, however, typically preferred to take the *National Tribune*, which made its debut in October 1877. The paper—edited in Washington by the slick-haired and walrus-mustached pension attorney George Lemon, who carried "between the bones of his leg" the rebel bullet that struck him at the battle of Bristoe Station in October 1863—quickly outgrew its headquarters on G Street and moved in later years to a five-story brick building on New York Avenue. Lemon was a man of business acumen and "indomitable pluck," but this merely fueled civilian suspicion that the paper was simply another flavor of activism in an era of troubling labor unrest. The *Tribune* no doubt argued eloquently for arrears

("We firmly believe that every man who went to the front during the war and helped to save the country earned a pension," one editorial began, "and that the least that the rescued and prosperous Nation can in decency offer him is $8 a month"), but subscribers understood the newspaper's utility rather differently. Much like the *Veteran's Advocate*, the *Tribune* provided ordinary rank-and-file veterans with the coveted opportunity to share their most horrific war stories with a wide audience. Every day, bundles of letters arrived in Washington—each author hopeful that typesetters donning ink-spattered aprons might very soon hunch over newfangled machines to fix his words above the fold. Arthur S. Fitch of the 107th New York, for example, contributed a few "tragic scenes" of the battle at Dallas, Georgia. A veteran of the 51st Pennsylvania remembered his beloved colonel coughing up an enemy bullet. An Illinois veteran challenged his comrades to best his company's record of losses throughout the war, while Chauncey Fish of the 9th New York Heavy Artillery attempted to explain the peculiar sensation of being wounded on the field of battle. Ex–prisoners of war shared their "pitiful" and bone-chilling tales of Salisbury, Libby, and Andersonville. In the pages of the *Tribune*, they met with none of the withering skepticism that they had come to expect from civilians. (Indeed, by the 1880s, Union veterans had compiled so many examples of northern newspapers carping about pension claims and demeaning needy soldiers that they began running the most contemptible excerpts in a regular column, "The Hue and the Cry.") In contrast, in *their* paper, the old boys could openly contemplate some "suggestive" comparisons, like the contrast between the "risks incurred by those who staked their money on the preservation of the Union and those who offered their lives in its defence." "Our ex-soldiers succeeded in putting down the rebellion of the slaveholders," one veteran wrote. "The enemies who now confront them are those of their own household, the ingrates who owe whatever prosperity they now enjoy to the value of the men who saved the Republic." Sentiments such as these only enhanced the veterans' intrinsic sense of alliance and fraternity. According to one veteran, this was the "great, important work" that the soldiers' papers accomplished.[17]

In regular columns and in letters to the editor, the veterans wandered back to the war's battles, "fighting them over" one by one. The paper allowed ex-soldiers to swap stories as they sought to assemble their own coherent narrative of the past. An article about Sherman's March to the Sea prompted Kentucky infantryman J. P. Coleman to lend his "testimony" that there was neither "willful" nor "wholesale destruction of property" when blue-coated columns penetrated Georgia in 1864. In turn, veterans rehabilitated the performance of Lew Wallace at Shiloh, "vindicated" the Union right at Franklin, and rectified the mortality rates at Florence and Salisbury. Sometimes the dialogue became particularly heated, and former comrades argued endlessly over every last tactical detail.[18]

Not infrequently, these volleys of pen and ink assisted in reuniting two long-lost friends. Abraham Kile was examining the *Tribune* in the parlor of his Muscatine, Iowa, home one July evening in 1902 when he noticed a passing reference to one Samuel Bloomer, a veteran who now made his home near Stillwater, Minnesota. Persuaded that Bloomer was an old companion from his days in the Veteran Reserve Corps, Kile decided to address a brief letter to him. When Bloomer received the note, he immediately confirmed Kile's suspicion, and the two began a regular correspondence. "I oftimes wonder how many of our old comrades are living or what has become of them," Bloomer replied in one of his letters to Kile. "Tell me about your wife and family . . . how well I should like to see you." Veterans impatient to find an old messmate or unwilling to trust fate could, for 25 cents, purchase a classified advertisement in the *Tribune*.[19]

Reading the contributions of former comrades cheered many veterans. Seventeen-year-old Logan Meade Boren, an Illinois lad "named after two of the bravest generals of the war," contended that the *Tribune* had a most salubrious effect on his father, a crippled veteran of the 14th Illinois. "It does him a great deal of good to read in *The Tribune* of the battles in which he took part," the boy wrote. John Rutt, a Michigander who spent three months in the Lynchburg and Belle Isle prison camps, likewise yearned for stories from "any of my comrades who served with me in prison." There was also Captain Grenville Sparrow of the 17th Maine, who dutifully maintained a 300-page leather-bound scrapbook bursting with tattered clippings from the *Tribune*. He even went to the trouble of indexing the book's contents, from "After Battle" to "Wilderness Battlefield."[20]

Not surprisingly, newspapers like the *Tribune* became important hubs of information about fraternal societies organized by and for Union veterans. Naturally, the papers reported on the activities of the various posts and departments of the Grand Army of the Republic. Founded by the former regimental surgeon Major Benjamin Stephenson in Decatur, Illinois, in April 1866, the Grand Army not only provided pecuniary aid for impoverished veterans, but "solace and psychological guidance" for those bewildered by civilian life. "No organization," one Hoosier ex-soldier insisted, "has ever existed that had better or more ennobling principles." One grateful soldier noted the "gladness and hope" that the Grand Army had brought to innumerable "sad and weary hearts."[21]

Though it has been routinely dismissed by historians as the brainchild of Republican partisans who self-interestedly sought support at the ballot box, handbooks and financial records reveal that the Grand Army was one of the most significant social-welfare organizations of the nineteenth century. Following the roll call and the delivery of the adjutant's and quartermaster's reports at weekly meetings, officers were instructed to ask if any comrade was "sick or in distress," or if any member had knowledge of "deserving soldiers or sailors" in need of assistance. These veterans were eligible to draw benefits from the post "relief fund," which outfitted soldiers with artificial limbs and muslin bandages, defrayed the cost of medical procedures and funerals, and kept poverty-stricken veterans in heated homes for the winter. Sometimes, relief-fund disbursements were all that sustained veterans supporting large families between pension payments. Around the country, comrades delivered "benefit lectures" to reimburse relief funds.[22]

In addition to monetary aid, the GAR relief committees assisted "penniless and helpless" veterans in securing employment. Headquartered on Boston's Pemberton Square, the Department of Massachusetts established the Veterans' Rights Union and Employment Bureau, while the Department of New York operated its own Bureau of Employment and Emergency Fund. And for $12 per year, comrades could purchase life insurance through the Indianapolis-based GAR Beneficial Association. "To the Grand Army of the Republic more than to any other order," wrote Major General John Alexander Logan's widow, Mary, "do the unfortunate look for aid. If a comrade is sick, he sends to his post for sympathy and help. If he seeks employment, he can rely upon his comrades to vouch for him. He knows that when the end comes he will be laid to rest by the members of his post, and that a stone will mark his last resting-place."[23]

The Grand Army was only one among hundreds of veterans' organizations competing for membership in the decades after the war. Survivor associations represented every echelon of military life, from individual regimental companies to the various Union field armies. The men of Company A of the 25th Massachusetts Volunteer Infantry, for example, convened annually in Worcester around the anniversary of Cold Harbor, the battle in which they suffered most "severe losses." Together, these reunions were opportunities for the old vets to "talk over the trials and hardships through which we passed"—including the harrowing experience of imprisonment at Andersonville, something they were "willing to forgive, but could never forget." Perhaps unavoidably, these gatherings prompted veterans to examine the cynicism they shared for northern society and the former rebels. In 1888, Corporal Walter S. Bugbee registered his disgust "with all the gush over the blue and the gray," declaring that "the rebels were [merely] half licked." He volunteered to help drown his former enemies in the Gulf of Mexico. The following year, in an after-dinner speech, one comrade reminded the crowd that "no one but a soldier knows the sacrifices" required that the nation might live. On yet another occasion, a veteran affectionately known as Old Dan "brought down the house" with his entertaining comparison of "Campaigns at Home and in the Army."[24]

Regimental and brigade reunion associations were ubiquitous. Beginning almost immediately after Appomattox, many fighting units, aiming "to perpetuate the bonds of comradeship . . . and to cherish with a holy love the memory of those of our companions, who fell in the good cause for which we risked our own lives," formed organizations and adopted prudently worded constitutions and by-laws. A need to honor the dead and celebrate the living animated the old boys everywhere. Complementing the work of veterans' newspapers, these associations functioned as essential "sites of memory," honoring the dead and providing social support for the living. The 52nd Illinois Veteran Volunteer Infantry Reunion Association, for instance, assembled annually on the second Wednesday of September, hoisting high banners emblazoned with the names of those hallowed fields where its members fought and their beloved comrades died—including Shiloh, Corinth, Iuka, Kennesaw Mountain, and Bentonville. Supplementing the important work of the Grand Army, local regimental reunion associations likewise maintained emergency funds for the relief of needy, ailing, or homeless comrades.[25]

Men also cherished links beyond the "order of battle." Veterans who shared distinctive wartime experiences like imprisonment or dismemberment allied in well over sixty local, state, and national ex–prisoner-of-war associations and in the ranks of the Crippled Soldiers Association. Others remembered the war as members of the Military Order of the Loyal Legion of the United States, the National Association of Civil War Musicians, the National Association of Naval Veterans, the Society of the Ram Fleet, the Union Veteran Army, the National *Sultana* Survivors' Association, and the Congressional Medal of Honor Holders Association. In 1905, a few dozen veterans living near Denver, Colorado, who had fought the rebels at Pittsburg Landing, Tennessee, in April 1862, even organized the National Association of the Battle of Shiloh Survivors. Through regular meetings and "discussions relating to personal incidents [involving the battle]," these veterans hoped to sustain the memory of what they regarded as the war's "most decisive and least understood" battle. The Denver veterans addressed letters to thousands of their fellow Shiloh survivors, including men like Iowa Sergeant Rodney Tirrill, whose distinct limp was a mute reminder of the shell wound he suffered on the battle's first day. Tirrill answered the circular and, at the first annual meeting of the association, called to order at the Plymouth Congregational Church in Minneapolis on August 14, 1906, he was elected senior vice commander. Like many of those who gathered that afternoon in Minnesota, Tirrill was unable to forget those momentous hours he passed with the rebel enemy in the brambles of the Hornet's Nest. Referring to the battle as though it were a chronic illness, he wrote, "I have had Shiloh ever since the sixth day of April 1862."[26]

Some civilians could not divine the purpose of formal veterans organizations, which seemed only to imperil cherished republican values. Local newspaper editors brashly questioned the motives of the curious new associations rising from the war's embers. "Comrades, people may and sometimes do criticize soldier's meetings," an Illinois veteran began. "Let them if they will . . . it is right we should meet just as we meet today, for it brightens the eye, it quickens the pulse, it stirs the blood of every old soldier, aye and more, it intensifies his devotion to his flag." Perhaps the most "ridiculous criticism," however, was leveled at the men of the Grand Army of the Republic. Citing the order's "unworthy and dangerous" officers, "rash pledges," "extra judicial oaths," secretive meetings, and categorical "selfishness," the United Presbytery of Keokuk, Iowa, declared the GAR to be "inconsistent with the principles of the United Presbyterian Church." Once again, civilian sentiments such as these only invigorated the belief held by many veterans that their experiences could "never be understood" by those "who shared not" in like perils. "The dangers and hardships of the service made stronger ties of friendship than civil life ever offered," one veteran explained to a dubious civilian. "Men, side by side, sharing the same privations, facing the same perils, and struggling to maintain the same glorious principles in years of sanguinary war, must form attachments that will endure while life lasts."[27]

Though they routinely dismissed quizzical looks from civilians, Union veterans remained profoundly troubled by their perception that the public neither understood nor appreciated their sacrifices. Diligently, they worked to ensure that their war stories would not only be safeguarded, but that they would reach well beyond the meeting hall, the old soldiers' newspaper column, and the reunion campfire. Many veterans thus took up their fountain pens and worked tirelessly on some seven hundred company, regimental, battery, brigade, division, corps, and army histories—attractive, tightly bound, and gilded volumes that they expected might serve as "an inspiration to the generations to come." "[These histories are] written not only for the survivors of the war," affirmed Andrew Elmer Ford, who served as the regimental historian for the 15th Massachusetts Volunteers, "but [are composed] for their children and their children's children."[28]

The preparation of a unit history was a grueling—even a "very thankless"—task, requiring years of determined spadework and enterprising collaboration. Ford, for example, spent months scouring the Massachu-setts State Archives and the "regimental chest" on deposit at the Ameri-can Antiquarian Society in Worcester for material; he also personally interviewed dozens of comrades at regimental reunions. Eugene B. Payne used regimental gatherings as an opportunity to gather "scraps of Dia-ries" for his history of the Fremont Rifles. Though he relied on his own extensive diaries to compose a history of the 10th Maine, John Mead Gould asked his comrades to assist in pinpointing the unit's locations and fighting strengths. Asa Bartlett, who "carried the 12th New Hamp-shire Regiment on his heart," was tasked with preparing the unit's his-tory. He spent the better part of a decade soliciting detailed reminiscences of Chancellorsville and Gettysburg from his comrades, now scattered throughout New England. Some of the old boys grew so impatient for the book's publication that they chided Bartlett for his fanatical attention to detail, an affliction that debilitated many other regimental historians. Other units, especially eager to see their regiment's history in print, appointed regimental history "committees" that, in turn, designated com-rades to complete individual chapters. A few regimental historians were paid "outsiders"—frustrated writers who advertised their services in vet-erans' papers. Despite the psychic burden of the task, faulty memories, and recurring spells of "discouragement," most of the ex-soldiers perse-vered; only outsiders, without personal investment, failed to see histories through to publication.[29]

Especially in later years, regimental chroniclers relied on a swelling number of published sources relating to the war. Most significantly, they made use of *War of the Rebellion: A Compilation of the Official Records of the Union and Confederate Armies*, a 128-volume set published by the War Department in the last two decades of the nineteenth century. During the 1870s, diligent clerks combed through the War Department attic, collect-ing official reports, correspondence, and general orders into an "authentic" record of the war. The first fruits of their labor appeared in print in July

1881, and by 1890, forty volumes had been published, documenting the war through Chancellorsville. The editors released the last of the set's nearly 140,000 pages and 1,500 battlefield maps in June 1900. Confederate sources, sometimes underrepresented in the *Official Records* (despite the fact that "over ninety large boxes" of Confederate materials had been shipped up from Richmond at the end of the war), were valuable wells of information, too. Hosea Whitford Rood, the custodian of the Grand Army Memorial Hall in Madison, who doubled as the regimental historian of the 12th Wisconsin Volunteers, maintained a subscription to Sumner Archibald Cunningham's *Confederate Veteran*, the leading periodical for southern ex-soldiers. An amateur historian, Rood quickly learned the value of triangulating evidence. "It is best to have here the views of men from the other side," he wrote. Veterans also relied heavily on other regimental histories and published papers in their work. Seeking inspiration during a stubborn spell of writer's block, the author of the 88th Pennsylvania's regimental history "carefully studied" the literary style of the many unit histories he owned. Addresses delivered to Military Order of the Loyal Legion of the United States commanderies, which first appeared as pamphlets and were eventually anthologized, were likewise esteemed sources, as were the stirring Wednesday evening lectures presented to the members of the Rhode Island Soldiers and Sailors Historical Society in Providence.[30]

Although scholars have disparaged regimental histories for "bur[ying] or distort[ing] the 'real war' in a sea of 'sentimentalism,'" these volumes were, more often than not, robustly argued exposés of the cause, course, and consequences of the war that "closely evaluated the unanticipated demands that the Civil War had placed on the men at arms." Ohio ex-soldier Jacob Smith, for example, underscored "the tolls, dangers, labor, and hardships of the common soldiers while in the discharge of the duties belonging to that sphere in life" in *Camps and Campaigns of the 107th Regiment.* Civic recognition of these privations, Smith contended, would supply sufficient compensation for his labors. Edward Lord began his regal history of the 9th New Hampshire Volunteers by explaining that "the growing evil of slavery" was "the real source of trouble" that had precipitated war. "The emergency was great," Lord continued, "but no one even dreamed how terrible a sacrifice of precious human lives was to be laid on the country's altar in expiation for the injustice done the African Negro." In the foreword he penned for *We Were the Ninth*, the history of a predominately German regiment from Cincinnati, Gustav Tafel set out to explain the "events leading up to the outbreak of hostilities." "The United States, developing rapidly and on a grand scale, had become the marvel of the modern world," he began. "Yet the North and the South had long been antagonistic. Clearer and clearer, and more and more precisely, the issue came into focus: slavery."[31]

These arguments, along with the feverish desire to reach a wide public audience, sallied forth in dozens of personal memoirs, war histories, and short sketches written by veterans. Taken together, these writings offer overwhelming testimony of the need of Union veterans to record and remember their war. While the American Revolution produced several notable soldier memoirs, and Confederate soldiers wrote several classic histories, the literary productivity of Union veterans was unrivaled. Captain Daniel Eldredge did not "hibernate" after the war; instead, his memories of service in Captain Israel Littlefield's Company K of the 3rd New Hampshire streamed steadily forth from his fountain pen. Considering that there were yet fragments of lead "perceptible to the touch" wedged between the tendons of his left forearm—the result of the cruel gunshot wound he received at Deep Bottom, Virginia, in July of 1864—Eldredge's labors were even more impressive. The twenty-four-year-old began writing one afternoon in November 1865, expecting that his narrative would consume no more than "a half dozen sheets of foolscap." Each day, writing from memory alone, he toiled on his manuscript—each new word sending currents of pain traveling up his fractured limb. Wincing with each word, he wrote up the scenes as they flashed before his eyes: "Let us take a walk through the [hospital] building and see the sick and dying," he began one day. "Here is one yellow as saffron, suffering from jaundice; there is another, whose speech is being slowly but surely cut off by that dreadful disease, diphtheria, yonder another suffering from the effects of an unknown disease which causes him to sleep for two or three days almost without intermission . . . on the right hand lays a poor unfortunate who is complete[ly] prostrated by diarrhea in its worst form; on our left hand is a victim of fever whom death has been struggling for." As the weeks and months passed, Eldredge's pain did not diminish (following an unsuccessful attempt to remove the lead shards in October 1866, his doctor, James Phillips, conceded final defeat). Still, the stack of completed pages grew ever more imposing. By the summer of 1867, when Eldredge finished, he had written over 600 pages, illustrated with hand-drawn maps depicting the siege operations against Charleston, the Bermuda Hundred campaign, and the assault on Fort Fisher.[32]

Like many veterans, Eldredge "had to grope [his] way through the writing process." "On some days I write half a dozen lines, upon other days none; occasionally a whole month goes by without a single word being written," he commented, "and if the reader wonders that I am puzzled to connect all the parts properly and that I skip from one locality to another without warning, he must be ungenerous and uncharitable." Rhode Island cavalryman George Bliss was "not a little puzzled" about how to author a "satisfactory" and "connected" story, and Solon Pierce, who started writing immediately after his return home to Wisconsin, had "many misgivings" about the "painstaking" labor of composition. R. W. Browne cautioned that his soldiers' tale was "very crudely told," as he was not one "of those 'd—d littery fellers.'" But while their prose was often "unremarkable" (at least in the estimate of literary scholar Daniel Aaron), veteran memoirists and historians more than compensated for any mechanical or stylistic deficiencies with their "candor and sincerity." These memoirists testified

about the experience of war and openly revealed the indelible imprint
it had left on their minds. Veterans shared a genuine desire to convey a
meaningful and exact record of their exploits—to "sustain the truth of
history" and to contribute to the already sprawling historiography of
the rebellion. They understood their writings as "a living rebuke" to
rose-colored sentimentality.[33]

In the 1880s, an itch to publish prompted thousands of northern veterans to supply war "sketches" for *Century Magazine*, an illustrated
monthly first published in 1881. *Century* was the self-appointed "cultural
steward" of late-nineteenth-century America, offering readers a healthy
variety of essays, illustrations, and short stories. Between 1884 and 1887,
Union and Confederate veterans—especially officers—were invited to
submit articles chronicling the exploits and personalities of the rebellion.
So popular—not to mention profitable—were these tales that Robert
Underwood Johnson and Clarence Clough Buel, the magazine's editors,
collected and rereleased the war stories as *Battles and Leaders of the Civil
War*, a four-volume series that remains in print today.[34]

Yet neither *Century* nor its civilian readership shared the ends of the
iron-willed ex-soldiers determined "to write the war as they fought it."
Century's editors and the reading public wanted only to peer through the
field glasses of the high command, to ride in the saddle with the officers.
They sought a bloodless war in which little was at stake, save the reputation of the cigar-chomping, whiskey-guzzling generals who moved armies
around like rooks on a chessboard. "Our plan is to have the Great Battles
described *as battles* with all their individuality, as one might characterize
men, describing their important features, events, incidents, heroic actions,
etc.," Johnson explained to former Confederate General James Longstreet.
"Especially desirous to avoid disputed points," Johnson exacted from
series contributors the "picturesque and significant features," the "individual examples of heroism," and narratives "lightened by anecdotes" and "as
much color and incident as possible." Dangling hefty royalties under their

noses, Buel and Johnson persuaded Union and Confederate officers like George McClellan, Joseph Eggleston Johnston, John Imboden, Fitz John Porter, Daniel Harvey Hill, William Franklin, Henry Kyd Douglas, and William Rosecrans to contribute articles to the series. Only seldom did the work of common soldiers, who were much less likely to tempt potential subscribers, actually appear in print. When veteran Joseph Pope submitted an article for consideration, the editors informed him that the essay duplicated information that would likely be covered in a forthcoming piece by Don Carlos Buell, the gnarled commander of the Army of the Ohio. "We thank you for taking the trouble to inform us so particularly regarding your design, and we regret that we cannot avail ourselves of [your] offer." One Iowan who fought at Shiloh concluded that there was an unequivocal "lack of respect" for the testimony of "Private soldiers."[35]

Indeed, after many hours of determined writing, hundreds of veterans received the news that the war sketches they had excitedly mailed off to the "book-lined, paper-strewn" *Century* editorial offices on Union Square in New York City would not be published. " 'I fear we shall not be able to use it'" became the editors' refrain in replies to impatient ex-soldiers. "We are very crowded for space in which to print War material," Johnson explained to John Collins after the Philadelphia veteran proudly submitted his war sketch. Buel admonished an Andersonville survivor inquiring about the fate of his manuscript on "life and death in rebel prisons" that "it might be four or five weeks before we examine it or arrive at a decision." In any case, Buel added frankly, "There is little likelihood we will be able to use much of it." Veterans' memories were literally irreconcilable with the glamorized war peddled by the editors. The editors told poor Oscar Jackson that they were "uninterested" in his gritty piece on Corinth unless he devoted considerably more space "to the picturesque and incidental side of the battle," while New Yorker George Kilmer's essay on the postwar lives of maimed soldiers was, not surprisingly, returned without comment.[36]

Such frank rejection no doubt came as a most crippling blow to Thomas Lee, who, after four years in the ranks of the 20th Indiana, collected a shell wound to the head at Second Manassas and gunshot injuries in the right hand and right leg at the Wilderness and at Spotsylvania Court House. ("I am nearly totally disabled from all the wounds and injuries that I received in battles and siege in the war," he explained.) An unmarried carriage maker who came to America from Ireland without kin, Lee was admitted to the Central Branch of the National Home for Disabled Volunteer Soldiers in Dayton, Ohio, in September of 1877. Lee was so harassed by his horrific past that he spent "over ten years" alone in his dimly-lit room, hunched over a wooden desk in the corner, chronicling his "war record" in forty manuscripts, twenty orders of battle, and some one hundred hand-drawn troop position maps. "My manuscripts weigh about thirty pounds," Lee explained immodestly, "and are mostly of uniform size and in book form."[37]

Yet even the overwhelming likelihood of editorial rejection did not dissuade Union veterans, who continued to submit their treasured manuscripts and coarse memories to *Century*. Ex-soldiers pitched their potential contributions in every conceivable way, touting their participation in obscure engagements and their inimitable knowledge of military events. "As you have had so many articles in relation to the Army of the Potomac, some articles in reference to the Western Army would not be out of place," one Hoosier veteran reasoned. "I am sure I could write you up a good one." With no small dose of conceit, Charles L. Baker assured *Century*'s editors that he possessed "ample material" for "a most entertaining" and "most interesting historical article." Other veteran writers, virtually indigent, persisted in their quest for literary success out of necessity. An unemployed veteran named Charles Kimmel of Dayton, Ohio, pleaded with *Century* to publish routine excerpts from his meticulous war diary. "I am a poor laboring man with a large family," he explained. "If you deem it a good investment, what would you gentlemen give me to send you monthly sketches to your valuable magazine?" "Stooped, gray, and wrinkled," pocked with scars from gunshot wounds received the day he was captured at the battle of the Crater, Robert K. Beecham was more direct, noting that as he was aging, another "sojourn in the poorhouse" was looking especially forbidding. "Of course it is not honor I am looking for now, but a chance for bread and butter," the hollow-eyed veteran of the Iron Brigade, an inveterate critic of slavery, confessed from his pathetic shanty in Antelope County, Nebraska. "Physically played out," Beecham's deepest worry was pecuniary. "I am willing to work cheap," he insisted. "I can do a great deal of writing for $100." Persistence would pay off for Beecham, although not with the editors at *Century*. In 1911, he scored a plum contract with A. C. McClurg for a new history of the battle of Gettysburg.[38]

⇢═◉═⇠

It is not at all surprising that needy veterans like Kimmel and Beecham sought real income by peddling their war stories. Not only were their pensions wholly inadequate, but, for so many of the war's survivors, being a veteran was "work." A squall of invitations to annual banquets, regimental reunions, association meetings, and anniversary celebrations overwhelmed many veterans, as did requests to deliver testimony on behalf of comrades seeking pension increases and summons to address Grand Army campfires and assemblies of local schoolchildren. This was especially true of veterans like Corporal James Tanner and drummer boy Martin Pembleton, who achieved recognition and renown on what became known as "the old soldier circuit." Tanner, who enlisted in the 87th New York Volunteers as a plucky seventeen-year-old, fought his way up the Peninsula in the spring of 1862. In late August, his regiment stared down "Stonewall" Jackson's troops at Second Manassas and anchored the right of the Union line. The New Yorkers weathered a "terrific shelling" from Jackson's artillery, but a mortar ripped into Tanner—necessitating the amputation of both legs. For the rest of his life, he walked with a cane and a pair of Dr. Ben-

jamin Frank Palmer's patented wooden prosthetics. He nonetheless maintained a grueling speaking schedule, traveling from New York to Nebraska
to address regimental reunions and state and national Grand Army
encampments eager to hear the "legless" corporal. Pembleton, who was
conscripted as the regimental musician for the 104th Pennsylvania, found
his way to York, Nebraska, after the war and began advertising himself as
"A Whole Band in One Man," boasting that he played "six instruments at
one time, no traps or wires." Banging on his "old army drum that went
through nearly four years of war," he performed old war songs in Grand
Army post rooms across the country.[39]

Regimental histories, war sketches, newspaper accounts, and magazine articles also required work—careful review, close editing, and correction. "Old soldiers do not like to be defrauded . . . by false report," one
Wisconsin Grand Army man explained. These tasks not only demanded
mastery of the emerging historiography of the war's military campaigns—
knowing exactly what had been written and by whom—but also required
veterans to stockpile statistics. The "rhetoric" of mortality statistics in particular, as historian Drew Gilpin Faust has noted, "provided the language
for a meditation on the deeper human meaning of the conflict." Gustavus
Biver prepared lengthy tables "showing the organization and number of
the Union and Confederate Armies" during the rebellion. On the ruled
pages of his tattered "Army Book," Allen Fahnestock meticulously compiled the totals of killed, wounded, missing, and captured for each company of the 86th Illinois Volunteers. All the same, an Andersonville
survivor named Gustavus Gessner urged the members of his Ohio Union
Ex-Prisoners of War Association to assist him in tallying the men who
starved in rebel prisons.[40]

Far more ambitious in scope were the statistical endeavors of veterans like Frederick Phisterer, William Fox, Frederick Dyer, and Thomas
Livermore. Phisterer was an authentic war hero who earned the Congressional Medal of Honor after wresting a federal artillery battery from

the hands of the rebels at Murfreesboro in December 1862. After culling through army orders and provost marshal reports, he published (and dedicated to the men of the Grand Army of the Republic) his "statistical record" of "the numbers and organization of the armies of the United States." In 1889, after a decade of thoroughly inspecting the muster rolls of every federal regiment, Fox, the colonel of the 107th New York Volunteers and president of the Society of the Twelfth Army Corps, published his nearly 600-page *Regimental Losses in the American Civil War*. The colonel aimed to remedy the "dearth" of published, official statistics "essential to the history of the war." The volume not only classified Civil War deaths by cause, but also compiled a list of the "three hundred fighting regiments" that had sustained the greatest casualties in battle. Thirsting for "public recognition" of their hardships, veterans regarded *Regimental Losses* as an essential reference work among a growing shelf of books documenting the war. Significantly, Fox devoted an entire chapter to "the colored troops," which could be used to supply empirical evidence of their praiseworthy performance on the war's battlefields. Fox computed losses by "regiment, brigade, state, and battle," and, to establish "some idea of the desperate character of the fighting during the American Civil War," compared the conflict's "terrible costs" with fatalities in both the Crimean and Franco-Prussian wars. "What limit is there to the toll of blood exacted from a regimental thousand during a long and bloody war?" he demanded. Fox volunteered no response to his question, but succeeded in evidencing the conflict's horrors.[41]

Even more thorough and wide-ranging than Fox's opus was the Connecticut drummer boy Frederick H. Dyer's colossal *Compendium of the War of the Rebellion*. Its 4,000 manuscript pages filled three oversized volumes. Dyer had worked as a traveling salesman after the war; while on the road, he met dozens of former comrades who, upon learning that they were in the presence of a veteran, became especially eager to share their own war records. Dyer filed away many of these statistics in the folds of his enviable memory. "It used to be a favorite trick of his," one Des Moines journalist recalled, "to stand up in an audience of 500 or 1,000 old soldiers and challenge any to name a regiment whose record of service he could not give." Dyer's travels convinced him that a reference book fixing the "vital statistics" of the Union armies could be commercially successful and, even more important, psychologically satisfying. He went at it with tough determination, sequestering himself at a tiny desk in his bedroom, sometimes "for weeks at a stretch," for five years. He was frequently "at it before breakfast" and could be heard tapping away on his primitive typewriter until after midnight. Dedicating the finished product "to all of my Comrades, fallen or surviving," the *Compendium* included an alphabetical and chronological register of "campaigns, battles, engagements, and skirmishes," as well as "concise" histories and casualty counts for every "Regiment, Battalion, [and] Battery" mobilized to suppress the rebellion. One reviewer touted the books as "the most monumental war record" produced by one man.[42]

Dyer's *Compendium* made more of a mark than Thomas Leonard Livermore's *Numbers and Losses in the Civil War in America*. Relying exclusively on the *Official Records* and other published sources, Livermore invited future historians to correct his inevitable errors with "patient labor" in the muster rolls "on file in the War Department." He chose to ignore Lost Cause arguments about the crushing superiority of northern arms, and likewise "refused to make invidious comparisons between Union and Confederate forces." Perhaps as a veteran of the "Fighting Fifth" New Hampshire (which had suffered greater total losses in battle than any other federal regiment during the war), he was impervious to comrades who brandished statistics to prove their worth. Yet in the end, even Thomas Livermore could not deny the psychic power of these numbers for ex-soldiers, who, as war psychiatrist Jonathan Shay has observed of more recent veterans, shared a "deadly addiction" to truth—an insatiable "obsession to know the complete and final truth of what they and the enemy did and suffered in their war and why." Mortality statistics were, in a very real sense, "trophies" of war. In the face of civilian skepticism, they acknowledged reality.[43]

--=○○=--

Union veterans not only massed statistics, but also participated in a "massive traffic in objects" that, as historian Joan Cashin has shown, began when the shooting did. Soldiers poached anything they could get their hands on: enemy muskets, bayonets, cartridge boxes, shell fragments, cast-iron kettles, belt plates, and jackknives. They pressed sweet gum leaves and magnolia blossoms between the pages of pocket Testaments, whittled fence rails into walking sticks, and lugged heavy rocks in their knapsacks. One veteran from Vermont crowed that during his service, he had filched "a few relics" from "almost every field." Others deliberately sought out the ugly material culture of chattel slavery—balls and chains, whips, and iron shackles. Even grisly human remains—including bullet-riddled limbs and hollow, sun-bleached skulls—became highly coveted battlefield souvenirs.[44]

After the war, these trophies comforted veterans seeking validation of their service, assuming what historian James Marten has called a "grail-like" renown. In the 1880s, Samuel Bloomer, a one-legged veteran from Stillwater, Minnesota, proudly exhibited the threadbare remnants of his unit's regimental colors in a gilded frame he placed in his living room. Grenville Sparrow treasured two small pieces of the "glorious flag" of the 17th Maine Volunteers, riddled with holes from the musketry fire of a dozen campaigns. One Vermont soldier similarly cherished both a metal canteen "with plug and strap" and the gold-trimmed Confederate officer's frock coat that he seized in the charge on Petersburg's Fort Gregg—"a relic," he said, "no one can have for love nor money." "I have been offered as high as $50 many times for the coat," he remarked, adding that only the memories it conjured rivaled the garment's "value." "The soldier who will carefully preserve everything in his possession connected with the struggle through which he has passed, and bequeath the same uninjured to his children," one writer advised, "will leave them in possession of a prize that a millionaire might well covet."[45]

The holiest of all relics were objects that conjured memories of "great personal peril" on the battlefield—pocket watches damaged in battle, Bibles discolored by ash or the mud of a pounding march, uniforms torn by musketry fire, and copper cents that had stopped bullets with but a moment to spare. Of course, many veterans unwillingly carried such relics with them for years after the war. At Savage's Station, an aptly named fight during the Seven Days campaign, a rebel Minié ball struck Vermont infantryman Orlando Williams. Upon examining the wound, Williams's regimental surgeon determined that the slug had stubbornly wedged itself behind his left eye, making extraction virtually impossible. Five years later, long after his return home to Winhall, Vermont, a "choking sensation" roused Williams from his slumber. After a few spiteful coughs, the startled veteran removed from his mouth the disfigured Confederate round.[46]

Reunions and battlefield excursions became irresistible opportunities to gather relics. G. M. Bradt & Company in Chattanooga, which advertised "the largest and best" assortment of "genuine war relics" in the nation, was a popular destination for blue-coated soldiers in the 1880s. The merchant's "exposition salesroom" displayed "large sections of pine and oak trees" riddled with solid shot; guns, pistols, knives, sabers, bayonets, ramrods, cartridge boxes, belts, drums, canteens, and "all kinds of bomb shells" collected from the Chickamauga, Lookout Mountain, Missionary Ridge, New Hope Church, Allatoona Pass, Kennesaw Mountain, Dallas, and Resaca battlefields. Among veterans, however, no destination was more popular for relic hunting than Gettysburg. For decades veterans raked the fields where they once fought, searching for shards of the past. When a park official spotted one aging veteran prying a rock from Devil's Den, the old soldier grew defensive. "I helped put that bundle of rocks into American history," he said, "and I guess I can now have a piece of 'em." On the occasion of the battle's silver anniversary in 1888, one veteran returned to Gettysburg hoping to retrieve a piece of the leaden projectile that wounded him on the third day of the battle. To the amusement of incredulous onlookers, who enjoyed a "hearty laugh" at this so-called "splendid spectacle," the veteran passed the afternoon "on his hands and knees," combing the sacred soil. Only darkness ended his search.[47]

A number of veterans loaned personal treasures and objects gathered from their travels to local Grand Army of the Republic posts. Grand Army men everywhere, from Rockville, Connecticut, to Peninsula, Ohio, festooned their otherwise mundane meeting spaces with these "priceless" relics. In many post rooms, not a single square inch of wall space went unused. Two canteens, two knapsacks, three muskets, five cannonballs, and even splinters purportedly snatched from Grant's coffin were on display at the Stannard Post in Burlington, Vermont. The Philadelphia post named for Major General George Meade even boasted the mounted head of its namesake's sturdy Morgan horse, Old Baldy. Desiring the most genuine artifact possible, two Union veterans exhumed the equine from his fresh grave under the cover of darkness on Christmas Day in 1882.[48]

Grand Army of the Republic posts depended on relics in their ongoing struggle to wrest recognition and understanding from civilians. For a week in mid-December 1886, an insolvent Hartford post sponsored a public exhibition of more than three hundred war relics on loan from its members. One of the largest public displays of relics, however, went up in a permanent exhibition installed at Chicago's Libby Prison War Museum—itself a "sacred relic" of the rebellion. In 1888, six Chicago investors moved the infamous Confederate prison by rail to a site on South Wabash Avenue. "It was a stupid plan," one former inmate snarled, "for the historic interest of the building was properly to be connected with its location, and there was something repellent in the thought of using as a show place a structure which represented so much pathetic tragedy." One former Libby inmate from upstate New York found it objectionable that the prison, which faced north in Richmond, would look west in Chicago. Civilians, averse to billeting such a painful reminder of the war on northern soil, predictably agreed—finding an odd moment of parity with the veterans. "Its presence will doubtless be offensive to those who profess any sentiment whatever," the *New York Herald* editorialized. Referencing the knots of ex-prisoners who earned their paltry living peddling war prints in the Windy City, the paper continued: "Already the war is being fought over again in the streets of Chicago, and the man with maps of Andersonville and border illustrations representing the horrors of that awful place abounds in the streets."[49]

Protests aside, the veterans came in droves to see Libby in Chicago when the facility was opened to the public in September 1889. One ex-prisoner recommended that his comrades visit the top floor first. "You can see the veritable scuttle holes, over what are now, as the prison stands, the north and the middle rooms," he exclaimed. A bevy of local ex-prisoner-of-war associations began hosting their meetings in the museum, and other former inmates volunteered as docents: "living relics" among the many cabinets of artifacts. All relished the unusual opportunity to mount tiny memorial plaques on the oak floorboards, denoting the "exact location" where they slumbered restively as inmates. A visit to Libby was mesmerizing for former inmates. After touring the museum and discovering the "auger hole" where he and other prisoners concealed "contraband" during their unhappy sojourn in Richmond, Indiana volunteer William Cockrum shipped off to Chicago the bullet-riddled army trousers he was wearing when the rebels bagged him as a prisoner on the second day at Chickamauga, imploring the curators to place them on public display.[50]

⚬⚬⚬

Visiting the Libby Prison War Museum allowed ex-prisoners to wrestle with their participation in the war—an intimate process duplicated on battlefields throughout the land. Veterans thought of themselves as custodians of their battlefields, and they assumed the role with urgency and solemnity. Much like relic collecting, the practice of marking and memo-rializing battlefields began well before the shooting stopped. While mark-ing time near Murfreesboro, Tennessee, during the epic summer of 1863, the Hoosiers, Ohioans, Illinoisans, and Kentuckians who fought in Colo-nel William Babcock Hazen's brigade erected a "quadrangular pyramidal shaft" in the cedar wood where they had endured a "murderous shower of shot and shell" the previous December during the battle of Stone's River. Two enlisted soldiers from the 115th Ohio Volunteers finished the mon-ument by chiseling moving inscriptions for the dead. In Vicksburg, Mis-sissippi, a few months later, Union soldiers unveiled a marker where Confederate General John Pemberton surrendered the besieged city and all-important river port to Ulysses S. Grant. Then, scarcely seven weeks after Appomattox (and only one week before receiving their discharge papers and starting for home), the bronzed veterans of the 16th Massa-chusetts Light Battery and the 5th Pennsylvania Heavy Artillery quarried local red sandstone and constructed two doleful monuments "in honor of the patriots who fell" in the two battles at Manassas—positioning one atop Henry House Hill for the slain of July 1861 and the other at the Deep Cut for the dead of late August 1862. The veterans capped both monuments with leaden missiles mined from the battlefields.[51]

Veterans also flecked their battlefields with regimental monuments and tiny flank markers in the years after the war—animating in granite and marble brutal charges and implausible counterattacks. In 1870, one apprehensive veteran asked if the "gallant deeds" of his and other regi-ments were to be "erased from the tablet of memory." "The war and all connected with it was a stern reality," he wrote, imploring public officials to underwrite the construction of soldiers' monuments on battlefields and town squares. "Are the people willing to forget the blood spilt on their behalf by their fellow citizens?"[52]

To be sure, many monuments did not appear until several decades after the war—what historian Timothy B. Smith has called "the golden age of battlefield preservation." Often brandished as evidence that Union veterans only returned to the war after many years of lethargy, the monument-building epidemic of the late 1880s and early 1890s ultimately reveals very little about the inner workings of veterans' memories. First, monuments had steep price tags, and despite the importance of honoring dead comrades, the care of the living came first. Grand Army of the Republic posts and other regimental associations struggled as it was to meet the daily living expenses and medical needs of ailing comrades, and they could hardly justify expensive monuments when so many ex-soldiers lodged in county poorhouses. Indeed, the sudden flood of monuments that appeared in the late nineteenth century reveals much more about the initial reluctance of both northern civilians and state and federal governments to honor the sacrifices of Union soldiers—yet another potent reminder of just what an inhospitable place the immediate postwar North was for the blue-coated soldiers fettered to their inimitable past.[53]

As battlefield "custodians," Union veterans remonstrated against the placement of monuments exalting the rebels. "I do not believe there is another nation in the civilized world that would permit a rebel monument to stand upon its soil for a single day, and I can see neither wisdom nor patriotism in building them here," one Ohio veteran declared in a dedicatory speech for his unit's regimental monument at Gettysburg in 1887. "Hallowed ground" was, in the words of one Union veteran, no place "to vaunt treason and glorify rebellion." Prodding the few ex-rebels who ventured to Gettysburg in the 1870s and 1880s to "leave for home in a huff," Union veterans quickly commandeered the fields as a place to "impress upon all, especially the young, the great principles for which we fought and suffered." "It has been said that the battles and victories of the late war ought not to be celebrated, because they were battles against and victories over our own countrymen," New York veteran Orlando B. Potter remarked.

"I cannot agree with this sentiment. They were battles for the supremacy and preservation of our constitution and government." "The war for the defense of the Nation's life," an Ohio veteran echoed, "was right, wholly right, eternally right, and the war made to destroy the Republic and build up the slave power was wrong, wholly and eternally wrong."[54]

Although immediate postwar regulations prohibiting the construction of Confederate monuments were lifted at Gettysburg and other battlefields in the 1880s, Union veterans persisted in their strident opposition. While they registered no objection to informational waysides describing rebel battle movements, they loudly opposed anything approaching esteem for treason. "We are heartily in favor of marking the Rebel lines, but we want the Government to do that work, not Rebels," one Pittsburgh Grand Army post declared. "You know that they do not care for history. When they erect their monuments it is to honor their dead and vaunt their rebellious acts. We don't propose to have that." Significantly, it was not a veteran at all, but the impressively whiskered New Hampshire–born artist John Bachelder (appointed by Congress as the official government "historian" of the battle of Gettysburg) who, endeavoring to offer visitors a more "complete picture of the battle," led the charge to reverse the prohibition on Confederate monuments.[55]

Even after rebel monuments began to materialize, Union veterans continued to search for meaning on blood-soaked battlefields. Scores of Grand Army posts pitched tents on the Gettysburg battlefield in the 1870s and 1880s, tottering down their old battle lines in the crimson twilight of a Pennsylvania summer. While resting on the Quincy granite tablet marking the position of his 88th Pennsylvania Volunteers, George W. Grant stared vacantly across Oak Ridge as the "soft breezes sang a gently-turned requiem." "Again I saw the mighty armed hosts, the blue and the gray, clashing in battle, dealing pain and death and scattering sorrow," he wrote. "The forms in blue were again behind the stone wall, and I noted familiar faces; and yonder the gray line vainly striving to advance; then the blue line springing forward . . . and I heard again the glad shouts of victory!"[56]

Union veterans longed for the opportunity to visit their "rugged battlefields," if only to make sense of their personal contributions to bedeviling engagements. A number of men organized their own southern excursions. One Hoosier planned a trip to Virginia and learned where to hire a "Negro carriage driver" who was "well posted in regard to Confederate localities" by thumbing through the *Guide to Richmond and the Battlefields*, printed by the Richmond, Fredericksburg & Potomac Railroad. In the summer of 1913, a wrinkled and graying Illinois veteran residing at the National Home for Disabled Volunteer Soldiers in Dayton pleaded for swift consideration of his pension increase appeal so that he might afford an autumn journey to Chattanooga, Atlanta, Corinth, and Shiloh with his beloved old comrades. Henry Baltzell, another Illinois ex-soldier, traveled by rail to Georgia with his son, Oliver. Together, father and son spent the better part of a day inspecting the overgrown outlines of the federal rifle pits at Allatoona Pass and, before returning north, scaled Lookout Mountain and Missionary Ridge, tented on an old army campsite near Rome, Georgia, and explored the newly dedicated Chickamauga battlefield in a newfangled "touring car." In addition to these independently organized trips, regimental and brigade associations arranged formal excursions "back to the battlefields" and other minor sites made famous by the "stirring events" of the war. The National Association of the Battle of Shiloh Survivors, for instance, organized annual pilgrimages to Pittsburg Landing. In mid-September 1902, the men of the McCook Brigade Association boarded a Pullman "Headquarters Special" at Dearborn Station in Chicago bound for "the beautiful battlefield country" along the Nashville, Chattanooga & St. Louis Railway. Seeking to resolve the "many points that are now shadowy and vague," the veterans assembled and wept where so many of their comrades had fallen at Kennesaw Mountain.[57]

—•━◉━•—

Union veterans shared experiences, narratives, and, most devastatingly, a deep sense of betrayal after the war. Feeling spent, discarded, and replaced, they turned, in dwindling numbers, to each other. In the decades after Appomattox, four men who had not known each other during the war (though they had all served in midwestern regiments) moved to Minneapolis and joined a local Grand Army post in St. Paul. Mark Flower, Henry Hicks, J. J. McCardy, and Henry Castle became fast friends. "Fraternity," Castle wrote, "is the bond that unites us." For twenty-six years, welded together by "common suffering" and "mutual devotion to the cause for which we fought," the men gathered to share their Thanksgiving feast at McCardy's home. In later years, ornate menu cards were prepared to announce the afternoon's bounty. Around the dinner table, accompanied by their wives, the old soldiers rehearsed their stirring tales of the war.[58]

Near the turn of the century, the odd quartet prompted one newspaperman to observe that the war had "touched the depths" of its veterans' souls. Delivering a now famous and oft-quoted Memorial Day address at a Grand Army of the Republic gathering in the southern New Hampshire town of Keene in 1884, Oliver Wendell Holmes, Jr., put it yet another way—the "awful orchestra" of the battlefield, he wrote, had noiselessly "set apart" Union veterans from a civilian world still grappling with the implications of a conflict that—perhaps even more convincingly than the beehive of immigration and the new smokestacks of the late nineteenth century—announced the arrival of modernity.[59]

These old soldiers lived somewhere between the past and the present, between the dead and the living, between innocence and guilt. Because of this liminal existence, no one, save another comrade, could ever truly *know* a Union veteran. He lived on as an enigma, an impossible riddle—casting a long and unwelcome shadow over a generation of Americans who were ideologically unprepared for the horrific consequences of the Civil War.

For their part, civilian men and women harbored skepticism about veterans and their secretive organizations—helpless to understand the need for so many rituals, so many reunions, so much reminiscing. The war they preferred to remember in popular culture was not at all the war the veterans fought and continued to live. Every time a short story, novel, or sheet music peddled sectional reconciliation—forgiveness and forgetfulness—veterans were forced to question why they had fought and what they had won. Paradoxically, then, because it further estranged veterans, the public's demand for "bygones to be bygones" only provoked the defenders of the Union to "wave the bloody shirt" more vigorously. Painful personal legacies of the war clashed with the sterilized public optimism that too many historians have assumed was the entire story of Civil War memory.[60]

CHAPTER 4

—⟫◆⟪—

LIVING MONUMENTS

Endure them all. You must. You have no choice.
And to no one—no man, no woman, not a soul—
reveal that you are the wanderer home at last.
No, in silence you must bear a world of pain,
subject yourself to the cruel abuse of men.

—HOMER, *THE ODYSSEY*

ANYONE IN WASHINGTON CITY who took the time to peruse the classified advertisements in the *Daily National Intelligencer* the first week of May 1866 could not have missed the curious notice about the "novel, unique, and interesting" public exhibition temporarily installed at Seaton Hall, a Masonic temple on the corner of Ninth and D streets that routinely hosted charitable exhibitions, concerts, and minstrel shows. "No one should fail to see this Grand Exhibition," the announcement exhorted. From ten o'clock in the morning to seven o'clock in the evening, men, women, and children were invited—for 25 cents each—to peruse a display of more than 250 carefully lettered manuscripts prepared by Union soldiers and sailors who had lost their right arms during the rebellion. The exhibit would last but a week, so time was of the essence: "This will be the only opportunity afforded the Washington public to witness this splendid collection of manuscripts."[1]

Among the manuscripts displayed in Seaton Hall was one belonging to an honorably discharged Illinois corporal named Jonathan McKinley Allison, who now earned his living selling butter-churns in his hometown on the Mississippi. In August 1862, Allison enlisted in Company I of Colonel James Martin's 111th Illinois Volunteer Infantry. For well more than a year, the regiment had simply marked time—performing mundane garrison duties in Kentucky, Tennessee, and Alabama. Some of the soldiers no doubt wondered if they would ever encounter the enemy. But those fears were laid to rest on Friday, May 13, 1864, as General William Tecumseh Sherman continued his relentless drive toward Atlanta. With their new comrades in Brigadier General Giles A. Smith's Fifteenth Corps brigade, the 111th Illinois was ordered to wait for the enemy behind some improvised breastworks along Camp Creek, near the tiny Western & Atlantic Railroad depot of Resaca, Georgia.

The following afternoon, as Confederate General John Bell Hood's men pummeled the opposite end of the federal line, Martin's troops did their best to keep Confederate General Leonidas Polk's men from joining the main rebel assault. After several hours of blistering skirmish fire, Smith's men were instructed to charge the enemy. A few minutes before six o'clock that evening, with the brigade (drawn up in "double lines") guiding on the 111th Illinois, the blue-coated soldiers dashed into the muddy creek and moored themselves on the opposite bank. The federal pioneer corps could not construct rifle pits quickly enough, as the rebels intuitively leveled their muskets and delivered a "close, destructive, and well-directed fire." Artillery shells raked Smith's muddy troops, claiming dozens of casualties. One of those missiles hurtled toward Jonathan Allison. He fell to the ground, his right arm oozing blood. Surgeons amputated the limb that evening.[2]

Allison spent the rest of his war in hospital wards, but he at least returned home with his regiment in July 1865. Eager to learn a trade, he enrolled in classes at a local college. That fall, as he dedicated himself to his studies, Allison learned of a curious competition for the thousands of men who, like him, had lost their right arms and were learning to write left-handed. The competition was the brainchild of William Oland Bourne, who no doubt sought to boost subscriptions to the *Soldier's Friend*, but likewise hoped to "induce the men to become skillful penmen, in order to fit themselves for lucrative and honorable positions." Bourne offered generous cash premiums as a reward—including individual prizes of $200, $150, $100, and $50. While he preferred "brief essays on patriotic themes," he insisted that entrants would be judged only on the artistry of their penmanship. Contestants need not worry about literary talent; they could copy a published work in their hand if they chose. Indeed, the official rules required that each entrant supply only his full name and postal address; regiment, company, and rank; a succinct military history, identifying the engagement in which his arm was lost (or, in the case of disease, the circumstances surrounding the amputation); and a notarized affidavit certifying that prior to the war, he was right-handed.[3]

Just a week before the January 1 submission deadline, Allison removed several sheets of lined parchment and began to write. He meditated on the difficulties he encountered finding meaningful employment, noting that civilians "invariably" recommended that he was only fit to keep a saloon. "I don't think the lives of so many brave soldiers were spared on fields of strife and death," he wrote, so that they could assume such a "low, mean, base calling as a 'Saloonkeeper.'" While he believed that all who had served in the Union armies were deserving of gratitude and respect, Allison also thought that maimed and dismembered soldiers were especially worthy of renown. "One legged soldiers may think I have forgotten them, but no. I do not desire to detract from their honor or praise due to them," he wrote. "We are the *living monuments* of the late cruel and bloody Rebellion. We now retire from fields of blood and carnage to prepare to act another part in the great 'drama' of life."[4]

Allison recognized that by losing a limb he had gained an unusual "authority" over the war's history. His wounds lent realism and authenticity to his experiences, something that other veterans seeking to explain the brutality of the war could only hope to approximate. Like thousands of his fellow amputees, he embraced his rare capacity to keep alive the war's historical memory. The postbellum North, after all, largely lacked the battle-scarred environment and haunting ruins that loomed eerily over the southern landscape. "Very soon [after the war]," author Rossiter Johnson remembered in an early history, "the only remaining indications of the great contest [in the north] were the battle-flags in the State-houses and arsenals, the framed portraits of President Lincoln and his ablest Generals, the occasional cannon-trophies in village greens and city squares, and the more than occasional crutches and empty sleeves." Only with regular glimpses of scarred and maimed soldiers, then, did northern civilians come face-to-face with the realities of the war's devastation. "The vast army of your comrades who have gone through life with empty sleeves, shattered limbs and broken health," veteran Charles W. Kepler informed the grizzled ranks of Crocker's Iowa Brigade at a biennial reunion held in mid-September 1898, "all stand as living testimonies of the magnitude and frightfulness of that great war."[5]

Legions of men missing arms and legs after the Civil War were a riddle for those civilians seeking reconciliation. Throbbing stumps weeping a foul brew of pus and blood were hardly an advertisement for the kind of glorious, sanitized war the public wanted to remember. While previous scholars have argued that the beelike productivity of prosthetics manufacturers left Union amputees somewhat "invisible," only a fraction of empty sleeves actually wore artificial limbs. For some amputees, this was a deliberate choice. Others opted against artificial limbs because they felt them awkward, unpleasant, and ill fitting. "An artificial arm hangs too heavy on my weak stump," one Wisconsin veteran groused, "and the strap or belt which goes around the breast chokes me, so I [can] hardly speak." Thus, despite some stunning innovations in the burgeoning artificial-limb industry, including ball-and-socket ankle joints and spring-loaded thumbs, prosthetics failed "to bind up the nation's wounds." Union veteran amputees instead continued to function as challenging—and at times revolting—"sites of memory." As one observer remarked soon after Appomattox, an empty blue coat sleeve proved to be "a *weapon* more powerful than that with which they conquered the Rebellion." Empty sleeves were not only symbols of rebel defeat, but also emblems of Union victory. Unlike the endless rows of mute, white headstones, they could speak and be heard.[6]

Nonetheless, the power of the empty sleeve was deceiving. Though incontestable, the physical pain of stumps and scars was, in the end, ineffable. As one "empty sleeve" testified, "I have an honorable scar that speaks plainer than words of deeds gone by." Civilians used the power of language to dignify injuries; they casually dismissed ghastly wounds as badges of honor and then left veterans to stew alone, with only their pain. Paeans to the "eloquence" of an empty sleeve effaced a world of anguish and torment. Despite the valiant effort of amputees who "waved the bloody shirt"—those ex-soldiers who used their bodies to debate the meaning and legacy of the southern rebellion—the chasm of experience alienated veterans and civilians once more. And for those soldiers without visible scars, the outlook was even worse.[7]

⇥◉⊂⊷

Empty sleeves peopled a living "republic of suffering" in post–Civil War America. "In our streets, in our offices, on our farms, everywhere we meet 'empty sleeves,'" the *Soldier's Friend* remarked soon after the war. "Sleeves that the wind blows against broken ribs, whips about crippled bodies; sleeves whose emptiness tells of arms blown off in battle; of arms lost in strife for the life of a nation; of arms shattered with the flag in hand." On the town green in nearly "every northern village," it seemed, one encountered "limbless and armless" veterans, "ruined in health" and "dependent on their friends for sympathy and the comforts of life."[8]

Indeed, the loss of a limb rendered many veterans unable to take care of themselves or their families. When a Confederate shell tore into the ranks of the 32nd Massachusetts at Petersburg's Fort Hell, it shattered the right arm of Private Henry H. Meacham, who, before the war, worked as a carriage maker in the small town of Russell. After a pounding seven-mile journey over rough roads to the division hospital, a surgeon examined the private, ordered up morphine, and amputated his lifeless limb. That evening, Meacham passed a "long and sleepless night," confronting the sobering reality that he was "crippled for life." Returning home to an ill wife and forced to abandon his trade, Meacham opted to make a living out of his soldier's tale. In 1869, he self-published his thirty-two page pamphlet *The Empty Sleeve: Or, The Life and Hardships of Henry H. Meacham in the Union Army*, which he retailed for 25 cents per copy, eager "to place myself and wife in comfortable circumstances."[9]

Like Meacham, more than a few amputees attempted to translate their "suffering into a salable commodity." "Working hard to earn an honest livelihood," but with merely "one arm to paddle his own canoe," a New York infantryman published *Only a Private*, an "imperfect sketch" of that sweltering third day at Cold Harbor, when a mischievous Confederate shell ripped away his right arm. One-armed and one-legged George M. Reed, who styled himself as a "wreck of manhood," peddled a tiny broadside that featured an original prose poem in which he recounted the loss of his limbs at Shiloh. David B. Tanner, a Rhode Island artillerist who lost his right leg supporting Doubleday's division along the fence-lined Hagerstown Turnpike at Antietam, made an earnest appeal for public support in his 1870 leaflet *"Our Limbs Are Lost! Our Country Saved!"* The "crippled and enfeebled" Tanner found it nearly impossible to provide for his wife and three young children. His throbbing stump continued to eject splinters of bone, flummoxing doctors who sought to fit him with a prosthetic appliance. For his part, A. O. Goodrich put his experiences "on the Peninsular Campaign" to music in an eighteen-stanza song that he printed up and hawked on the streets of Detroit. None of these tracts, of course, became bestsellers. But that was beside the point. Similar to the growing number of ordinary Americans who put their pens to paper and published their life stories in the mid nineteenth century, these soldiers did not seek literary immortality. Rather, in the simple act of crafting a narrative—even one that was so wooden as to lack all color and emotion—these men sought to make sense of the war indelibly inscribed on their bodies.[10]

⇥▬◉◯▬⇤

It was that same, intrinsic need to explain the war that compelled so many amputees to enter William Oland Bourne's left-handed penmanship competition. Indeed, few were able to keep their entries to the seven-page limit Bourne imposed in the contest rules. During the summer of 1865, the editor printed up scores of handbills to announce the contest and its distinguished panel of judges, which included Governor Fenton; William Cullen Bryant, the editor of the *New York Evening Post*; George Curtis, the political editor of *Harper's Weekly*; and the noted New York City philanthropists William E. Dodge, Jr., and Theodore Roosevelt, Sr. Appeals for left-handed manuscripts appeared in newspapers across the country.[11]

One-armed veterans excitedly forwarded their manuscripts—carefully coiled around wooden rollers to ensure safe delivery—to the *Soldier's Friend* editorial office in New York City. Some entrants undoubtedly sought nothing more than their fifteen minutes of fame, offering prolix sketches of daring martial feats and appending to their entries lengthy lists of the harrowing battlefields where they had fought. Frank Valleraux, an Illinois artillerist, "wished to find out how [his] writing would compare," while a young soldier dismembered at Chickamauga simply hoped to learn how many empty sleeves the war had produced. Still others, as the historian Frances Clarke has pointed out, sought only to demonstrate that if amputation had damaged their bodies, it could not seize their spirit of self-determination. "There is only one way to arrive at independence," one amputee declared soon after returning to his home in New England. "Learn immediately to write with your left hand."[12]

The much-touted contest moved nearly 300 amputees to submit writing samples. Overwhelmed by the response, Bourne announced that he would sponsor a second competition the next year. In a handbill addressed "To the Left Armed Corps of the Union," he declared that the second round of competitors would vie for $500 in premiums, to be divided equally among ten winners. Each premium carried the name of a Union officer who would, in turn, forward a handwritten letter of congratulations to the recipient. During the second competition, another 115 carefully inked essays, their words perfectly slanted to the left, arrived at No. 12 Centre Street in New York City.[13]

Bourne intended to publish a gilded volume containing the submitted essays and vowed to reserve a complimentary copy for each entrant—a moving testament to the depth and breadth of suffering after the war. Union amputees keenly understood that they had been afforded an opportunity to speak to the public—and to posterity. The thought of seeing their words carefully typeset and bound excited them. "I do not write for the Premiums because I know that I cannot get mine," one New Hampshire veteran prefaced his submission, "but I should like a book to see what the left armed men can do." Likewise, a New York sergeant who lost his right arm while storming Marye's Heights at Fredericksburg looked forward "with joyful anticipations" to the publication of the tome, as it would "embrace the history of many of my brave comrades with whom I have fought." "Truly such a book," the soldier added, "will be prized next to the Bible itself."[14]

Yet Bourne's contest was about more than adding "a little to the book"; it was also about claiming membership in one of the war's most exclusive guilds. Samuel Carpenter, who lost his right arm in battle at Dalton, Georgia, explained with pride that he was "in the 'brotherhood.'" In his contest submission, Frank H. Evans expressed what many one-armed ex-soldiers had already suspected: there was a "secret history connected with the empty coat sleeve which none can understand who have not had the misfortune to lose an arm." "Bitter disappointments" and "ruined hopes" belonged especially to his comrades who had lost a limb. One amputee firmly maintained that "only such of those who have experienced something similar" could grasp the depths of his suffering.[15]

The one-armed contestants took seriously their responsibilities as stewards of the war's history, even if they were often rather self-conscious about their intellectual abilities. They persevered because they held firm to the belief that the nation at large had an obligation to remember their sacrifices. Henry Krahl, a bearded Iowa farmer who enlisted in the 13th United States Infantry and lost his arm to a shell wound at the battle of Arkansas Post in 1863, insisted that it was "the *duty* of every one, belonging to *our band*" to contribute a specimen of left-handed penmanship. Unwilling to hide his injury, Krahl sat for a tintype profile, proudly displaying his missing right arm and the excess skin puckering awkwardly around the stump. George Warner echoed that it was his "*duty* to write something whether it meets with the approbation of all or not," while James Lee declared that he would submit an essay, despite being "no scholar." All the same, though he questioned his ability to fashion a narrative "suitable for publication" and cautioned that Bourne would "no doubt find ... serious mistakes in both spelling and grammar," Ohio amputee Seth Sutherland submitted the very first contest entry.[16]

These men assumed that because their bodies bore "living witness" to

the realities of the war, it ultimately mattered little how clumsy and bela-
bored their entries were. "Veteran scars" were, in the estimation of one-
armed Philip Faulk, "enduring, priceless mementoes" that irrefutably
established "the price of liberty and Union." "An empty sleeve," remarked
Albion Winegar Tourgée, who became one of reconciliation's most outspoken opponents, "shows that the heart beneath it beat warm with devotion." Indeed, contemporaries frequently deployed the adjective "eloquent"
to describe an empty sleeve generated by the war. "If we cannot find [an
ex-]soldier who is a speaker," one Harvard trustee declared in preparation
for the College's Triennial Festival of Alumni, "we can find one with an
empty sleeve. Let him hold that up and we shall all acknowledge that it is
full of eloquence." "There is a strange history connected with each of those
empty sleeves," one amputee contended. "A history of hardships such as
only the soldier knows of long marches now through the rain and cold . . .
of fearful conflicts amid roaring shells and hissing bullets, rattling of musketry and thunder of cannon, shouts and yells of excited men and groans
of the dying and wounded." As Maine poet David Barker concluded in
stanzas that were widely reprinted in the years immediately after the war,
"What a tell-tale thing is an empty sleeve!"[17]

Alongside their writing samples, some veterans, such as Henry C.
Allen and John F. Chase, included photographs prominently displaying
their pinned-up coat sleeves. Allen, who rode with the 1st Massachusetts
Cavalry, explained in the essay attached to his photograph that he
"wanted to bring a mark home with me to show that I had been where
danger came near me." Allen got his wish on September 14, 1863, at
Rapidan Station, Virginia. "I have that mark and so conspicuous that all
can see it and I am proud of it." Chase, who, at the age of eighteen,
enlisted in the 5th Maine Battery, survived a "grievous" wound at Chancellorsville in May 1863—only to defy death once again two months
later at Gettysburg. On the second day of the battle, the 5th Maine

unlimbered its six Napoleon guns on the "saddle" between Culp's Hill and East Cemetery Hill. One of the guns spewed a round of canister without warning. As the cannon recoiled, a bewildered Chase tumbled to the ground in a squall of lead that tore away his right arm, detached his left eye, and pockmarked his face and shoulders with more than forty scars. Comrades carried the twenty-year-old captain to the rear and left him for dead (only a feeble whimper two days later managed to land him a stretcher bound for the field hospital on Seminary Ridge). The startling reality of these photographs—a right arm missing near the shoulder; a mangled body stained by more than forty scars, the result of "peaces [*sic*] of fragments of a case shot"; a young volunteer robbed of both hands— illustrated the dismal results of what one Vermont enlisted man rather aptly described as "this unholy and ungodly conflict."[18]

Each of the competitors supplied compelling evidence of the war's ugly realities. In his essay, an Indiana veteran who described the war as a "carnival of death" remembered the "heavy rains," the prevalence of "measles or typhoid fever or some other disease," and the seemingly endless rows of "new made graves." Although sketch artists had published hundreds of drawings in northern newspapers depicting scenes from the war, entrants struggled to describe for their readers the vicious, haunting sounds and tormenting emotions of the battlefield. Philip Faulk's composition depicted "the hell of carnage" and "the mangled be-dabbled with blood" on Virginia's Cedar Mountain battlefield; he testified that "the demonic scream of the death dealing shell" yet rang in his ears. Phineas Whitehouse wrote about Fredericksburg, his first battle, by describing the files of men who "trembled from head to foot" because "the scenes of death around them" were "more than their hearts and nerves could bear." William Connor described "the discordant sounds of a battle" in his manuscript, recounting the "shrieks of the wounded and groans of the dying . . . the neighing of wounded horses, the soar of artillery, the rattle of mus-

ketry, the yells of deadly charges, and the shouts of victorious hosts."
Finally, R. J. Dickinson wrote that he hoped "never to see again" the sights
he witnessed in the 127th Illinois. "Men mangled and torn in every conceivable shape," he exclaimed, "oh! The horrors of war!"[19]

For still other veterans, battle was such a sirocco of emotion that it
could not be accurately conveyed in narrative form. The Ohio cannoneer
John Blanchard inked a tribute to the right hand he lost in a nasty skirmish prior to the battle of Stones River in the unpretentious verse of
"Amputated," while New Hampshire soldier Phineas Whitehouse contributed the mournful stanzas of "My Crippled Arm":

> *A rebel bullet's madness*
> *Shattered that arm on Spotsylvania's field*
> *And many hours of pain and days of sadness*
> *In gloom succeeded, 'ere the ugly fracture healed.*

At once holding his former enemies accountable for his wound and con-
demning their stubborn act of treason ("madness"), Whitehouse wrote
unreservedly, and with conviction—flouting any tendency to "let bygones
be bygones."[20]

Whitehouse's missing limb ensured that he could not view the war
dispassionately. His injury demanded meaning. Like so many of the contestants, he delighted in the fact that the preservation of the Union "tore
up by the roots" the oligarchic and "infamous system of slavery." "The
inauguration of a causeless and bloody Rebellion by the Slaveholders of
the South undeceived us, and revealed to us our utter ignorance of the
civilization begotten of slavery," John Stewart declared. Though he stopped
short of declaring emancipation the war's principal aim, J. A. Lantz, an
Akron, Ohio, native who lost his right arm at First Winchester, betrayed
his interpretation of the war when he referred to it as the " 'Great Slaveholders Rebellion.'" For his part, Alfred Whitehouse offered no academic

explanation for the rebellion; the war came, he wrote, because "the time had arrived for Right Justice and Liberty to enter into fierce combat with Wrong Unjust and Oppressive principles of every satanic Kind."[21]

Having imbued the war with great purpose, then, some contestants naturally professed pride in having sacrificed their limbs for the cause. "[Dismemberment] is sacred to those who have been actively engaged in our late war," one veteran reflected, "not because [the war] was domestic, but because it was between democracy and aristocracy, freedom and slavery, the freedom of the white as well as the black, the suppression of the wicked to the freedom of the just." Echoing these sentiments, a soldier who lost his right arm at Spotsylvania asked if he and his one-armed comrades could "regret even the loss of our strong right arm[s]," being as they were, torn from their bodies in the defense of "the most sacred rights of humanity." E. R. Wise declared that he "did not regret" the arm he left at Gettysburg, insisting that he was "rather proud that I could lay on the altar of my country such an offering for such a cause."[22]

"I am not ashamed to own the cause, nor through what means I was made what I am," one veteran explained. "The empty chair at the fireside, and the empty sleeve in the old blue uniform ... will remind us," John Lawford contended in his entry, "that through such sacrifices as these are the blessings we now enjoy purchased." Henry Krahl boasted that he was a "deep and lasting memento of the war for the Union," while Alva Williams alleged that he sacrificed his arm at South Mountain for the "sacred cause" of preserving "our glorious fabric of Freedom, Unity, and the Republic." This bombast was no hollow triumphalism; in the space of these painstakingly crafted essays, Union veterans explained—both to the nation and to each other—just what the war meant.[23]

While many among the larger Union veteran population purported that experience had estranged them from civilians, amputees were rather exceptional in claiming that their disfigured bodies equipped them with cultural and political power. "The maimed and crippled ones, with the widows and orphans," Iowa veteran T. S. Bailey declared, "speak with living tongues of the crimes of Copperheads and open Rebels." Armless veterans brazenly called for their former enemies to reap retribution. In his manuscript, Alvin Dibble even volunteered to "string up around the Capitol, each rebel of you, on a gibbet, high as Haman's!" David Yates, who claimed to be the first Ohioan to shed blood during the war, likewise dreamt of hanging "trembling traitors" on a "well-earned scaffold" with the halyard from one of the Army of the Cumberland's battle flags. An amputee from Connecticut observed that Confederates deserved retribution, for "thirsting for glory and sure of success," they had waged a "crusade against the Old Flag" and "fell in the hopeless struggle of wrong against right."[24]

Indeed, the competitors took advantage of the rare opportunity afforded by Bourne's contest to demand a national reconciliation that refused to compromise the righteousness of Union victory. The contest could not have been more perfectly timed, for Reconstruction seemed to be spiraling out of control by the minute. Despite declaring himself the "Moses" of the freed people and vowing repeatedly to "make treason odious," Andrew Johnson, the impetuous Tennessee tailor in the White House, spent the summer of 1865 cranking out pardons for former rebels, propping up antebellum political leaders that wasted no time belting the South with restrictive "black codes." Emboldened by their escape from retribution and humiliated by the facts of emancipation, many white southerners turned violent. Not infrequently donning their old gray uniforms, Confederate veterans rode roughshod over the South, terrorizing newly freed slaves, their carpetbagger allies, and anyone who dared to imagine biracial democracy as the war's charge.

"Justice should be done to the perpetrators and leaders of the wicked rebellion," beseeched Ezra Dayton Hilts, the New York cannoneer with piercing eyes and a boyish face who lost his arm at Williamsburg, Virginia, in May 1862 when his gun discharged prematurely. "Our work is

On May 23 and May 24, 1865, more than 200,000 men from the Union armies strode down Pennsylvania Avenue beyond a wooden reviewing stand erected on the front lawn of the White House. As civilians lined the nation's avenue, they cheered wildly—unable to understand that for the men in the ranks, this was no victory parade, but a funereal march.

When most Americans think of Union veterans, they envision the feeble grandfathers who extended the olive branch to their former enemies. Photographs of Union and Confederate veterans reconciling at the Angle—the site where the battle of Gettysburg came to its bloody climax—were staged and then widely reproduced, reinforcing the cultural triumph of reconciliation.

For Union veterans, the Civil War did not end at Appomattox. The road ahead was long and uncertain—riddled with guilt, doubt, and even destitution. Soldiers often described their military service as a form of enslavement. At the end of the war, then, many felt a certain kinship with the newly freed slave, an interpretive linkage made by Julian Scott in his majestic painting *Going Home*.

In the months after Appomattox, some returning soldiers were greeted with welcome-home ceremonies like this one, held in Philadelphia. Paradoxically, by celebrating the Union victory as something unquestionably achieved—by extending triumphal arches across town greens and paying lip service to veterans in their newspaper editorials and indulgent orations—many northern civilians not only dismissed the extent to which the war left "unfinished work," but also foreclosed opportunities for veterans to heal.

While northern civilians looked with indifference on the plight of Union veterans, Vincent Colyer was determined to help. As the visionary Superintendent of the New York State Soldiers' Depot, he provided nourishment, sanctuary, and words of caution for many hundreds of veterans returning home in 1865.

At least 50,000 Union soldiers returned from the war missing a limb. Although prosthetic appliance manufacturers competed for business, many veterans opted not to wear notoriously uncomfortable artificial limbs. Their empty sleeves thus became profound, public reminders of the war's corporeal costs. Private William Sargent, pictured here, lost both of his arms in the ranks of the 53rd Pennsylvania at the battle of Seven Pines, Virginia.

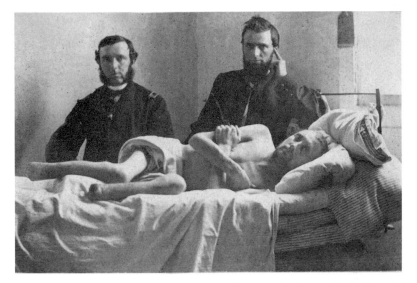

Calvin Bates was a corporal in the regiment that, perched atop Little Round Top, secured the Union left at Gettysburg with a storied bayonet charge. Yet even in the 20th Maine, there was not enough glory to go around. Bates was taken prisoner the following year at the Wilderness and packed off to Andersonville, where he was subjected to months of mistreatment, malnourishment, and exposure. His feet were amputated shortly after his release. Taken just nineteen days after Appomattox, this photograph illustrates how the war's misery marched on.

Starved and sunbaked in notorious Confederate prison camps like Andersonville, ex–prisoners of war were the most embittered—and least understood—Union veterans. The prison experience frayed their nerves and shattered their minds, necessitating the creation of local, state, and national survivor associations like the one depicted above.

Though many destitute veterans relied on monthly pension checks, securing a claim was about more than financial aid. For many, it was an opportunity to share war stories—and have them accepted as truth. Eastman Johnson depicted this effort in his 1867 oil on canvas *The Pension Claim Agent*, in which a one-legged Union veteran recounts his doleful tale to the staid visitor who will file his claim in Washington.

The National Home for Disabled Volunteer Soldiers provided some disabled and destitute veterans a place to live out their lives. Surrounded by their former comrades, the inmates of these facilities could not help but marinate in their memories. Here, veterans gathered in the majestic Putnam Library at the Central Branch of the National Home in Dayton to fight their battles "over again."

More than 51,000 veterans of the American Civil War journeyed to Gettysburg, Pennsylvania, in 1913 to participate in the Peace Jubilee. They feasted on bounteous meals and listened to countless speeches; many observed that it was the final act of Union veteranhood. Yet while reconciliation was celebrated onstage, sectional animosities lingered in the hearts and minds of the former combatants.

Even in the twilight of their lives, Union veterans sought outlets for their war stories. Private Orlando Learned served in the 16th Illinois Volunteer Infantry; in 1931, clutching a bullet-riddled, thirty-six-star flag he salvaged from the Vicksburg Campaign, the octogenarian found a captive audience—his two-and-a-half-year-old grandson.

Albert Woolson—a drummer boy from Duluth, Minnesota, who went off to war with the 1st Minnesota Heavy Artillery at the age of seventeen—was the very last survivor of the Union armies. He became something of a celebrity before his death in 1956.

not yet finished." Hilts hoped that he might persuade the "people of the South" to "turn from the 'error of their way' and swear allegiance" to the restored government: "I would not pardon rebels, especially the leaders, until they should first kneel in the dust of humiliation and show by their deeds that they sincerely repent." Norman Vroman hoped that the "judgment of those that are in the right" would direct the course of Reconstruction. A former New York artillerist concurred, reasoning that the crucial months after Appomattox were "no time for reaction or imbecility."[25]

In an essay that he titled "Plain Dealing with the South," Thomas Sanborn, a bearded Vermont infantryman who lost his arm when an enemy round tore through his elbow at Poplar Grove Church in September 1864, acknowledged that "in passing from the narrow gauge of slavery to the broad gauge of freedom, something more is necessary than to throw away the old rules . . . the whole dimensions and proportions are to be remodeled." For the balance of Sanborn's life, the neuralgic pains that besieged his jaundiced frame and the discomfort of his government-issued artificial limb offered him a keen reminder of the war's consequences—and sharpened his commitment to the war's unfinished business. Like his fellow contestants, the Vermonter thought that his dismembered body was an apt metaphor for the nation and its elusive quest for racial justice.[26]

In his contest entry, Henry Allen made the connection between his maimed body and the political struggles over Reconstruction explicit. The Massachusetts cavalryman was casting about for an essay theme when Andrew Johnson vetoed a Republican-sponsored measure to extend the charter of the Freedmen's Bureau. Staffed disproportionately by mangled veterans like Oliver Gray, who lost an arm tussling with Barksdale's Brigade at Gettysburg, and Frederick Gaebel, thrice wounded during the war, the bureau was the federal agency charged with mitigating the difficult transition from slavery to freedom. Conceiving of their service "as part of a broader mission to secure the fruits of victory," these veterans and their civilian counterparts, led by the bureau commissioner, one-armed Major General Oliver Otis Howard, sought to protect the civil and political rights of newly freed men, women, and children. Allen became so incensed by Johnson's action that he began a poem, imploring his comrades to "gather 'round the standard" and to "blow the bugle" once more:

> *Many wounded yet remain*
> *Tell me, comrades, true and loyal*
> *"Have our sufferings been in vain?"*
> *Must this Union be severed*
> *And "our flag" be rent in twain?*
> *Must the "Freedmen" still be bounded*
> *In slavery's wicked, hellish chains?*[27]

Will Thomas posed this very question in the neatly lettered essay he submitted to Bourne. Thomas, who lost his right arm only eight months before during the attack on Fort Fisher, North Carolina, was an African-American—a veteran of the 5th United States Colored Infantry and one of the nearly 190,000 black soldiers who fought for the Union. He entered the contest "not to compete for the prizes," but to voice "a colored man's view on the subject of the war." On behalf of his black comrades, Thomas demanded social and political rights. "Since . . . we have shared alike in the dangers and vicissitudes of war, ought we not to partake in all the immunities pertaining to the rights of citizens, even, as our Anglo Saxon brothers?" he asked. Recalling the "zeal and fidelity to the Union" of African-American soldiers in battles like Olustee, Fort Wagner, Milken's Bend, New Market Heights, and Honey Hill, Thomas sought belated recognition of the contributions of black troops in suppressing the rebellion. The black soldier in blue, he argued, like the empty sleeve, spoke volumes about the meaning and legacy of the Civil War.[28] As such compelling reminders of the war's transformations, African-American veterans experienced not only the derision and indifference accorded to their white comrades, but also the slings and arrows of northern racism.[29]

Yet white amputees, at least, cheered the "sable arm" in their contest entries—and circled around the flickering memory of black contributions to the war effort. In searching for the meaning of their injuries, disfigured veterans became especially committed to the cause of emancipation and racial equality. Henry Krahl esteemed the "fidelity and courage" and "the strong arm and the steady valor" of the black soldier in battle. Charles Edmonds expressed pride that he fought "Side by Side with Sambo" in an essay that lauded the U.S. Colored Troops who "so nobly dared" and "freely bled" to aid the Union cause. In his account of the fighting around Nashville, John W. Reynolds not only lauded the performance of the black regiments, which "charged first" and whose "dead strewed the ground at the abatis," but insisted that their performance exceeded the efforts of the white volunteers.[30]

In his essay, Conrad Dippel, a soldier who emigrated from Saxony and fought with the 37th Wisconsin Volunteers, described his June 1864 trip from the improvised Petersburg field hospital where surgeons amputated his right arm—a devastating loss for one who made his living as a plasterer and stonemason—to the general hospital at City Point. Along the way, Dippel spotted a knot of rebel prisoners under the watchful eye of United States Colored Troops. "This gave me really the greatest satisfaction," Dippel wrote, who claimed to have "forgot all my sufferings in reflecting how quick Providence turns the luck of man and does justice to everyone."[31]

That white veterans in a society riddled by the ugliest racism rallied to the defense of their disabled black comrades commends to us the powerful bond shared by amputees. As one *Harper's Weekly* political cartoonist recommended immediately after the war, at least between two dismembered veterans, "a man knows a man." This image depicted two legless veterans—one white, one black. Leaning on crutches, the maimed veterans clasped hands. "Give me your hand, Comrade! We each lost a leg for the good cause; but thank God, we never lost heart!"[32]

⊶⫶⊷

After sifting through the reams of foolscap submitted by the contestants, Bourne announced the winners of his first contest in the *Soldier's Friend*. The Soldiers' and Sailors' Union of the District of Columbia made preparations for a public exhibition of the essays that would benefit the flood of disabled veterans lingering in Washington-area military hospitals. A hive of volunteers swarmed the Seaton Hall exhibition room, the "handsomest room of any kind" in Washington, to set up the exhibit. Workers removed Albert Bierstadt's majestic oil painting of Oregon's Mount Hood, which had been on display the month of April, to make room for the left-handed manuscripts, displayed on narrow tables that crammed the exhibition space. Festooning the hall were large American flags, interrupted only by carefully lettered mottoes and handsomely framed portraits of Union commanders, including Generals Hancock, Sherman, Grant, and Burnside. On the east wall, gilded letters proclaimed: OUR DISABLED SOLDIERS HAVE KEPT THE UNION FROM BEING DISABLED. Around the room, placards conveyed other patriotic messages: UNION AND LIBERTY, DISABLED, BUT NOT DISHEARTENED, THE EMPTY SLEEVE, THE LEFT HAND, and THE ARM AND BODY YOU MAY SEVER, BUT OUR GLORIOUS UNION, NEVER. A rebel battle standard that had been captured by federal troops during the desperate fighting at Fort Fisher, North Carolina, in January 1865 was placed on proud display, adjacent to deliberately enlarged images of Andersonville's spindly survivors.[33]

The display opened to the public on the evening of Tuesday, May 1, 1866. The 5th United States Cavalry's brass band provided patriotic melodies as the spectators began to mill outside the hall. A few minutes before nine o'clock, the president of the Soldiers' and Sailors' Union took the stage and introduced Nathaniel Prentice Banks, the impressively mustached general who led Union armies in both the Shenandoah Valley and Red River campaigns. "The people should take a lesson from this exhibition and faithfully discharge the duty they owe the soldier," he declared. The empty sleeve had done his duty in battle; now it was time for the civilian to do his duty in peace.

When Banks finished his remarks, the Speaker of the U.S. House of Representatives, Schuyler Colfax, delivered remarks lauding "the deeds of Farragut, of Sherman, of Sheridan, and of Grant." "Empty sleeves," he maintained, "continue to remind us of the war." Bourne had hoped that President Johnson might be in attendance to close out the evening— indeed, he had called on him at the White House the previous week—but tellingly, the pardon-issuing president did not show.[34]

In the ensuing days, a great number of visitors strolled through the narrow aisles of the display. Some could hardly stomach the exhibit. One visitor from Macon, Georgia, prepared a review laden with sarcasm. "The exhibition of Left-Hand Penmanship was opened last evening at Seaton Hall," he began, "a grand display of Union flags, speechifying, etc., and Gen. Banks and Colfax discoursed largely upon the patriots who were disabled by 'rebel bullets,' and who were now going to 'encounter the trials of this world, boldly, with the left hand.'" One newspaper added that the exhibit was simply more loathsome bloody-shirt waving, managed by "Radical Members of Congress" lurking backstage.[35]

General Grant visited the manuscripts, many of them produced by his troops, one memorable evening. Another prominent exhibition-goer was Rev. George F. Magoun, president of the newly opened Iowa College in Davenport. With "very great pleasure," he studied the manuscripts, later commenting on the "indomitable spirit and high purpose of the brave and precious young men who have given their right hands to their country." Fanny Fern, one of the most popular humorists of the day, had a similar reaction to the display, commending Bourne and the exhibition organizers in her nationally syndicated newspaper column. "I was glad that they placed it on record that an American soldier is still wide-awake and hopeful, though he may be so hacked and hewed to pieces that not half his original proportions remain," Fern gushed. "I wanted to sing 'Hail Columbia,' and the 'Star Spangled Banner,' and 'John Brown,' and 'Yankee Doodle,' to the top of my lungs."[36]

Like many other civilians who encountered soldiers with empty sleeves and missing legs immediately after the war, Magoun and Fern allowed soaring celebrations of wartime virtue and courage to short-circuit any consideration of postwar realities. Even the most genuine "soldier's friends," including men like Vincent Colyer, were so eager to mend the wounds of the war that they decreed bodily dismemberment a fulfilling "honor." On the Fourth of July 1865, Colyer and a few prominent New Yorkers gathered in the patriotically appointed City Assembly Rooms to extol the wards of maimed soldiers from nearby Central Park Hospital. Rev. William Adams of the Madison Square Church delivered welcoming remarks. "We congratulate you for the scars you bear upon your persons," Adams began, and "we congratulate you that you have such a subject for contemplation." Although the *New York Tribune* reported that the "festival" was "a sad spectacle," describing the dozens of feeble men "disfigured with scars and bruises," it quickly noted that "we err: these wounds will yet be, as they are now, their proudest decorations, and shall ever win from their countrymen the rewards they so well deserve." The ink on the Appomattox surrender documents was hardly dry and, already, northern civilians were shrouding the war's scars in the fabric of forgetfulness. Content to observe the wounded in a tidy exhibition, civilians looked toward a future of freewheeling prosperity and national unity—marveling at their own empathy.[37]

⋅═◉═⋅

But like Bourne's contestants, many maimed and disfigured veterans refused to go quietly into the dusty pages of history. "The misguided and misled current of sentimental gush which has found a lodging place in the hearts of some cannot move the men who spent years on the field of strife to preserve the Union," the *Washington Republican* observed. As one-armed Wallace Moore concluded, "Politicians may forget—Soldiers will remember." In late 1866, a Hoosier empty sleeve confronted an office seeker who called upon the audience at a political rally to "forget the unpleasantness of the past." Bounding from his seat near the front row and holding his stump in the air, the ex-soldier responded, "No sir, not 'til that grows out!" In 1868, the *New Orleans Times* carped about the brazen one-legged soldier "waving his crutch all over the North, with the declaration that the 'War is not yet over.'"[38]

Even as white northerners grew increasingly weary of Reconstruction, one newspaper reported that "every empty sleeve and every crutch" objected to "State-rights and Ku Kluxism." One amputee submitted a tart letter to the editor of the *Chicago Inter Ocean* in September 1874. "For months, I have read in your columns accounts of outrages upon white and colored Republicans," he began.

This morning I told my wife to bring out my old blue coat. She did so, and as I gazed upon the dingy, moth-eaten garment, I noticed again that ragged hole through the sleeve. A bullet entered there while we were before Atlanta. I have one arm now, and wear an empty sleeve. I do not grumble, I am content, only my wish is that my good arm may not have been taken in vain. Even if tears came to my wife's eyes, and perhaps to mine, as we gazed at that old coat, does not matter. . . . But while I am willing to cease regrets for my losses during the rebellion, I do not wish that the country, the Union, shall be again imperiled. We whipped those rebels, we pardoned them, traitors though they were; but now, they are practicing the same tactics that they were in 1861. The Times *and* Tribune *and other Confederate sheets may talk of "carpet-baggers" and "niggers" if they please, but it is the disruption of the Union that they are after. . . . There are 1,000 old veterans in Chicago to-day who think as I do, and we are glad that there is one paper in the city that will not by implication even wink at this new assertion of State sovereignty as taught by the "color liners."*

Simply signing his letter "An Empty Sleeve," this cantankerous veteran urged his countrymen to consider both his disabled body and the "great task remaining" before them.[39]

Still other amputees lacked the poise and resolve of these soldiers. Some simply refused to contemplate an unhappy life of dependency—the kind of life scorned and derided by the striving culture of the late nineteenth century. An infantryman whose Kennesaw Mountain wound "never healed" and had resulted in "constant" suffering deemed himself an insufferable "burden on everyone" before taking his own life. "Don't cry for me," he admonished in the suicide note he left for his brother. "I have done an nuff [*sic*] of that." Citing discontent at home, one dismembered Vermont soldier hanged himself from a tree; in 1869, "under the influence of liquor," one-armed Jack Gilligan brutally assaulted his wife. Clearly, not every amputee was willing (or able) to divine purpose and dignity in an "honorable scar."[40]

And of course, not all veterans returned with scars and wounds that were visible. David Merrill, a Yale student who trudged his way up the Virginia Peninsula between the York and James rivers with George McClellan's Army of the Potomac in the spring of 1862, almost lamented that he had seen "hard pieces of shell whistle by within four feet—had the dirt thrown in my face by a Minnie ball—have laid two hours in a hole with thirty guns . . . and had five eight inch shells burst over head," and yet somehow emerged "unscathed." "Haven't got a scratch to show for it," he observed, and "have never had anything wounded except my feelings."[41]

Indeed, many (if not most) soldiers returned to civilian life "prematurely broken down," atrophied by years spent exposed to the elements and disease in unsanitary army camps. An exhausted Eugene Payne was convinced that his "arduous and difficult" service in the dank Vicksburg trenches accounted for the measles, chronic diarrhea, pneumonia, and malarial diseases that imperceptibly attacked his delicate frame. So frequently was one Maine physician called upon to diagnose the unsavory condition of the veterans in his community that he prepared a printed pamphlet demonstrating the "probable effect" of malarial poisoning on surviving soldiers. Joseph Duso was taken with "swamp fever" in the swamps and bayous of Louisiana. Decades later, when his engorged joints and "crooked leg" rendered him incapable of working, his wife resorted to a dreary life in the local poorhouse.[42]

In 1892, John Shaw Billings, who served as an army medical inspector, concluded "the exertions, privations, and anxieties of military service . . . must necessarily have lowered the vitality and diminished the power of resistance to subsequent exposure and causes of disease." After years of hoarding extant vital statistics, Billings demonstrated what he knew intrinsically—that veterans were significantly more likely than non-veterans to suffer from chronic illnesses and disease. Figures he mined from Massachusetts revealed that veterans were twice as likely as adult civilian males to suffer from consumption and rheumatism; nearly seven times as likely to develop heart disease; and some fifty-five times more likely to contract diarrheal diseases. Mortality records from Ohio confirmed similarly disproportionate rates of consumption, heart and kidney diseases, and diarrhea among the Union veteran population.[43]

Nervous disorders, mental "aberration," and insanity were equally menacing. According to Horace Porter, a Connecticut regimental surgeon, these afflictions were "so very common" among veterans "that they have been almost overlooked." "The life of our soldiers of the late war was one of continuous hardship to the nervous system," Porter explained in an address to the Northern Kansas Medical Society. "For every one hour of battle there were hundreds of hours of the brain tension of expected danger." According to another New England physician, the "tiresome watches of sleepless nights," the "vicissitudes of climate," and relentless exposure to an "unhygienic environment" accounted for the "common nervous troubles" and "idiotic leer" of old soldiers. He began applying the term *neurokinesis* to describe the effects of war on "nerve structures." Porter embraced this diagnosis as a way to legitimize for a doubting public—and most especially for a skeptical Pension Bureau—that veterans aged "so early," ached "so greatly," and "so often" lagged behind in the "struggle for existence" because of the oppressive years they had passed in camp and on the battlefield. "No country can afford to treat its brave men grudgingly," he insisted.[44]

Diagnostic language undoubtedly aided veterans "at a loss to give a name" to their ailments, but ultimately had little influence with the public at large. "There are a great many people who speak of the old Vets as being cranks, and never stop to think what makes them so cranky," one veteran appealed. "But if they had been brought through what some of these so-called cranks have, they would see that there is a cause of all of this crankiness."

Supposing you, who are so full of egotism, that judge others without thought, were placed all day out on the bare pavement with nothing to protect you and were ordered to lay down and let ten men shoot at you from a distance of say from 1,000 to 5,000 feet away, and you lay there without food or water, with every nerve strained to the highest tension, and you had to do that every two or three months during the year for four or five years, say nothing of the other hardships. Do you not think your nerves would be unstrung and you would be called cranky too?

Though the veteran cautioned that not all ex-soldiers were of "the same temperament," he contended that "the majority" felt the lingering effects of shrieking shells.[45]

Albert Orville Wright would no doubt have agreed. Born in Rome, New York, in 1842, Wright passed his boyhood in northwestern Ohio before landing at Beloit College in Wisconsin. After his graduation in 1864, he attended the Union Theological Seminary, returned to the Badger State, and was installed as pastor of the Congregational Church in Waterloo. Interested in the social sciences, Wright became active in reform circles. In 1896, while serving as the president of the National Conference of Charities and Correction, he crisscrossed his home state in a probe of its care for the insane. The "sinfulness and misery" he discovered astounded him. In nearly every county insane asylum and poor farm, from Dane and Outagamie counties to Fond du Lac, he met "totally disabled" and "insane" veterans existing as "county charges" without government pensions. Wright assembled a list ("the first attempt ever made to compile a list of insane soldiers," he boasted) of nearly 100 veterans entirely dependent on local support—including men like Private Christian Fisher of the 45th Wisconsin Volunteers, who resided in the new Northern Hospital for the Insane on the west bank of Oshkosh's Lake Winnebago. After suffering a severe shell wound to his head, Fisher returned to Wisconsin in a state of confusion, incapable of speaking. The old soldier wandered about as a pauper until he was "picked up" by local authorities. In a Manitowoc prison cell, he waited for the insane hospital to begin accepting patients. In other cases, the veterans Wright encountered were "so insane" that they could provide no account of themselves. One veteran, who continued to don his "soldier's clothes," was unable to offer "any rational account" of his identity, although he snapped to attention and obeyed military commands almost "automatically."[46]

More than any other cohort of soldiers, the survivors of southern

prison hells experienced enduring psychological injuries. The trials of captivity, the humiliation of starvation, and the omnipresence of death in
places like Andersonville and Camp Lawton indelibly marked Union ex-
prisoners of war. Although the northern public was initially receptive to
their unimaginable tales of suffering, ex-prisoners too found themselves
engaged in yet another battle—a costly struggle for elusive healing and
understanding.

CHAPTER 5

---◆---

CAPTIVE MEMORIES

First I will transform you—no one must know you.
I will shrivel the supple skin on your lithe limbs,
Strip the russet curls from your head and deck you out
In rags you'd hate to see some other mortal wear;
I'll dim the fire in your eyes, so shining once—
Until you seem appalling to all those suitors,
Even your wife and son you left behind at home.

—HOMER, *THE ODYSSEY*

"**T**HIS IS NO ordinary meeting," Joseph O'Neall explained. "It is a meeting of ex-prisoners who preferred to starve and rot rather than sacrifice their honor, or falter in the discharge of their duty." Shortly after eleven o'clock in the morning on June 15, 1882, nearly 2,000 blue-coated veterans filed into Memorial Hall on the oak-shaded grounds of the National Home for Disabled Volunteer Soldiers in Dayton, Ohio. After only a few moments, the men completely filled the chairs that lined the parquet floors of the flag-festooned auditorium—requiring many to take their seats in the galleries. O'Neall, who fought in the ranks of the 35th Ohio Volunteer Infantry, delivered the welcoming remarks. He was a survivor of Andersonville, the Confederacy's contemptible prisoner-of-war camp in southwestern

Georgia. He and his comrades had assembled in Dayton that morning for the third annual reunion of the Ohio Union Ex-Prisoners of War Association, one of more than sixty organizations maintained by the serried survivors of rebel prison pens.[1]

Edwin Beach, the Ohio association's president and a fellow former inmate of the southern stockade, approached the podium next. "We should fully comprehend and be actuated by the fact that there is embodied in our lives, individually and collectively, a thrilling part of the history of the late war," he declared. Beach found it appropriate that the ex-prisoners convened in a hall dedicated to disabled Union soldiers. Like those veterans who sported pinned-up blue coat sleeves or hobbled around on makeshift wooden legs, ex–prisoners of war perceived themselves as important citadels of Civil War memory. "We helped to make history," one survivor of Richmond's Libby prison maintained. "We are the living witnesses . . . we should leave our testimony before we go."[2]

In the postbellum years, "thousands of living witnesses all over the land," like those who convened in Dayton, became wardens of the war's most difficult history. "It is a sacred duty we owe to our fallen comrades, to ourselves, and to posterity," Andersonville survivor Gustavus Gessner from Ohio maintained, "to spare no effort to make the true story of our sacrifices and sufferings as inmates of rebel prison pens a part of the history of the war for the Union." Estranged by their captivity and seething with resentment, ex–prisoners of war sought to detail every last act of cruelty—each torment and each persecution they endured in the hands of the enemy. One Ohio cannoneer assured his fellow inmates that if there was life beyond Andersonville—something about which he was not entirely certain—that he would do "all in his power to spread abroad knowledge of our treatment, and arouse the sympathies of our friends to action in our behalf."[3]

Historians know that hatred for the enemy often motivates soldiers on the front lines to continue fighting. Among prisoners of war, however, these feelings, fortified with humiliation and disgrace, become intensely personal. Not surprisingly, then, Union ex-prisoners emerged from captivity with an unquenchable thirst for revenge. But they also felt an intrinsic need to tell their stories to as many civilians as possible. According to the modern war psychiatrist Jonathan Shay, "if they are to heal," survivors of war "need to voice their grief" publicly with "some mix of formal social ceremony" and some "informal telling of the story." Only then can they feel as though they are not "alone."[4]

Yet the truth of the prison experience was, in the words of Gustavus Gessner, "so appalling and so unlike anything that has taken place during modern times among civilized nations" that no one in possession of their faculties could believe it. Civilians accused ex-prisoners of stoking the war's embers—of embellishing their tales in a calculating, incendiary way. Each time they told of the "desolation, cruelty, and death" of Andersonville, ex-captives were dismissed as partisans intent on spoiling the peace.[5]

To be sure, even former prisoners were sometimes skeptical of their memories. One Norwegian-born Wisconsin soldier, snatched as a rebel prisoner at Chickamauga, marveled that anyone who passed "any length of time" mired in Andersonville's filth "could come out alive and be with you now." In an address that he delivered years later to an Iowa ex-prisoner gathering, Andersonville survivor Alson Blake queried, "Can it be possible that I endured all that suffering and am still living to tell this dreadful tale?" "It seemed more like a dream than reality," one ex-prisoner explained, "that such cruelty could exist." Flummoxed by the fact that he survived, Robert Hale Kellogg pointedly asked George Whitney, a trusted regimental comrade from Connecticut with whom he endured months of rebel captivity, "Were we really ever in Andersonville?"[6]

Physically ravaged and emotionally devastated by their implausible past, ex-prisoners needed public understanding and meaningful recognition even more than other veterans. And at first, it seemed as though they would get it. When a steady trickle of reports about "barbarities" in rebel prisons swelled into a flood, the U.S. House of Representatives empowered a five-member Special Committee (composed of northern congressmen) to provide "a faithful and true official history of the wrongs and sufferings endured by the national soldiers and loyal citizens at the hands of the confederate authorities." In the spring and summer of 1865, trade publishers frenziedly inked dozens of contracts with ex-prisoners for tell-all memoirs of days passed in rebel prison. Finally, a military tribunal convened in Washington to hear the wrenching evidence (much of it delivered in person by hundreds of repatriated prisoners) that would condemn Captain Henry Wirz to hang for war crimes. Born in Zurich in 1822, Wirz immigrated to the United States at the age of twenty-seven. Reed-thin, he had brooding, sinister eyes and wore a dark, oily beard. When the war broke out, he went off to fight for the Confederacy in a Louisiana outfit. Wounded in battle outside of Richmond in the spring of 1862, Wirz was shuffled off to a desk job at Libby prison, an old tobacco warehouse on the James River. When swelling numbers of captives necessitated a new prisoner-of-war camp, trusting Confederate authorities opted to hand Wirz the keys to Andersonville.[7]

Despite their deep knowledge of Wirz's crimes, however, most northern civilians possessed remarkably short attention spans. Especially when it came to contemplating the war's most painful legacies, northerners felt little sense of urgency. After all, the war had ended, the Union had been saved, the prisoners had returned home, and Wirz had swung from the gallows. By the end of the decade, then, ex-prisoners not only lacked formal outlets for their memories, but friendly audiences for their tales. Prison stories, civilians thought, would unnecessarily conjure up the demons of the past. Ironically enough, it was this unwillingness to countenance the past that rendered ex-prisoners more irascible, more vocal, and ultimately unable to heal. Now, the former captives who, during many sweltering months in Andersonville, felt as though they were utterly forsaken by their government, experienced betrayal once more.

--=◐◑=--

"No wartime experience," writes the historian David Blight, "caused deeper emotions, recriminations, and lasting invective than that of prisons." Former inmates remained under the spell of wretched places like Anderson ville and Cahaba, Florence and Belle Isle, for the rest of their lives. What happened in Civil War prisons beggared description. The informal prisoner exchanges common in the early months of the war gave way in 1862 to an official cartel (the combined energy of Confederate General Daniel Harvey Hill and his federal counterpart, Major General John Adams Dix), but the mass enrollment of African-American troops the following year resulted in its collapse. Confederate officials, fuming from Richmond, refused to exchange captured black men in blue—whom they considered to be rebellious slaves—on equal terms with white southern soldiers. At the precise moment that the war escalated in scale and fury, the Union and Confederate brass lacked any meaningful policy to facilitate prisoner exchange—more content to, in the words of a recent historian, "regard prisoners not as men, but as mere pawns to be used and then callously discarded in pursuit of national objectives." Throughout the South, overcrowded prison camps guarded by bloodhounds and pistol-wielding sentinels teemed with Union soldiers who lacked adequate food supplies, fresh drinking water, and medical attention.[8]

By the spring of 1864, one prison site in the pine wilderness of southwestern Georgia had achieved a monopoly on this brand of misery. Andersonville was a "dismal" outdoor stockade near Americus that provided precious little cover for prisoners roasting in the "torrid heat." By

August, the rebel wardens had herded more than 30,000 blue-coated captives into the twenty-six acre camp, which was bounded both by upright, slave-felled timbers and the "dead line," a line of pitch pine stakes beyond which no prisoner could venture. With little food and a lethargic brook supplying the camp's only water (and also its notorious dysentery), Andersonville slowly devolved from prison site to extermination camp. Life hardly existed in the surreal stockade; not "a spear of grass" nor "one green twig" could subsist there. "I [have] seen men weeping, praying, and cursing," wrote one former inmate. "I [have] seen them beg for bread and cry for water, which they were too weak to get. I [have] seen twenty skeleton bodies laid out and ready for the dead call." Some 13,000 men—or nearly one in three Andersonville inmates—perished before the prison was liberated in May 1865 and those fearful "gates of Death" clanged shut for the last time.[9]

Even in a world turned upside down by a ruinous and destructive war, no Civil War landscape was riddled with more death or infused with more uncertainty than Andersonville. "Of all places of distress and misery and suffering which I have ever seen," the Connecticut inmate Ira Emory Forbes recorded in his diary, "this is the worst." Without food, some men, reduced to skeletons, resorted to scraping through dirty latrines for sustenance. "Sunken eyes, extended cheek bones, and regular claw fingers, they seemed to haunt me for days," one Indiana inmate recalled in his memoir. Another inmate, this one from New York, recalled with "pity and disgust" his fellow prisoners, their "withered, filth and dirt begrimed skin, parchment-like in appearance, drawn tightly over their fleshless bone." Equally haunting was the vile, suffocating "stench" that emanated from the oozing, maggot-infested heaps of the dead.[10]

What made Andersonville such an epic human disaster was not merely "exposure to privation and physical suffering," but the way that the rebels' murderous captivity "wrecked constitutions and deranged minds." "It was anguish and despair," wrote one Massachusetts ex-prisoner, "which killed quite as much as actual starvation and disease." One Minnesota captive reported that under such punishing conditions, even the brawniest of soldiers gradually surrendered their last shred of humanity. "Suffering was so universal," he wrote, "that we lost all fellow feeling and had no interest in the dead or dying unless they were our own friends and acquaintances." Solon Hyde's imprisonment destroyed all "reason, sense, [and] feeling." Numerous inmates noted that in rebel prison, "idiocy" conquered hopelessly "shattered" and "dethroned" minds. Countless were the "bright intellects whose morning sun went down at noon."[11]

For most of these men, the sun would remain eternally set leaving behind an eventide of despair. In an address he delivered at a Union ex-prisoner-of-war reunion in Kansas, Joseph Waters resolved that a period of captivity in Andersonville could "never be effaced." "It is a plague we remember by its holocaust," he vowed. After his release from captivity, A. A. Hyde realized that his world had forever changed. "I was more than glad to be at home," he explained, "although home was new to me." For weeks, the ex-prisoner awoke "several times each night," feeling "intensely . . . of that wretched misery." Gilbert Sabre "lurked mournfully" in the "dark sepulchers" of the still-fresh prison scenes blinking before his eyes. "I sometimes forget that I am again surrounded by friends and humanity, and become despondent and oppressed." "A person hardened to all sorts of wretchedness for nineteen long months," he explained, "is often apt, for some time after, to overlook his freedom." In his memoir, Ezra Hoyt Ripple echoed that encountering old friends "braced me up so that for a time I forgot my sickness, but when I went to bed that night, I was to remain there . . . most of the time in delirium, in which the dogs, the prison, the rebel cavalrymen who took me back, and the old transport all contributed to keep me in terror and trouble night and day." Many former inmates dreaded hunger for the rest of their lives. "Starvation," wrote a survivor, "is a horror which, once suffered, leaves an impression that is never erased from the memory."[12]

There was no greater measure of just how profoundly their lives had been altered than the alarmed reactions of their friends and family back home. "Their arms and legs look like coarse reeds with bulbous joints," the *Chicago Medical Examiner* reported. "Their faces look as though a skillful taxidermist had drawn tanned skin over the bare skull, and then placed false eyes in the orbital cavities." Those who had been afflicted with scurvy returned with loose or missing teeth, ossified skin, and extremities so swollen that they assumed a "purplish" hue. Some survivors were so depleted, so ravaged, and so emaciated that their loved ones did not even recognize them upon their return. "I was so changed in appearance that nobody knew me, not even my mother," one ex-inmate recollected of his return home to Wisconsin. "I almost wished then that I had died at Andersonville."[13]

In other words, in the weeks and months immediately following their repatriation, it was difficult for even the most hard-edged skeptic to deny the base realities of Civil War prisons. The evidence was everywhere—tangible and immediately perceptible. Few could refute the brooding, life-less stare of an emaciated, lice-infested Andersonville survivor. Even those unacquainted with ex–prisoners of war could rely on the tidal wave of personal narratives and prison memoirs produced in the first years after the war. By 1868, at least thirty-four titles penned by Union ex–prisoners of war were available—many of them sold door-to-door by their desperate authors.[14]

⋅→⊨◉═⊨←⋅

Yet familiarity breeds contempt. "Made very uneasy by these reports," northern civilians rather quickly grew less receptive to tales of rebel prisons. "One class have accepted them as true; another have felt them to be exaggerated; still another have pronounced them wholly false, fictions purposely made and scattered abroad to inflame the people against their enemies, and doing great injustice to the South," one observer concluded. In an editorial review of Warren Lee Goss's *The Soldier's Story of His Cap-*

tivity, published in 1867, one literary critic candidly confessed: "We do not like to read such narratives. They are too remindful of the late sorrow, and we would for our own taste discourage their publication." Many prisoner autobiographies, in the words of one editor, "never took" commercially. Lee & Shepard, the Boston-based publisher of Union army medical inspector Augustus Choate Hamlin's clumsily titled Andersonville tell-all *Martyria*, mourned when it barely "got back [the] advertising bill in amount by sales, without saying anything about profits." Indeed, as early as the 1870s, blue-coated prison survivors aching to see their stories in print began turning to local bookbinderies and homegrown printers. They'd grown impatient with major publishing firms who, unfortunately for the ex-prisoners, understood their market—and Civil War memory— all too well. Others, many without means to underwrite costly self-publication fees, consigned their beloved manuscripts to the oblivion of dusty attics and dank cellars. By 1879, Ohioan John McElroy, an Andersonville survivor, could judiciously lament that "the country has heard much of the heroism and sacrifices of these loyal youths who fell on the field of battle, but it has heard little of the still greater number who died in the prison pen."[15]

Ex-prisoners were not only censored, but openly defamed and maligned. Northern men and women reproached ex-prisoners as "fuller of bitterness than of patriotism," alternating between allegations of sensationalism and outright deceit. The son of a Pennsylvania veteran who survived the miseries of the rebel prison camp at Salisbury, North Carolina, regretted that "people seem to think that prisoners were well used ... I think it is a shame that such cruel things should be said about our soldiers." After turning the last page of John McElroy's *Andersonville*, one Kansas man looked up a local survivor mentioned in the tome. "I have been reading a book ... on Southern prisons, and I would ask you if the truth is told in regard to them," he brazenly queried. Desperate, Warren Lee Goss sought anything that might "more thoroughly convince" the public that Andersonville "was not a myth but a hell that tried American endurance and fidelity and courage more than its battlefields." But in an age of sectional reconciliation, Goss's plea went unheard; a "fading away of the painful memories of the war" was writing these men "out of history." "The people in the North," Andersonville survivor Francis Roy confided to the editor of the *Veteran's Advocate*, "are forgetting all about what the boys suffered during the war."[16]

⊶⥱◉⥃⊷

And so these veterans did what they had done so well while enduring captivity—they relied on each other for healing, comfort, and empathy. "Though no man holds dearer his regimental comrades," one Libby prison survivor maintained, "there is a stronger affection that binds together in remembrance of hardship and suffering those who were prisoners of war." "No one who has not had experience of the miseries of confinement in southern prisons," Lester Phelps echoed in a moving letter to a fellow Andersonville inmate from Connecticut who had been carted off to the Georgia prison hell just two days before his twenty-first birthday, "can realize or imagine suffering and horrors there endured, nor the patriotism and loyalty of those who endured it."[17]

Condemned to wrestle with the horror wedged into the deepest and darkest recesses of their memories, the ex-prisoners acknowledged each other as "fictive kin." They proudly dedicated memoirs to their "comrades in suffering" and wrote to one another for the rest of their lives; they addressed emotional letters to "brother captive" and lovingly signed them "fellow prisoner." Understanding the healing power of sharing their stories, they neither glamorized nor embellished the prison experience. They told the truth as they knew it. When they stumbled over a niggling detail, or when their powers of recollection grew feeble and dim, they asked a fellow ex-prisoner for assistance. Robert Hale Kellogg would quite often, at the request of an inquiring comrade, search the groaning shelves of prison memoirs and "finely bound" reports that lined the second-floor study of his Ohio home for information. And just as regimental comrades diligently scoured their diaries and wracked their memories to aid the authors of unit histories, ex-prisoners called upon each other to proofread and to edit the first drafts of their books. Before publishing *Andersonville*, for example, John McElroy solicited comments from hundreds of fellow ex-inmates. The feedback he received no doubt contributed to the book's mammoth size, and to its unrivaled commercial reception.[18]

Remarkably, ex-prisoners always knew where they could find one another. In 1910, floodwaters stranded Robert Kellogg, who was on a business trip, near Granville, Ohio. Instinctively, he called upon Rev. Thomas Sheppard, a veteran of eleven battles who passed ten months in Andersonville. Sheppard, hailed as the "Andersonville Chaplain" by those who remembered the prayer services he conducted in the pen, was elated to see his old comrade. Sheppard invited him to spend the evening swapping tales of the stockade. "His aged wife was upstairs, ill, and his daughter out, so we had a good, quiet talk by ourselves," Kellogg recalled. "I may never see him again, but shall always remember this visit."[19]

⋅⊷══⊶⋅

Within a decade of their return north, rebel prison survivors moved to formally establish a national organization of ex–prisoners of war. In 1873, prison survivors Warren Lee Goss and Charles Shaw formed the National Union Survivors of Andersonville and Other Southern Military Prisons. This alliance of more than twenty state and local associations of ex-prisoners endeavored to strengthen "ties of fraternal fellowship and sympathy" among survivors and sought to "secure justice" to the veterans by "joint action." Goss and Shaw also delineated among the order's objectives the correction of "false statements"; the defense of historical records, prison artifacts, and incarceration sites; and the pronouncement of "the truth of our hardships." These orders were not only repositories of memory and places to mourn, but exclusive spaces in which survivors shared and worked through the "burning, scalding crucible of the rebel prison pen." In these guilds, men whose invisible scars were elsewhere dismissed could "stand by each other."[20]

Participation in these organizations fortified survivors by validating the truth of even their most impossible stories. Membership applications asked veterans to provide their rank and regiment, as well as the specifics of their capture and release. Applicants were only successful if they averred that they had remained loyal to the flag during their imprisonment and had never taken an oath of allegiance to the Confederacy. In keeping with the organization's objective of preserving and documenting history, membership blanks entreated those who had "ever been subjected to any barbarous and cruel tortures" to provide a description on the reverse side of their application. Extant rosters from local and state associations suggest that the national organization commanded a sizeable membership. An 1883 roster for the Ohio Association of Union Ex-Prisoners of War boasted more than 1,600 members, and a surviving 1884 register for the New York City association listed the names of more than 200 active members.[21]

Former prisoners genuinely prized the oversized membership certificates issued by the associations. Printed on parchment enriched by gilded trimming, elaborate seals, and looping signatures, these diplomas aimed to lend the survivors a measure of credibility. Members could also acquire brass medallions, which they proudly affixed to their lapels with red, white, and blue ribbons. The badges, embossed with the words, "A Survivor of Southern Military Prisons, 1861–1865," depicted one of Wirz's snarling bloodhounds mounting a fugitive Andersonville inmate. To ornament their medallions, prison survivors could also purchase—for a modest 35 cents each—tiny brass bars stamped with the names of the stockades in which they suffered. One veteran acquired seven bars for his badge: Libby, Danville, Savannah, Blackshear, Millen, Macon, and Andersonville.[22]

At ex-prisoner gatherings, the "roll call" worked in tandem with the certificates, badges, and bars. After calling a meeting to order, the presiding officer would reel off the names of rebel prisons—from the well-known Libby, Belle Isle, and Andersonville to the lesser-known Mayo Tobacco House, Marshall, and Leggetts. Upon hearing the name of their incarceration site, members stood for a somber and affecting moment of acknowledgment. At a Massachusetts gathering in 1894, attendees responded to the names of some twenty-five pens. Often, especially at annual banquet meetings, shield-shaped placards bearing the names of "hell's own houses of despair" adorned the walls.[23]

Yet even the roll call achieved little in contrast to the storytelling that occurred at monthly meetings and annual reunions. At last, the ex-prisoners had a space in which they could express themselves "frankly and freely," uninhibited by doubt, disdain, or disbelief. In 1882, Ohio state association reunion attendees erupted into "deafening cheers" when A. D. Streight announced that Andersonville "never had a parallel" in history. "People say these are exaggerations, but not one-half has been told," he declared. The Chicago-based Western Andersonville Survivors' Association concluded each evening of its annual reunion sessions by inviting ex-prisoners to deliver five-minute speeches; annual reunions of the Illinois, Iowa, Massachusetts, and Connecticut associations likewise ended with long "recitals of personal experiences." The *Boston Journal* reported that such storytelling was "a great jollification" for the former inmates. At an ex-prisoner meeting in Centralia, Illinois, for example, Comrade Green's "graphic" rehearsal of his Andersonville days "got the boys thoroughly enthused." When he published his memoir, a gritty Massachusetts survivor named Amos E. Stearns set aside the dedication page for the members of the Massachusetts state association, those "congratulating comrades" who had helped him to work through his surreal history.[24]

Each survivor association created a figurative space in which veterans could gather to heal and grieve. The District of Columbia Association of

Ex-Union Prisoners of War was exceptional in that it also provided its members with their own physical meeting space. In April 1887, after months of gathering in a bevy of hotel lobbies, fraternal lodges, and members' homes, the association leased two adjoining rooms in the Corcoran Building downtown. Officers invited ex-prisoners to make these rooms their "resting place" when downtown. Rings of tobacco smoke curled into the air most evenings as the veterans reminisced. John McElroy, who had recently moved to Washington to become the *National Tribune*'s managing editor, donated a "handsomely framed" copy of Thomas O'Dea's *Andersonville Prison* for display in one of the rooms. The heartrending lithograph, an aerial view of the stockade sketched from memory and dedicated to former inmates, brought "tears to many eyes" of those assembled for an evening of storytelling.[25]

Equally affecting were the "precious" prison relics that festooned this and other meeting spaces. After calling gatherings to order with pine gavels created from stockade timbers, presiding officers frequently invited members to highlight treasured items from their own collections. "With touching appeal" during one Connecticut state association meeting, Norman Hope displayed the "small but unique collection" of broken knives, forks, and spoons that he had procured from various prisons. After one ex-prisoner banquet in Grand Rapids, Clark Wakeman, a private from the 21st Michigan who was captured at Chickamauga, exhibited the tin cup that once held his meager rations. Frank Smith, who ventured to Andersonville on a souvenir-hunting expedition in 1883, prepared an arresting exhibition in Toledo for the Tri-State Association of Union Ex-Prisoners of War. A frail section of the deadline served as the focal point for Smith's display. At a meeting of the New England association, a relic display included a tiny vessel containing dark red earth from Andersonville and an old, tarnished kettle from Millen.[26]

These relics, like the gatherings themselves, nurtured recollection and corroborated the horrors of rebel prisons. Rather than objects of glory, like bullets or bayonets, these mementoes were the stuff of survival. Recognizing the explanatory power of these relics, one survivor traveled to Andersonville, pulled a log from the stockade, pried rusty barbs from the north gate, and sawed a segment of pitch pine from the deadline. The veteran passed months hewing the lumber into splinters, intending to furnish a relic "free to all who were imprisoned at Andersonville." (When high demand rendered postage costs insurmountable, he began retailing the relics, attaching to each relic a certificate of "genuineness.") "Every comrade who gets a relic should take it to his local paper and exhibit it to the editor," he recommended, believing that the objects might, by reminding northern civilians that a place like Andersonville existed, generate "a favorable opinion" toward ex-prisoners. "I know of no possible way to get so many notices in newspapers throughout the country as by this means," he wrote.[27]

⋅–≡⊙⊂≡⋅–

The hard truth was that while ex-prisoner-of-war associations sustained prison survivors, they had scarcely moved the hearts and minds of the northern public. If anything, ex-prisoner meetings contributed to even greater public suspicion and scorn. Men and women peppered ex-inmates with glib questions about the object of their reunions. "Are they to advertise your wounds and sufferings?" one passenger on a train conveying survivors to an Illinois ex-prisoner reunion allegedly asked. Northern civilians were convinced that the reunions were held merely "to perpetuate hatred for the South." "The people generally do not fully understand the full scope of [our] meaning when [we] say we are ex-prisoners of war," one veteran insisted. The trouble, as Chicago's *Inter Ocean* observed, was that so long as ex-prisoners gathered, "the object of the war" could not be "forgotten, nor its results lost."[28]

Brimming with insult and feeling betrayed, many associations redoubled their efforts to "inculcate in the minds of the American people a

proper regard" for the fallen and a "true appreciation" of their past sufferings. As "stewards" of the past, they leveled stern challenges to those who
sought to "soften" the appalling history of rebel prisons. Numbering the
dead became a chief concern. In 1876, when Jefferson Davis contended in
a widely reprinted, venomous letter that the mortality rate among Confederate prisoners detained in Chicago's Camp Douglas, Ohio's Johnson's
Island, and New York's Elmira prison "exceeded" that of Union soldiers in
his own stockades, the National Association responded in kind. Drawing
on official reports and the testimony of southern leaders, President Goss
averred that the morality rate in rebel prisons "was about three times as
great as that in Union prisons." A few years later, after Frederick Phisterer's
Statistical Record overlooked the death tolls for Millen, Cahaba, and several
other notorious prison camps in the Deep South, Ohio state association
President Gustavus Gessner, who passed many years making exhaustive
tallies of the dead and living, demanded from Secretary of War Robert
Todd Lincoln an "official admission" of the "gross inaccuracy" of Phisterer's
numbers. "The most convincing proof of the truth of the story of . . . sufferings endured by the Union prisoners of war," he explained, "is the appalling
death rate which prevailed in the various prisons of the South." The
National Association followed with a braying resolution that condemned
Phisterer's oversights.[29]

By the late nineteenth century, ex-prisoners yearned for anything that
might rectify their feelings of abandonment and neglect. Increasingly, they
sought to distinguish themselves as the most courageous lot among the Civil
War's common soldiers, whose battlefield heroics and acts of martial splendor were—by the 1880s and 1890s—heralded by a rising generation of
Americans who knew the war as only a distant memory. The war was now
the province of history; the threat of a second rebellion had subsided, and the
thorny questions of Reconstruction, if not resolved in a way that achieved
justice for African-Americans, were nevertheless settled. To be sure, this new

interest in all things martial rarely extended to genuine concern for the fate of the veteran. By the turn of the century, Americans had done so much to trumpet the common soldier's courage that any veteran who begged for assistance was immediately perceived as less than manly. Nonetheless, ex-prisoners hoped that by emphasizing the more inspiring aspects of their captivity, they could earn the elusive respect they deserved.[30]

With great fervor, prison survivors wrote about heart-pounding escape attempts—of burrowing under Andersonville's red clay and slinking through the fingers of the Georgia woods under the cover of darkness. Prisoners began illustrating personal memoirs with detailed blueprints of their stockades, very much reminiscent of the hand-drawn battlefield maps that many soldiers included in their published accounts. In the last decade of the nineteenth century, they likewise returned to their incarceration sites and erected markers, obelisks, and columns that paid tribute to their courage and conviction.

They reminded him that the prisoner of war had been abandoned by his government—banished to the precipice of hell. Many ex-captives also began arguing that it was easier to face death on a battlefield. William Lyon devoted an entire chapter of his memoir to the contrast between the "loyalty" required on the field of battle and the "bravery" demanded in the prison pen. "The prisoner," he maintained, "has nothing to inspire or encourage him. The music is gone. There are no words from his officers to help him but the long, monotonous days and dreary, sleepless nights." Joseph Twichell explained in a Memorial Day address on the New Haven green that while "patience" and "endurance" were "incidental to service in the field," the cruel monotony of captivity demanded a perpetual "halo of super human fortitude."[31]

Insisting that those who suffered in rebel prisons "gave their lives for their country as though they had fallen in battle," the survivors were adamant that they deserved to be counted among the war's most "heroic" soldiers. One ex-prisoner even boasted that he returned home to Massachusetts bearing "more scars" after his brief tenure in Andersonville than his "old comrades" who had evaded captivity. "For more than twenty-three centuries, civilized mankind has drawn inspiration and example from the patriotism and valor of those who fell on the field of Marathon in delivering Greece from the yoke of Persia," Gustavus Gessner explained. "It ought not to be considered inappropriate to speak of the 'heroic' dead of Andersonville." Augustus Hamlin similarly urged the readers of his Andersonville history to look beyond "the glittering and inspiring pomp of war," confident that they might find something dauntless and daring in the hollow eyes of an Andersonville inmate. Yet in the late nineteenth century, haunted minds were hardly "honorable scars." Despite their determined appeals, prisoners' stories were still "too horrible for civilized people to contemplate." The collective memory of the war was simply too powerful, too entrenched, and too satisfying to resist.[32]

⋆⟞◉⟝⋆

The ex-prisoners made one last attempt to earn a place in the war's history. Survivor associations encouraged their members to rally public support for legislation that would establish an "ex-prisoner pension." Writing into the law the harrowing consequences of rebel captivity, they asserted, was "an act of justice," signaling that the nation had at last deemed injuries to "mental faculties" worthy and heroic. (The proposed bill also served a practical purpose, for the daunting evidentiary demands of existing legislation rendered it "utterly impossible" for many former prisoners to successfully secure a pension claim. Gustavus Gessner, for instance, argued that it was easier for a "one-hundred days man" who "never fired a gun" to secure a pension, for, unlike ex-prisoners, he could at least supply supporting testimony from a regimental officer or surgeon.) An indignant Nathan Goff petitioned Congress to consider the prison pension bill, a "very modest demand" because the "Government had not taken any action in doing any thing for the men that suffered in Rebel prisons." "Teach us that Republics are not ungrateful," the Iowa association urged the Committee on Invalid Pensions in a petition bearing dozens of unsteady signatures.[33]

Despite the heap of handbills and petitions agitating for pensions and at least four efforts to secure the passage of a prisoner bill in Congress, the survivors continued to meet with a dogged and, at times, unlikely opposition. The chin-whiskered Connecticut Senator Joseph Roswell Hawley, who led a brigade into battle at Olustee and a division forward at Petersburg, pledged his determined opposition, as did a number of Grand Army of the Republic posts. "If this bill passes as it stands," the Alexander Hays Post No. 3 in Pittsburgh resolved, "it will include many who are not entitled to a Pension because of having no disability." A neighboring post unanimously adopted a resolution opposing this obvious money "grab." Challenged to a "contest of suffering," prison survivors, for one, sneered at the notion that the Grand Army of the Republic was a parochial pension lobby. While more than a few Andersonville veterans secured their pecuniary rewards through the passage of so-called "private pension bills" (special measures approved in the wee hours of the morning by a "unanimous consent" request in a largely abandoned House chamber), the recognition afforded by a singular pension rating for ex-prisoners went unrealized—and was rendered moot when President Benjamin Harrison signed the Dependent Pension Act of 1890 into law, permitting all loyal and honorably discharged "persons who served ninety days or more in the military or naval service of the United States during the late war of the rebellion" to receive monthly disbursements from the federal treasury.[34]

⋄⊷⊙⊶⋄

For ex–prisoners of war, the pension battle constituted the final campaign of their long struggle to find a measure of healing in public acknowledgment. Beginning in the 1890s, attendance at ex-prisoner-of-war meetings ineluctably declined as the aging survivors made one final escape—this one from their earthly bondage. "The old boys are going home," Robert Kellogg observed in one of his last letters to George Whitney. Ex-prisoners receded from public view nearly as swiftly as they had emerged and took their uncomfortable memories to their graves. Although their tales never "captured" the public, their rituals, relics, and reunions nonetheless indulged each other in the face of withering distrust. More so than any other cohort of Union veterans, ex–prisoners of war learned that "memory" was something they could neither live with—nor without.[35]

CHAPTER 6

———✦———

A DEBT OF HONOR

Now along came this tramp, this public nuisance
Who used to scrounge a living round the streets of Ithaca

———

Well he came by to rout the king from his own house
And met Odysseus now with a rough, abusive burst:
"Get off the porch, you old goat, before I haul you
Off by the leg! Can't you see them give me the wink,
All of them here, to drag you out—and so I would
But I've got some pangs of conscience. Up with you, man,
Or before you know it, we'll be trading blows!"

———

A killing look, and the wily old soldier countered, "Out of your mind?
What damage have I done you? What have I said?
I don't grudge you anything,
Not if the next man up and gives you plenty.
This doorsill is big enough for the both of us—
You've got no call to grudge me what's not yours."

—HOMER, *THE ODYSSEY*

HIS PARENTS AND young sister looked on as the one-legged veteran, sporting his blue uniform once more, leaned into his crudely made wooden crutch. The Springfield musket he shouldered throughout the war was mounted in a position of prominence on the paneled wall, just beneath the exposed rafters of their modest cabin. Adjacent to the weapon, his empty cartridge box and old army canteen—its tin lurking beneath an olive patina—were suspended from two pegs. A stout man in a tailored suit with perfectly manicured dundrearies carefully inspected the soldier, furiously scribbling notes as the veteran regaled all with his mournful tale. Peeling apples in the corner, the old soldier's sister braced herself for the wrenching moment when that cussed rebel projectile hurtled toward her brother's leg. She had heard this story too many times before. From the farming communities of the Midwest to the rural villages of New England, this was a scene duplicated many times in the years after the Civil War: the arrival of the pension claim agent.[1]

Of the myriad obstacles confronted by Union veterans, few were as protracted and public as securing a pension claim. Thousands of tattered brown envelopes, bulging with decades of pleading correspondence and yellowed applications, exhaust the stacks of the National Archives Building in downtown Washington, D.C. Collectively, they reveal the fierce determination with which veterans confronted both a cynical citizenry and a labyrinthine bureaucracy. Throughout the last decades of the nineteenth century, the so-called "problem of the pensioner" convinced many observers and policy-makers that Union veterans posed a genuine "threat" to the republic they once battled to save. For many "totally destitute" ex-soldiers "suffering for actual necessaries of life," then, obtaining a pension was worrisome and discouraging, requiring both invasive examinations and unmanly pleas for aid. Sometimes, veterans fought for years to demonstrate the merits of their claims. An old soldier from Elkhart, Indiana, sardonically observed that it took physicians "less than fifteen minutes" to presume him physically fit for army service, but required "more than fifteen years" for pension examiners to determine that he was physically unable to support himself. "If the United States has been as slow in examining into the physical condition of us fellows when the war broke out, in 1861, as it is today in examining our condition when we ask for a pension," he contended, "the country would have gone to [hell] long ago." In the end, securing a pension meant wresting from the public elusive recognition of soldiers' sufferings and sacrifices on the battlefield. By demanding pensions, veterans insisted that the public make good on a "sacred debt" and, in the process, demanded that they remember the cause and consequences of the American Civil War. "That this generation and all that shall follow may learn the real lessons of the war and may appreciate and understand what our liberties cost," veteran Eliakim Torrance declared from his home in Minnesota, "this is the lesson the soldier of the Union is trying to teach."[2]

⊶⊷⊙⊷⊶

Federal benefits for veterans were not without precedent when Billy Yank came marching home. In the age of the early republic, thousands of "suffering soldiers" who fought in the Revolution finally received compensation when Congress passed the Federal Pension Act in 1818. Similarly, the federal government made provisions for veterans of the War of 1812 and Mexican War by issuing warrants for coveted government lands in the Lower Missouri Valley. But politicians in Washington were still too riveted to republicanism and its scorn for standing armies to embrace anything that approached a fixed ideology of veterans' rights. While "shatter[ing] nearly forty years of resistance against awarding lifetime pensions" for veterans, these early provisions did not result from a national consensus about the rights of veterans; they no doubt established a veteran's "right to appeal for assistance," but hardly declared him "automatically entitled to aid." Indeed, most civilians eased lingering reservations by resolving that pensions and bounties would "gradually decrease in importance."[3]

Those hopes, of course, became some of the first casualties of the war.

In an effort to "promote voluntary enlistments" and to cheer an army still licking the wounds of First Bull Run, in the summer of 1861, Congress established federal pension benefits for volunteers wounded on the field of battle. Rife with "uncertainties and discrepancies," the measure made but a fitful commitment to care for him who had borne the battle. A year later, confronted with the mounting costs of war, Congress approved more sweeping legislation granting monthly pensions to those Union soldiers who were completely disabled in the service. Rates were determined by rank; officers received $30 per month, while privates were pensioned at $8 per month. Men wounded though not "totally" incapacitated were pensioned at a rate commensurate with the severity of their injuries. The bill, which Secretary of the Interior John Palmer Usher deemed "the wisest and most munificent enactment of the kind ever adopted by any nation," also made provisions for the widows of those veterans whose untimely deaths were attributed to injuries received in battle or diseases contracted while in the service. "The aid and relief of wounded and disabled soldiers," Secretary of War Edwin Stanton assured veterans and their families, "is . . . a subject that will commend itself strongly to every patriotic heart."[4]

Even amid the war, however, many northerners voiced concerns about the "extravagant, if not insupportable" albatross placed annually around the neck of the federal treasury. For one, Pension Commissioner Joseph Barrett winced at the swelling cost of caring for the disabled, which, by the time of Appomattox, was approaching $9 million per year. The burden (like the pension laws themselves) only seemed to multiply. In a July 1864 measure, Congress introduced uniform, "statutory" pension rates for soldiers who had lost their sight, lost the use of both arms, or lost the use of both legs. Within just two years, legislators had prescribed some fifteen permanent rates for specific disabilities—each of which testified in grisly detail to the consequences of the battlefield. Suddenly, the government found itself making good on claims for "total disability in one arm and one leg"; for the "loss of a leg above the knee causing inability to wear an artificial limb"; and for the "loss of an arm at the shoulder joint." By 1873, the volume of pension laws was such that Hoosier Senator Daniel Pratt, the Republican who presided over the Senate Committee on Pensions, introduced a measure "consolidating" the existing tangle of legislation. "So many changes have been introduced from time to time, so many sections and parts of sections repealed or modified," the senator insisted, "that it is a task of no small magnitude to deduce what is the existing law." To a thicket of statutory rates for "specific" disabilities, the Consolidation Act added three "grades" of pensionable afflictions. These grades nodded to those veterans who required the services of a full-time medical attendant; those who were deemed "unable to perform manual labor"; and those who suffered a wound or an injury deemed "equivalent to the loss of a hand or foot."[5]

In the public mind, this maddening maze of legislation confirmed the nation's "largesse" and, even more significantly, canceled any outstanding or future debts owed to the soldiers who put down the rebellion. "We are flippantly told that our pension laws are ample and the most beneficent in the world," one Hoosier general explained, "and that no ex-soldier has the right to find the least fault with the generosity and paternal care of our government . . . tauntingly told that our ex-soldiers should be more than thankful, and that no nation in the world can show such a grand total of pensioners."[6]

Despite "such loud and bombastic boastings," however, the federal government not only paid piddling attention to those soldiers whose injuries were not immediately visible, but its legislation made "no promise of ongoing relief." Veterans were quick to point out the "innumerable defects" of the "restricted," "incomplete," and "niggardly" laws, "passed when the subject of pensions was not understood." First, evidentiary demands on applicants were too rigorous. When War Department or Navy Department records failed to provide sufficient evidence that the claim being prosecuted originated on the battlefield, the law required veterans to supply a sworn affidavit by a commissioned officer who "had personal knowledge" of the circumstances relating to the wound or injury. In cases lacking *any* record of a wound or injury, applicants were required to submit the testimony of the surgeon or assistant surgeons who treated him. While the Pension Bureau no doubt had an obligation to foil scoundrels filing fraudulent claims, more often than not, these provisions refused pensions to worthy ex-soldiers. One New Hampshire veteran knew several comrades "entitled to a pension, beyond a doubt" (including one man who lost all of his teeth to scurvy in Andersonville, and another who recovered in a field hospital whose records were subsequently captured and destroyed by the rebels), who could not secure an allowance "for lack of medical evidence." Frustrated applicants could be found "in every neighborhood." "Sometimes the regimental surgeon who treated them is dead, or cannot be reached, so that his affidavit may be taken," another comrade noted, not only supposing that applicants remembered the names of their attendants, but assuming that the surgeons would perfectly recall each of their patients. Veterans railed against Section 4717 of the Revised Statutes, which imposed a five-year limit on applicants who, owing to the lack of evidence on file either at the War Department or the Navy Department, were obliged to gather supporting testimony from distant sources. "What every veteran most desires," one veterans' newspaper explained, "is a simple law, which can easily be defined, and yet is stringent enough to prevent fraud."[7]

Equally affronting was the "unjust" behavior of the unbelieving bureaucrats who reviewed applications. Despite presenting testimony from a fellow Andersonville ex-inmate, two lieutenants, and several neighbors, Wisconsin veteran Ole Steensland was branded a liar and had his claim for a disability pension rejected not once, but twice. "I must say that that hurt," he confessed. "The people of my town and county have had confidence in me as an honest man." A fellow Badger State ex-soldier had his case "repeatedly rejected" because War Department logs erroneously recorded his regiment's debut on the firing line at Shiloh. All the same, the Pension Bureau's medical examiners routinely earned the ire of veterans dependent on their jaundiced judgments. At the bureau's Boston agency, Daniel Eldredge let out a shriek and recoiled from the forceful grip of a skeptical examining surgeon who appeared to have no regard for his wounded left arm, fractured by a rebel Minié ball at the battle of Deep Bottom. "You lie when you say that hurts you," the startled surgeon replied. "Damn it! Do you think we're a set of damned fools here and don't know when a man's 'playing it'?" When assessing William Olsen's claim of "heart trouble," pension examiners required the aging ex-soldier to "strip entirely nude and climb up and down a steep stairway on his hands and knees." "They ought to be retired to some warmer place, the door locked and the key lost," one veteran fumed.[8]

Underwriting these grievances was the conviction that pensions were "not a gratuity," but, much like enlistment bounties, a "debt of honor" owed to suffering soldiers. "It is a common mistake, on the part of the pensioners and the public," explained one veteran from New York, "to suppose that a pension given by the Government is a mere gratuity to its patriotic soldiers. This is not so. To give a pension to a soldier disabled by wounds, injuries, or diseases . . . is merely the fulfillment of a CONTRACT made by the United States with every man who enlists in its military service." George Wilson, an Illinois private who passed long months in rebel captivity at Macon, Georgia, and at the Race Course in Charleston, South Carolina, also demanded that the government fulfill its contract with his comrades. "The soldier did not go to the fight for the miserable $11 a month, but to save his country," he snarled. A pension seemed but a small price to pay for a Union preserved and saved from the scourge of slavery; "an army that had wrought such results," one ex-soldier announced, "cannot be forgotten, and . . . should not forget itself."[9]

Nonetheless, what animated so many veterans to demand more liberal pension laws were the inescapable examples of anguish, insolvency, and destitution all around them. "There is no little suffering among [us]," one New England Grand Army man observed. Post relief funds disbursed assistance to those "helpless" men "receiving no pension or aid from the Government" and made appeals to sister posts on behalf of worthy comrades, like the Pennsylvania cannoneer who, "able to do but very little labor," scraped by in "a very rude shanty." In 1888, the surgeon general of the Grand Army of the Republic reported that "the reports of destitution and sickness that I have received this year . . . are simply appalling." At great expense, county almshouses took charge of the nearly 30,000 ailing veterans—a full army corps—denied admission to state and federal soldiers' homes. In Wisconsin, so many Union soldiers died penniless that in 1887 the state legislature passed an act defraying the funeral and burial expenses of any honorably discharged, "indigent" ex-Union soldier. Even veterans who were fortunate enough to receive a pension often found the government's largesse wholly "insufficient" to support a family. Despite winning a pension claim, twenty-nine-year-old Philip McGuire, who lost a leg on the third day at Gettysburg, was unable to feed his wife and three children—all under the age of ten—on $8 per month. He reluctantly turned to the local overseer of the poor. Tragically, one veteran of Champion Hill and Missionary Ridge—who carried "a burden upon his soul . . . too great to bear"—found the relief he needed only by placing the barrel of a .32-caliber Smith & Wesson revolver to his temple and squeezing the trigger.[10]

Resolving to fight "the battle of the Veterans" in the face of such humiliation, the comrades clenched their teeth for one more long campaign. "We will not go hungry and wander around the streets looking for work and be refused it because we are old soldiers," one veteran from St. Paul vowed. "Let us stand together, and if we must starve let us starve together, and the disgrace that will accrue to an ungrateful people will be a just retribution." "For the sake of common decency," one-armed Lucius Fairchild pleaded, "I want every old soldier kept out of the common pauper house . . . and in common decency, I want them to have bread, and I want them to have butter on it, too." New committees and organizations sprang to life. The Grand Army of the Republic appointed a five-member Pension Committee, which included the double amputee James Tanner, to report to Congress the condition of men who had "made drafts of blood, of limbs, suffering, and life." Adopting the motto "Unity Is Our Strength," a new guild known as the Union Veteran Army sought to secure "justice and honor" to "all those who faithfully served the Government during the rebellion." In October 1882, heeding the call of a New York City Grand Army of the Republic post, some 150 ex-soldiers gathered to form the Veterans' Rights Union, pledging to work "tirelessly" in the interest of veterans' "privileges and rights." Chapters quickly reached across the country. "This is no child's play," advised the president of the Kansas chapter. "Knowing our rights let us dare to maintain them and stand elbow to elbow as in the days that have past [sic]." These organizations did not focus entirely on pension reform legislation; they also sought to secure western land grants for ex-soldiers and to impose hiring preferences for those veterans seeking federal employment. "We believe the Government should keep its implied contract with its Defenders as faithfully as it has its expressed contract with its Bondholders," the Maryland chapter decreed. Ultimately, by demonstrating the depth and breadth of need within their ranks, comrades sought to topple the stubborn notion that pension applicants were loathsome beggars—or, even worse, "deadbeats," "deserters," "coffee-coolers," "bounty jumpers," and "paupers upon the community"—who had thoughtlessly exchanged their sacred honor for government alms.[11]

Late-nineteenth-century Americans pointed to the impatient and argumentative tone adopted by these organizations as damning evidence of Union veterans' "arrogance" and conceit. To be sure, these men craved acknowledgment and agonized over their legacies. Nevertheless, their shrill demands reveal far more about the cultural triumph of reconciliation than they do about any unsavory pride. Albion Winegar Tourgée made precisely this point in the short preface that he penned for his

1885 tome *The Veteran and His Pipe*, a cutting collection of essays in which a one-armed Union ex-soldier and his briar wood pipe, devotedly nicknamed "Blower," lampoon sectional reunion. So many had "succeeded in forgetting" the "immortal cause" won by the Union soldier, Tourgée contended, that it was scarcely surprising to find the veteran "remembered chiefly as a pensioner." "There was a time when the Union saviours were heroes," one veteran wistfully lamented a few years later, "when the people couldn't do enough for them; when words of kindness and praise were on every lip for them." But as the "roar of the cannon was hushed," the "din of musketry" faded, and as odes to "shared valor" replaced the heroism of ideas, northerners developed "a preference for the picnic ground over the cemetery on Decoration Day." The "hate and bitterness" of the war were "put out of sight." Some even began looking forward to that not-so-far-off day when the last "pension-beggar" would be "securely planted."[12]

It is no coincidence that the most passionate appeals for (and the most determined opposition to) "veterans' rights" came as the waves of sentimentalism and sectional reconciliation reached high tide. Like the veterans who depended on them, pensions were "cultural symbols" that kept the southern rebellion and its consequences alive and resonant. To pension a Union soldier was to pronounce suffering endured on behalf of the Union as worthy of remuneration and to generate a "massive redistribution of capital" from the conquered, "capital-poor South" to the victorious North. By rendering ex–rebel soldiers ineligible for benefits, the Union pension bureaucracy functioned as a poignant reminder of the stubborn facts of the rebellion—and held Confederate treason in open, deliberate contempt. While the Pension Bureau's ever-multiplying demands on the federal budget hardly inspired public support for veterans' benefits, in the end, the nation had little desire to revisit the dreadful results of the war so painstakingly documented in pension applications. Significantly, one Nebraska Grand Army man even dismissed the unremitting charges of vice and swindle at the Pension Bureau as a symptom of willful forgetfulness among civilians. "We find that many of our prominent citizens are apt to forget the dark days of the rebellion, and [thus] it becomes quite popular, periodically, to raise the cry of pension fraud."[13]

⊷══◎═══⊶

Grover Cleveland, for one, had little desire to reflect on the war. Not only had he hired a Polish substitute, the hapless Buffalo sailor George Benninsky, to fight for him in the ranks of the 76th New York Volunteers (political foes made sure to remind the electorate of Cleveland's unwillingness to take a stand for the Union and alleged that the president displayed no regard for Benninsky during or after the war), but the portly president was the first Democrat elected to the White House since Appomattox. Trusting that his election had at last removed the stains of slavery and secession from Democratic robes, Cleveland set out "to restore harmony between the North and the South" and to display a "spirit of conciliation" toward the South. "How wicked," he wrote, is "the traffic in sectional hate." "It surely cannot be wrong," he continued, "to desire the settled quiet which lights for our entire country the path to prosperity and greatness." Not surprisingly, the former Buffalo mayor and New York governor became the bête noir of Union veterans. His appointment of high-ranking former rebels to cabinet posts and ambassadorships sparked outrage. "It makes us hot to see traitors honored and representatives of the Lost Cause . . . now acting as ministers and consuls in every foreign country," Milton Garrigus thundered at a regimental reunion in Indianapolis. "Treason does not seem now to be odious." Most conspicuous among Cleveland's appointments was his selection of Arkansan Augustus Garland, an ex–Confederate senator once vetted for Jefferson Davis's cabinet, to serve as attorney general.[14]

The president likewise demoralized many veterans by vetoing hundreds of special acts granting pensions and pension increases to individual ex-soldiers (only one private pension bill had been vetoed prior to Cleveland's presidency). Cleveland exhibited his narrow understanding of the war's consequences in especially unreserved veto messages. In late June 1884, Charles Wright, laboring under the punishing throb of a horrific gunshot wound that he received two decades earlier at Third Winchester, determined to end his suffering by committing suicide. His devastated widow, Laura, appealed to Congress for the relief of a private pension bill, resolving that her late husband's "wound was so great that it caused temporary insanity, under the influence of which he destroyed himself." Cleveland was hardly convinced. "There is not a participle of proof that I can discover tending to show an unsound mind," he declared upon returning the bill to the House without approval, "unless it be the fact of his suicide." "The bounty of the Government may without injustice be withheld from one whose soldier husband received a pension for nearly twenty years, though all that time able to labor, and who, having reached a stage of comfortable living, made his wife a widow by destroying his own life." Recalling the canvas banner fastened to the Treasury Building during the Grand Review—the banner that had pledged a "debt of gratitude" to the nation's "loyal soldiers"—one Indiana infantryman purported it was with "ghoulish glee" that the president dismissed private-pension measures. "It is a burning shame and disgrace," the Hoosier bewailed, "that a great nation with its vaults overflowing with surplus money should allow its worthy soldiers to suffer for the necessaries of life."[15]

Opposition to Cleveland rose to new heights on February 11, 1887, when the president vetoed a Grand Army-sponsored bill that granted a monthly pension to any Union soldier or sailor who had served ninety days and was now incapable of living independently. A "vast" army of Union veterans, Cleveland assured in his veto message, had "contentedly resumed their places in the ordinary avocations of life"; the few who hadn't only desired to be made "simple objects of charity." Besides, the president maintained, nearly a quarter-century had elapsed since the war; it was time for the nation to "move on." And so "with [a] single stroke of his pen," one cross ex-soldier vowed, Grover Cleveland "consigned nearly

20,000 old soldiers to the poorhouse." "Mr. Cleveland," the *National Tri-bune* editorialized, "has taken the responsibility for the continuance of a world of sorrow and misery—of poverty and wretchedness beyond description." Smarting with righteous resentment, the veterans challenged the chief executive for slurring the Grand Army of the Republic as a "gang . . . eager for an opportunity to swindle and commit perjury." Petitions pleading for Congress to override the president's veto poured into Washington.[16]

Cleveland's determination to preside over a truly reunited nation manifested itself yet again only a few months after his rejection of the dependent pension bill. In April, Adjutant General Richard Drum hinted to stocky, walrus-mustached Secretary of War William Crowinshield Endicott that it was time to return to the South the scores of rebel flags and regimental colors that were collecting moth holes in the cluttered attic of the War Department Building in Washington. Cleveland's embrace of the proposal triggered "indignant protest" from Union veterans, who regarded the president's consent as final confirmation of "his sympathy with the rebellion." "May God palsy the hand that wrote this order," a pale and forbidding Lucius Fairchild roared before an audience of Grand Army men in Harlem. One Louisville, Kentucky, GAR post offered to pony up the funds necessary to conserve the captured standards in federal archives, if only the president would countermand his ill-considered decree. Expressions of "profound regret" about the battle-flag order even stood in as dedicatory remarks for the impressive new soldiers' monument installed on the town common in Brattleboro, Vermont.[17]

In mid-June, resolutions recording the "unanimous" dissent of ex-soldiers arrived on the president's desk from around the country. A profound sense of betrayal animated these resolves, for it was in "good faith" that the veterans had entrusted their "sacred trophies" to the War Department. Many veterans connected the battle flag order to Cleveland's veto of the dependent pension bill; in both instances, the federal government had abrogated an implicit contract with the soldiers of the Union in the name of sectional reconciliation. "We must not be asked to forget the sufferings and the pleasures of the days when we rallied around the flag and saved the Union," one Pennsylvania GAR post asserted. Keeping the captured, bullet-riddled banners "in a conspicuous place" would remind the nation of the perilous costs of treason. While an impatient northern press tagged the old soldiers "misguided," embittered "fools" waving the "bloody shirt" of sectional hate, the veterans who protested Cleveland's order did not "cherish" animosity. Unable to forgive and forget, these ex-soldiers sought an acknowledgment of their accomplishments that peace and fraternity foreclosed.[18]

Wishing only to be rid of the veteran "problem," President Cleveland quietly countermanded his directive to Secretary Endicott. "I have today considered with more care than when the subject was orally presented to me, the action of your Department," he wrote. "I am of the opinion that the return of these flags in the manner thus contemplated, is not authorized by existing law nor justified as an Executive act." Eight days later, the president declined an invitation to attend the much-hyped July Fourth reunion of Pickett's Division and the Philadelphia Brigade at Gettysburg's High Water Mark.[19]

⁂

Emboldened by their victory over Cleveland in the battle-flag dispute, veterans renewed their efforts to secure the passage of a general pension bill. "The time has come," affirmed a resolution passed at the 1888 Grand Army National Encampment held in Columbus, "when the soldiers and sailors of the war for the preservation of the Union should receive the substantial and merited recognition of the Government." The election to the presidency that fall of Republican Benjamin Harrison, a veteran of the 70th Indiana Volunteers who fought courageously at Peachtree Creek and New Hope Church, made the task simpler. Harrison was known for his unwavering support of pension benefits. Not only was he the principal author of the Dependent Pension Act vetoed by Cleveland, but the Hoosier statesman had shepherded more than a hundred individual pension bills to passage, observing that the flush financial times of the 1880s did not occasion the "use [of] an apothecary's scale to weight the rewards of men who served the country."[20]

Harrison signaled the dawn of a new era in the struggle for pensions with his brazen appointment of "Corporal" James Tanner, a veteran of the Grand Army's Pension Committee and a sought-after speaker at veterans' meetings and reunions, as pension commissioner. Tanner, the New Yorker who lost both legs at the battle of Second Manassas, pledged that so long as he superintended the Pension Bureau, "no man who wore the blue and laid it off in honor" would "ever feel the necessity or be permitted to crawl under the roof of an alms house for shelter." "Compelled to stump through life on two cork feet," one newspaper editor observed, Tanner had no shortage of empathy for his fellow maimed and crippled ex-soldiers. "I will drive a six-mule team through the Treasury," he vowed. "God help the surplus!" To be sure, the indefatigable Tanner wasted no time, dusting off thousands of pension applications that had moldered for decades in the bureau's archives because their petitioners had neglected to produce two supporting witnesses. Insisting that he would not "hunt for merely technical reasons" to deny the veterans their rightful pensions, the commissioner "eased the evidentiary demands" on men pursuing claims, a move that, of course, retroactively added scores of soldiers to the nation's roll of honor.[21]

The press, of course, objected to Tanner's steadfast, "surplus busting" tactics with sniping editorials. "Before the close of this administration," one editor predicted, "the treasury will be as hollow as a bass-drum." Even Grand Army men who devotedly championed the legless commissioner snickered at the media's more lighthearted caricatures of the Pension Bureau during Tanner's brief tenure. One satirist, for example, told the story of an aging veteran who approached Corporal Tanner in hopes of obtaining a pension. With pride, the soldier reported that he had been wounded at Gettysburg. "At Gettysburg," the corporal exclaimed, "That is first rate! It will be easy to get a pension for wounds received at Gettysburg." The commissioner then proceeded to ask about the nature of the man's wound. "Well," he replied, "a monument fell on me."[22]

Tanner invited more intense enemy fire when, paying scant attention to the Confederate veterans in the audience, he delivered closing remarks at a Scotch-Irish Convention in Columbia, Tennessee, on May 10, 1889. "The wolf of want must in common decency be driven from the door of the maimed or diseased veteran," the commissioner declared. "Last week," he continued, "a man of good character, who had trod many a battlefield at the head of a thousand men . . . was found by an officer of one of the charitable institutions of New York City, with his old wife, eking out a miserable existence in an attic room, trying to subsist on twenty cents a day."

For twenty years and under varying circumstances I have plead[ed] the cause of my comrades who wore the blue. For twenty years I have been able to only plead, but now I am thankful that at these finger tips there rests some power and as that power is mine I broadly say that I propose just as soon as possible to call in every one of the certificates of pension . . . and re-issue them on the basis of the truth that no man ought to be down on the pension roll of the United States for less than the miserable pittance of $1 per week.[23]

By early summer, Tanner's unblushing effrontery became a serious liability for the administration. Allegations of misconduct prompted Secretary of the Interior John Willock Noble to demand a congressional investigation of the Pension Bureau. After a summer of blistering exchanges with the secretary, it was with deep regret in September that Tanner submitted a letter of resignation. A relieved Harrison promptly acknowledged the dispatch. In mid-October, the president swiftly dammed a torrent of reproach from fellow veterans by appointing Green Berry Raum, who, as a brigade commander, fought his way up the slopes of Missionary Ridge, as the next pension commissioner. The Illinois-born Raum shared Tanner's convictions, but not his braggadocio, doing his level best to satisfy the bureau's vocal critics while taking care of his loyal comrades.[24]

The Grand Army kept up their advocacy, too, entering resolutions in support of a new Dependent Pension bill to provide monthly disbursements of $12 to all disabled soldiers and sailors honorably discharged from the Union armies and navies. The bill worked from the premise used by Corporal Tanner—that the government had a responsibility to pension old soldiers even if they could not demonstrate that their infirmities were service-related. For a few comrades, worried about the order's reputation as "obnoxious" pension beggars, this was a step too far. "Your reputation is made by your enemies," one Illinois soldier declared, urging his comrades to withdraw their proposal. "The enemies of the Grand Army of the Republic are many, and they are powerful and strong." Nonetheless, braced by editorials in veterans' newspapers, most old soldiers persisted in their efforts until the Republican Congress took up the measure. To render it more "palatable," legislators posited the bill as a measure to relieve veterans' dependents. Innocent children and heartbroken spouses were, unlike begging veterans, deemed "worthy" of public aid.[25]

On June 27, 1890, Congress passed the Dependent Pension Act and Harrison signed it into law. In a sense, James Tanner was vindicated. (Congress, on the other hand, was not, with voters handing control of the House of Representatives to the Democrats in a withering rout of the Grand Old Party.) But what was once deemed a "substantial reward" was now merely "balm to middle or old age." The federal government had acted, only too late. And even then, sociologists, Democrats, and the press registered their opposition to a law "unsound in principle" and "absurd in application," certain in its immodesty to "stimulate dishonesty and dependence." Such commentary provoked Frank Bell—who, after being shot through the lung at Antietam, lost a leg at Gettysburg—to respond with an open letter to the editors of *Century Magazine* in 1891. "It is true that the large majority of our old comrades are poor men," he began. Rehearsing the difficulties that Union veterans faced upon their return to civilian life, Bell contended that it was "dire necessity, not want of patriotism," that had prompted the plea for the Dependent Pension Act. "As a survivor of the late war I cannot but feel deeply when I see the motives of my comrades impugned," he wrote. "I frankly admit that I do feel proud of my comrades and their record in the war for the Union. The humblest one who volunteered and followed the old flag has thereby earned the right to have his name inscribed upon the roll of honor and to be cherished and remembered through all time and eternity."[26]

Rhetoric in opposition to pensions was even more deafening in the new century. The memory of the war, one incensed observer noted in 1904, "would pass out if the promoters of pensions would decently permit [the public] to forget it." In the aftermath of the First World War, as brigades of maimed and disabled doughboys returned home, government propagandists routinely deployed the "worn out" and "emasculated" figure of the Civil War pensioner as a cautionary tale. These writers argued that with "good moral character" and a dash of "determination," the newest legion of American veterans might avoid the "pitiable dependence" of Billy Yank. Questioning the character of the pensioners, the critics made their case: the Civil War veteran was a nuisance who only saddled the nation with debt and doleful memories. Peddling the notion that physical rehabilitation could "fully restore" even the most worn-out soldiers, propagandists rejected not only the grim consequences of combat, but the blue-coated ex-soldier himself.[27]

Historians have long pointed out the "increasing liberality" of military pensions after the Civil War, marveling at the munificence of the federal government in an age of lemon-sucking fiscal conservatism. The persistent lobbying of Union veterans and their organizations no doubt secured upwardly adjusted rates, relaxed evidentiary requirements, and the full payment of arrears. But these legislative successes, only achieved after bruising political battles, failed to wrest from the public an enduring recognition of the human and emotional costs of the war; alternatively, they merely confirmed that there was indeed "another" civil war—between Union veterans and northern civilians. By the end of the nineteenth century, the public viewed the Civil War pension system as a problem—not a paradigm. Critics argued that pension disbursements fostered malice, apathy, even debauchery among Union veterans—and they invited anyone with doubt to take a stroll through the unsavory wards of the National Home for Disabled Volunteer Soldiers.[28]

CHAPTER 7

———✦———

THIS DEGRADATION OF SOULS

"Would to god this drifter had dropped dead—"
"Anywhere else before he landed here!"
"Then he'd never have loosed such pandemonium."
"Now we're squabbling over beggars!"
"No more joy in the sumptuous feast . . ."
"Now riot rules the day!"

—HOMER, *THE ODYSSEY*

CLOUDS OF COAL SMOKE stained the sky as Paul James Lindberg and the men of the 61st Illinois Volunteer Infantry broke camp at St. Louis's Benton Barracks and, beneath a melancholy drizzle, trudged off to the "seat of war."[1] Fifty-five years old upon enlistment, the Mexican War veteran turned Chicago boilermaker was ancient by army standards. A paddle-wheel steamer conveyed Lindberg and his comrades to a berth on the Tennessee River called Pittsburg Landing, where they arrived on the last day of March 1862. Six days later, in the oak forests high above the Landing, the Prairie State men traversed East Corinth Road, within a mile of the small log church the locals called Shiloh. The rebels cut through the woods, emerging before dawn. Remaining "well forward" throughout three enemy attacks, the 61st Illinois took 75 casualties in its first battle. Among those reported wounded was Paul Lindberg. A rebel ball struck him square in the right knee, an injury (sufficiently serious for even a young man) that necessitated his discharge from the army that August.[2]

In December 1867, afflicted with regret and savaged by aches, Lindberg moved into the newly opened Northwestern Branch of the National Asylum for Disabled Volunteer Soldiers in Milwaukee, Wisconsin ("Asylum" was not changed to "Home" until the 1870s). Unable to secure employment, he had, in his own words, "gradually descended to that intermediate stage," where "the substance of dignity is all gone, but its shadow—shame—remains." With "nothing to do but kill lice and time," the veteran passed hours at the tiny desk in his "cold and uncomfortable" room, scribbling old adages, droll yarns, and most often incoherent meditations into the voluminous daybooks he referred to as his "Lunatic Memorandum." What emerged most plainly in Lindberg's trembling hand was the complex portrait of a man tortured by both the "frightful visages" of his past and the inertia of the asylum. "If you had to sit in my place for one whole day," he wrote, "you would be enabled to give an infallible definition of Vertigo from personal experience."[3]

There were plenty of things to weary Lindberg at the National Asylum: the gluttonous bedbugs that invaded the barracks each summer; the thick, foul-smelling air, made even more oppressive by the summer heat; the sour bread, rancid meat, "so-called" hash, and tasteless coffee served in the dining hall; the aberrant bands of inmates who roamed the halls and helped themselves to razors, postage stamps, and foolscap; the "insufferable" moans that emanated from the home-hospital; the insane men, "wrecks of former selves," who, screaming like "wild beasts," interrupted even the deepest sleep with their "pandemonium." And yet what distressed Lindberg most was the realization that he and every veteran who lived in a soldiers' home occupied a wretched middle ground—some uneasy space between the dead and the living, the past and the present, meaning and inconsequence. "Around me is

Silence," he scrawled one afternoon, "certainly not as of 'Death,' but of a 'Time When Life was Not.'" "I am," he concluded, the "living dead."[4]

On several occasions, Lindberg came perilously close to suicide. He sought a final discharge from that "dread sound of cannon" and those "agonizing groans of the dying" ringing in his ears, but ultimately realized that he could not take his own life. "There is nothing within," he conceded, "that is not dead already." Instead, the "Soldiers' Home Pariah" lived on in "this accursed place," scarcely able to contain his hatred and self-loathing. Sheltered from the public's gaze, Lindberg and his fellow inmates marinated in the memories of "grim-visaged war." As the renowned antislavery stump speaker Anna Dickinson noted, only on the grounds of a soldiers' home, teeming with one-armed and one-legged soldiers, could one encounter "the whole panorama of the war."[5]

The quest to establish a federal veterans' home met with "paralyzing delays" in the spring of 1865. On March 3, in the waning hours of its final wartime session, Congress approved legislation shepherded by the Republican Senator Henry Wilson of Massachusetts—the "Natick Cobbler"—establishing a National Asylum for Disabled Volunteer Soldiers. Perhaps owing to the "confusion and hurry" of its passage, Wilson's measure, as the historian Patrick Kelly has noted, was hardly "a considered policy designed to serve the long-term institutional needs" of Union veterans. For instance, the bill included an impossible provision appointing one hundred civic leaders (including the Sanitary Commission's cantankerous Henry Bellows) to a corporation tasked with organizing and administering the asylum. At least four attempts to convene the appointees proved abortive, arresting the development of the NADVS for more than a year. Only in the spring of 1866, after Congress scrapped the corporation, empowered a board of managers, and appointed dour-looking Major General Benjamin Franklin Butler to lead the government's efforts

did plans for a national asylum come to fruition. Butler drafted blueprints for three NADVS campuses—including an Eastern Branch in
Togus Springs, Maine; a Central Branch in Dayton, Ohio; and a Northwestern Branch in Milwaukee, Wisconsin. Even then, Butler and his colleagues anticipated that "most of the disabled soldiers would be cared for
otherwheres," and doubted the "expediency" of erecting buildings "which
might never be occupied."[6]

Fortunately, a few soldiers' allies had anticipated not only the need for
a veterans' asylum, but also the halting response of the federal government. Foremost among them was the impressively bearded governor of
New Jersey, Marcus Lawrence Ward. Selfless to a fault, politics was almost
an afterthought for the Newark native. In 1863, he secured from the New
Jersey legislature a generous appropriation to fund a home for his state's
maimed soldiers. Perched high atop a knoll that afforded ex-soldiers commanding views of Newark, the New Jersey Home for Disabled Soldiers
and Sailors was located in an old U.S. General Hospital barracks abandoned by the army. Dozens of one-armed, one-legged, and partially blind
veterans requiring constant attention—including men like William Cock-
roft, who carried in his bladder an iron ball released from a rebel mortar
during the siege of Petersburg—settled in when the home opened its
doors on July 4, 1866, many months before the National Asylum for Disabled Soldiers began admitting members.[7] In other states, where the legislatures made inadequate provisions for either the short- or long-term
needs of maimed veterans (a measure to create a state veterans' home twice
failed to earn the endorsement of the Ohio legislature, while a "lack of
public interest" resulted in New York deserting its plans for an asylum),
the loyal women of local soldiers' aid societies—not only somewhat dis-
concerted about the end of their war work, but profoundly disturbed by
the returning soldiers—maintained temporary shelters for those honorably discharged Union soldiers "unable to support themselves."[8]

These physically and emotionally drained volunteers were much relieved when the Eastern Branch of the National Asylum began admitting disabled and destitute veterans on November 10, 1866. Perched outside of Augusta on a sprawling, 900-acre-campus near Togus Springs, the home "filled up to its capacity with rapidity," receiving nearly 450 veterans within the year. More than 100 residents arrived directly from the poorhouses scattered about New England. To the astonishment of the Board of Managers, the need for a veterans' asylum was equally great in the Midwest, where the Central and Northwestern Branches opened in the spring and summer of 1867. Scores of pleading letters from "poor, scanty, miserable" veterans confirmed for Lewis B. Gunckel, the silvery-whiskered former Ohio state senator who served on the NADVS Board of Managers, the "importance of the work in which we are engaged."[9]

By the time General Butler submitted his annual report to the House Committee on Military Affairs in March 1868, exactly 1,000 soldiers were living in the National Asylum. Still, the number of applications from veterans hardly dwindled; each afternoon, mountains of letters from veterans seeking a home at a national asylum arrived at Butler's law firm in downtown Washington. Many hopefuls were homeless; R. J. Wolfe, a veteran who lived at the Milwaukee Branch, described his fellow inmates as "a truly pitiful looking set" of men fresh from the streets. Most were in desperate need of medical attention; "entirely helpless," they sought treatment for a long litany of ailments: anchylosis, asthma, boils, bronchitis, cataracts, constipation, consumption, contusions, debility, diarrhea, dropsy, dyspepsia, enuresis, epilepsy, exhaustion, fever, fistula, fractures, gangrene, gonorrhea, hernias, insanity, jaundice, kidney inflammation, lung disease, mental aberration, necrosis, neuralgia, orchitis, paralysis, pneumonia, sciatica, stomach ulcers, tapeworm, urethra strictures, variola, vertigo, and, yes, old wounds. Families unable to provide adequately for these veterans doubtless breathed a heavy sigh of relief upon receiving the word that an application for admission had been approved.[10]

Proud veterans who might have otherwise refused relief were persuaded to seek the assistance of the national asylums after the Board of Managers blanketed veterans' organizations with promotional circulars. These handbills contended that each branch was not "a hospital or alms-house, but a home," and sought to reassure distrustful veterans of the government's intentions. The managers also pointed out that since fines imposed by courts-martial—and *not* Congressional appropriations—provided the principal revenue stream for the home, the asylums were in fact "contributions" made by "bounty jumpers and bad soldiers to the brave and deserving." Application blanks, which required veterans to aver that they had neither aided nor abetted the rebellion, likewise reified the notion that accepting a room in the National Asylum was a reward for those who had selflessly rallied to the defense of the Union in its hour of peril.[11]

Despite this reassurance, more than a few veterans remained hesitant. Unlike pursuing a pension claim, when a veteran sought shelter, he announced that civilian life was too daunting. "The droll idea was still abroad in the land," one contemporary observed, "that people might generally be expected to earn their own living." As a result, many ex-soldiers framed their appeals to the Board of Managers rather tepidly, betraying both shame and disquiet. "I would never ask to trouble [the] institution if I could only find employment," New York veteran Peter Cassidy contended, explaining that he was a "one arm soldier" abandoned to "the storm" of civilian life. Others were quite simply reluctant to leave their families behind. The NADVS did not receive wives or children—a policy that prompted much discussion amongst the Board of Managers. "Losing a leg or an arm does not emasculate the soldier or destroy within him the parental feelings," Butler maintained. "Is it not due to those who fought our battles for us . . . to give them every comfort in their declining years? Is not the society of one's wife and children the greatest of all comforts?" One manager proposed the construction of a village of small cottages on the asylum grounds, where married soldiers might live "independently" with their families. Each family would tend a tiny garden to help defray the cost of their residence at the asylum. But in the end, the plan was abandoned, and the board contented itself by providing "outdoor relief" to those disabled men who refused to live apart from their families. For those veterans who resolved to live at the National Asylum, the managers wrote a provision into the by-laws that allowed inmates to forward pension payments (ordinarily surrendered in full upon admission) to dependent families back home. Still, pension payments were frequently mislaid. In Milwaukee, for example, local poorhouses sheltered some forty women whose husbands had accepted a room in the Northwestern Branch.[12]

⋯⊷⊜⊷⋯

Once a veteran determined to live at the National Asylum, he completed an application and mailed it to the Board of Managers, appending copies of his honorable discharge and his pension certificate. Though the *New York Times* reported that the managers "never refused admission to a soldier," admittance was by no means assured. Applicants fortunate enough to earn a place in one of the homes but without the means to provide for their own transportation received a voucher for the emotion-laden, iron-horse journey to Togus, Dayton, or Milwaukee. On several occasions, conductors unfamiliar with these vouchers indifferently ejected veterans from their trains, but these incidents were rare. At the train station, a carriage would collect incoming veterans and deliver them to the home grounds. Upon his arrival at headquarters, and following a physical examination by one of the home surgeons, each veteran was issued a "straight, single-breasted coat of army blue . . . fastened with shiny brass buttons bearing the Soldiers' Home insignia"; a vest; perfectly hemmed blue trousers; and a tightly-fitting, woolen McClellan cap. Stitched to their lapels with white thread, home veterans wore a square of red—an identifying "badge." According to young Elizabeth Corbett, whose father worked as a civilian manager at the Northwestern Branch, these uniforms often "had sentimental associations" for the veterans and did "a great deal for their self-respect."[13]

New inmates were next sorted into "companies" and escorted to the three-story, steam-heated barracks that they would learn to call home. Along the way, many new arrivals stopped to greet familiar faces, some of whom they had not encountered since the Grand Review. Letters to family back home were laden with reports of these unexpected reunions. Each man was assigned to a room furnished with a bed frame, spring mattress, linens, and a wardrobe. "Our beds are first rate," a Dayton veteran reported in a letter to his local GAR post; his only objection was "we got to make them ourselves." Inmates were also expected to tidy up their rooms for weekly Sunday inspections, and refusal to put away laundry or empty spittoons routinely landed men on the offenders' docket. A pallid Henry Crosby resolved never to end up on that list; he retained—for a dollar each month—a fellow inmate to "look after [his] bed, make it, sweep and mop."[14]

Soon, the veterans settled into the numbing routine imposed by the military officers who administered the homes. The familiar growl of a 12-pounder Napoleon announced the dawn each morning. Throughout the day, the strident songs of a bugle ("it is the bugle note that speaks loudest to me of the fullness of the past") beckoned the inmates to the dining hall, to the surgeon's call, and finally, as dusk settled in, back to the barracks. "One day is like another," one melancholic Connecticut ex-soldier who resided at the Eastern Branch lamented, and "one month or one year the same unfailing round." Ralph Tremain agreed that his life was "dwindling away" by the hour at the Central Branch. "Let the plague come and kill us all off," he implored, "and let the Rath of a just God rain fire and Brimestone upon [the home] that it may be treated like Sodom and Gomorah." Samuel Hynes, who also resided at the Central Branch, desperately sought relief from what he described as "pales" of monotony. The disabled Illinois veteran grew envious of men who worked for a living, noting that he was nothing more than a lowly "subject" under the strict control of the home's administrators. "The greatest trouble here," Milwaukee inmate Daniel Burke concluded, "is there is nothing for the soldier to busy his mind with ... no workshops [or] schools." They lived like "stuffed toads." Men like Dayton inmate Joel Campbell withered away in their beds, refusing to leave their rooms unless ordered by a floor corporal or a company sergeant.[15]

Despite the claims of these veterans, the asylums did offer inmates a few welcome digressions. Each branch maintained a well-stocked library (owing in part to routine donations from regimental reunion associations), and, on any given day, a veteran could be seen poring over tattered copies of Benson Lossing's *Pictorial History of the Civil War*; Frank Moore's *Rebellion Record*; Thomas Wentworth Higginson's *Young Folks' History of the United States*; Joel Tyler Headley's biographies of Grant, Sherman, and Farragut; or George Wood's *The Seventh Regiment: A Record*. Pipe and cigar smoke curled into clouds that filled the spacious reading rooms where veterans gathered to fight their battles over again. In amusement halls, the cheerful "clink" of billiard balls could be "heard all the time." At the Central Branch, inmates formed their own Grand Army of the Republic post and invited local veterans to the home for a lively campfire chat each month; they also formed the Historical and Monumental Society, aiming to "collect relics of every battle field of the late war" and "mementoes of the men who fought the battles." Similarly interested in preserving a record of their exploits, the men of the Eastern Branch hosted a variety of lectures on battles and leaders. On one memorable occasion, using maps that "traced all the points of attack" and the "different avenues leading to the battlefield," James Hall of the 2nd Maine Light Artillery delivered a "true to life" lecture on the battle of Gettysburg to the Veteran Soldiers' Debating Society. Dozens of theatrical troupes performed for applauding audiences each year in Memorial Hall, the majestic focal point of the Central Branch's sprawling, oak-lined campus. The theater at the Northwestern Branch also hosted traveling actors and, on several occasions, staged adaptations of *Uncle Tom's Cabin*, which proved to be popular among the old Boys in Blue. Summer band concerts, held outdoors under gaslit gazebos, were equally esteemed.[16]

Nonetheless, the men could not help but feel insufficient—even incarcerated. In a caustic pamphlet extending more than a dozen pages, one inmate insisted that Eastern Branch was nothing more than "a military prison." A resident of the Dayton home likened that facility to "the Bastille"; he even suggested that the asylum's managers were more villainous than the rebel wardens who manned the gates of Andersonville. "The name has gone out through all the Country that this is a Soldiers' Home," he wrote, "but let me tell you . . . this Home is a perfect Hell here on Earth . . . if there should be any other place that can surpass it in torment I do hope that I never shall be able to find it, especially in what few days I have to pass here on this Earth." "Keep away from here," another veteran admonished in a daybook teeming with curious aphorisms, "as long as there be a hearse to be had or a gutter to sleep in!" After the National Asylum became known as the National Home for Disabled Volunteer Soldiers in the mid-1870s, Elisha Reed, a veteran who was domiciled at the Northeastern Branch, quipped that NHDVS was actually shorthand for "Near Hell, Drive Very Slowly."[17]

Striving to live independent lives, men sought to leave the asylums as soon as practicable. Determined that their time at the home would be provisional, not permanent—and firmly convinced that they could make a living on their own—scores of veterans applied to the Board of Managers for honorable discharges. Michael Brannon, a Massachusetts soldier who left his right leg at Cold Harbor, informed Ben Butler that he had "made up [his] mind . . . never to go to any of the homes while I could make a living oute side." "I can do better outside the Home," disgruntled Togus inmate Terence O'Brien echoed in a letter to the home's governor, William Tilton. "I am competent to take care of myself." Clint Parkhurst lived at the Central Branch but a month before acquiring his discharge. "I got out as soon as I could," he sighed. "I couldn't endure the place."[18]

Many of the veterans who secured their coveted discharges were quickly reminded of civilian life's peculiar challenges; quite a few met with hard luck. A Pennsylvania private whose right hand was badly mangled at Spotsylvania's Bloody Angle was "obliged to seek shelter" in an almshouse after leaving the Milwaukee home convinced that he could earn his own living. After leaving the Dayton home, one-armed veteran Daniel Arnold, "broken down completely," was unable to provide for himself, either medically or financially. Following a short-lived marriage to a known Dayton prostitute, Arnold tracked hopelessly between the city's dodgy saloons and seamy brothels. He became so beastly drunk one evening that he loaded his revolver and fired two shots into the crowd at his preferred house of ill repute. Fifty-three-year-old West Virginia First Lieutenant Wirt Morris determined not to return to Togus when, after three months, the managers granted him a furlough. Morris, who had acquired a morphine habit in the army, meandered through the streets of Boston before landing in the padded jail cell in which he died a "violent death" of delirium tremens. In verse, a Wisconsin man with "strong misgivin' 'bout being cooped up in a Soldiers' Home" reconciled himself to living out the rest of his days as a "vag," not "through choice, but through misfortune."[19]

With much humiliation, others candidly admitted to the governors of the home that they had made a great mistake in seeking their release. An Ohio veteran named John Gaspar, who a year before received the discharge he had requested from the Dayton home, wrote a pleading letter requesting readmission. "I tried my best," he confessed, "but I feel I can't do so [any longer]." This was especially true of those former inmates whose family members proved unable or even unwilling to care for them. Thomas Fitzgerald reluctantly returned to the Dayton home after his brother, who only months earlier pledged unconditional support, declared him "half witted." After scarcely two years back at home in the Adirondacks, William Rooney grew "anxious" to return to the National Asylum; the throbbing wounds he collected at Antietam and Fredericksburg proved too great of a burden for his frail wife and their two young children to endure. Some men were "in and out" of the national home so "frequently" that their applications for readmission were denied. "Don't you think you have been admitted and readmitted about as often as one man ought to be?" a vexed Butler asked one inmate.[20]

Of course, not all veterans were willing to seek readmission. Some pitched makeshift "camps" in the fingers of the woods fringing the homes, maintaining access to the medical care and relief provided by the asylum while living as they pleased. In a shack erected near the Togus home, Daniel Mullett, an eccentric Vermont artillerist, "conducted experiments" and tinkered with his prototype for a "perpetual motion machine." A homemade clapboard sign affixed to the shed instructed prying visitors to KEEP OUT. A number of veterans rambled about from town to town and home to home, prompting home officials to print up circulars announcing missing inmates.[21]

Still others sought to reap the bounty of the Homestead Act of 1862, which offered squares of untamed western acres to any settler who pledged to live on and improve the land for at least five years. (In 1870, a supplement to the Homestead Act allowed Union veterans to count their military service toward the five-year requirement.) In late March 1871, a twenty-seven-year-old, one-armed Irish immigrant named Mathew O'Regan petitioned for a discharge so that he and fourteen of his fellow Dayton inmates might migrate west to try their hands at homesteading.

In addition to requesting that the Board of Managers furnish their transportation, these vigilant comrades requested readmission should the experiment fail. Lewis Gunckel heartily endorsed the proposal, presenting his own resolution to outfit the migrants with the woolen blankets, canvas tents, and suits of clothing necessary for their journey. Men like O'Regan and his comrades found new homes (and hope for new lives) in so-called "soldier's colonies" on the infinite plains of Kansas, Nebraska, and the Dakotas. In May 1883, for example, Captain James Bryson and a score of wounded veterans formed a joint-stock company, loaded a covered wagon, and made tracks for the solitude of Potter County, South Dakota. Together, they surveyed a town near the dusty banks of Artichoke Creek and christened it Gettysburg. On the wide open prairie, "the camp fires of Donelson, Chancellorsville, Corinth, Stone's River, Vicksburg, Champion Hill, of the Meridian and Red River campaigns burned as brightly . . . as in the days of old."[22]

⊷═◉═⊷

By the early 1870s, crippled veterans had filled to capacity each campus of the national home. Still, the applications kept arriving—even after the Board of Managers established both a Southern Branch on a sandy spit overlooking Fortress Monroe near Hampton Roads, Virginia, and a Western Branch, located a few miles beyond the city limits of Leavenworth, Kansas. During the summer of 1885, inspectors counted a shortage of forty-six beds at the Togus home and spied some ninety veterans sleeping in the corridors of the Central Branch. The following summer, dozens of disabled soldiers took to the streets and poorhouses of Milwaukee after being turned away from the grossly overcrowded Northwestern Branch. Michigan volunteer Charles McCally "wandered from poor farm to poor farm" that summer. Seeking to mend the lives of as many ailing and inveterate ex-soldiers as possible, the Grand Army of the Republic once again assumed the leading role in the Union veteran melodrama. For years, local posts had worked noiselessly to secure places for needy veterans in the branches of the national home. Now, the GAR took its advocacy to new heights—exhorting northern governors and state legislatures to establish state-funded soldiers' homes. From New England to the Midwest, Grand Army men told and retold policy-makers and public officials—including many "ready to deny the fact[s]"—about "the large number of veterans maintained at public expense in alms houses." "No old soldier ought to remain in distress, needy and suffering," Lucius Fairchild decreed. "If the Government of the United States will not do it, then the State should do it." Another Badger State veteran resolved that the "relief of indigent Union soldiers" was "a proper subject for legislative action." "They should have the benefit of our poor laws without being required to go to the poor- or alms-houses," he bellowed. "If our Senators and Representatives in Congress had done their duty or half fulfilled their promises to us *veterans*," alleged a sixty-year-old Ohio veteran who was wounded at Missionary Ridge, "few of us [would] need to apply at this late hour for relief." These appeals were persuasive. Between 1883 and 1887, state soldiers' homes multiplied—opening to men in Grand Rapids, Michigan; Bennington, Vermont; Quincy, Illinois; Chelsea, Massachusetts; Erie, Pennsylvania; Sandusky, Ohio; Marshalltown, Iowa; Minneapolis, Minnesota; Waupaca, Wisconsin; and Grand Island, Nebraska.[23]

While the state soldiers' homes were sometimes more attractive than the national asylum—the Wisconsin Veterans' Home, for instance, admitted veterans along with their wives and permitted the men to wear civilian clothing—more often than not, these facilities prompted criticism. Almost universally, the managers of state asylums required inmates to surrender most—if not all—of their monthly pension disbursements to the home coffers. "The obligation of the *state* governments to care for the disabled veterans of the war is *only secondary* in its nature, extending to the men whom the *general* government has failed to provide for," the Pennsylvania Soldiers' and Sailors' Home trustees explained. "When an ex-soldier becomes a charge upon any State government, it should be the privilege of the State authorities to require [his] pension." Most NHDVS veterans proved perfectly willing to substitute their pension certificates for room in a *federal* asylum. But few veterans seeking shelter in a *state* home—especially those who had been denied space in one of the national asylums—were willing to comply with these demands; the "saviors of the Union" deemed themselves "entitled to claim the benefits of the State Home Assylums [*sic*]." Numerous ex-soldiers abandoned the Pennsylvania Home rather than have their money, in the words of one veteran, "exacted and extorted" by deceitful managers. The discharge register of the Nebraska Soldiers' and Sailors' Home in Grand Island brimmed with veterans "unwilling to obey pension rules." Isaac Caplinger "refused absolutely" to file his pension certificate at the Adjutant's Office the third time he was readmitted to the Illinois Soldiers' and Sailors' Home; when questioned, he attempted to "run the gate without a pass," branded the guards "sons of bitches," and threateningly raised his heavy cane at the home police. Inmates of the Iowa Veterans Home sparked considerable "uproar" when they took the pension question all of the way to the State Supreme Court. "[This] institution," Commandant John R. Ratekin observed, "fed on firecrackers and bombshells."[24]

Given the significance that Union veterans assigned to their hard-won pension claims, it is hardly surprising that so many soldiers' home inmates looked askance at rules and regulations curtailing their monthly rewards. In pension decrees from civilian administrators, veterans perceived pocket-lining schemes instead of reasonable contributions toward their care. The managers at the Wisconsin Veterans' Home, one inmate explained, were "more dangerous than night robbers." Yet paradoxically, managers relied on pension rules as a part of their larger effort to shield inmates from the insidious, liquor peddling "harpies" who, around every state and national soldiers' home, it seemed, invited veterans to sip away the war—one shot of whiskey at a time.[25]

"Whiskey brings the most of them here," Milwaukee inmate Elisha Reed confessed ashamedly to his old comrade Hosea Rood, "and whiskey is taking the most of them out of here." In the wards of every state and national home, intemperance became the veterans' most "stubborn enemy." "I am effected with that disease drink," admitted Michigan infantryman George Ditzell, an inmate of the Grand Island home in his adopted state of Nebraska. Clint Parkhurst, an eccentric journalist who fought with the 16th Iowa at Shiloh and Atlanta before being carted off to Andersonville and Millen, consistently staggered about the NHDVS branches in both Dayton and Hampton "beastly intoxicated." The insomniac endured stubborn spells of self-loathing. One bout prompted Parkhurst to announce brazenly that he was a "Man Who Failed," condemned to a lonely soldiers' home "amid the wreck" of his "ruined dreams." "I sadly ponder on disastrous grief," he wrote, "[b]ut note the cunning skill of heartless fate." Civil War soldiers were, of course, notorious for hitting the bottle during the war, but the crushing despair and "chronic misfortune" of institutional life—the precise anguish experienced by men like Parkhurst, who felt as though they had left their "pride and self-respect behind"—caused many veterans to hide behind the mask of intoxication. Especially around the holidays and battle anniversaries, veterans turned to intoxicants; as the fourth anniversary of his left leg amputation approached in August of 1868, for instance, twenty-seven-year-old Dayton resident Charles Renold tipped the bottle so much that he became threateningly "boisterous" and earned for himself a dishonorable discharge.[26]

Managers attempted to "outflank" the local grogshop owners, who had always done their level best to ensnare unsuspecting soldiers. On home grounds, managers opened canteens where veterans congregated like "a gigantic hive of bees." The move met with questionable success. One Southern Branch inmate attributed his home's "uncongenial surroundings" to the newly opened "facilities for imbibing that foul and debasing concoction called beer." In 1899 alone, profits on the beers poured by the one-armed attendant of the Ohio Soldiers' and Sailors' Home Canteen exceeded an astonishing $45,000. The "old soldier" who manned the bar at the Northwestern Branch would not infrequently earn the ire of the comrade "entitled to his nickel's worth, not of foam but of actual beer." And many veterans continued to visit the local dive bars and stumbled about the streets neighboring the soldiers' homes, "attract[ing] unusual attention by the blue uniforms which they wear." "In the morning we see them passing along the street in small squads, on their way to the liquor saloons," one Milwaukee man wrote, "and at night they return stringing along, nine-tenths of them drunk."[27]

Intoxicated inmates disgusted local civilians and dismayed home managers. Under the influence of rum, one Togus inmate "made his debut as a phrenologist" in nearby Augusta. Charging into a milliner's shop on Water Street, the forty-six-year-old Mainer, a veteran of First Winchester and Cedar Mountain, attempted to measure attractive young customers' heads. Local police quickly responded and delivered the inmate to the home guards, who placed him in the lockup. James Frazier, a Massachusetts cavalryman who resided at the Central Branch, kept up "quite a disturbance" in an otherwise quiet Dayton neighborhood for several weeks, teetering from home to home as he made his way back to the asylum from the doggeries. "We are just tired of him keeping up a fuss," one homeowner protested. Blocks away, drunken ensembles leaned against downtown storefronts and begged for money from frightened pedestrians. Tipsy inmates likewise collected at the Third Street railroad depot and used "such language as a decent man would not want to listen to." One February afternoon in 1881, police in Bath, New York, discovered "vile" and "blasphemous" George Ackerly, an inmate of the Grand Army Home who had been wounded in the assault on Fort Fisher, "exposing his person in the most disgraceful manner" before a local widow, Mary Chepen, who was visiting with her daughter and a few female friends. A Western Branch inmate with whiskey-tainted breath hurled stones at passing civilians and confronted a woman on a Leavenworth street, vowing to "kick the shit out of her." It could hardly have been a surprise, then, when one Milwaukeean described soldiers' home inmates as "low," "beastly," and "unworthy." "I would not cut one rag or take one stitch to fix up a home for such ungrateful human beings," she self-righteously sneered.[28]

Following a brief visit to the Milwaukee home, Hosea Rood resolved that his fellow comrades were nothing more than "a drunken lot of old fellows." "It is a sad sight," he conceded in the weekly "Grand Army Corner" column that he penned for the Sunday edition of the *Madison Democrat*. "This degradation of the souls of these old men is worse than the shooting of their bodies in war." Incorrigible inmates made life inside the state and national asylums absolutely "wearying." They roamed the corridors and dining halls, refused to bathe or to go quietly to their quarters, robbed comrades of valuables (which they then pawned at "rum shops"), urinated in spittoons, upended inkstands, wrote "filthy and obscene notes" in library books, and resisted home authorities. "If liquors can be kept from the soldier, he makes no trouble," General Butler observed. "But when influenced with drink, he becomes uncontrollable, insubordinate, and vicious." A significant number of "beastly intoxicated" veterans assailed their fellow inmates with weapons, ranging from "vulgar and foul language" to pocketknives, wooden crutches, and hickory canes. Thomas Kenny, a grievously wounded Massachusetts ex-soldier who lived at the Togus home, became notorious for delivering "unprovoked and outrageous" blows to his ailing comrades. Indiana veteran Oran Bixler often returned to his quarters at the Western Branch in a foul state of intoxication. "He terrorizes not only the men in his own ward," one fellow resident complained, "but has made himself a nuisance to the whole company." The menacing soldier unfailingly threatened to "do up" his fellow comrades, "morally, mentally, and physically." Francis Worth, a New York cannoneer, prompted similar distress for the managers of the Western Branch. "The habit of this man is to get full of beer every day until quite intoxicated," one administrator began, "and then to annoy and disturb the men in quarters during the night." One night, he became so drunk that he toppled headlong down the stairs of his barracks, lacerating his wrist.[29]

Perhaps as many as a quarter of the residents suffered some form of mental anguish. Peter Mueller, at the Illinois state home recovering from a gunshot wound to his right side, melancholically muttered death wishes within earshot of home officials. "I think the war caused his nerves to be unsettled," his daughter confided in a letter to the home superintendent, expressing genuine sorrow that her father had "caused so much trouble." Joseph Lapp, an aging Shiloh veteran from Freeport, Illinois, who resided at the Western Branch, endured recurring delusions of persecution. Unable to remain in the barracks, he persuaded the home managers to grant him permission to sleep outdoors in a cheap canvas tent that he procured in Leavenworth. During obstinate fits of rage, Lapp would uproot flowers from the beds which colorfully ornamented the home grounds. On another occasion, he shredded his home uniform, made a fire on the ground near his tent, and burned the tattered remnants of cobalt. This behavior landed him in the "insane" ward, which teemed with "weak minded" inmates—many of whom were on their way to the Government Hospital for the Insane in Washington, D.C. (now St. Elizabeth's). Each home chartered special trains to ensure the safety of the patients. In 1894 alone, the Western Branch packed twenty-nine ex-soldiers off to the Government Hospital; the Central Branch forwarded twenty-six inmates, and the Eastern Branch shipped out ten. Unable to rely on the Government Hospital, state soldiers' homes filled county and state lunatic asylums from Connecticut to Nebraska with scores of "hopelessly insane" veterans.[30]

A number of home medical officials explained away the epidemic of insanity as one of the predictable consequences of intemperance. One acting surgeon at the Central Branch, for instance, testified before the U.S. House of Representatives that alcoholism and epilepsy frequently gave rise to insanity. Other managers were even less charitable. "I am very free to say that many of the complaints [of feeble-minded inmates] are imaginary," one Dayton home official declared. Conspicuously absent among most professional "explanations" of mental aberration, of course, was the specter of the war itself. In the late nineteenth century, psychiatrists were eager to attribute mental illness to personal or moral failings. While not every instance of insanity recorded in soldiers' home death and discharge records can be attributed to the horrors of combat, some cases are nonetheless quite revealing. A matron at the Illinois Soldiers' and Sailors' Home, left one such account in a description of her responsibilities "in and out" of Quincy's anguished and perplexed wards. As she made her rounds one wintry January evening, Emily Lippincott encountered "an insane man" who was fighting "his battles over again." He "fought the rebels all day," she wrote, "tearing his bed and clothes until exhausted."[31]

It was not uncommon for lonesome and dejected veterans—"simply tired of being an inmate of a soldiers home"—to take their own lives. James O'Donnell, an Irish immigrant who fought with the 93rd New York, made at least three attempts to take his own life "by Knocking himself in the head" before being transferred to the Maine Insane Asylum. Seven months to the day after his arrival at the Ohio Veterans Home, sixty-three-year-old Christian Cook hanged himself in his room. His body was interred in a plot on the home grounds. At the Northwestern Branch, men "disgusted with life" plunged deliberately into one of the four willow-shaded ponds dotting the grounds. A slender, tobacco-spitting "misanthrope" known to history only as "Charley the Boatman" sliced his throat one evening in the boathouse (his "solitary shelter"), surrounded by the silvery wads of tin foil that he had passed countless hours shaping into "cannon balls."[32]

Most commonly, men stretched across active railroad tracks or busy turnpikes near the homes and waited impatiently for steam locomotives or electric street cars to end their miseries. The conductor of a Missouri Pacific engine could not decelerate in time to spare the life of tortured David Geary, a veteran who resided at the Leavenworth home. The train struck the intemperate Hoosier square in the back, killing him instantly. Momentum heaved his lifeless body into the air, releasing it unceremoniously into a nearby puddle. "It is safe to say that two hundred of the inmates of the National Home have lost their lives from being run over by cars," Cornelius Wheeler, the governor of the Northwestern Branch, gloomily reported. The pathetic irony was hardly lost on him. Long after the rattle of musketry had been silenced and the sulfurous clouds of battle smoke had been dissolved, long after the folly of Chancellorsville and the fury of Chickamauga, these men arranged their own rendezvous with death—on railroad tracks. "It makes the heart sick," Wheeler wrote, "to read the record of such deaths among the gallant old heroes who helped to form the lines of blue, and stood between National life and National death." But their sorrow had finally—and forever—ceased.[33]

⋅⇥◉⇤⋅

Especially as the century wore on, funerals became part of the weekly routine at the soldiers' homes. Solemnly, the flag slid down to half-mast, announcing that "another" of the "brave defenders" was dead. Most veterans desired to be buried beneath a simple, government-issued headstone in the home cemeteries, and family members typically honored these wishes. Escorted by six pallbearers donning "plain black neckties," a wooden hearse conveyed each flag-draped casket, first to the chapel for a pithy eulogy ("what need be said further than that when his country was assailed by enemies, he buckled on the armor and went forth to do battle for freedom and right") and then to the old soldier's fresh grave. Smoke from the polished barrels of old Springfield muskets lingered stubbornly in the air as the firing squad released three rounds. "It is so," wrote a sullen

Western Branch inmate, "that these men, who have made the names of Grant and Sherman and Meade and Thomas and Sheridan immortal, re-cross the ghostly shore."

As the casket was lowered carefully into the earth, the home band performed a dirge. Huddled around the grave, the old soldiers mouthed the words:

> *He sleeps his last sleep;*
> *He has fought his last battle;*
> *No sound can awake him;*
> *To glory again.*[34]

EPILOGUE

PARADE REST

No more words, not now—
Athena stroked Odysseus with her wand.
She shriveled the supple skin on his lithe limbs,
Stripped the russet curls from his head, covered his body
Top to toe with the wrinkled hide of an old man
And dimmed the fire in his eyes, so shining once.

—HOMER, *THE ODYSSEY*

IN 1885, AN AGING Oscar Baldwin penned a letter to his former comrade William Rand. The two New Hampshire veterans wrote to each other often, recalling how they had waded through Louisiana's snake-infested bayous during the operations against Port Hudson. This letter, however, assumed a decidedly somber tone. "One after another of our comrades is dropping away," Baldwin wrote, predicting that in "a few years more," the "last roll call" would be sounded. His calculations were not far off. By 1890, a full company of Union veterans passed away each day. Ivory beards, "dimmed eyes," and "bended forms" became common among the survivors; the men who went to war in their twenties were now "cheered by the prat-tling joyful voices of their grandchildren." Once crowded dining halls in soldiers' homes, where conversation "used to turn to experiences at Spotsylvania Court House or Cold Harbor," grew emptier. Ulysses Grant, "Uncle Billy" Sherman, Phil Sheridan, and George Thomas were dead, "now at rest where battles and strife enter not." Membership in the Grand Army of the Republic declined precipitously, placing impossible financial strain on individual posts. Unable to pay the rent, some posts were forced to abandon the hallowed halls where they had gathered, swapped anecdotes, and stored relics for decades. Post relief funds no longer aided needy comrades, but rather "truck[ed] headstones to the cemeteries" and defrayed the cost of planting durable, cast-iron markers and American flags beside their graves. "We cannot tarry much longer," Private Dalzell assured the readers of the *Los Angeles Times*. "Bid the hungry and avaricious office-seeker and miser be patient! We shall soon be out of their way!"[1]

The Union veteran was dying. Yet even as he grew wrinkled and worn, his war memories endured. In 1890, William Hamilton Church described the tendency of his mind to wander back to "the land of the cypress and the pine." "Mighty hosts, booming cannon, shrieking shot and shell, the cheers of our men, the answering rebel yell, the double quick of troops to reinforce some hard pressed point in our line, men falling like autumn leaves; the wounded struggling to the rear . . . How plainly it all comes back," he noted. "Again [I] sniff the smoke of battle and [my] fingers tingle to the very tips. . . . The march, the bivouac, the battle, the horrors of Libby and Andersonville, little wonder is there that . . . [the] veterans sometimes live them over again." "Memory," proclaimed veteran Milton Carmichael, "is deeply engraved upon our hearts . . . and thear it will remain till life shall be no more." "We will always contend," he continued, "that we were eternally right and that they were eternally wrong."[2]

With the demise of the Boys in Blue imminent, many old soldiers grew increasingly alarmed when they deliberated the ultimate fortune of the war's memory. For three decades, they had struggled to keep alive "talk of the deeds that were done." But now, as Commander-in-Chief John Palmer declared in 1892 at the Grand Army's national encampment in

Washington, "a new generation stands where we stood." "They know nothing of the realities of war, or the dangers and hardships of a soldier's life," he insisted, "except when they read or hear from the lips of those who were actors in that great drama from 1861 to 1865." "Great deeds" were already "half-forgotten things." "Soon there will be none to answer the roll call," another veteran observed, tears welling in his eyes. "How little the present generation appreciates our past services, and suffering as soldiers." "An Old Veteran" echoed these sentiments in verse, for which the Massachusetts band leader Charles Adkins later provided a doleful melody:

> *Who will tell about the marching*
> *"From Atlanta to the sea,"*
> *Who will halt, and wait, and listen*
> *When they hear the reveille;*
> *Who will join to swell the chorus*
> *Of some old Grand Army song;*
> *Who will tell the world the story,*
> *When the "Boys in Blue" are gone?*[23]

Beneath the confident patriotism of the elderly Union veteran simmered resentment about the kind of peace that had been achieved in the half century since the war. In 1909, when the Commonwealth of Virginia contributed Edward Virginius Valentine's bronze Robert E. Lee to Statuary Hall in the U.S. Capitol, the men of the 127th Pennsylvania Survivors' Association registered their "earnest protest" and wish "that it will be removed without further request by the patriotic and loyal soldiers of the Union army." "We are willing to forgive," the Pennsylvanians resolved, "but we cannot exalt and put a premium upon [rebel] leaders and generals by placing them on a power and level with the Commanders and Generals of our northern army." Grand Army posts likewise erupted angrily in response to D. W. Griffith's *Birth of a Nation*, the 1915 silent epic in which conquered white southerners confront lustful African-Americans and a vengeful, club-footed Radical Republican congressman named Austin Stoneman (who closely resembled Pennsylvania's Radical Republican Congressman Thaddeus Stevens, one of the architects of the Fourteenth Amendment). "It makes out that the North was all wrong and the South right in the Civil War," the commander-in-chief of the Kansas GAR retorted. "It holds up the Ku Klux Klan as knight errants protecting the helpless." "While it pretends to teach history," echoed one Lawrence post, "it teaches a lie. It begets racial prejudice."[4]

There remains little doubt that many veterans—especially as they entered the twilight of their lives—began to wax nostalgic about the war. After all, the Civil War had managed to fold a lifetime of exhilarating experience into four short years, and the worst fears of veterans immediately after Appomattox—the outbreak of another full-scale deadly rebellion—went unrealized. "Many and frequent have been tribal feuds fought out to their bloody end," wrote Charles Paige, a New Hampshire veteran who served on the siege lines of Vicksburg and Petersburg. "But here," he admired, "how different . . . such a peace was never before achieved." And although he conceded the "bitterness" and desperation of the conflict, by century's end New York veteran George Kilmer celebrated the war's "counter currents of kindly feeling," which, he was delighted to add, had inevitably ignited "a hearty and general sentiment" of peace and reunion after Appomattox.[5]

Nonetheless, the extent to which survivors shouldered the work of reconciliation has been overstated—dramatized by iconic photographs of wrinkled old men extending their arms across the low, stone fence at Gettysburg's bloody Angle. As historian Fergus Bordewich has pointed out, such images were typically staged, the sentimental handiwork of journalists eager to announce that former enemies had at last reconciled. All the same, historian John Neff has argued that much-hyped reunions of the Blue and the Gray were "local and regional" affairs arranged by individual Grand Army posts, and should not be considered indicative of a consensus among veterans. Even that most striking reunion of Civil War veterans—the semicentennial gathering that brought more than 53,000 Union and Confederate survivors to the Gettysburg battlefield during the dry and hazy summer of 1913—proved to be substantially less than the "peace jubilee" its organizers sought and anticipated.[6]

Indeed, the most remarkable thing about the jubilee reunion is that it happened at all. Disbelieving Confederate veterans peppered reunion organizers with "inquiries" as to "whether or not they were to wear their Confederate uniforms, carry their Confederate battle flags, and bring their wives, daughters, or sisters," and demanded to know if "negro members of the G.A.R. would participate" in the commemorative exercises. "It has been rumored here that [the Gettysburg reunion will] be a rather one cided affair," one ex-rebel remonstrated, "that the confederate veterans would have to play second fiddle, that they would not be permitted to display confederate colors or even ware confederate uniforms on this occasion." While the state commissioners endeavored to reassure southerners of their good intentions in Pennsylvania, the Boys in Blue were somewhat less generous—insisting that they would permit their former enemies to carry the Stars and Bars only if they conveyed "the flag of our Country," too. "Unless your Commission should be willing to accept conditions of that nature," one incensed Union veteran wrote, "I doubt if the Celebration can be made one of 'Peace and Good Will.' " Predictably, northern newspapers fumed at "these Grand Army veterans who object to the presence of the Confederate uniform." "This is not to be a gathering of Northerners or of Southerners, but of American citizens, with one flag, one nation, and one history," the editor of the *New York World* explained. "This," he declared, "is what Gettysburg means in 1913." And "this" was exactly what many reporters were determined to foist on the veterans.[7]

During the reunion itself, while homage to national might and collective heroism ultimately won the day, the heat of sectional rancor rivaled the blistering temperatures "all over that great plain, on wooded ridge and open slope." In his opening remarks, the commanding general of the United Confederate Veterans proclaimed Robert E. Lee the "noblest and grandest soldier and man combined that the world has ever produced," lauded Stonewall Jackson as a "vigorous and skillful leader, who walked with God in prayer," and feted rebel horsemen John Hunt Morgan, Wade Hampton, and Nathan Bedford Forrest. "We believe we failed not because we were wrong," he declared, "but because you men of the North had more soldiers, better food, longer and better guns, and more resources than the men of the South." The following afternoon, when he assumed the stage to represent all of the northern armies, John Brooke (whose tiny brigade determinedly held the "stony ridge" for a crucial twenty minutes on the second day) responded in kind: "On this ground was fought the battle which assured the maintenance of the Great Republic." "It seems to me, as it seems to many," he continued, "that our Republic has been destined to convince the world that the language of the Constitution that 'all men are born free and equal' was not an idle boast." In the dining room of the Hotel Gettysburg on the final evening of the reunion, a Confederate veteran "aroused the anger of an old veteran in blue by abusing Lincoln." The verbal assault quickly deteriorated into a duel, and seven veterans "in a serious condition" were hurried to the Pennsylvania State Hospital.[8]

⊷═◎═⊶

Now in their mid-seventies, the Boys in Blue regarded the Gettysburg jubilee as "the High Tide or Climax of [their] service as Civil War veterans." Although they confronted abundant evidence that the wounds of the war remained open and raw, the reunion was, at the end of the day, "a glorious good time." Many relished the wealth and "good quality of the food" (codfish in cream, deviled crabs, smoked tongue and spinach, baked bluefish, turtle soup, macaroni au gratin, roast lamb, pot roast, and chipped beef each made appearances on the menu) and likewise welcomed the opportunity to pause "where once we met in death's struggle for the pres-ervation of Old Glory." Casting bended silhouettes at sunset, they stag-gered across the battlefield, combing for relics and "grasp[ing] the hand[s]" of comrades "with the enthusiasm of youth."[9]

On the train ride home, as the outline of Gettysburg grew smaller and their shiny badges caught the sun, the old boys undoubtedly considered how much life had changed around them—how much had changed while they marked time in the past. "So many of the old boys have answered Taps," one veteran from Indiana later remarked, "that those of us who are still here stand out somewhat in bold relief, like unto trees left standing in a forest of cut-over lands." In a bustling and brave new world, these ancient figures became cherished tokens of "simpler" times—men who were, at long last, worthy of celebration, awed regard, and "quiet rever-ence." In 1917, when some 8,000 Union veterans, most "grizzled gray" and "lean[ing] heavily on canes," paraded from Temple Place down to Bos-ton's Park Square, spectators crowded "the sidewalks on both sides of the streets, all along the parade route," waving flags and sending up "cheer upon cheer." One-armed George Lamphere, who fought and was cap-tured with the hard-luck 16th Connecticut, participated in the cavalcade and remembered parents allowing children to "press upon the line of the march, both to testify their respect to these venerable men and to secure for themselves vivid memories of them to carry into another generation." "I had never seen so many men, women, boys, and girls massed along a parade route," he later wrote. "The very lessening of members," one writer editorialized, "only served to emphasize the patriotic lessons of the hour."[10]

Indeed, the hundreds of Civil War veterans yet living became near-celebrities who rumbled down Main Street in shiny Model T's on Memorial Day. Now, they were more likely to garner headlines for quaint birthday parties, bouts of pneumonia, and fainting spells—and not for their political opinions, self-righteousness, or disquieting behavior. Observing that Union veterans "quietly faded away," Bruce Catton explained that the First World War in its "sheer incomprehensible magnitude seemed to dwarf that earlier war we knew so well." Increasingly, it was the veterans of that war—especially the tens of thousands of unemployed ex-doughboys who, in the summer of 1932, piled onto Washington-bound freight cars to demand payment of their promised service "bonuses"—who sparked controversy, outrage, and charges of inequity.[11]

Menacing no longer, Union veterans became "honorary grandfather[s]" for a country that, in the wake of an acute economic depression and on the eve of another devastating world war, was in desperate need of nostalgia. In January 1931, fawning letters and telegrams, including congratulatory messages from both Calvin Coolidge and Herbert Hoover, flooded into Londonderry, New Hampshire, when 102-year-old Joseph Lynde Day, the hometown hero, became the "oldest living Civil War veteran." In 1938, film crews and photographers again descended upon Gettysburg to capture for posterity the spectacle of those "remarkably spry" Civil War veterans "tenting on the old campground." In a matter of weeks, energetic construction crews had belted the battlefield with plank sidewalks and pitched sturdy canvas tents for some 1,600 soldiers and their escorts. Alert to the sectional bitterness that endured even at this late date, hoping to "avoid aged and sometimes fractious feelings," reunion organizers took measures to place the former enemies' camps at a reasonable distance.[12]

A decade later, with fewer than four dozen Union veterans still living, the Grand Army of the Republic held its eighty-second national encampment in Grand Rapids, Michigan. "I think this should be our last meeting," 107-year-old James A. Hard, who had traveled to the meeting from his home in Rochester, New York, hoarsely resolved between cigars. "There are just too few of us left to make any more worthwhile." The other veterans in attendance knew that Hard was right, but, then again, they had not come to Michigan to gavel the Grand Army into history. So together the men resolved to host one last national meeting the following year in Indianapolis. Slowly surveying the five bowed and feeble comrades whose wheelchairs were circled around him, Theodore Augustus Penland, ninety-nine years young (he had "told a little white lie" about his age to enlist in the army) realized that he would be the Grand Army's last commander-in-chief.[13]

The following August, in 1949, the reverent song of church bells greeted the six men who made it to Indianapolis for the last encampment. Joining Penland and Hard were four centenarians—the Duluth drummer boy Albert Woolson; Robert Barrett, a bearded and coarse Kentucky cavalryman; Charles Chappel, who, at seventeen, had enlisted in a New York infantry regiment; and Joseph Clovese, now legally blind, who had taken up arms for the Union outside of Vicksburg after escaping slavery in Louisiana. With colorful ribbons and bronze medals affixed to their lapels, they held the Grand Army's final business meeting in a cozy, carpeted room at the elegant Claypool Hotel. Hard attended in his wheelchair, but Barrett sank into a comfortable armchair. Clovese, Woolson, Penland, and Chappel shared a sofa. The memories, like the tears, flowed freely. "I love the Grand Army," Hard announced in a faltering voice, pausing to dry his eyes. "I love all of you, my comrades." Later that evening, the men were ushered into six separate automobiles for a "twilight parade." The procession passed by the nearly 100,000 spectators who lined the streets of downtown Indianapolis before looping triumphantly around Monument Circle.[14]

One by one, these veterans went to their eternal rest. Charles Chappel, who had collapsed from exhaustion during the last encampment, died just weeks after he returned home. "Daddy" Penland passed away the following September at the Veterans' Hospital in Vancouver, Washington, at the age of 101. More than six hundred flag-waving mourners turned out to pay their respects in his hometown of Portland, Oregon. Robert Barrett died in January 1951, and "Uncle Joe" Clovese followed that July in his adopted home state of Michigan. Each death prompted a spate of editorials from writers who at long last wondered what, exactly, the Union veteran had meant to America.[15]

With distance, Americans were finally ready to address with more focus the sacrifices of Union soldiers. No longer menacing reminders of the nation's rift, they were heroic symbols of what turned out to be a monumental turning point in American history. Led by the likes of T. Harry Williams and Bell Irvin Wiley, a profusion of popular books began exploring the experiences of common Civil War soldiers. Likewise, professional historians began rethinking the Civil War in light of the nation's victory in World War II. Although itself fragile, the postwar consensus papered over any doubts about the meaning of the Civil War. It was a "good war," fought for a noble purpose by hale and hearty men worthy of praise.

In March 1953, James Hard, who had bested pneumonia three times during his last decade, succumbed to complications from a leg amputation at the age of 111. After he was buried beneath a simple white headstone in Rochester's Mount Hope Cemetery, only Woolson remained. "I am proud to be the rear-guard for such a gallant group of soldiers," the Minnesotan declared. "He is the living symbol of the Union Armies," the Duluth Chamber of Commerce gloated. In the parlor of his home at 215½ East Fifth Street, on a bluff overlooking the mild waters of Lake Superior, Woolson passed his final days in a creaky wicker rocking chair—puffing on cheap cigars and responding to bundles of autograph requests from admirers far and wide. Among the adoring letters was one from John Gary Dillon, a twenty-three-year-old Akron, Ohio, native who was mesmerized by the survivors of the Grand Army. As a wide-eyed young boy, he had visited with a host of aging Ohio veterans—"Uncle Dan" Clingaman of Wauseon, who with pride recalled his journey to the seventy-fifth anniversary reunion at Gettysburg; John Henry Grate of Atwater, who had marched in the Grand Review with the 6th Ohio Cavalry; and Alvin Smith of Akron, an African-American veteran who remembered that he "brought a price of $765.50" on the slave auction block. Dillon began an enviable correspondence with Woolson, and, the very next summer, he was lurching toward Duluth on a Northern Pacific passenger car to meet the last survivor.

Many others came to grip, if only for a moment, the last living link to the Civil War. They posed for photographs, insisting, as did Dillon, that the old man put on his Grand Army hat. "We shook hands, looked into those eyes that had scanned more than a century, embraced him, and turned to wave goodbye," recalled Tennyson Guyer, another visitor from Ohio, "and right then, we knew we had been in the presence of one in a million—I felt as though Abraham Lincoln had touched me on the shoulder." Woolson's home lured so many tourists that the local police mounted "NO PARKING" signs along the stretch of road in front of the house. "Good Lord," Woolson's daughter breathlessly exclaimed several decades later. "Our home was just like Grand Central Station, especially on his birthdays."[16]

Each birthday prompted national media attention, a "succession of flashbulbs," and a frenzy of wire reports ("a lot of hullabaloo," as Woolson once put it). "Who'd of thought it?" he chuckled on his 107th in February 1954. "I'm getting to be a national monument." Western Union telegrams arrived from local, state, and national politicians and American Legion and VFW posts around the country. General Douglas MacArthur sent along a Remington electric razor, with the "compliments of one soldier to another." Hundreds of schoolchildren offered their birthday greetings with construction paper kepis. The front-parlor walls groaned under the weight of honorary citations, plaques, framed newspaper clippings, and signed photographs. The United States Congress even passed an "Act for the Relief of Albert Woolson," authorizing the Veterans' Administration to compensate the old man "for medical treatment and care required" after the enactment of the legislation. Although it seemed that he had little difficulty embracing the limelight, there was another, more introspective side to Woolson. He grew "saddened" whenever he talked about the war, a war in which "there was no glory." The old man was justifiably incredulous—perhaps even uneasy—that after so much suffering and sacrifice, he was the very last survivor. "He seemed to know," Guyer recalled, "that he was all alone in his memories." "I am the Grand Army of the Republic, all that is left of it," Woolson wrote only a few months before his death. "I am the 'Boys in Blue.'"[17]

Then, at forty-five minutes past nine o'clock on the morning of August 2, 1956, Albert Woolson died after a brief illness at St. Luke's Hospital. He was 109. Four days later, the funeral was held at the Minnesota National Guard's red brick Duluth Armory. Fifteen hundred men, women, and children elbowed their way into the building. Despite the eighty-five-degree heat, "hundreds more" watched as the hearse bearing Woolson's bronze casket wound its way to an unassuming corner of Park Hill Cemetery, shaded by giant trees. The Sons of Union Veterans of the Civil War executed the Grand Army of the Republic funeral ritual as fifes mournfully wailed the "Battle Hymn of the Republic." "Something deeply and fundamentally American is gone forever," the popular historian and *American Heritage* editor Bruce Catton wrote the following week in the cover story for *Life* magazine, "for the Grand Army of the Republic was the living link that bound us intimately to the great morning of national youth. As long as the Army existed—even though it was at last embodied in one incredibly old man, who stood alone without comrades—the great day of tragedy and of decision, was still a part of living memory. There was an open door into the past, and what we could see through that opening was magically haunted. . . . But when the final handful of dust drifted down on Albert Woolson's casket, and the last notes of the bugle hung against the sky, the door swung shut."[18]

Buried in Woolson's grave that afternoon was the wrenching struggle of the Union veteran, over at last.

ACKNOWLEDGMENTS

—◆—

I STARTED THINKING about Union veterans—and this book—nearly fifteen years ago. As a youngster, I joined several of the Civil War Roundtables that held monthly meetings near my home in northeastern Ohio. I eagerly awaited each meeting and formed lasting friendships with fellow members. John Gary Dillon, then a seventy-something Akron bachelor, was one of those friends. On many occasions, he recalled his visits with the last survivors of the Union army. He was a humble man of few words, but when he spoke of "his veterans," even after so many decades, he came to life. I listened to Gary's recollections of these old men with genuine awe; his stories functioned as a poignant reminder of just how recent the war truly was. How I wished that I, too, could visit with these men, if only for a few moments, to ask them what it meant to survive the Civil War.

Little did I know, I would spend the formative years of my academic life engaged in that very project—traveling the country in search of what these men left behind in their letters, diaries, Grand Army of the Republic records, and veterans' newspapers. And over the past five years, I have come to know and empathize with those whose stories it has been my privilege to tell. I have visited their hometowns, their monuments, their prison pens, and their battlefields; I have stalked the wards of their Soldiers' Homes, retraced their steps down Pennsylvania Avenue, and planted flags at their graves. The journey was at once heartbreaking and exhilarating, and it would not have been possible without the help of the brilliant archivists and librarians at the many institutions where I conducted research. Kerry Bryan and Hugh Boyd very graciously facilitated my visit to the Grand Army of the Republic Museum, a true national treasure that flies under the radar in a quiet northeastern Philadelphia neighborhood. Nan Card, the curator of manuscripts at the Rutherford B. Hayes Presidential Center, is an historian's dream. Her cheerful demeanor and knowledge of sources is unparalleled among the many archivists and librarians that I have encountered over the years. Rich Baker helped me to navigate the vast holdings of the United States Army Military History Institute, and James Amemasor of the New Jersey Historical Society made my research visit to Newark incredibly profitable. Fellow Civil War historian Glenn Longacre at the National Archives in Chicago was a researcher's delight, as were Debbie Hamm at the Abraham Lincoln Presidential Library in Springfield, Illinois; John Heiser at the Gettysburg National Military Park Library; Kathy Lafferty at the Kenneth Spencer Research Library in Lawrence, Kansas; Lin Fredericksen at the Kansas State Historical Society; Linda Hein at the Nebraska State Historical Society; friend Rich Saylor at the Pennsylvania State Archives; and Richard Pifer at the Wisconsin Historical Society. Gayla Koerting, the feisty state archivist of Nebraska and a Civil War scholar in her own right, deserves special mention. Gayla's foresight rescued the records of the Nebraska Soldiers' and Sailors' Home from the shredder when a state administrator deemed the case files "too depressing" to salvage. Gayla has spent the past two years painstakingly organizing these records at the Nebraska State Historical Society's offsite warehouse in downtown Lincoln. One humid August afternoon, she invited me into the warehouse to inspect the files, not yet catalogued for the public.

Charles Scott made my trip to Iowa City and the State Historical Society of Iowa worthwhile, and the cheerful Patricia Maus had boxes of Grand Army records waiting for me when I arrived at the Northeast Minnesota Historical Center in Duluth. Peg Williams and the folks of

Gettysburg, South Dakota, treated me like a celebrity when I arrived in their beautiful town. Brent Abercrombie was much help at the Indiana State Library. Joseph Ditta at the New-York Historical Society tracked down an obscure sermon for me. I also salute the reference librarians at the Houghton Library, Harvard University; the American Antiquarian Society; the Worcester Historical Museum; the Indiana Historical Society; the University of Iowa at Iowa City; the Ohio Historical Society; the Akron–Summit County Public Library in Akron, Ohio; the Dayton Metro Library in Dayton, Ohio; the Vermont Historical Society; Rhode Island Historical Society; Connecticut Historical Society; Connecticut State Library; the Huntington Library; the Library of Congress; the National Archives in Washington (and its regional branches in Waltham, Massachusetts; in Kansas City, Missouri; and in Manhattan); the New Hampshire Historical Society; the Maine Historical Society; the Massachusetts Historical Society; the Newberry Library; the Institute for Regional Studies in Fargo; the North Dakota State Archives; the Jerome Library at Bowling Green State University; the Albert and Shirley Small Special Collections Library at the University of Virginia; the Carol Newman Library at Virginia Polytechnic Institute; the Butler Library, Columbia University; the New-York Historical Society; the New York State Archives; the Montana Historical Society; the Adams County [Pennsylvania] Historical Society; and the Minnesota Historical Society.

Two lengthy research trips crucial to this project were funded by one of Yale's John F. Enders Fellowships. I offer my sincere thanks to Allegra di Bonaventura, a historian whose work I deeply admire, for steadfastly believing in this project. My beloved undergraduate alma mater, Gettysburg College, offered me an adjunct professorship in the Department of Civil War Era Studies as I started writing. Gettysburg provided me with a welcoming and intellectually stimulating environment in which to finish the project, and for that I thank Provost Christopher Zappe and Vice Provost Jack Ryan. At Gettysburg, conversations with my brilliant colleagues Allen Guelzo, Ian Isherwood, and Peter Carmichael kept reminding me what, exactly, I was doing. Cathy Bain, the administrative assistant in Civil War Era Studies, kept me fed and stocked our office with my favorite dark roast. Lincoln M. Fitch became my able teaching assistant and ensured that I could spend much-needed time at the keyboard. Finally, there is Brianna Kirk, my abundantly talented and brilliant student assistant, who streamlined the notes, filled in more than a few holes in the narrative, and accompanied me on a last-minute trip to the National Archives.

David Blight believed in this project and, more importantly, in me. I thank him not only for the care with which he mentored me, commented on my work, and supported my every endeavor at Yale, but also for sharing an order of scallion pancakes each week at our favorite New Haven dive. He encouraged me to follow the sources, even when they led to interpretations that directly challenged his own. He is a giant in the field not only because of his monumental work, but also because of his kindness and generosity. Joanne Freeman is also a talented scholar, and she offered many important insights at crucial stages of this project. Her keen sense of the historian's craft made this book far better than it might have been otherwise. Bruno Cabanes is more than a colleague; he is a dear friend. Evidence of his enormous influence on my development as a scholar can be found on every page. The graduate seminar on postwar trauma that he led with the psychiatrist Deane Aikins was one of the very best courses I took while at Yale.

Years ago, Matthew Norman fanned the flames of my interest in Civil War veterans in his stimulating undergraduate seminars at Gettysburg College. I owe a great deal of my development as a scholar to Matt's friendship, reassurance, and constructive criticism. It was Matt who taught me how to ask questions about the past. Allen Guelzo has taught and continues to teach me many things—how to write, how to master source material, and how to tolerate academic life. I think his mentorship and example are very evident in the pages of this book. My debts to him are enormous.

I continue to be amazed at the generosity and accessibility of my colleagues who write Civil War history. Jim Marten encouraged me to tackle this project when I phoned him in a fit of panic four years ago, believing that his brilliant book *Sing Not War* had hopelessly sabotaged my ambitious plans. Since then, Jim and I have worked together on several panels and projects. Lesley Gordon offered me the chance to try out ideas in the pages of *Civil War History*; Terry Johnston published an early draft of my chapter on Andersonville survivors in the *Civil War Monitor*, and Peter Carmichael gave me the opportunity to meet Seraphim Meyer, the only Union colonel court-martialed at Gettysburg, in an essay for his anthology on Civil War cowardice. Fellow travelers on the veteran beat Barbara Gannon, Megan Kate Nelson, and Brian Craig Miller (the latter two are charter members of Civil War history's "three name club") have offered welcome encouragement.

Various friends have read and commented on portions of this manuscript or on early drafts, including Matthew Norman, Evan C. Rothera, and Glen Robbins. Evan likewise passed along several leads from his diligent work at both the Library of Congress and the Southern Historical Collection. I am also grateful to the many people who commented on the conference papers that I have delivered over the last few years. Paul Cimbala, Frances Clarke, Greg Downs, Judith Giesberg, and David Zonderman helped me to ask new questions of my material. Randal Allred invited me to deliver some remarks about Union veterans at the Popular Culture Association/American Culture Association meeting in Boston, which was a delightful experience. Mark Dunkelman invited me to deliver a talk to the Rhode Island Civil War Roundtable, which was similarly enjoyable. And the book is no doubt better because I had the opportunity to participate in the "Understanding Battlefield Trauma from a Long Historical Perspective" working group at the Future of Civil War History Conference, hosted by the Civil War Institute at Gettysburg College.

Behind every author is a great editor, and I am proud that mine is

Katie Henderson Adams. From the very beginning, Katie understood and believed in this book, and her keen editorial eye vastly improved every paragraph. Cordelia Calvert and everyone at Liveright/W. W. Norton have been a dream to work with.

For three years, Sean and Erin Joyce made New Haven home. I thank them for their friendship and for providing me with much-needed time away from this manuscript. The staff of the Bruegger's Bagels in the Amity section of New Haven, where I penned the first words of the book, consistently brightened my days. My in-laws, David and Susan Herrmann, provided some welcome time away from New Haven. They lost their dining room table to a blizzard of paper and books on more than one occasion.

My mother and father are the best parents a son could ever ask for, and their love, support, and encouragement—both emotional and financial—made this journey possible. They have waited very patiently to read the words preceding these acknowledgments. And they might have read them sooner had I taken their sage advice: "Write it up, you've done enough research." I only wish that my grandfathers, Willard Jordan and Dick Klar, had lived to see this book.

Finally, there is Allison, who deserves to be listed as a coauthor. She has lived with this book longer than anyone. She accompanied me on countless research trips, took hundreds of pages of notes, and read and edited every single word—from the earliest drafts to the final product. She sacrificed much for this book, and it is fair to say that it still wouldn't be finished without her. For that reason, among many others, this modest acknowledgment is simply not enough.

Brian Matthew Jordan
Gettysburg, Pennsylvania
November 1, 2014

NOTES

LIST OF ABBREVIATIONS

ASSpCL	Albert and Shirley Small Special Collections Library, University of Virginia
DSMC	Dakota Sunset Museum Collection, Gettysburg, South Dakota
GARMA	Grand Army of the Republic Museum Archives, Philadelphia
GNMPL	Gettysburg National Military Park Library, Gettysburg, Pennsylvania
InHIS	Indiana Historical Society, Indianapolis
JGDC	John Gary Dillon Collection, Akron
KaHS	Kansas Historical Society, Topeka
KSRL	Kenneth Spencer Research Library, University of Kansas, Lawrence
LoC	Library of Congress
MaineHS	Maine Historical Society, Portland
MinnHS	Minnesota Historical Society, St. Paul
NA	National Archives
NARA	National Archives and Records Administration
NDSU	North Dakota State University, Fargo
NeMinnHC	Northeast Minnesota Historical Center, Duluth
NHDVS	National Home for Disabled Volunteer Soldiers
NHS	Nebraska Historical Society, Lincoln
NHHS	New Hampshire Historical Society, Concord
NJHSL	New Jersey Historical Society Library, Newark
OR	Official Records of the War of the Rebellion
PaSA	Pennsylvania State Archives, Harrisburg
RHPC	Rutherford B. Hayes Presidential Center, Fremont, Ohio
SHSIo	State Historical Society of Iowa, Iowa City
SUoNYB	State University of New York at Binghamton Special Collections
USAMHI	United States Army Military History Institute, Carlisle, Pennsylvania
WHM	Worcester Historical Museum, Worcester, Massachusetts
WiHS	Wisconsin Historical Society, Madison
WiVMA	Wisconsin Veterans' Museum Archives, Madison
WOB	William Oland Bourne

INTRODUCTION: WHEN THIS CRUEL WAR WAS "OVER"

1 J. Matthew Gallman's synthetic treatment of the northern home front, for example, notes that "problems" of readjustment were "short-lived." Patrick J. Kelly argues that soldiers' homes and pension money prevented most veterans from living unstable lives. See Gallman, *The North Fights the Civil War: The Home Front* (Chicago: Ivan R. Dee, 1994), 181; and Kelly, *Creating a National Home: Building the Veterans' Welfare State, 1865–1900* (Cambridge: Harvard University Press, 1997). The image of veterans "clasping hands across the stone wall" has been popularized most recently by the final episode of Ken Burns's documentary *The Civil War* (1990). See especially Eric Foner, "Ken Burns and the Romance of Reunion," in *Who Owns History? Rethinking the Past in a Changing World* (New York: Hill & Wang, 2002), 189–204. See also James Marten, "Not a Veteran in the Poorhouse," in Gary W. Gallagher and Joan Waugh, eds., *Wars Within a War: Controversy and Conflict over the American Civil War* (Chapel Hill: University of North Carolina Press, 2009). Gerald F. Linderman, *Embattled Courage: The Experience of Combat in the American Civil War* (New York: Free Press, 1987), 271, 274. For the argument that Union veterans, together with northern civilians, retreated into a world of romance that overlooked racial realities, see David W. Blight, *Race and Reunion: The Civil War in American Memory* (Cambridge: Harvard University Press, 2001); and Edward Tabor Linenthal, *Sacred Ground: Americans and Their Battlefields* (Urbana: University of Illinois Press, 1991), quote on 91.

2 Stuart McConnell, *Glorious Contentment: The Grand Army of the Republic, 1865–1900* (Chapel Hill: University of North Carolina Press, 1993); James Marten, *Sing Not War: The Lives of Union and Confederate Veterans in Gilded Age America* (Chapel Hill: University of North Carolina Press, 2011).

3 Bell Irvin Wiley, *The Life of Billy Yank: The Common Soldier of the Union* (Indianapolis: Bobbs-Merrill Co., 1952); James M. McPherson, *For Cause and Comrades: Why Men Fought in the Civil War* (New York: Oxford University Press, 1997); Earl J. Hess, *The Union Soldier in Battle: Enduring the Ordeal of Combat* (Lawrence: University Press of Kansas, 1997); Michael Barton, *Goodmen: The Character of Civil War Soldiers* (University Park: Pennsylvania State University Press, 1981); Chandra Manning, *What This Cruel War Was Over: Soldiers, Slavery, and the Civil War* (New York: Alfred A. Knopf, 2007). For a useful meditation on common-soldier literature, see Jason Phillips, "Battling Stereotypes: A Taxonomy of Common Civil War Soldiers," *History Compass* 6, no. 6 (2008): 1407–1425. On republicanism and common soldiers, see Charles Royster, *A Revolutionary People at War* (Chapel Hill: University of North Carolina Press, 1979).

4 Dave Grossman, *On Killing: The Psychological Cost of Learning to Kill in War and*

Society (New York: Little, Brown & Co., 1995); James Marten, " 'Exempt from the Ordinary Rules of Life': Researching Postwar Adjustment Problems of Union Veterans," *Civil War History* 47, no. 1 (2001): 57–71.

This complicates, of course, the pervasive notion that the war augmented the power of the nation-state, and challenges historians who have pointed to the Civil War as the origin of augmented federal authority. See Richard Franklin Bensel, *Yankee Leviathan: The Origins of Central State Authority in America, 1859–1877* (Cambridge: Cambridge University Press, 1990); Melinda Lawson, *Patriot Fires: Forging a New American Nationalism in the Civil War North* (Lawrence: University Press of Kansas, 2002); and Heather Cox Richardson, *The Greatest Nation of the Earth* (Cambridge: Harvard University Press, 1997).

5 Oliver Wendell Holmes, *Dead, Yet Living: An Address* (Boston: Ginn, Heath & Co., 1884), 6.

6 George Templeton Strong, diary entry, 10 April 1865, in *The Diary of George Templeton Strong*, ed. Allan Nevins and Milton Halsey Thomas (New York: Macmillan Co., 1952), 578–579.

7 Illinois correspondent quoted in Mark Wahlgren Summers, *A Dangerous Stir: Fear, Paranoia, and the Making of Reconstruction* (Chapel Hill: University of North Carolina Press, 2009), 39; Steven E. Woodworth, *While God Is Marching On: The Religious World of Civil War Soldiers* (Lawrence: University Press of Kansas, 2001), 291.

Works exploring the northern homefront have multiplied in recent years. See Michael Thomas Smith, *The Enemy Within: Fears of Corruption in the Civil War North* (Charlottesville: University of Virginia Press, 2011); Mark E. Neely, Jr., *The Union Divided: Party Conflict in the Civil War North* (Cambridge: Harvard University Press, 2002); and Robert M. Sandow, *Deserter Country: Civil War Opposition in the Pennsylvania Appalachians* (New York: Fordham University Press, 2009). Some scholars have begun to question just what Union victory meant. See John R. Neff, *Honoring the Civil War Dead: Commemoration and the Problem of Reconciliation* (Lawrence: University Press of Kansas, 2005); and Jim Downs, *Sick from Freedom: African-American Illness and Suffering During the Civil War and Reconstruction* (New York: Oxford University Press, 2012).

8 Nina Silber, *The Romance of Reunion, Northerners and the South, 1865–1900* (Chapel Hill: University of North Carolina Press, 1993); and Silber, *Gender and the Sectional Conflict* (Chapel Hill: University of North Carolina Press, 2008), 48. For the "democracy of devastation," see Stephen Ash, *Middle Tennessee Society Transformed, 1860–1870: War and Peace in the Upper South*, 2nd ed. (Knoxville: University of Tennessee Press, 2006), 172; and Earl J. Hess, "A Terrible Fascination: The Portrayal of Combat in the Civil War Media," in Paul A. Cimbala and

Randall M. Miller, eds., *An Uncommon Time: The Civil War and the Northern Home Front* (New York: Fordham University Press, 2002), 26.

9 Silber, *Gender and the Sectional Conflict*, and *Daughters of the Union: Northern Women Fight the Civil War* (Cambridge: Harvard University Press, 2005).

10 On the Lost Cause, see Charles Reagan Wilson, *Baptized in Blood: The Religion of the Lost Cause, 1865–1920* (Athens: University of Georgia Press, 1987); and Wolfgang Schivelbusch, *The Culture of Defeat: On National Trauma, Mourning, and Recovery* (New York: Metropolitan Books, 2003).

11 On Hendershot, see H. E. Gerry, *Camp Fire Entertainment and True History of Robert Henry Hendershot, The Drummer Boy of the Rappahannock* (Chicago: Hack & Anderson, 1900); and Bruce Catton, *Waiting for the Morning Train: An American Boyhood*, 2nd ed. (Detroit: Wayne State University Press, 1987), 216. On Catton, see also David W. Blight, *American Oracle: The Civil War in the Civil Rights Era* (Cambridge: Harvard University Press, 2011).

12 Catton, *Waiting for the Morning Train*, 216–218, quotes on 218, 190.

13 Gregg Zoroya, "Number of Homeless Iraq, Afghanistan Vets Double," *Army Times*, 26 December 2012; Zoroya, "Red Tape Trauma," *USA Today*, 12 June 2013; see also Kate Taylor, "Veterans of Iraq War, Some Argue, Also Deserve a Parade," *New York Times*, 7 February 2012.

CHAPTER 1: A DAY FOR SONGS AND CONTESTS

1 The chapter titles and epigraphs are drawn from the first work of history to narrate the travails of a veteran's homecoming, Homer's *The Odyssey*. See Homer, *The Odyssey*, trans. Robert Fagles (New York: Penguin Books, 1996), 192. For an insightful reading of the psychological trauma of war in *The Odyssey*, see Jonathan Shay, *Odysseus in America: Combat Trauma and the Trials of Homecoming*.

2 *Hartford Daily Courant*, 24 May 1865; *Philadelphia Daily Age*, 24 May 1865; *Philadelphia Inquirer*, 24 May 1865; Albert Franklin Blaisdell, *Stories of the Civil War* (Boston: Lee & Shepard, 1890), 193–194; James Monroe Wells, *With Touch of Elbow; or, Death Before Dishonor: A Thrilling Narrative of Adventure on Land and Sea* (Philadelphia and Chicago: John C. Winston Co., 1909), 270; Rossiter Johnson, *The Story of a Great Conflict: A History of the War of Secession* (New York: Bryan, Taylor & Co., 1894), 530; Alonzo Leighton Brown, *History of the Fourth Regiment of Minnesota Volunteers* (St. Paul: Pioneer Press, 1892), 422–425; *OR*, series I, vol. 46, part 3, pp. 1194–1196; D. G. Crotty, *Four Years Campaigning in the Army of the Potomac* (Grand Rapids, Michigan: Dygert Bros. & Co. Printers and Binders, 1874), 193–194; J. Howard Wert, "Incidents of the Grand Review at Washington," ed. G. Craig Caba, in *Lincoln Herald* 82 (Spring 1980): 337–340; William G. and Janet B. Davis, eds., *The Diaries of William T. Clark* (Lancaster,

Pennsylvania: Lancaster County Historical Society, 1988); Allan Nevins, ed., *A Diary of Battle: The Personal Journals of Colonel Charles S. Wainwright, 1861–1865*, 2nd ed. (New York: Da Capo Press, 1998), 524–530; Oscar Osburn Winther, ed., *With Sherman to the Sea: The Civil War Letters, Diaries, and Reminiscences of Theodore F. Upson* (Bloomington: Indiana University Press, 1958), 175–178; Milton Garrigus, address at the third reunion of the 39th Indiana Volunteers, 30 September 1886, in Civil War Miscellany Collection, Box 3, Folder 25, InHS; Charles McKenna, diary entry, 24 May 1865, in Charles McKenna Diary, Carol Newman Library, Virginia Polytechnic Institute; letter "to mother," 28 May 1865, in Letters—1865, MS 93-005, Carol Newman Library. Many other scholars have written about the Grand Review. See Charles Royster, *The Destructive War: William Tecumseh Sherman, Stonewall Jackson, and the Americans* (New York: Alfred A. Knopf, 1991); Stuart McConnell, *Glorious Contentment: The Grand Army of the Republic, 1865–1900* (Chapel Hill: University of North Carolina Press, 1993); Georg R. Sheets, *The Grand Review: The Civil War Continues to Shape America* (York, Pennsylvania: Bold Print, 2000); Dixon Wecter, *When Johnny Comes Marching Home* (Boston: Houghton Mifflin Co., 1944); and Gary W. Gallagher, *The Union War* (Cambridge: Harvard University Press, 2011); Benjamin Brown French, diary entry, 24 May 1865, in Donald B. Cole and John J. McDonough, eds., *Witness to the Young Republic: A Yankee's Journal, 1828–1870* (Hanover, New Hampshire and London: University Press of New England, 1989), 478.

3 *Harper's Weekly*, 10 June 1865; *Hartford Daily Courant*, 24 May 1865; *North American*, 24 May 1865; "Abstract of the Proceedings of the Board of Trustees," special meeting, 19 May 1865, in *Twenty-First Annual Report of the Board of Trustees of the Public Schools of the City of Washington* (Washington, D.C.: McGill & Witherow, Printers, 1866), 71; J. Howard Wert, "Incidents of the Grand Review at Washington," 337; John Mead Gould, diary entry, 23 May 1865, in John Mead Gould Diary, Collection 1033, vol. 8 (1865–1867), MaineHS. See also Charles Royster, *The Destructive War: William Tecumseh Sherman, Stonewall Jackson, and The Americans* (New York: Alfred A. Knopf, 1991), 406–409; *New York Herald Tribune*, 24 May 1865; *Daily National Intelligencer*, 24 May 1865.

4 "The Grand Review," *Philadelphia Inquirer*, 24 May 1865; Garrigus, reunion address, 30 September 1886, Civil War Miscellany Collection, InHS.

5 John Mead Gould, *History of the First—Tenth—Twenty-Ninth Maine Regiment* (Portland, Maine: Stephen Berry, 1871), 576; Winther, ed., *With Sherman to the Sea*, 176; John Mead Gould, diary entry, 23 May 1865, in John Mead Gould Diary, Collection 1033, vol. 8 (1865–1867), MaineHS; F. A. Gast, "A Chaplain's Reminiscences," in Allen D. Albert, ed., *History of the Forty-Fifth Regiment Pennsylvania Veteran Volunteer Infantry* (Williamsport, Pennsylvania:

Grit Publishing Co., 1912), 316–317; *Daily National Intelligencer*, 24 May 1865; *Hartford Daily Courant*, 24 May 1865; Ulysses S. Grant, *Personal Memoirs of U.S. Grant* (New York: Charles Webster & Co., 1885), 2:535; Thomas Leonard Livermore, *Days and Events, 1860–1866* (Boston and New York: Houghton Mifflin Co., 1920), 472; Crotty, *Four Years Campaigning in the Army of the Potomac*, 194.

6 Gould, diary entry, 23 May 1865, in Gould Diary, MaineHS; Lyman Jackman, diary entry, 23 May 1865, in Lyman Jackman Papers, Box 1, NHHS; Jackman, *History of the Sixth New Hampshire Regiment*, 325–329.

7 French, diary entry, 24 May 1865, in Cole and McDonough, eds., *Witness to the Young Republic*, 478–479; Walt Whitman, *The Complete Prose Works of Walt Whitman*, vol. 1 (New York and London: G. P. Putnam's Sons, 1902), 126; Gould, diary entry, 23 May 1865, in Gould Diary, MaineHS.

8 Lois Bryan Adams, *Letter from Washington, 1863–1865*, ed. Evelyn Leasher (Detroit: Wayne State University Press, 1999), 263, 265, 267; Joseph W. Morton, ed., *Sparks from the Campfire; or, Tales of the Old Veterans* (Philadelphia: Keeler & Kirkpatrick, 1899), 127–128; J. W. Anderson, "The Grand Review," in Oscar Lawrence Jackson, *The Colonel's Diary* (Sharon, Pennsylvania: privately published, 1922), 219; Gould, diary entry, 23 May 1865, in Gould Diary, MaineHS.

9 Marian Hooper to Mary Louisa Shaw, letter, 28 May 1865, in Ward Thorton, ed., *First of Hearts: Selected Letters of Mrs. Henry Adams* (Bloomington, Indiana: Author House, 2011), 6; Edwin C. Hall, "The Story of the Tenth Vermont Regiment, 1862–1865," in Edwin C. Hall Papers, Box 1, Folder 27, Vermont Historical Society, Barre, Vermont; Kathryn Allamong Jacob, *Testament to Union: Civil War Monuments in Washington, D.C.* (Baltimore: Johns Hopkins University Press, 1998), 59.

10 Dixon Wecter, *When Johnny Comes Marching Home* (Boston: Houghton Mifflin Co., 1944), 128; "The Closing Tableau of the Great American War," *Columbian Register*, 27 May 1865; William T. Clark, diary entry, 24 May 1865, in *The Diaries of William T. Clark*; French, diary entry, 24 May 1865, in Cole and McDonough, eds., *Witness to the Young Republic*, 479; "The Grand Review," *Wisconsin State Register*, 27 May 1865; George Whitfield Pepper, *Personal Recollections of Sherman's Campaigns in Georgia and the Carolinas* (Zanesville, Ohio: Hugh Dunne, 1866), 468; Sarah Jane Hill, *Mrs. Hill's Journal—Civil War Reminiscences*, ed. Mark Krug (Chicago: R. R. Donnelley & Sons, 1980), 327.

11 Pepper, *Personal Recollections*, 464–468; *Daily National Intelligencer*, 25 May 1865; *Daily Cleveland Herald*, 26 May 1865; Brown, *History of the Fourth Regiment of Minnesota Infantry*, 424; Mary Logan, *Reminiscences of the Civil War and Reconstruction*, ed. George Worthington Adams (Carbondale and Edwardsville:

Southern Illinois University Press, 1970), 125–127; William Tecumseh Sherman, *Memoirs of General William T. Sherman*, 2nd ed. (New York: D. Appleton and Co., 1904), 2:377–379; Alexander Downing, *Downing's Civil War Diary*, ed. Olynthus B. Clark (Des Moines: Historical Department of Iowa, 1916), 276–277; Wert, "Incidents of the Grand Review at Washington," 339; Jacob Roemer, *Reminiscences of the War of the Rebellion, 1861–1865*, ed. L. A. Furney (Flushing, New York: For the Estate of Jacob Roemer, 1897), 291; Blaisdell, *Stories of the Civil War*, 196; Gould, diary entry, 24 May 1864, in Gould Diary, MaineHS; W. W. Belknap, ed., *History of the Fifteenth Regiment, Iowa Veteran Volunteer Infantry* (Keokuk, Iowa: R. B. Ogden & Son, Printer, 1887), 490–491; Stacy Dale Allen, ed., *On the Skirmish Line Behind a Friendly Tree: The Civil War Memoirs of William Royal Oake, 26th Iowa Volunteers* (Helena, Montana: Farcountry Press, 2006), 322–323.

12 David Bittle Floyd, *History of the Seventy-Fifth Regiment of Indiana Infantry Volunteers* (Philadelphia: Lutheran Publication Society, 1893), 391; Brown, *History of the Fourth Regiment of Minnesota Infantry*, 423; Hill, *Mrs. Hill's Journal*, 327; Joseph Heft Diary, Southern Historical Collection, Wilson Library, University of North Carolina, Chapel Hill, North Carolina; Holberton, *Homeward Bound*.

13 George Templeton Strong's diary, for instance, reported that the newspapers were "full of the grand parade and review at Washington." Strong, diary entry, 25 May 1865, in Allan Nevins and Milton Halsey Thomas, eds., *The Diary of George Templeton Strong: The Civil War, 1860–1865*, vol. 3 (New York: Macmillan Co., 1952), 601; John R. Kinnear, *History of the Eighty-Sixth Regiment, Illinois Volunteer Infantry* (Chicago: Tribune Company's Book and Job Printing Office, 1866), 119; *Daily Ohio Statesman*, 24 May 1865; *Hartford Daily Courant*, 24 May 1865; *Albany Evening Journal*, 24 May 1865; see also *Coshocton Democrat*, 24 May 1865; "The Armies of the Republic," *Philadelphia Inquirer*, 25 May 1865; *Daily National Intelligencer*, 31 May 1865; Lois Bryan Adams, *Letter from Washington, 1863–1865*, 265; Evelyn Leasher, "Introduction," in *Letter from Washington*, 18.

14 "Our Grand Review," *Neighbor's Home Mail: The Ex-Soldier's Reunion and National Campfire* 4, no. 2 (February 1877): 28; Michael Hendrick Fitch, *Echoes of the Civil War as I Hear Them* (New York: R. F. Fenno, 1905), 344; Kinnear, *History of the Eighty-Sixth Regiment*, 120. An Ohio infantryman noted that enthusiasm among the troops for military reviews had "played out." See Jacob Allspaugh, diary entry, 24 May 1865, Special Collections, University of Iowa Library, Iowa City, Iowa; William B. Westervelt, *Lights and Shadows of Army Life: From Bull Run to Bentonville*, ed. George S. Maharay (Shippensburg, Pennsylvania: Burd Street Press, 1998), 260.

15 "Review of the Armies," in Morton, ed., *Sparks from the Campfire*, 134; William

H. Barron to "dear friend Emma," letter, 27 May 1865, in William H. Barron Letter, Carol Newman Library, Virginia Polytechnic Institute; Joshua D. Rilea, diary entry, 15 May 1865, in Joshua D. Rilea Diary, SC 1274, Abraham Lincoln Presidential Library; "Veteran of 92 is Dead," *Oregonian*, 25 July 1915; Edmund Spencer Packard, diary entry, 15 May 1865, WiHS; for other accounts of soldiers filing through the war-torn landscape of Virginia on the way to the Grand Review, see Henry A. House Diary, MinnHS; Israel Taggart Moore, diary entry, 7 May 1865, in Israel Taggart Moore Diary, Bruce Catton Papers, Box 48, The Citadel Archives and Museum; and Wert, "Incidents of the Grand Review at Washington," 340.

16 General Orders No. 41, Department of the Cumberland (1865), as quoted in Program of the Twentieth Annual Reunion of the Society of the Army of the Cumberland [September 1889], in William Stanley Mead Collection, Box 2, Folder 1, InHS; Alfred Seelye Roe, *The Thirty-Ninth Regiment Massachusetts Volunteers, 1862–1865* (Worcester, Massachusetts: The Regimental Veteran Association, 1914), 294; Patrick Sloan as quoted in James B. Swan, *Chicago's Irish Legion: The 90th Illinois Volunteers in the Civil War* (Carbondale: Southern Illinois University Press, 2009), 229; untitled newspaper clipping in the Stannard Post No. 2 Grand Army of the Republic Scrapbook, Vermont Historical Society, Barre, Vermont.

17 Henry Evans, *Grand Army of the Republic Almanac for 1879* (Worcester, Massachusetts: Noyes, Snow & Company, 1878), 33; David W. Lowe, ed., *Meade's Army: The Private Notebooks of Lt. Col. Theodore Lyman* (Kent: Kent State University Press, 2007), 382; General Francis A. Walker, "Oration," in *Report of the Twentieth Annual Reunion, Society of the Army of the Potomac, at Orange, New Jersey, June 12–13, 1889* (New York: Macgowan & Slipper, Printers, 1889), 30; Elijah Cavins, draft of speech for Grand Army of the Republic reunion [circa 1900], in Elijah Cavins Papers, Box 2, Folder 3, InHS.

18 Albion W. Tourgée, *The Story of a Thousand: A History of the 105th Ohio Volunteer Infantry*, ed. Peter C. Luebke (reprint ed.; Kent, Ohio: Kent State University Press, 2011), 381; see also William Bircher, *A Drummer Boy's Diary: Comprising Four Years of Service with the Second Regiment Minnesota Veteran Volunteers, 1861–1865* (St. Paul: St. Paul Book & Stationary Co., 1889), 191; Steven J. Ramold, " 'We Should Have Killed Them All': The Violent Reaction of Union Soldiers to the Assassination of Abraham Lincoln," *Journal of Illinois History* 10 (Spring 2007): 27–48; Adelaide Smith to Bruce Catton, letter, circa May 1957, in Bruce Catton Papers, Box 45, Folder 7, The Citadel Archives and Museum; and Irwin C. Fox, diary entries, pp. 25, 28, in Irwin C. Fox Diary, ASSpCL; Hervey Eaton to "dearest Mother," letter, 20 April 1865, in Hervey

Eaton Civil War Letters, ASSpCL; Hosea Rood, *Story of the Service of Company E, and of the Twelfth Wisconsin Regiment of Veteran Volunteer Infantry in the War of the Rebellion* (Milwaukee: Swain & Tate, 1893), 448; see also Richard McCadden, letter to his brother, 29 May 1865, quoted in Mark Dunkelman, *Marching with Sherman: Through Georgia and the Carolinas with the 154th New York* (Baton Rouge: Louisiana State University Press, 2012), 177; and Peter Haley, undated reminiscence, Grand Army of the Republic Papers, Box 1, Folder 1, State Historical Society of North Dakota, Bismarck, North Dakota.

19   Bret Harte, "The Second Review of the Grand Army" [originally published 1 July 1865], in Faith Barrett and Cristanne Miller, eds., *"Words for the Hour": A New Anthology of American Civil War Poetry* (Amherst: University of Massachusetts Press, 2005), 174–175. George Hitchcock, who served in the ranks of Company A of the 21st Massachusetts, was one veteran who was moved by Harte's poem. Decades after Appomattox, Hitchcock revised and expanded his wartime diary. In the concluding pages, Hitchcock quoted extensively from "The Second Grand Review," lamenting the absence of so many beloved, departed comrades. Hitchcock, "An Army Diary in the War for Freedom," vol. 2, in George Hitchcock Diary, Massachusetts Historical Society, Boston, Massachusetts.

20   Oscar Cram to Ellen Cram, letter, 5 May 1865, in Civil War Document Collection, Box 29, Folder 5, USAMHI; Tourgée, *The Story of a Thousand*, 381; Charles Edgar Abbey, diary entries, May 1865, in Charles Edgar Abbey Civil War Papers, American Antiquarian Society; Stephen P. Chase, diary entries, 27 May 1865, 28 May 1865, 6 June 1865, and 8 June 1865, in *Civil War Times Illustrated* Collection, 2nd series, Box 31, USAMHI; for another example of a veteran little impressed by the review and more interested in his return home, see Peter Boyer, letter to his father, 28 May 1865, in Boyer Family Papers, Harrisburg *CWRT* Collection, Box 18, USAMHI. On desertion, see Guy Taylor to Sarah Taylor, letter, 25 June 1865, in *Letters Home to Sarah: The Civil War Letters of Guy C. Taylor, 36th Wisconsin Volunteers*, ed. Kevin Alderson and Patsy Alderson (Madison: University of Wisconsin Press, 2012), 280–281; George Jarvis, letter, 16 July 1865, in Civil War Manuscript Collection, George Jarvis Papers, Box 15, Folder 2, Manuscripts and Archives, Sterling Memorial Library, Yale University; R. Jacobus to Marcus L. Ward, letter, 1 June 1865, in Marcus L. Ward Papers, Box 9, Folder 15, NJHSL.

21   George Shuman to Fannie, letter, 12 June 1865, in Harrisburg Civil War Roundtable Collection, Box 11A, USAMHI; F. N. Boney, ed., *A Union Soldier in the Land of the Vanquished: The Diary of Sergeant Mathew Woodruff, June–December 1865* (University: University of Alabama Press, 1969), 88–89; Delavan S. Miller,

A Drum's Story and Other Tales (Watertown, New York: Hungerford-Holbrook Co., 1909), 185.

22 William T. Clark, diary entry, 6 July 1865, in *The Diaries of William T. Clark*; John Mead Gould, diary entry, 27 May 1865, in John Mead Gould Diary, MaineHS; Lyman Jackman, *History of the Sixth New Hampshire Regiment in the War for the Union* (Concord, New Hampshire: Republican Press Association, 1891), 369.

23 Jacob Harrison Allspaugh, diary entry, 2 June 1865, in Jacob Harrison Allspaugh Diary, Special Collections, University of Iowa Library.

24 W. Frank Cox to Edward, letter, 2 May 1865, in Civil War Document Collection, Box 29, Folder 2, USAMHI; Samuel B. Chase as quoted in Harry H. Anderson, "The Civil War Letters of Lieutenant Samuel B. Chase," *Milwaukee History* 14, no. 2 (1991): 54.

25 Gould, *History of the First—Tenth—Twenty-Ninth Maine Regiment*, 579; Gould, diary entries, 26 April 1865 and 30 June 1865, in Gould Diary, MaineHS; see also James Ewer Kendall, *The Third Massachusetts Cavalry in the War for the Union* (Maplewood, Massachusetts: William Perry Press, 1903), 252; Ida M. Tarbell, "Disbanding the Union Army," *McClure's Magazine* (March 1901): 402; Francis T. Moore as quoted in Thomas Bahde, ed., *The Story of My Campaign: The Civil War Memoir of Captain Francis T. Moore, Second Illinois Cavalry* (DeKalb: Northern Illinois University Press, 2011), 253.

26 William H. Church to Ella Church, letters, 9 June 1865 and 4 July 1865, in William H. Church Papers, WiHS; E. B. Quiner, *The Military History of Wisconsin in the War for the Union* (Chicago: Clarke & Co., 1866), 447; see also Isaac Newton Carr, diary entry, 15 July 1865, in Isaac N. Carr Papers, Box 1, SHSIo.

27 Sam Evans to his father, letter, 7 May 1865, in Robert F. Engs and Corey M. Brooks, eds., *Their Patriotic Duty: The Civil War Letters of the Evans Family of Brown County, Ohio* (New York: Fordham University Press, 2007), 346. Evans's sentiment was not uncommon. In May 1865, military commanders were dispatched to Concord, Tennessee, to quell fighting between Union and Confederate veterans. In the weeks after Appomattox, Union veterans "wreaked vengeance" on their former foes throughout eastern Tennessee. See Noel Fisher, *War at Every Door: Partisan Politics and Guerrilla Violence in East Tennessee, 1860–1869* (Chapel Hill: University of North Carolina Press, 2001), 157. Henry Weldo Hart to "my dear wife," letter, 9 May 1865, in Civil War Small Manuscripts Collection—Henry Weldo Hart Letters, Carol Newman Library, Virginia Polytechnic Institute; Arlon Atherton to his wife, letter, 11 May 1865, in Arlon Atherton Papers, Box 1, Folder 3, NHHS; see also Irwin C. Fox, diary entry, p. 28, in Irwin C. Fox Diary, ASSpCL.

28 William H. Barron to "dear friend Emma," letter, 27 May 1865, in William H.

Barron Letter, Carol Newman Library, Virginia Polytechnic Institute; Lucius Wox quoted in Holberton, *Homeward Bound*, 67; see also Private John W. Haley, diary entries, 19 May and 3 June 1865, in Ruth L. Silliker, ed., *The Rebel Yell and the Yankee Hurrah: The Civil War Journal of a Maine Volunteer* (Camden, Maine: Down East Books, 1985), 277, 280; Ellis Spear, "The Return Home," in *The Civil War Recollections of General Ellis Spear*, ed. Abbott Spear, Andrea C. Hawkes, Marie H. McCosh, Craig L. Symonds, and Michael H. Alpert (Orono, Maine: University of Maine Press, 1997), 190; Edwin Eustace Bryant, *History of the Third Regiment of Wisconsin Veteran Volunteer Infantry* (Madison: Veteran Association of the Regiment, 1891), 337; William T. Clark, diary entry, 21 June 1865, in *The Diaries of William T. Clark*; Henry Clay Fike to Lucy Fike, letters, 6 May 1865 and 17 May 1865, Fike Papers, Box 3, Folder 3, KSRL; see also Taylor Peirce to Catherine Peirce, letter, n.d., in Richard L. Kiper, ed., *Dear Catherine, Dear Taylor: The Civil War Letters of a Union Soldier and His Wife* (Lawrence: University Press of Kansas, 2002), 408; Chapin Warner to Father and Mother, letter, 31 May 1865, in Civil War Papers, reel 2, Massachusetts Historical Society; unidentified soldier to "mother," letter, 28 May 1865, in Letters, 1865, MS 93-005, Carol Newman Library, Virginia Polytechnic Institute.

29 Edmund Burritt Wakefield, letter to "Dear folks at home," 29 June 1865, Wakefield Family Papers, Section 2—Wakefield Correspondence, College Archives and Special Collections, Hiram College Library, Hiram, Ohio; William H. Church, letter, 6 July 1865, Church Civil War Papers, WiHS; Edmund Spencer Packard, diary entry, 29 May 1865, Packard Diary, WiHS; see also J. H. Thomas to Gov. Stephen Miller, letter, 23 June 1865, in Minnesota Governor's Records, MinnHS; John W. Pratt, diary entry, 9 August 1865, Pratt Diary, Special Collections, University of Iowa Library.

30 John W. Haley, diary entry, 31 May 1865, in Silliker, ed., *The Rebel Yell and the Yankee Hurrah*, 279; William H. Church, letter, 6 July 1865, Church Civil War Papers, WiHS; on the preparation of muster-out rolls, see also John C. Fleming to his parents, letter, 12 June 1865, in John C. Fleming Papers, Box 1, Folder 84, Newberry Library; Richard Oglesby to J. B. Barrett, Thomas H. Hobbs, Charles W. Ravy, and James D. Johnson, letter, 28 July 1865, in Richard Oglesby Correspondence, Series 101.014, Illinois State Archives; Lot Abraham, diary entry, 29 July 1865, Lot Abraham Papers, Box 1, Special Collections, University of Iowa Library, Iowa City, Iowa; Henry Hoskins, diary entry, 17 June 1865, SC 2745, Abraham Lincoln Presidential Library; Hervey Eaton to "my dearest Mother," letter, 31 May 1865, Eaton Civil War Letters, ASSpCL; Irving Bronson Memoir, in Bruce Catton Papers, Box 45, Folder 9, The Citadel Archives and Museum; and Samuel Cormany, diary entries, 12 August 1865, 16 August 1865, and 17

August 1865, in James C. Mohr, ed., *The Cormany Diaries: A Northern Family in the Civil War* (Pittsburgh: University of Pittsburgh Press, 1982), 576–578.

31 Lyman Jackman, diary entry, 1 August 1865, in Lyman Jackman Papers, Box 1, NHHS; John Whiting Storrs, *The Twentieth Connecticut: A Regimental History* (Ansonia, Connecticut: Press of the Naugatuck Valley Sentinel, 1886), 170; Lucien B. Crooker, Henry Stedman Nourse, and John G. Brown, *The Story of the Fifty-Fifth Regiment, Illinois Volunteer Infantry in the Civil War* (n.p.: W. J. Coulter, 1887), 438; Allen Diehl Albert, ed., *History of the Forty-Fifth Pennsylvania*, 187; D. G. Crotty, *Four Years Campaigning in the Army of the Potomac*, 204–205; Irving Bronson Memoir, Bruce Catton Papers, Box 45, Folder 9, The Citadel Archives and Museum.

32 *The National Cyclopaedia of American Biography* (New York: James T. White & Co., 1897), 7:541; H. W. French, *Art and Artists in Connecticut* (Boston: Lee & Shepard, 1879), 123–124.

33 Ibid.

34 *The National Cyclopaedia of American Biography* 7:541; H. W. French, *Art and Artists in Connecticut* (Boston: Lee & Shepard, 1879), 123–124; George C. Rable, *God's Almost Chosen Peoples: A Religious History of the American Civil War* (Chapel Hill: University of North Carolina Press, 2010), 213.

35 Patricia Catherine Click, *Time Full of Trial: The Roanoke Freedmen's Colony, 1862–1867* (Chapel Hill: University of North Carolina Press, 2001), 38.

36 *Documents of the Senate of the State of New York* (Albany: Comstock & Cassidy, Printers, 1864), 3:66.

37 *Report of Vincent Colyer*, 19–20.

38 *Daily National Intelligencer*, 24 May 1865; J. W. Rumpel to "dear Father," letter, 27 May 1865, in H. E. Rosenberger, ed., "Ohiowa Soldier," 148; "Sunday Night's Dispatches from Washington," *Daily Ohio Statesman*, 29 May 1865; *Milwaukee Sentinel*, 11 August 1865; see also "Crime in Our Cities," *Daily Age* (Philadelphia), 3 June 1865, and *The Soldiers' Guide in Philadelphia*, copy in Herbert Deuel Civil War Collection, Carol Newman Library, Virginia Polytechnic Institute; *Davenport* (Iowa) *Daily Gazette*, 7 August 1865; "Rev. William White Williams' Appeal for the Fourth of July," *Journal of the American Temperance Union and New York Prohibitionist* 29, no. 7 (July 1865): 109; Wecter, *When Johnny Comes Marching Home*, 150–151; James Henry Avery as quoted in Karen Jean Husby and Eric J. Wittenberg, eds., *Under Custer's Command: The Civil War Journal of James Henry Avery* (Washington, D.C.: Brassey's, 2000), 156; "Rev. William White Williams' Appeal for the Fourth of July," 109; see also *Davenport Daily Gazette*, 28 July 1865 and 29 July 1865; Colyer, *Report of Vincent Colyer*, 17–18, Nicholson Collection, Huntington Library; "A Soldier Robbed," *Soldier's Friend*, April 1865, American Antiquarian Society; Theodore

J. Karamanski, *Rally 'Round the Flag: Chicago and the Civil War* (Lanham, Maryland: Rowman & Littlefield, 2006), 241; "Advice to Returned Soldiers," *Soldier's Casket* (June 1865): 365, Nicholson Collection, Huntington Library. The diary of an Iowa soldier named Isaac N. Carr reported that "stealing" was rampant. "A pocket book stole last night," he jotted in his diary. See Isaac N. Carr Papers, Box 1, SHSIo.

39 "Value of a Soldier's Discharge," *Ashland Times*, 23 November 1865; *Philadelphia Inquirer*, 4 July 1865; Perry O. C. Nixon, memoir (circa 1907), in Perry O. C. Nixon Collection, KSRL; Perry O. C. Nixon Pension File, RG 15, NA; *Grand Army Journal*, 14 May 1870; Henry C. Welcher to Marcus L. Ward, letter, 5 September 1869, in Marcus L. Ward Papers, Box 4, Folder 2, Special Collections, Alexander Library, Rutgers University, New Brunswick, New Jersey; see also "Tricks on the Soldiers," *Coshocton Democrat*, 10 July 1865.

40 Massachusetts captain quoted in Warren Wilkinson, *Mother, May You Never See the Sights I Have Seen: The Fifty-Seventh Massachusetts Veteran Volunteers in the Last Year of the Civil War* (New York: Harper & Row, 1990), 363; *OR*, series III, vol. 5, pp. 301–306. For important interpretations of movement and space in Civil War America useful here, see Yael Sternhell, *Routes of War: The World of Movement in the Confederate South* (Cambridge: Harvard University Press, 2012); and Holberton, *Homeward Bound*, 39–52.

41 Charles Addison Partridge, *History of the Ninety-Sixth Regiment, Illinois Volunteer Infantry* (Chicago: Brown, Pettibone & Co., Printers, 1887), 478–479; Irving Bronson Memoir, in Bruce Catton Papers, Box 45, Folder 9, The Citadel Archives and Museum; Winther, ed., *With Sherman to the Sea*, 180.

42 Francis Moore in Bahde, ed., *The Story of My Campaign*, 253–254; Andrew F. Sperry, *History of the 33rd Iowa Infantry Volunteer Regiment* (Des Moines: Mills & Co., 1866), 186–187. For similar comments, see George M. Shearer, diary entry, 31 May 1865, Shearer Diary, Special Collections, University of Iowa Library.

43 Holberton, *Homeward Bound*, 143; "Homeward Bound," *Soldier's Friend*, June 1865; *History of the Thirty-Sixth Regiment Massachusetts Volunteers* (Boston: Rockwell & Churchill, 1884), 307; see also Ida M. Tarbell, "Disbanding the Union Army," *McClure's Magazine* (March 1901): 400–412; Wecter, *When Johnny Comes Marching Home*; and Russell F. Weigley, *Quartermaster General of the Union Army: A Biography of M. C. Meigs* (New York: Columbia University Press, 1958), 329–330. Chester D. Berry, ed., *Loss of the* Sultana *and Reminiscences of Survivors* (orig. published 1891; reprint ed., Knoxville: University of Tennessee Press, 2005), 9; William N. Fast to the editor of the *Toledo Blade*, letter, 6 December 1885, Fast Family Papers, Box 1, Folder 2, Center for Archival Collections, Bowling Green State University; see also W. A. Huld, quoted in Berry, ed., *Loss of the* Sultana, 183.

44 Spear, "The Return Home," in *Civil War Recollections*, 190, and J. W. Rumpel to "dear Father," letter, 27 May 1865, in H. E. Rosenberger, ed., "Ohiowa Soldier," *Annals of Iowa* 36, no. 2 (Fall 1961): 147–148; Ulysses S. Grant to Edwin M. Stanton, 28 June 1865, *OR*, series III, vol. 5, p. 60; Hiram Blaisdell to his wife, 5 May 1865, Civil War Manuscripts Collection, Blaisdell Family Papers, Box 6, Folder 13, Sterling Memorial Library, Yale University; Partridge, *History of the Ninety-Sixth Regiment*, 477; Francis Hamilton to Marcus L. Ward, letter, 26 June 1865, in Marcus L. Ward Papers, Box 10, Folder 5, NJSHL; Harvey Hyde to Marcus L. Ward, 25 June 1864, Ward Papers, Box 10, Folder 4, NJHSL.

   It is important to note here the psychological effects of army demobilizations made individually or without all members of a fighting unit, something trauma specialists have learned much about in the aftermath of Vietnam. See, for example, Jonathan Shay, *Odysseus in America: Combat Trauma and the Trials of Homecoming* (New York: Simon & Schuster, 2003).

45 See William C. Wright, "Joel Parker," in Paul A. Stellhorn and Michael J. Birkner, eds., *The Governors of New Jersey, 1664–1974* (Trenton: New Jersey Historical Commission, 1982), 132–135; Emerson Opdycke, 19 August 1865, in Glenn V. Longacre and John E. Haas, eds., *To Battle for God and the Right: The Civil War Letterbooks of Emerson Opdycke* (Urbana and Chicago: University of Illinois Press, 2003), 304; Jennifer L. Weber, *Copperheads: The Rise and Fall of Lincoln's Opponents in the North* (New York: Oxford University Press, 2006); Louis Powers to Marcus L. Ward, letter, 8 June 1865, in Marcus L. Ward Papers, Box 9, Folder 17, NJHSL; James Sherman to Marcus L. Ward, letter, 24 June 1865, in Marcus L. Ward Papers, Box 10, Folder 4, NJHSL; William Gillette, *Jersey Blue: Civil War Politics in New Jersey, 1854–1865* (New Brunswick, New Jersey: Rutgers University Press, 1995), 311; Amos Featherolf to Marcus L. Ward, letter, 9 June 1865, in Marcus L. Ward Papers, Box 9, Folder 18, NJHSL. For similar complaints, see "Waterford," letter, 28 June 1865, in William B. Styple, ed., *Writing and Fighting the Civil War: Soldier Letters from the Battlefront*, 2nd ed. (Kearny, New Jersey: Belle Grove Publishing Co., 2004), 359–360.

46 2nd Illinois Artillery to Richard J. Oglesby, in Richard Oglesby Correspondence, Series 101.014, Illinois State Archives; William H. Church, letter, 6 June 1865, in Church Civil War Papers, Box 1, Folder 2, WiHS.

47 Similar fears of a Copperhead conspiracy "behind the lines" emerged when an Ohio unit made its return to Columbus in mid-June. Addressing comrades at a welcome-home reception, one ex-soldier made a plea for "three groans for the Copperheads." See "Chickens Coming Home," *Coshocton Democrat*, 21 June 1865.

   "John Mason's Return," *New York Observer and Chronicle*, 27 July 1865; see also Gerber, *Disabled Veterans in History*, introduction.; Elizabeth's letter is refer-

enced in Andrea R. Foroughi, ed., *Go if You Think It Your Duty: A Minnesota Cou-*
ple's Civil War Letters (St. Paul: Minnesota Historical Society Press, 2008), 301.
For similar civilian sentiments, see E. Brooks to Henry Spencer Parmelee, letter,
19 May 1865, in Henry Spencer Parmelee Papers, Civil War Manuscript Collec-
tion, Group 619, Box 20, Folder 9, Sterling Memorial Library, Yale University;
Logan, *Reminiscences of the Civil War and Reconstruction*, 137–138. *Cleveland Plain*
Dealer, 23 May 1865; "Our Returning Soldiers," *Milwaukee Daily Sentinel*, 31
May 1865.

48 *Milwaukee Daily Sentinel*, 31 May 1865; "Reception of the 115th Reg't," *Ohio*
Repository, 5 July 1865; Gallagher, *The Union War*, 3. For a probing exploration of
republicanism and citizen soldiers in another American army, see Charles Royster, *A Revolutionary People at War: The Continental Army and American Character,*
1775–1783 (Chapel Hill: University of North Carolina Press, 1979); for the "cultural expectations" of a citizen-soldier army during the Civil War, see Wayne
Wei-Siang Hsieh, *West Pointers and the Civil War: The Old Army in War and Peace*
(Chapel Hill: University of North Carolina Press, 2009). "Homeward Bound,"
Soldier's Casket 5 (May 1865): 318; *Daily National Intelligencer*, 23 May 1865, as
quoted in Gallagher, *The Union War*, 27; "Peace—The Boys Are Coming Home,"
Coshocton Democrat, 24 May 1865, and the assurance of the *Ohio Repository*, 5 July
1865, that the members of the 104th Ohio Volunteers would "soon lay aside their
blue, and, as useful members, mix again in society." "The Returning Soldiers,"
Trenton State Gazette, 7 June 1865.

49 Oliver P. Morton as quoted in William Dudley Foulke, *Life of Oliver P. Morton,*
Including His Important Speeches, vol. 1 (Indianapolis: Bowen-Merrill Co., 1899),
445; remarks delivered by Illinois Governor Richard J. Oglesby at a reception for
Macoupin County's returning soldiers in Richard Oglesby Correspondence,
Series 101.014, Illinois State Archives; Mattie Morrison in *Soldier's Casket* 5
(October 1865): 686–688.

50 *Cleveland Plain Dealer*, 23 May 1865; *Coshocton Democrat*, 24 May 1865; Committee on Commemorating the Service of Yale Men in the Civil War Records,
Sterling Memorial Library, Yale; J. R. Adams to Arthur Wright, letter quoted in
undated newspaper clipping, Box 1, Folder 1, Committee on Commemorating
the Service of Yale Men in the Civil War Records, Sterling Memorial Library,
Yale; James Hovey to Arthur Wright, letter, undated, and Horace James to Wright,
letter, 20 July 1865, Box 1, Folder 2, Committee on Commemorating the Service
of Yale Men in the Civil War Records, Sterling Memorial Library, Yale; *New York*
Tribune, 20 June 1865; *Trenton State Gazette*, 8 June 1865; "The Soldiers at Harrisburg," *Gettysburg Republican Compiler*, 12 June 1865; unidentified soldier to "my

dear wife," letter, 4 July 1865, in Letters from a Civil War Union Soldier, MS 96-005, Carol Newman Library, Virginia Polytechnic Institute.

51 Wecter, *When Johnny Comes Marching Home*, 143; Gallman, *The North Fights the Civil War*, 180–181; Charles H. Lynch, diary entry, 29 June 1865, in *The Civil War Diary 1862–1865 of Charles H. Lynch* (Hartford: privately printed, 1915), 158; Dearing, *Veterans in Politics*, 51; Carl Russell Fish, "Back to Peace in 1865," *American Historical Review* 24, no. 3 (April 1919): 435–443; James Lorenzo Bowen, *History of the Thirty-Seventh Regiment, Massachusetts Volunteers in the Civil War* (Holyoke, Massachusetts, and New York: Clark W. Bryan, 1884), 430; Allen, ed., *On the Skirmish Line*, 323; Anthony Waskie, *Philadelphia and the Civil War: Arsenal of the Union* (Charleston, South Carolina: History Press, 2011), 190.

Cornelius Wheeler, in his "Sketch of the Services of Company I, Second Regiment Volunteer Infantry," noted the "hundreds of beautiful girls strewing our roadway with flowers" as the lead Iron Brigade regiment entered the grounds of the Wisconsin State Capitol. Wheeler, "Sketch," in Cornelius Wheeler Papers, Box 1, WiHS.

52 Colyer, *Report of Vincent Colyer*, 28–29, 20–21, 47.

53 Ibid., 16, 20, 13, 40.

54 Joshua Rilea, diary entry, 11–12 June 1865, in Joshua D. Rilea Diary, SC 1274, Abraham Lincoln Presidential Library; William S. Hotchkin, diary entry, 4 July 1865, in William S. Hotchkin Diary, ASSpCL; S. C. Rogers, 9 June 1865, reprinted in *Davenport Daily Gazette*, 17 June 1865. Rogers reported that the situation did not improve in Davenport, either. "No hearts respond to ours in Iowa!" he wailed. "Shame! Shame!" The Burlington, Iowa, newspaper later commented that Davenport civilians were "too busy making money out of Uncle Sam's boys ... to extend them that welcome which should greet them everywhere." *Davenport Daily Gazette*, 13 June 1865. Allen L. Fahnestock, "Fahnestock Army Book," entry for 11 June 1865, in Allen L. Fahnestock Papers, SC 472, Abraham Lincoln Presidential Library.

55 *Boston Daily Advertiser*, 14 June 1865; William Haines as quoted in Edward G. Longacre, *To Gettysburg and Beyond: The Twelfth New Jersey Volunteer Infantry, II Corps, Army of the Potomac, 1862–1865* (Hightstown, New Jersey: Longstreet House, 1988), 291; William Haines Pension File, RG 15, NARA; Writers Program of the Works Progress Administration in New Jersey, *New Jersey: A Guide to Its Past and Present* (New York: Stratford Press, 1939), 629; see also Gillette, *Jersey Blue*, 311. Francis O'Keefe to Marcus L. Ward, letter, 24 June 1865, in Box 10, Folder 4, Marcus L. Ward Papers, NJHSL; Leander Stillwell, *The Story of a Common Soldier of Army Life in the Civil War, 1861–1865* (Kansas City, Missouri: Franklin Hudson Publishing Co., 1920), 277; Leander Stillwell Pension File, application no. 1,356,880, certificate no. 1,131,481, C 2486110, RG 15: Civil War Pension Files, NARA; Moore, in Bahde, ed., *Story of My Campaign*, 255.

56 Fenton quoted in Colyer, *Report of Vincent Colyer*, 48.

57 Charles Wainwright as quoted in Nevins, ed., *A Diary of Battle*, 527; Registers of Cases in Records of the St. Elizabeth's Hospital, RG 418, Entry 64, Box 1, NARA.

58 George Hitchcock, in "An Army Diary in the War for Freedom," vol. 2, in George Hitchcock Diary, Massachusetts Historical Society; Wilbur Fisk, letter, 26 July 1865, in Emil and Ruth Rosenblatt, eds., *Hard Marching Every Day: The Civil War Letters of Private Wilbur Fisk, 1861–1865* (Lawrence: University Press of Kansas, 1992), 342; Edmund Burritt Wakefield, 16 July 1865, in Wakefield Family Papers, Section 2, Wakefield Correspondence, College Archives and Special Collections, Hiram College Library; *The Carnegie Foundation for the Advancement of Teaching—Sixteenth Annual Report of the President and of the Treasurer* (Boston: Merrymount Press, 1921), 173; unidentified veteran, letter, n.d., to Arthur Wright, Box 1, Folder 1, Committee on Commemorating the Service of Yale Men in the Civil War Records, Sterling Memorial Library, Yale. Veterans of subsequent wars have experienced this phenomenon; see Samuel Hynes, *The Soldier's Tale: Bearing Witness to Modern War* (New York: Penguin Press, 1998). On the eve of demobilization, civilians also mused about how dramatically the country had changed. See Elizabeth Bowler to James Madison Bowler, 14 May 1865, in Foroughi, ed., *Go if You Think It Your Duty*, 292–293; Charles O. Musser as quoted in Barry Popchock, ed., *Soldier Boy: The Civil War Letters of Charles O. Musser, 29th Iowa* (Iowa City: University of Iowa Press, 1995), 211–212.

CHAPTER 2: STRANGER AT THE GATES

1 Fenton as quoted in Colyer, *Report of Vincent Colyer*, 17.

2 On the citizen soldier ideal, see John Clark Ridpath, *The Citizen Soldier: His Part in War and Peace* (Cincinnati: Jones Brothers Publishing Co., 1891); and Marcus Cunliffe, *Soldiers and Civilians: The Martial Spirit in America, 1775–1865* (Boston: Little, Brown & Co., 1968).

3 On the size of the pre–Civil War armies, see Caroline Cox, "The Continental Army," in *The Oxford Handbook of the American Revolution*, ed. Edward G. Gray and Jane Kamensky (New York: Oxford University Press, 2013), 162; K. Jack Bauer, *The Mexican War, 1846–1848*, revised ed. (Lincoln: University of Nebraska Press, 1992), 397; and James M. McPherson, *Battle Cry of Freedom: The Civil War Era* (New York: Oxford University Press, 1988), 250, 313.

4 "A Carnival of Crime," *New Haven Daily Palladium*, 4 August 1865.

5 Nathaniel Hawthorne as recollected in Henry Bright to Lord Houghton, 18 November 1870, in Thomas Weymss Reid, ed., *The Life, Letters, and Friendships of Richard Monckton Milnes, First Lord Houghton*, 3rd ed. (London, Paris, and

Melbourne: Cassell & Co., 1891), 2:242. Hawthorne's fears are well known among scholars. See Richard Severo and Lewis Milford, *The Wages of War: When America's Soldiers Came Home, From Valley Forge to Vietnam* (New York: Simon & Schuster, 1989), 125; Larry M. Logue, *To Appomattox and Beyond: The Civil War Soldier in War and Peace* (Chicago: Ivan R. Dee, 1996), 86; W. J. Rohrbaugh, "Who Fought for the North?" *Journal of American History* 73, no. 3 (December 1986): 695–701; Lee O. Harris, *The Man Who Tramps: A Story of To-Day* (Indianapolis: Douglass & Carlon, Printers, 1878), 17; John Clark Ridpath, *The Citizen Soldier*, 51–52; Lorien Foote, *The Gentlemen and the Roughs: Violence, Honor, and Manhood in the Union Army* (New York: New York University Press, 2010); William L. Burton, *Melting Pot Soldiers: The Union's Ethnic Regiments* (Ames: Iowa State University Press, 1988); E. D. Townsend, "General Orders No. 101," 30 May 1865, in *OR*, series III, vol. 5, p. 43.

6 "They Are Afraid of Us," *Soldier's Friend* (June 1866); Phineas P. Whitehouse Pension File, RG 15, NA; Whitehouse to WOB, 27 April 1867, Bourne Papers, Manuscript Division, LoC; See also *Milwaukee Sentinel*, 31 May 1865; *Daily Ohio Statesman*, 9 June 1865; *Plain Dealer*, 17 May 1865; *Portsmouth Journal of Literature and Politics*, 10 June 1865; and letter to Mary Ashley, 7 May 1865, in "Georgetown, D.C. Letter, 1865," Carol Newman Library, Virginia Polytechnic Institute; "Baltimore," *Philadelphia Inquirer*, 13 June 1865; "The Liquor Order," *Jackson Daily Citizen*, 16 June 1865; A. L. Roumfort, "A Proclamation," 31 May 1865, reprinted in the *Philadelphia Inquirer*, 1 June 1865; *Hartford Courant*, 8 June 1865. For a detailed and useful treatment of Harrisburg in the Civil War, see William Miller, *Civil War City: Harrisburg, Pennsylvania, 1861–1865* (Shippensburg, Pennsylvania: White Mane Books, 1990); *Soldier's and Sailor's Almanac for 1865* (New York: Protestant Episcopal Society for the Promotion of Evangelical Knowledge, 1865), 39; "Advice to Returned Soldiers," *Soldier's Casket* (June 1865): 365, copy in Nicholson Collection, Huntington Library; see also "Our Returning Soldiers," *Lowell Daily Citizen and News*, 29 May 1865; "The Returned Soldiers," *Lowell Daily Citizen and News*, 26 August 1865.

7 "Our Returning Soldiers," *Lowell Daily Citizen and News*, 29 May 1865; advertisement for J. Fortune & Company in *Boston Herald*, 16 June 1865.

8 John Alexander Logan as quoted in W. S. Morris, L. D. Hartwell, Jr., and J. B. Kuykendall, *History 31st Regiment Illinois Volunteers, Organized by John A. Logan*, reprint ed. with a foreword by John Y. Simon (Carbondale: Southern Illinois University Press, 1998), 174; "The Army of the Tennessee," *Chicago Tribune*, 11 July 1865; Ellis Spear, "The Return Home," 192–194.

9 William Henry Jones to mother and brother, 16 July 1865, in American Historical Manuscripts Collection, Box 6, Folder 51, Special Collections and University

Archives, Kent State University Library; Edwin Coles to Marcus Ward, letter, 9 February 1866, and Henry A. Black to Marcus Ward, letter, 18 February 1866, in Marcus L. Ward Papers, Box 11, Folder 17, NJHSL; Daniel Eldredge, manuscript history of the 3rd New Hampshire Infantry (dated 1867–1869), in Daniel Eldredge Papers, NHHS. Rioting among returned veterans was such a problem in New Haven that the editor of the city's newspaper suggested that if the ex-soldiers could not be "paid off" and summarily "sent away," then the city would have to consider closing its "low groggeries." "Rum and Riot in New Haven," *New Haven Palladium*, 10 August 1865.

10 *Davenport Daily Gazette*, 31 July 1865 and 2 August 1865; Sperry, *History of the 33rd Iowa*, 188–193. See also Isaac Newton Carr, diary entry, 11 July 1865, in I. N. Carr Papers, Box 1, SHSIo.

11 Longacre, *To Gettysburg and Beyond*, 288–290; "Another Riot," *New York Times*, 22 June 1865; "Rows Among Returning Soldiers," *Philadelphia Public Ledger*, 25 July 1865; "Shameful," *Illustrated Daily Age* [Philadelphia], 28 June 1865; "Murder and Robbery near Bloomington, Ill.," *Chicago Tribune*, 4 July 1865.

12 Robert Hale Strong, *A Yankee Private's Civil War*, ed. Ashley Halsey (Chicago: Henry Regnery Co., 1961), 214–216.

13 Ibid., 216–217.

14 *Plain Dealer*, 1 July 1865; "Rumors of Violence in Bellaire and Zanesville," *Daily Ohio Statesman*, 16 June 1865; "The Contagion of Crime," *New York Tribune*, 15 July 1865; "A Carnival of Crime," *New Haven Daily Palladium*, 4 August 1865; Edith Abbott, "The Civil War and the Crime Wave of 1865–70," *Journal of the American Institute of Criminal Law and Criminology* 9, no. 1 (May 1918): 226–227; "Rows Among Returning Soldiers," *Philadelphia Public Ledger*, 25 July 1865; "Shameful," *Illustrated Daily Age*, 28 June 1865; *Philadelphia Inquirer*, 21 August 1865; "Increases of Crime," *Lowell Daily Citizen*, 12 August 1865; "Epidemics of Crime," *Daily Cleveland Herald*, 17 July 1865; "Crime in Chicago," *Milwaukee Daily Sentinel*, 25 August 1865; "A Deluge of Crime," *New Hampshire Statesman*, 1 September 1865; *Ohio Repository*, 26 July 1865; "The City," *Philadelphia Press*, 21 July 1865; and "Crime in the East," *Daily National Intelligencer*, 20 July 1865. See also Betty B. Rosenbaum, "The Relationship Between War and Crime in the United States," *Journal of Criminal Law and Criminology* 30, no. 5 (January-February 1940): 722–740; "Riot by Returned Soldiers at Concord, N.H.," *Albany Argus*, 29 July 1865; "Incipient Riot at Concord, N.H.," *Hartford Courant*, 28 July 1865; *New York Herald*, 27 July 1865; *North American*, 28 July 1865.

15 On alcohol use and abuse in the federal army, see Steven J. Ramold, *Baring the Iron Hand: Discipline in the Union Army* (DeKalb: Northern Illinois University

Press, 2010), 123–179; Foote, *The Gentlemen and the Roughs*, 29–31, and "Whiskey in the Army," *Army and Navy Journal*, 15 April 1865; "Temperance Tracts," *Soldier's Friend*, September 1865; "Song of the Decanter," *Soldier's Friend*, January 1868; "Drunk," *Summit County Beacon*, 15 June 1865.

16 "A Subject for the Insane Asylum," *Philadelphia Inquirer*, 2 August 1865; *Smith's Hand Book and Guide in Philadelphia* (Philadelphia: G. Delp, 1871), 148; *New York Daily Evening Post*, 22 July 1865; *Annual Report of the Adjutant General of the State of New York—Register of the Fifteenth and Sixteenth Artillery in the War of the Rebellion* (New York and Albany: Wynkoop Hallenbeck Crawford Co., 1898), 265; *New Albany Daily Ledger*, 15 January 1866. One particularly embarrassing spectacle involving drunken veterans occurred in Gettysburg on July 4, 1865. Yet awaiting their discharges, the soldiers of the 50th Pennsylvania were ordered to participate in the cornerstone-laying ceremony for the soldiers' monument in the Gettysburg National Cemetery. After Major General Oliver Otis Howard delivered an oration, the soldiers made their way into town, "drank rather freely," and became "badly used up" in a saloon near the Diamond. Civilians loudly "complained of [the veterans'] disorderly conduct." See Lewis Crater, diary entries, 4–5 July 1865, in Lewis Crater Diary, Special Collections, University of Iowa Library.

17 On alcohol and temperance reform in nineteenth-century America, see Ronald G. Walters, *American Reformers, 1815–1860* (New York: Hill & Wang, 1978), 123–143; and W. J. Rohrbaugh, *The Alcoholic Republic: An American Tradition* (New York: Oxford University Press, 1979).

18 "Speech of J. B. Merwin, U.S.A., on Boston Common, June 17th," *Wisconsin Chief*, 30 June 1865; John Marsh, *Temperance Recollections: Labors, Defeats, Triumphs* (New York: Charles Scribner & Co., 1866), 341–342; "Six Men in Jail for Rum-Selling," *Ithaca Journal and Advertiser*, 27 January 1866; WOB to the New York State Liquor Dealers' Association, in *Soldier's Friend*, August 1867.

19 John Mead Gould, diary entry, 13 October 1865, in John Mead Gould Diary, Maine Historical Society, Portland, Maine.

20 Frederick Walster, diary entries, 8 October 1865 and 3 December 1865, in Civil War Manuscripts Collection—Frederick Walster Diary, Special Collections and University Archives, Glenn G. Bartle Library, State University of New York at Binghamton, Binghamton, New York.

21 W. B. Emmons, diary entry, 13 July 1865, in W. B. Emmons Diary, Special Collections, University of Iowa Library, Iowa City, Iowa.

22 Henry Wood as quoted in Salvatore G. Cilella, Jr., *Upton's Regulars: The 121st New York Infantry in the Civil War* (Lawrence: University Press of Kansas, 2009), 402.

23 For a fine example of a soldier who was disoriented upon his return home, see

David W. Blight, ed., *When This Cruel War Is Over: The Civil War Letters of Charles Harvey Brewster* (Amherst: University of Massachusetts Press, 1992), 21.

24 W. P. Conrad and Ted Alexander, *When War Passed This Way* (Greencastle, Pennsylvania: Lilian Besore Memorial Library, 1982), 332–333; Eric Paul recollection in Hosea Rood, "Grand Army Corner," newspaper clipping, in Box 2, Folder 2, Grand Army of the Republic Memorial Hall Collection, WiVMA.

25 William Wallace Hensley, autobiography, n.d., in William Wallace Hensley Papers, Carol Newman Library, Virginia Polytechnic Institute.

26 Unidentified Pennsylvania soldier as quoted in Miller, *Civil War City*, 220.

27 Avery as quoted in Husby and Wittenberg, eds., *Under Custer's Command*, 158.

28 Roemer, *Reminiscences of the War of the Rebellion*, 302–303.

29 Arlon Atherton, letter to his wife, 6 August 1865, in Arlton Atherton Papers, Box 1, Folder 3, New Hampshire Historical Society, Concord, New Hampshire; for similar sentiments, see "Peace," in *Connecticut War Record* 2, no. 10 (May 1865), microfilm copy at Connecticut State Library, Hartford, Connecticut.

30 Samuel Cormany as quoted in James C. Mohr, ed., *The Cormany Diaries: A Northern Family in the Civil War* (Pittsburgh: University of Pittsburgh Press, 1982), 567, 571–573, 575–576, 578–581, 582–586.

31 Isaac Newton Carr, diary entry, 15 July 1865, in Isaac N. Carr Papers, Box 1, State Historical Society of Iowa, Iowa City, Iowa. "They Are Afraid of Us," *Soldier's Friend* (June 1866), copy at American Antiquarian Society, Worcester, Massachusetts; *Davenport Daily Gazette*, 17 July 1865, copy at State Historical Society of Iowa, Iowa City, Iowa; "Keeping a Disorderly House," *Illustrated Daily Age*, 24 July 1865; "Crime—Two Murders in Michigan," *New York Daily Evening Post*, 3 August 1865, and "Divorce Made Easy," *Coshocton Democrat*, 11 September 1866. See also Thomas P. Lowry, *The Story the Soldiers Wouldn't Tell: Sex in the Civil War* (Mechanicsburg, Pennsylvania: Stackpole Books, 1994), 173–174. Divorce rates climbed steadily in the decades after the war, a trend many contemporary observers suspected was not unrelated to war. See "Divorce in the United States," *National Tribune*, 21 March 1889.

32 "A Carnival of Crime," *New Haven Daily Palladium*, 4 August 1865.

33 Franklin B. Hough, *History of Lewis County in the State of New York* (Albany: Munsell & Rowland, 1860), 287; Louis B. Filler, *The Crusade Against Slavery, 1830–1860* (New York: Harper & Row, 1960), 17; *Methodist Quarterly Review* (January 1882): 69–71; *Boston Investigator*, 31 March 1852; *School Journal* 62 (June 15, 1901): 679; WOB, *Poems of Hope and Action* (New York: G. P. Putnam, 1850); Charles F. Cooney, "The Left-Armed Corps," *Civil War Times Illustrated* 23, no. 2 (1984): 40–41.

34 *School Journal* 62 (June 15, 1901): 679; Thomas Jones to Dear Sister Maggie,

letter, 24 July 1865, in Richard M. Trimble, ed., *Brothers 'til Death: The Civil War Letters of William, Thomas, and Maggie Jones, 1861–1865: Irish Soldiers in the 48th New York Volunteer Regiment* (Macon, Georgia: Mercer University Press, 2000), 97.

35 Phineas Whitehouse to WOB, 27 April 1865, in WOB Papers, Manuscript Division, LoC; David Montgomery, *Beyond Equality: Labor and the Radical Republicans, 1862–1872* (New York: Alfred A. Knopf, 1967), 3–4; "An Unemployed Veteran," *Boston Daily Advertiser*, 18 October 1865; John Niven, *Connecticut for the Union: The Role of the State in the Civil War* (New Haven: Yale University Press, 1965), 429–432.

36 *Soldier's Friend* (November 1865); *Grand Army Journal*, 30 April 1870; *Soldier's Friend* (June 1866); "Our Unemployed Soldiers," *Daily Ohio State Journal*, 10 May 1865; Leonard Bacon to "My Dear Son," letter, 2 September 1865, in George S. Burkhardt, ed., *Double Duty in the Civil War: The Letters of Sailor and Soldier Edward W. Bacon* (Carbondale: Southern Illinois University Press, 2009), 175.

37 *George P. Rowell & Co.'s American Newspaper Directory* (New York: George P. Rowell & Co., 1869), 264; *Soldier's Friend* (March 1868); *Soldier's Friend* (June 1866); "One of Sherman's Boys" to WOB, in *Soldier's Friend* (August 1866).

38 WOB, "Is It True?" *Soldier's Friend* (November 1865); Thomas Croker, "The Returned Soldier," *Soldier's Friend* (November 1865); "Work for Soldiers," *Soldier's Friend* (November 1867); see also George S. McWatters, *Knots Untied; or, Ways and By-Ways in the Hidden Life of American Detectives* (Hartford: J. B. Burr & Hyde, 1872), 49–50.

39 "Employment for Returned Soldiers," *Daily Trenton State Gazette*, 13 June 1865; John Owen to John Blutchford, letter, n.d., in James Valentine Campbell Papers, Valeria Campbell Materials, Box 3, Bentley Historical Library, University of Michigan; United States Sanitary Commission, *Supplement to Document No. 90: Bureau of Information and Employment, June 14, 1865* (Washington, D.C.: McGill & Witherow, Printers and Stereotypers, 1865), 2.

40 Between 15 August 1865 and 20 November 1865, 211 veterans filed résumés with the Bureau of Information and Employment in Detroit. Some 102 veterans were unable to find work. See Applicant's Register for the Bureau of Information and Employment—Detroit Branch, in James Valentine Campbell Papers, Valeria Campbell Materials, Box 4, Bentley Historical Library, University of Michigan.

41 *New York Herald*, 9 August 1865; "Our Unemployed Veterans," *New York Herald*, 11 August 1865; "Parade of Unemployed Veterans," *New York Herald*, 12 August 1865; Moses King, *Handbook of New York City* (Boston: Moses King, 1893), 608.

42 Rufus L. Robinson to WOB, 30 September 1865, in WOB Papers, Manuscript

Division, LoC; "History of Applicants for Aid," Charlestown Overseer of the Poor Records, Box 1, Massachusetts Historical Society; Clarence D. Long, *Wages and Earnings in the United States, 1860–1890* (Princeton: Princeton University Press, 1960), 144; "An Unemployed Veteran," *Boston Daily Advertiser*, 18 October 1865.

43 Edward Crapsey, *The Nether Side of New York; or, The Vice, Crime and Poverty of the Great Metropolis* (New York: Sheldon & Company, 1872), 111–115; see also T. J. Jackson Lears, *Rebirth of a Nation: The Making of Modern America, 1877–1920* (New York: HarperCollins, 2009), 71–72.

44 Crapsey, *The Nether Side of New York*, 111–115.

45 "A Mendicant Soldier," *Soldier's Friend* (November 1865); see also "The Returned Soldier," *Soldier's Friend* (November 1865); "Injustice to the Soldiers," *Soldier's Manual*, September 1868; *Soldiers' and Sailors' Half Dime Tales* 1, no. 2 (May 1868). Indeed, so stereotypical had the image of the one-armed beggar become in the years after the war that enterprising civilians who had been dismembered in railroad accidents began to disguise themselves in uniforms of federal blue and beg on Broadway. See "News Brief," *Grand Army Journal*, 3 June 1871; "Where Is the Nation's Gratitude?" *Soldier's Friend* (March 1868); "Duty to the Soldier," *Grand Army Journal*, 3 June 1871; *New York Herald*, 9 January 1866.

46 C. P. Van Wyck, as quoted in the *Daily Iowa State Register*, 19 April 1866; *La Crosse Democrat*, as quoted in Dearing, *Veterans in Politics*, 53; "Work for Soldiers," *Soldier's Friend* (November 1867); *Soldier's Record*, 16 January 1869, copy at Connecticut State Library, Hartford, Connecticut; *Grand Army Journal*, 14 May 1870; Benjamin Tinkham Marshall, ed., *A Modern History of New London County, Connecticut*, vol. 1 (New York: Lewis Historical Publishing Co., 1922), 238; "The Organ Grinding Nuisance," *Philadelphia Daily Evening Bulletin*, 26 May 1868; George S. McWatters, *Knots Untied; or, Ways and By-Ways in the Hidden Life of American Detectives* (Hartford: J. B. Burr & Hyde, 1872), 49–50; *Soldiers' and Sailors' Half Dime Tales* 1, no. 2 (May 1868); Phineas Whitehouse, "My First Battle," manuscript dated August 1866, in William Oland Bourne Papers, Manuscript Division, LoC.

47 "Coroners' Inquests," *New York Times*, 2 October 1865; New York Civil War Muster Roll Abstracts, rolls 1037–1038.

48 "Self-Murder—A Man Commits Suicide," *Illustrated Daily Age*, 27 November 1865; *New York Tribune*, 27 November 1865; "Sad Cases of Suicide," *Boston Herald*, 30 November 1865; "Suicide of a Soldier of the First Massachusetts Regiment," *Boston Daily Journal*, 23 March 1866; "Singular Case of Suicide," *New York Daily Evening Post*, 28 September 1865.

49 *Davenport Daily Gazette*, 7 June 1865; William Quentin Maxwell, *Lincoln's Fifth*

Wheel: The Political History of the United States Sanitary Commission (New York: Longmans, Green & Co., 1956), 286–287. Though the USSC began shuttering its offices, it miraculously mustered the strength to launch a "Historical Bureau," tasked with compiling the records, archives, and printed reports of local offices. See F. Browning to Valeria Campbell, letter, 26 March 1866, in James Valentine Campbell Papers, Valeria Campbell Materials, Box 3, Bentley Historical Library, University of Michigan.

50 Bellows as quoted in Maxwell, *Lincoln's Fifth Wheel*, 28; George M. Fredrickson, *The Inner Civil War: Northern Intellectuals and the Crisis of the Union* (Urbana and Chicago: University of Illinois Press, 1965); Michael B. Katz, *In the Shadow of the Poorhouse: A Social History of Welfare in America* (New York: Basic Books, 1986), 60–61, 68–69, 76–78; Robert H. Bremner, *The Public Good: Philanthropy and Welfare in the Civil War Era* (New York: Alfred A. Knopf, 1980).

51 Robert H. Bremner, *The Public Good: Philanthropy and Welfare in the Civil War Era* (New York: Alfred A. Knopf, 1980), 146; Bellows as quoted in Bremner, *The Public Good*, 146, and Attie, *Patriotic Toil*, 245; Henry Bellows to Stephen G. Perkins, Esq., Document 67, in *Documents of the U.S. Sanitary Commission*, vol. 2 (New York: United States Sanitary Commission, 1866), 6–10; Knapp as quoted in Jeannie Attie, *Patriotic Toil: Northern Women and the American Civil War* (Ithaca: Cornell University Press, 1998), 243–244; see also Valeria Campbell to "Miss Brayton," 19 September 1865, in James Valentine Campbell Papers, Valeria Campbell Materials, Box 3, Bentley Historical Library, University of Michigan.

52 Frances M. Clarke, *War Stories: Suffering and Sacrifice in the Civil War North* (Chicago: University of Chicago Press, 2011), 6–7, 48–50; W. Fletcher Thompson, *The Image of War: The Pictorial Reporting of the American Civil War* (New York: Thomas Yoseloff, 1960), 184; Mark E. Neely, Jr., and Harold Holzer, *The Union Image: Popular Prints of the Civil War North* (Chapel Hill: University of North Carolina Press, 2000). On the "good death," see Faust, *This Republic of Suffering*, 6; John McElroy as quoted in Ezra Hoyt Ripple, *Dancing Along the Deadline: The Andersonville Memoir of a Prisoner of the Confederacy*, ed. Mark A. Snell (Novato, California: Presidio Press, 1996), 5–6; Charles W. Dodge to WOB, 23 September 1865, in WOB Papers, Manuscript Division, LoC.

53 Thomas Fitzgibbon to Francis Willett Shearman, letter, 8 April 1865, in Francis Willett Shearman Papers, Box 1, Folder 1, Bentley Historical Library, University of Michigan; Sean A. Scott, *A Visitation of God: Northern Civilians Interpret the Civil War* (New York: Oxford University Press, 2011), 244; See Elizabeth Leonard, *Lincoln's Avengers: Justice, Revenge, and Reunion After the Civil War* (New York: W. W. Norton & Co., 2004); Leonard, *Lincoln's Forgotten Ally: Judge Advo-*

cate General Joseph Holt of Kentucky (Chapel Hill: University of North Carolina Press, 2011).

54 James Dalzell, "The Blue and The Gray," poem in *Soldier's Friend* (December 1867), copy at American Antiquarian Society, Worchester, Massachusetts; Blight, *Race and Reunion*. For similar sentiments, see also "Forget The Soldier?" in *Soldier's Friend* (January 1868). For the literature on reunion, see Blight, *Race and Reunion*; Silber, *The Romance of Reunion*; Blum, *Reforging the White Republic*; and Richardson, *West from Appomattox*.

55 "The Voice of a Soldier," *Soldier's Friend* (June 1867), copy at American Antiquarian Society, Worcester, Massachusetts.

56 Quoted in the *Argus and Patriot*, 1 November 1866; "What a Soldier Thinks," *Soldier's Friend* (July 1867); "From the 20th Regiment," *Connecticut War Record* 2, no. 10 (May 1865); William Henry Church to Ella Church, 5 June 1865, in William H. Church Civil War Papers, Folder 2, WiHS.

57 Robert J. Rothwell, undated letter to WOB, in MS 1273, Civil War Records, Box 3, Butler Library, Columbia University; Robert J. Rothwell Pension File, RG 15, NA.

58 James M. Dalzell, "The Veterans Begging," *Soldier's Friend* (March 1868); James Dalzell Pension File, RG 15, NA; "Forget the Soldier?" in *Soldier's Friend* (January 1868), American Antiquarian Society; On the *Inter Ocean*, see *A History of the City of Chicago: Its Men and Institutions* (Chicago: Published by the Inter Ocean, 1900), 319; *Inter Ocean*, 14 July 1877, 26 December 1874, 10 September 1881; *Delmarva Star*, 9 March 1924; *Cleveland Herald*, 17 September 1883; see also Eugene Payne, address to the Fremont Rifles, in Eugene Payne Speech, SC 2701, Abraham Lincoln Presidential Library.

59 Henry H. Baltzell, memoir, in Henry Baltzell Memoir, SC 2717, Abraham Lincoln Presidential Library; "A Soldier's Retrospect," *Soldiers' and Sailors' Half Dime Magazine* (1868).

60 William Oland Bourne, "Out of Work," *Soldier's Friend* (October 1865).

CHAPTER 3: ITHACA AT LAST

1 "The Soldiers' Reunion," *Daily Iowa State Register*, 5 June 1867; *The History of Iowa County, Iowa* (Des Moines: Union Historical Co., 1881), 490; Augustus Vignos Compiled Service Record, RG 94, NARA. Vignos fought with the 107th Ohio Volunteers and lost his right arm in the fight for Blocher's Knoll on the first day of the battle of Gettysburg. Active on the veteran circuit, he became the postmaster of Canton, Ohio, where he went into business peddling pocketknives.

2 "The Soldiers' Reunion," *Daily Iowa State Register*, 5 June 1867; *The History of Iowa County, Iowa*, 490.

3 Gerald Linderman, *Embattled Courage: The Experience of Combat in the American Civil War* (New York: Free Press, 1987), 267, 268, 271, 275, 278, 280. Linderman may have based his periodization on the earlier and equally important study of Union veterans by Mary R. Dearing, *Veterans in Politics: The Story of the G.A.R.* (Baton Rouge: Louisiana State University Press, 1952). Though she cautioned that "it would be easy to underestimate the veterans' importance" in the 1870s, Dearing deemed the decade "the quiescent years." Dearing, *Veterans in Politics*, 185. Stuart McConnell, in his more recent study of the Grand Army of the Republic, wrote that immediately after the war, "Northern soldiers showed little inclination to dwell on the war." McConnell, *Glorious Contentment*, 20. See also Earl J. Hess, *The Union Soldier in Battle: Enduring the Ordeal of Combat* (Lawrence: University Press of Kansas, 1997). Historians, most notably James Marten, consider Union veterans "creatures of the Gilded Age." One measure of Linderman's influence on the field is the percolation of his "hibernation" thesis into the realm of popular military history. "At first the veterans, young men still, turned aside thoughts of the war and what it cost," writes Lance Herdegen in his military history of the Iron Brigade. See Herdegen, *The Iron Brigade in Civil War and Memory: The Black Hats from Bull Run to Appomattox and Thereafter* (El Dorado Hills, California: Savas Beatie, 2011), 599.

4 Frederick Walster, diary entry, 13 October 1865, in Civil War Manuscripts Collection, Frederick Walster Diary, Special Collections and University Archives, Glenn G. Bartle Library, State University of New York at Binghamton; *Davenport Daily Gazette*, 20 June 1865; *Constitution of the Grand Veteran League of New Hampshire* (Concord: McFarland & Jenks, 1865); John A. Johnson to A. Willich, 22 October 1866, John A. Johnson Collection, WiHS; Allen Fahnestock, diary entry, 28 August 1865, in Allen Fahnestock Diary, Abraham Lincoln Presidential Library.

5 Sarah McLean to Edgar McLean, letter, 5 July 1865, Edgar McLean Papers, Box 1, Folder 57, Newberry Library. Cleary, whose "rambling during the whole period," according to one deponent, "has been always upon matters relating to the civil war," was later admitted to the Northern Hospital for the Insane near Oskosh, Wisconsin. His condition did not improve, and nobody at the asylum could "get any rational talk from him, but incoherent language relating to army life." See Affidavit of William Cunningham on Patrick Cleary, 28 February 1896, in A. O. Wright Papers, Box 2, WiHS.

6 Oliver Perry Newberry, letter, 30 December 1864, Oliver Perry Newberry Papers, Box 1, Folder 12, Newberry Library; Oliver Perry Newberry Pension File, application no. 268,369, certificate no. 531,366, RG 15, Records of the Veterans Administration, Civil War Pension Files, NARA; Oliver Perry Newberry to

Cousin Fanny, 16 September 1867, Oliver Perry Newberry Papers, Box 1, Folder 15, Newberry Library; Lydia Elizabeth Newberry to "dear Brother," 25 January 1866, Oliver Perry Newberry Papers, Box 1, Folder 13; Lydia Elizabeth Newberry to Walter Newberry, 5 August 1867, Oliver Perry Newberry Papers, Box 1, Folder 14.

7 *Grand Army Journal*, 16 July 1870; C. D. Clark, "Grierson's Raiders," *Soldiers' and Sailors' Half Dime Tales* 1, no. 1 (1868): 3.

8 Eugene Payne, speech to the Fremont Rifles, in Eugene Payne Speech, SC 2701, Abraham Lincoln Presidential Library; Eliakim Torrance, address, 4 July 1866, Ell Torrance Papers, Box 34, MinnHS. For the blood-soaked history of Reconstruction, see George C. Rable, *But There Was No Peace: The Role of Violence in the Politics of Reconstruction* (Athens: University of Georgia Press, 1984); James G. Hollandsworth, *An Absolute Massacre: The New Orleans Race Riot of July 30, 1866* (Baton Rouge: Louisiana State University Press, 2001); and James K. Hogue, *Uncivil War: Five New Orleans Street Battles and the Rise and Fall of Radical Reconstruction* (Baton Rouge: Louisiana State University Press, 2006); Samuel Dickson to Samuel Bloomer, 31 August 1866, Box 2, Folder 3, Samuel Bloomer Papers, MinnHS; Illinois veteran as quoted in Summers, *A Dangerous Stir*, 135; Dearing, *Veterans in Politics*, 102, 107; Eugene Payne, speech to the Fremont Rifles, in Eugene Payne Speech, SC 2701, Abraham Lincoln Presidential Library; T. S. Atlee, editorial, in *Grand Army Journal*, 18 June 1870.

9 James J. Creigh, *Oration and Poem Delivered Before Right Honorable Legion of Veterans of Chester and Delaware Counties, Pennsylvania* (West Chester, Pennsylvania: W. W. Miller, Bookseller, 1866), 19; Summers, *A Dangerous Stir*, 47; *The Union Must and Shall Be Preserved: National Convention of Union Soldiers and Sailors Held at Cleveland, Ohio, Monday, Sept. 17, 1866*; Butler as quoted in *The Great Republic*, 4 October 1866, copy at American Antiquarian Society; "The Ku Klux Outrages," *Grand Army Journal*, 25 March 1871; on the Klan, see also *Grand Army Journal*, 13 May 1871; Creigh, *Oration and Poem*, 15. See also John R. Neff, *Honoring the Civil War Dead: Commemoration and the Problem of Reconciliation* (Lawrence: University Press of Kansas, 2005), and Barbara A. Gannon, *The Won Cause: Black and White Comradeship in the Grand Army of the Republic* (Chapel Hill: University of North Carolina Press, 2011).

10 "Soldier's Monuments," *Grand Army Journal*, 6 August 1870; *Report of the Thirty-Ninth Annual Reunion of the 52nd Illinois Veteran Volunteer Association* (Chicago: Binner-Wells Co., 1906), 14–15; Stephen P. Chase Diary, *Civil War Times* Illustrated Collection, 2nd series, Box 31, United States Army Military History Institute; W. H. Doll, undated remarks delivered at reunion of the 6th Indiana Volunteers, in Box 1, Folder 13, William Stanley Mead Collec-

tion, InHS; Wilson Hopkins as quoted in John Schildt, *Roads to Antietam* (Chewsville, Maryland: Antietam Publications, 1985), 107.

11 Creigh, *Oration and Poem*, 15; John Haley, 9 June 1865, in Silliker, ed., *The Rebel Yell and the Yankee Hurrah*, 283; McConnell, *Glorious Contentment*, 24; Susan-Mary Grant, "Reimagined Communities: Union Veterans and the Reconstruction of American Nationalism," *Nations and Nationalism* 14, no. 3 (July 2008): 498–519.

12 For more on the "distinctiveness" of Union veterans, see also Marten, *Sing Not War*, chap. 6; "Returned Soldiers," in *Soldier's and Sailor's Almanac for 1865*, copy in Nicholson Collection, Huntington Library; on veterans as "cranks," see *Relief Guard*, 30 August 1890, copy at MinnHS; for the references to "tiresome back numbers," see Union Veterans' Union circular, dated 4 July 1905, in Union Veterans' Union Records, Box 1, MinnHS; and George N. Lamphere, "Experiences and Observations of a Private Soldier in the Civil War," in George N. Lamphere Papers, Institute for Regional Studies and Archives, NDSU.

13 A. V. Randall, letter to "Comrades," 12 September 1913, in 104th Pennsylvania Survivors' Association Records, Box 1, GARMA; on the personal significance of discharge dates, see O. W. Baldwin to William A. Rand, letter (1887), in William A. Rand Papers, Box 1, Folder 1, NHHS; Erie L. Ditty, "Memoirs of a Lieutenant in the Civil War," in Stearns Family Papers—Civil War Correspondence, Box 4, Folder 2, Carol Newman Library, Virginia Polytechnic Institute; Lyman Jackman, diary entries, 30 September 1865, 6 May 1874, and 12 May 1874, in Lyman Jackman Diaries, 1862–1901, NHHS; *Veterans of the War Whom All Should Assist: Almanac and History of the Late Rebellion, 1860–1865* (New York: Soldiers' & Sailors' Publishing Co., 1869); *Souvenir, Principal Events and Battles of the Rebellion* [circa 1885], copy in Captain G. F. Sparrow Collection, Envelope 3, MaineHS. *Soldier's and Sailor's Almanac for 1869*.

14 Hayes as quoted in Brian Matthew Jordan, "Fighting for South Mountain: How the Army of the Potomac Won a Crucial Battle but Lost Control of Its Legacy," *Civil War Monitor* 2, no. 2 (Summer 2012): 52–59, 77–79. On Hayes and Civil War memory, see also Brooks D. Simpson, "The Good Colonel: Rutherford B. Hayes Remembers the Civil War," Fourteenth Annual Hayes Lecture on the Presidency, 16 February 2003, copy at Rutherford B. Hayes Presidential Center.

15 Wallace Evan Davies, *Patriotism on Parade: The Story of Veterans' and Hereditary Organizations in America, 1783–1900* (Cambridge: Harvard University Press, 1955), 105; Dearing, *Veterans in Politics*, 117, 119; *Proceedings of the First to Tenth Meetings, 1866–1876, of the National Encampment, Grand Army of the Republic* (Philadelphia: Samuel P. Town, Printer, 1877), 10; *Soldier's and Sailor's Almanac for 1869*; *Soldiers' and Sailors' Half Dime Tales* 1, no. 1 (1868); William T. Collins,

"The Grand Army Journal," *Grand Army Journal,* 6 May 1871; *Grand Army Journal,* 30 December 1871; Lloyd Lewis, *The Assassination of Abraham Lincoln: History and Myth,* revised ed. (Lincoln: University of Nebraska Press, 1994), 312–313; *Leavenworth Bulletin,* 2 July 1871; *St. Alban's Messenger,* 20 May 1870; Alex C. Botkin, *Legislative Manual of the State of Montana* (Helena: James B. Walker & Co., 1895), 165.

16 Davies, *Patriotism on Parade,* 107; Marten, *Sing Not War,* 147–148; *Soldier's Record,* September 1875; *Relief Guard,* 30 August 1890, MinnHS; *Weekly Knight and Soldier,* KaHS; *N. W. Ayer & Sons American Newspaper Annual* (Philadelphia: N. W. Ayer & Sons, 1884), 938; *The Veteran's Advocate,* 22 April 1884, 5 February 1884, and 9 December 1884, NHHS.

17 Davies, *Patriotism on Parade,* 106; "Earning a Pension," *National Tribune,* 31 January 1889. On the *National Tribune,* see Richard Allen Sauers, *"To Care for Whom Who Has Borne the Battle": A Research Guide to Civil War Material in the* National Tribune (Jackson, Kentucky: History Shop Press, 1995); Richard Allen Sauers, *Fighting Them Over: How the Veterans Remembered Gettysburg in the Pages of the National Tribune* (Baltimore: Butternut & Blue, 1998), i; Ezra de Freest Simons, *A Regimental History: The One Hundred Twenty-Fifth New York State Volunteers* (New York: E. D. Simons, 1888), 159, 258, 259. Theda Skocpol notes that Lemon "launched the National Tribune . . . in order to agitate for arrears legislation." See Skocpol, *Protecting Soldiers and Mothers: The Political Origins of Social Policy in the United States* (Cambridge: Harvard University Press, 1992), 116–117; Arthur S. Fitch, "Thick of the Fight: Some Tragic Scenes at the Battle of Dallas, Ga.," *National Tribune,* 15 November 1883; "William J. Bolton," *National Tribune,* 29 November 1883; William Kutz, "Beat It Who Can," *National Tribune,* 3 January 1884; Chauncey Fish, "Wounded in the Back," *National Tribune,* 20 March 1884; George Pettibone, "The Heavy Mortality at Salisbury," *National Tribune,* 6 September 1883; Perry I. Quick, "The Pitiful Experience of a Union Prisoner in Southern Pens," *National Tribune,* 6 December 1883; H. C. Cartwell, "As to the Dead-Line," *National Tribune,* 27 September 1883; see, for example, "The Hue and the Cry," *National Tribune,* 1 February 1883. According to the editor of one veterans' newspaper, nearly "every day" civilians derisively asked, " 'What is your object in publishing a soldier's paper?'" "Our Object," *Soldier's Record,* 26 September 1870; *Weekly Knight and Soldier,* 5 October 1887; "A Suggestive Comparison," *National Tribune,* 18 January 1883. Similarly, Hoosier veterans delighted in the Indianapolis *American Tribune,* a weekly Grand Army newspaper, which compared the soldiers' sacrifices with the treasonous "disloyalty" of the Copperhead Democrats back home. On the *American Tribune,* see James H. Madison, "Civil War Memories and 'Pardnership Forgittin',' 1865–1913," *Indiana Magazine of*

History 99, no. 3 (September 2003): 206; "Our Object," *Soldier's Record*, 26 September 1870.

18 J. P. Coleman, 22 December 1882, in *National Tribune*, 25 January 1883; for another example of a veteran compelled to write up his experiences after perusing the pages of the tribune, see Asbury Thornhill, undated letter, in Asbury Thornhill Letter, KaHS. "Pittsburg Landing: A Review of the Mooted Points," and "Vindication of the Right Wing by A Participant," *National Tribune*, 1 February 1883; David H. Smith, "Mortality at Florence and Salisbury," *National Tribune*, 23 August 1883; see, for example, Walter B. Norton, "The Last Word About the First Shot," *National Tribune*, 24 April 1884; Charles Ruff, "Who Opened the Battle of Gettysburg?" *National Tribune*, 15 November 1883; "How General Reno Was Killed," *National Tribune*, 13 September 1883; George D. Moore, "Were Spears Used at Knoxville," S. F. Brown, "A Comrade Who Saw the Spears," and Austin Curtin, "Another Comrade Who Never Saw the Spears," in *National Tribune*, 1 November 1883; see also Sauers, *Fighting Them Over*, ii, 79–81. On the struggle over who fired the first shot at Gettysburg, see J. David Petruzzi, "Opening the Ball at Gettysburg: The Shot That Rang For Fifty Years," *America's Civil War* 19, no. 3 (2006): 30–36.

19 Abraham Kile to Samuel Bloomer, 12 July 1902, and Samuel Bloomer to Abraham Kile, 17 December 1902, in Samuel Bloomer Papers, Box 2, Folder 6, MinnHS. See also Henry Irving to Wright Gilbert, 19 November 1900, in Wright Gilbert Papers, Carol Newman Library, Virginia Polytechnic Institute.

20 Logan Meade Boren, *National Tribune*, 25 January 1883; John Rutt, *National Tribune*, 1 February 1883; George Sparrow, "W-A-R Scrapbook," in Captain G. F. Sparrow Collection, MaineHS. Elijah Cavins likewise kept a scrapbook of clippings from the *National Tribune*. See Elijah Cavins Collection, Box 2, Folder 11, InHS.

21 Mark C. Carnes, *Secret Ritual and Manhood in Victorian America* (New Haven: Yale University Press, 1989), 14. On the history of the Grand Army of the Republic, see Robert Burns Beath, *History of the Grand Army of the Republic* (New York: Bryan, Taylor & Co., 1889); McConnell, *Glorious Contentment*; Dearing, *Veterans in Politics*, 80–85; James Pickett Jones, *Black Jack: John A. Logan and Southern Illinois in the Civil War Era* (Tallahassee: Florida State University Press, 1967), 273–275; Marcus Benjamin, "Patriotic Societies of the Civil War," *Munsey's Magazine* 15 (1896): 322–331; Mary Logan, *Reminiscences of the Civil War and Reconstruction*, 145–148; and General Orders No. 19, circular, 30 December 1868, in Grand Army of the Republic, Morrison Post No. 80 [Morrison, Illinois] Records, Abraham Lincoln Presidential Library; Elijah Cavins, draft of speech for Grand Army of the Republic reunion, circa 1900, in Elijah Cavins Papers,

Box 2, Folder 3, InHS; Joseph Wright Johnson, undated Grand Army notes, in Joseph Wright Johnson Papers, Box 1, Series 3, Folder 1, NHS.

22 This impression of the Grand Army has been shaped most significantly by Dearing, *Veterans in Politics*. Ritual Book of Johnston H. Skelly Post No. 9, Grand Army of the Republic, in Johnston H. Skelly Post No. 9, Grand Army of the Republic Collection, Box 9, Adams County Historical Society; Charity Fund Ledger Book, in Grand Army of the Republic Collection, Sedgwick Post. No. 17 Records, Box 3, USAMHI; Quartermaster Report of J. K. Taylor Post No. 182, dated 30 June 1882, in J. K. Taylor Post No. 182 Collection, Box 11, GARMA; Skelly Post Financial Records, in Box 5, Johnston H. Skelly Post No. 9, Grand Army of the Republic Collection, Adams County Historical Society; E. W. Kinsley Post No. 113, Grand Army of the Republic, minutes for 15 April 1872, in Kinsley Post Minute Book (1872–1876), E. W. Kinsley Post No. 113 Papers, Carton 1, Massachusetts Historical Society; "Prompt Response," *Summit County Beacon*, 19 May 1880; see, for example, remarks of veteran O. S. Hinsdale, who promised to reimburse the relief fund upon receipt of his next pension payment, in minutes of John Fulton Reynolds Post No. 5, Grand Army of the Republic, 7 March 1898, Post Minute Book, Reynolds Post No. 5 Records, Folder 2, Institute for Regional Studies, NDSU. Relief payments were dispersed so frequently and routinely that some posts authorized relief committees to "use their discretion" rather than insist on the acquiescence of the membership at-large. See Farragut Post No. 28, Grand Army of the Republic minutes, 25 February 1885, in Farragut Post No. 28 Minute Book, vol. 3, Department of New Jersey, Grand Army of the Republic Collection, NJHSL. On relief fund benefit lectures, see, for example, tickets for E. B. Walcott Post No. 1 Relief Fund Benefit, 16 October 1894, featuring a lecture by Col. Nicholas Smith, "War Songs and Their Influence," in Augustus Gordon Weissert Papers, Box 5, Folder 7, WiVMA; "The Grand Army," *Daily Inter Ocean*, 11 December 1880; "At Grand Army Hall," *Evening News*, 17 January 1887; "Grand Army of the Republic," *Philadelphia Inquirer*, 20 January 1871.

23 Post meeting minutes, 13 January 1891, in Minute Book [1891–1896], E. W. Kinsley Post No. 113, Grand Army of the Republic, E. W. Kinsley Post No. 113 Papers, Carton 1, Massachusetts Historical Society; "Introduction and Greeting," *Official Souvenir Program of the Twenty-Fourth Annual Encampment* (Boston: George H. Richards, Jr. & Co., 1890); *The Boston Almanac and Business Directory*, vol. 59 (Boston: Sampson, Murdock & Co., 1894), 386; George H. Herbert, *The Popular History of the Civil War in America* (New York: F. M. Lupton, 1885), 443–444; Grand Army of the Republic Beneficial Association circular, n.d., in Charles Henry Wilson Papers, Box 6, Folder 2, NHS; Logan, *Reminiscences of the Civil War and Reconstruction*, 149.

24 Reunion Record Book in Company A, 25th Massachusetts Association Records, WHM; see also Amos Edward Stearns, *Narrative of Amos E. Stearns, Member Co. A., 25th Regiment, Massachusetts Volunteers, A Prisoner at Andersonville* (Worcester, Massachusetts: Franklin Rice, 1887); and Joseph Waldo Denny, *Wearing the Blue in the Twenty-Fifth Mass. Volunteer Infantry* (Worcester, Massachusetts: Putnam & Davis, 1879), 370–373.

25 George E. Goodrich, "Thirty-Fourth Massachusetts Regiment Association Circular," 1 December 1870, copy on Civil War Papers Microfilm, reel 2, Massachusetts Historical Society; *Soldier's Casket* (November 1865): 643, Nicholson Collection, Huntington Library; Henry Dillon, address to reunion of the Sixth Wisconsin Battery Association [circa 1881], in Henry Dillon Papers, Box 2, Folder 13, WiHS; circular for Veteran Association of the 134th New York State Volunteer Infantry [circa 1889], Henry B. Bradt Family Papers, New York State Archives; on "sites of memory," see Jay Winter, *Sites of Memory, Sites of Mourning*; and Winter, *Remembering War in the Twentieth Century*; Minutes of Reunions, 1868–1872, 52nd Illinois Veteran Volunteer Infantry Reunion Association Records, Abraham Lincoln Presidential Library; 34th Illinois Volunteers Veterans Association Records, Lincoln Presidential Library; see, for only one example, the minutes of the Company A, 25th Massachusetts Association, 3 June 1875, in Reunion Record Book, Company A, 25th Massachusetts Association Records, WHM.

26 Ex-prisoner-of-war associations will be treated in greater detail in chap. 5. See also Brian Matthew Jordan, "Captive Memories: Union Ex-Prisoners of War and the Work of Remembrance," *Civil War Monitor* 1, no. 1 (2011); "Federal Soldiers' and Sailors' Societies," *Detroit Journal Year-Book* (Detroit: Detroit Journal Co., 1890), 64. On the Crippled Soldiers Association, see J. A. Underwood, General Order No. 9, Crippled Soldiers Association, *Kansas Knight and Soldier*, 1 May 1887; partial list of organizations found in William Stanley Mead Collection, Box 1, Folder 10, InHS. On the Military Order of the Loyal Legion, a society for Civil War officers, see Robert Girard Carroon and Dana B. Shoaf, *Union Blue: The History of the Military Order of the Loyal Legion of the United States* (Shippensburg, Pennsylvania: White Mane Publishing, 2001); on the Union Veteran Army, "organized for the purposes of securing justice and honor to all those who faithfully served the Government during the rebellion," see Charles Henry Wilson Papers, Box 6, Folder 3, NHS; on the National Association of Naval Veterans, see Cameron Rotblat, "Last in the Hearts of Their Countrymen: Union Naval Veterans and the Struggle for Naval Memory," seminar paper, Yale University, May 2012 (copy in author's possession); *Proceedings of the First Annual Meeting of the National Association of the Battle of Shiloh Survivors, Minneapolis, Minnesota, August 14, 1906*; circu-

lar for Battle of Shiloh Survivors Association [circa 1917], Isaac N. Carr Papers, Box 6, Folder 6, SHSIo; Samuel Meek Howard, *The Illustrated Comprehensive History of the Great Battle of Shiloh* (Kansas City, Missouri: Franklin Hudson Publishing Co., 1921), 181–185; Benjamin F. Gue, *History of Iowa: From the Earliest Times to the Beginning of the Twentieth Century*, vol. 4 (New York: Century History Co., 1903), 264; *Journal of the Senate of the Forty-second General Assembly* (Des Moines: State of Iowa, 1927), 1604.

27 The 82nd Illinois Volunteers Association, for example, was subjected to some of these journalistic slights. See Mark A. Dluger, "A Regimental Community: The Men of the 82nd Illinois Infantry Before, During, and After the American Civil War" (Ph.D. diss., Loyola University of Chicago, 2009), 397–398; *Dayton Daily Empire*, 1 September 1866; *Daily Ohio Statesman*, 19 September 1866; Address of Illinois veteran, as quoted in *Report of the Thirty-Ninth Annual Reunion of the 52nd Illinois*, 15; "The Braying of Asses," *Grand Army Scout and Soldiers' Mail*, 16 August 1884. Responding to the attack, Grand Army comrades offered up evidence of their charitable work. "It can be safely alleged that the humblest comrade of the Grand Army has done and is doing more unselfish work for the amelioration of the condition of his unfortunate fellow men than the foremost and influential of the men who . . . blather in denunciation of an organization about which they apparently know nothing," they retorted. "And we believe that it can be proved that in real, genuine charity the Grand Army is doing a work unequalled by any denomination of the Christian church in the land, to say nothing of the set of pharisaical fools calling themselves the United Presbytery of Keokuk"; Ohio veteran, address at 1878 reunion, as quoted in Charles Dana Miller, *Report of the Great Reunion of the Veteran Soldiers and Sailors of Ohio* (Newark, Ohio: Clark & Underwood, 1879), 304–305, Nicholson Collection, Huntington Library; *Report of the Thirty-Ninth Annual Reunion of the 52nd Illinois*, 14–15; for similar sentiments, see Samuel Graham to J. B. Whitaker, letter, 10 April 1868, in J. B. Whitaker Collection, Box 1, Folder 26, KSRL.

28 A. E. Ford as quoted in minutes of the 15th Massachusetts Association meeting, 21 October 1897, in Record Book of the 15th Massachusetts Association, 15th Massachusetts Collection, Folder 3, WHM; see also Andrew Elmer Ford, *The Story of the Fifteenth Regiment Massachusetts Volunteer Infantry in the Civil War, 1861–1864* (Clinton, Massachusetts: Press of W. J. Coulter, 1898); Stephen Z. Starr, "The Grand Old Regiment," *Wisconsin Magazine of History* 48, no. 1 (1964): 21–31; Crompton B. Burton, " 'The Dear Old Regiment': Maine's Regimental Associations and the Memory of the American Civil War," *New England Quarterly* 84, no. 1 (March 2011): 104–122; Hess, *The Union Soldier in Battle*.

29 Orton Clark, regimental historian of the 116th New York, to John Mead Gould,

letter, 16 March 1870, John Mead Gould Collection, Folder 1, MaineHS. On the arduous process of researching and writing, see also newspaper clipping relating to the publication of the 15th Connecticut regimental history, dated June 1892, in Sheldon Thorpe Collection, North Haven Historical Society; A. E. Ford as quoted in minutes of the 15th Massachusetts Association meeting, 21 October 1897, in Record Book of the 15th Massachusetts Association, 15th Massachusetts Collection, Folder 3, WHM; Eugene Payne quoted in minutes of the 34th Illinois Volunteers Veterans' Association, 27–30 August 1900, in 34th Illinois Volunteers Veterans' Association Records, Folder 1, Abraham Lincoln Presidential Library; Woodbury Dana to Gould, 25 July 1870, in John Mead Gould Collection, Folder 2, MaineHS; Thomas Clark to Gould, letter, 25 February 1871, in Gould Collection, Folder 3, MaineHS. See also Joseph L. Horr, circular and proof sheets for *History of the First Battalion, Thirteenth Infantry*, in Joseph L. Horr Papers, Carol Newman Library, Virginia Polytechnic Institute; Daniel Hall to Asa Bartlett, letter, 21 March 1892; John F. Marsh to Asa Bartlett, letter, 20 March 1897; Albert Merrill to Asa Bartlett, 12 April 1896, and Wes Chancellor to Asa Bartlett, letter, 26 February 1889, in Asa Bartlett Papers, Box 1, Folder 6, NHHS; *Proceedings of the Bar Association of the State of New Hampshire* 1, no. 1 (Concord: Rumford Press, 1900–1903), 87. See also David T. Thackery, *A Light and Uncertain Hold: A History of the Sixty-Sixth Ohio Volunteer Infantry* (Kent, Ohio: Kent State University Press, 1999), 235; and Cilella, Jr., *Upton's Regulars*, 435–457. Even veterans who remained "ambivalent" about their experiences in the ranks contributed "personal incidents" to regimental historians. Peter C. Luebke, "Introduction," in Tourgée, *The Story of a Thousand*, xxi; Starr, "The Grand Old Regiment," 24–25; Burton, " 'The Dear Old Regiment,' " 104, 112; on the "outsiders" as regimental historians, see especially Mark H. Dunkelman, *Brothers One and All: Esprit de Corps in a Civil War Regiment* (Baton Rouge: Louisiana State University Press, 2004), 268–275.

30 Starr, "The Grand Old Regiment," 25; *The War of the Rebellion: A Compilation of the Official Records of the Union and Confederate Armies*, serial no. 130 (Washington, D.C.: Government Printing Office, 1881–1901), iii–xxi; Joan Waugh, *U.S. Grant: American Hero, American Myth* (Chapel Hill: University of North Carolina Press, 2009), 169–170; *The War of the Rebellion: A Compilation of the Official Records of the Union and Confederate Armies*, serial no. 130, vi; comments of Hosea Rood in Grand Army of the Republic Memorial Hall Records, Box 3, Folder 1, WiVMA; on Rood, see Thomas J. McCrory, *Grand Army of the Republic, Department of Wisconsin* (Black Earth, Wisconsin: Trails Books, 2005), 53–54, 296–297; John A. Simpson, *S. A. Cunningham and the Confederate Heritage* (Athens: University of Georgia Press, 1994); and Marten, *Sing Not War*, 149–152; Hosea Rood,

"Grand Army Corner" column, undated, in Grand Army of the Republic Memorial Hall Records, Box 2, Folder 2, WiVMA; John Vautier as quoted in Luebke, "Introduction," xxv; William Marvel, "Introduction and History of the Military Order of the Loyal Legion of the United States," in *Biographical Sketches of the Contributors to the Military Order of the Loyal Legion of the United States*, comp. Marvel (Wilmington, North Carolina: Broadfoot Publishing Co., 1995), 3–6; see also Soldiers' and Sailors' Historical Society Collection, Reports and Constitution, Box 2, Folder 21, Rhode Island Historical Society. For an excellent example of a veteran who deployed these sources in his writing, see Ezra A. Carman, *The Maryland Campaign of September 1862, Vol. 1: South Mountain*, ed. Thomas G. Clemens (El Dorado Hills, California: Savas Beatie, 2010), xv–xvi.

31 For works characterizing regimental histories as a sentimentalized genre, see Linderman, *Embattled Courage*, 280; McConnell, *Glorious Contentment*; Blight, *Race and Reunion*; and Alice Fahs, *The Imagined Civil War: Popular Literature of the North and South, 1861–1865* (Chapel Hill: University of North Carolina Press, 2003), 313–314. My argument here builds on Robert Hunt, *The Good Men Who Won the War: Army of the Cumberland Veterans and Emancipation Memory* (Tuscaloosa: University of Alabama Press, 2010), 1–8, 42–43; M. Keith Harris, "Across the Bloody Chasm: Reconciliation in the Wake of Civil War" (Ph.D. diss., University of Virginia, 2009), 20, 149n215, 178–181, quote at 179; and Gallagher, *The Union War*, 65–70; Jacob Smith, *Camps and Campaigns of the 107th Regiment Ohio Volunteer Infantry*, ed. Mark L. Gaynor (Navarre, Ohio: Indian River Graphics, 2000), 4. Similarly, Evan Morrison Woodward noted that his "object" in writing a history of the Second Pennsylvania Reserves was to provide the public with "insight into the life of a soldier." Woodward, *Our Campaigns: The Second Regiment Pennsylvania Reserve Volunteers, 1861–1864*, ed. Stanley W. Zamonski (Shippensburg, Pennsylvania: Burd Street Press, 1995), xiii; Edward Oliver Lord, *History of the Ninth Regiment, New Hampshire Volunteers in the War of the Rebellion* (Concord, New Hampshire: Republican Press Association, 1895), 1–2; Gustav Tafel, "Foreword," in Constantine Grebner, *We Were the Ninth: A History of the Ninth Regiment, Ohio Volunteer Infantry, April 17, 1861 to June 7, 1864*, 2nd ed., trans. and ed. Frederic Trautmann (Kent, Ohio: Kent State University Press, 1987), 3.

32 The historian Earl J. Hess has written that northern veterans "produced the most voluminous collection of memoirs to come from any American war." Hess, *The Union Soldier in Battle*, 196. On the significance of veterans' memoirs, see also Craig A. Warren, *Scars to Prove It: The Civil War Soldier and American Fiction* (Kent, Ohio: Kent State University Press, 2009). See also Harris, "Across the Bloody Chasm," 181; Linderman, *Embattled Courage*, 266; Daniel Eldredge, letter

to Pension Bureau, 21 December 1883, in Daniel Eldredge Pension File, application no. 119,073, certificate no. 80,269, RG 15, Records of the Veterans Administration, Civil War Pension Files, NARA; Daniel Eldredge, manuscript history [1865–1867], in Daniel Eldredge Papers, NHHS.

33 Hess, *The Union Soldier in Battle*, 161; George Bliss, "Reminiscences of Service in the 1st Rhode Island Cavalry," dated 11 April 1877, in Soldiers' and Sailors' Historical Society Collection, Box 2, Folder 4, Rhode Island Historical Society; Solon Pierce, *Battlefields and Campfires of the Thirty-Eighth* (Milwaukee: Daily Wisconsin Printing House, 1866), preface; R. W. Browne to Robert Underwood Johnson, letter, 18 August 1887, in *Century* Collection, Civil War Letters, Box 117, Rare Books and Manuscripts Division, New York Public Library; Hess, *The Union Soldier in Battle*, 161; Daniel Aaron, *The Unwritten War: American Writers and the Civil War* (New York: Alfred A. Knopf, 1973), xiv. On soldiers' war memoirs in general, see Samuel Lynn Hynes, *The Soldiers' Tale: Bearing Witness to Modern War* (New York: Penguin Books, 1997), esp. xiii. See also *Western Veteran*, 29 October 1890; T. G. Boss to *Century Magazine*, letter, 12 March 1886, in *Century* Collection, Civil War Papers, Box 117, Rare Books and Manuscripts Division, New York Public Library; Daniel R. Ballou, "The Military Services of Major General Ambrose Everett Burnside," n.d., in Soldiers' and Sailors' Historical Society Collection, Box 2, Folder 3, Rhode Island Historical Society; Hunt, *The Good Men Who Won the War*, 2–3.

34 Mark J. Noonan, *Reading* The Century Illustrated Monthly Magazine: *American Literature and Culture, 1870–1893* (Kent, Ohio: Kent State University Press, 2010), x; On the *Century* "War Series," see Noonan, *Reading* The Century Illustrated Monthly Magazine, 154–175; Blight, *Race and Reunion*, 164, 173–174; and Waugh, *U.S. Grant*, 169–171. See also Clarence Clough Buel and Robert Underwood Johnson, eds., *Battles and Leaders of the Civil War*, 4 vols., reprint ed. (New York: Thomas Yoseloff, 1956).

35 Robert Underwood Johnson to James Longstreet, 3 April 1884, in Letterbook 1, Robert Underwood Johnson Letterbooks, Rare Books and Manuscripts Division, New York Public Library; Robert Underwood Johnson to Adam Badeau, 8 April 1884; Johnson to Joseph E. Johnston, 8 April 1884; Johnson to James P. Smith, 5 June 1884, and Johnson to Pierre G. T. Beauregard, 24 April 1884, in Letterbook 1, Robert Underwood Johnson Letterbooks, Rare Books and Manuscripts Division, New York Public Library; Clarence Clough Buel to Joseph Pope, 3 July 1885, in Letterbook 5, Robert Underwood Johnson Letterbooks, Rare Books and Manuscripts Division, New York Public Library; A. P. Lowery to Editors, *Century*, 30 December 1885, in *Century* Collection, Civil War Papers, Box 126, Rare

Books and Manuscripts Division, New York Public Library; on *Century's* "elitism," see also Blight, *Race and Reunion*, 178–181.

36 Robert Underwood Johnson to John Collins, 11 August 1885, in Letterbook 5, Robert Underwood Johnson Letterbooks, Rare Books and Manuscripts Division, New York Public Library; William Allen White, *The Autobiography of William Allen White* (New York: Macmillan, 1946), 385; Clarence Clough Buel to Warren Lee Goss, 7 May 1885, in Letterbook 4, Robert Underwood Johnson Letterbooks, Rare Books and Manuscripts Division, New York Public Library; Oscar Jackson to Editors, *Century*, letter, 28 September 1886, in *Century* Collection, Civil War Letters, Box 123, Rare Books and Manuscripts Division, New York Public Library; George Kilmer to Editors, *Century*, letter, 14 December 1890, ibid., Box 125.

37 Thomas Lee to Editors, *Century*, 3 February 1888, in *Century* Collection, Civil War Letters, Box 126, Rare Books and Manuscripts Division, New York Public Library; entry for Thomas Lee in Historical Register of the National Home for Disabled Volunteer Soldiers (National Archives Microfilm Publication M1749, 282 rolls); Blight, *Race and Reunion*, 180–181; on the National Home for Disabled Volunteer Soldiers, see also Patrick J. Kelly, *Creating a National Home*.

38 P. B. Bowser to Editors, *Century*, letter, July 1885, and Charles H. Baker to Editors, *Century*, letter, 28 October 1888, both in *Century* Collection, Civil War Letters, Box 117, Rare Books and Manuscripts Division, New York Public Library; Blight, *Race and Reunion*, 180–181. John D. Billings to *Century*, 27 April 1885, and William Birney to *Century*, 22 January 1885, both in *Century* Collection, Civil War Letters, Box 117, Rare Books and Manuscripts Division, New York Public Library; Blight, *Race and Reunion*; Charles Kimmel to Editors, *Century*, 16 March 1886, in *Century* Collection, Civil War Letters, Box 125, Rare Books and Manuscripts Division, New York Public Library; and Robert K. Beecham to Editors, *Century*, 11 February 1885, in *Century* Collection, Civil War Letters, Box 117; Robert K. Beecham Pension File, application no. 269,727, certificate no. 335,303, RG 15, Records of the Veterans Administration, Civil War Pension Files, NARA; Michael E. Stevens, ed., *As if It Were Glory: Robert Beecham's Civil War from the Iron Brigade to the Black Regiments* (Lanham, Maryland: Rowman & Littlefield, 1998), ix–xxiv; Robert K. Beecham, *Gettysburg, The Pivotal Battle of the Civil War* (Chicago: A. C. McClurg & Co., 1911).

39 Charles D. Barney to Laura E. Cooke, 1 May 1867, Papers of the Neilson, McClew, Barney and Related Families, Box 1, Folder 2, ASSpCL; for the sheer volume of these requests, see William Olin Letterbook, vol. 2, William Olin Papers, Massachusetts Historical Society; see also McConnell, *Glorious Contentment*; William E. Roscoe, *History of Schoharie County, New York, 1713–1882*, vol. 2 (Syracuse: Truair,

Smith & Bruce, Printers and Binders, 1882), 445–446; "James Tanner," *Washington Post*, 4 October 1927; "Remarkable Career of the Legless Soldier," *New York Times*, 11 February 1894; advertisement for Palmer Patent Leg in the *Grand Army Gazette*, copy at American Antiquarian Society; "Encampments of Other Days: Corporal James Tanner's Reminiscences of Veterans and Their Reunions," *Washington Post*, 8 October 1902; John A. Joyce, *Jewels of Memory* (Washington: Gibson Bros., 1895), 123–124. On the "old soldier circuit," see also Marten, *Sing Not War*; "The Whole Man in One Band," advertisement for M. L. Pembleton in "G.A.R. Records," unfiled box, GARMA.

40   Cornelius Wheeler as quoted in newspaper clipping, 9 February 1885, in Cornelius Wheeler Papers, Box 1, WiHS; Faust, *This Republic of Suffering*, 265; Gustavus E. Biver to Editors, *Century*, letter, 25 September 1889, in *Century* Collection, Civil War Papers, Box 117, Rare Books and Manuscripts Division, New York Public Library; Allen Fahnestock, "Army Book," Allen Fahnestock Papers, Abraham Lincoln Presidential Library. William Stanley Mead kept a list of casualties in Company E of the 6th Indiana Volunteers on five typewritten legal pages. See William Stanley Mead, list of casualties, in William Stanley Mead Collection, Box 2, Folder 4, InHS; Gustavus E. Gessner, loose prisoner-of-war tallies, in Gustavus E. Gessner Papers, Box 1, Folder 4, RHPC.

41   Walter F. Beyer and Oscar F. Keydel, *Deeds of Valor: How America's Heroes Won the Medal of Honor* (Detroit: Perrien-Keydel, 1901), 129–130; Frederick Phisterer, *Statistical Record of the Armies of the United States* (New York: Charles Scribner's Sons, 1883); see also Faust, *This Republic of Suffering*, 258; Society of the Army of the Potomac, *Report of the Fourteenth Annual Reunion* (New York: MacGowan & Slipper, Printers, 1888), 90; William F. Fox, *Regimental Losses in the American Civil War, 1861–1865*, reprint ed. (Dayton: Morningside Books, 1985), preface; John Page Nicholson, *Catalogue of Library of Brevet Lieutenant Colonel John Page Nicholson* (Philadelphia: n.p., 1914), 294. Fox reported that "days, and often weeks" were spent compiling the statistics on individual regiments. Fox, *Regimental Losses*, preface. See also Faust, *This Republic of Suffering*, 258–259; Fox, *Regimental Losses*, 2, 37, 52; Mark E. Neely, Jr., *The Civil War and the Limits of Destruction* (Cambridge: Harvard University Press, 2008), 208–209. Like Fox, the Wisconsin veteran Hosea Rood grew weary of civilians "belittling" the rebellion. Wielding statistics and making comparisons to other military conflicts, Rood insisted that "in the last hundred years, the world has seen no other such fighting." See Rood, "Don't Belittle the Civil War," undated newspaper clipping in Grand Army of the Republic Memorial Hall Collection, Box 16, WiVMA. On the relationship between white Union veterans and their black comrades, see Gannon, *The Won Cause*; Andre Fleche, " 'Shoulder to Shoulder as Comrades

Tried,'" *Civil War History* 51 (June 2005): 175–201; and Norwood P. Hallowell, "The Negro as a Soldier in the War of the Rebellion," paper delivered to the Military Historical Society of Massachusetts, 5 January 1892, in *Papers of the Military Historical Society of Massachusetts*, reprint ed. (Wilmington, North Carolina: Broadfoot Publishing, 1990), 13:287–314.

42 Frederick H. Dyer, *A Compendium of the War of the Rebellion*, 3 vols., reprint ed. (New York and London: Thomas Yoseloff, 1959); Bell Irvin Wiley, "Introduction," in Dyer, *A Compendium of the War of the Rebellion*, vol. 1 (New York and London: Thomas Yoseloff, 1959), i–iv; *Des Moines Register and Leader*, 26 April 1908, as quoted in Wiley, "Introduction," i–iv. Even today, many Civil War military historians rely on Dyer's *Compendium* as a reliable source for casualty numbers.

43 Thomas Livermore, *Numbers and Losses in the Civil War in America, 1861–1865* (Boston and New York: Houghton, Mifflin & Co., 1900), 34; Thomas L. Livermore, "The Numbers in the Confederate Army, 1861–1865," in *Papers of the Military Historical Society of Massachusetts*, reprint ed. (Wilmington, North Carolina: Broadfoot Publishing, 1990), 13:315–344; Neely, Jr., *The Civil War and the Limits of Destruction*, 209; "Regimental Losses in the American Civil War," *United Service* 2 (1889): 99–101. On the Fifth New Hampshire, see also the splendid regimental history by Mike Pride and Mark Travis, *My Brave Boys: To War with Colonel Cross and the Fighting Fifth* (Hanover, New Hampshire: University Press of New England, 2001); Shay, *Odysseus in America*, 87; Cashin, "Trophies of War"; Jim Weeks, *Gettysburg: Memory, Market, and an American Shrine* (Princeton: Princeton University Press, 2003), 102. Weeks argues that the "possession of a relic thought to be associated with a personal combat experience could authenticate that experience and reduce the battle's magnitude and horror." While relics no doubt did the former, they were helpless to do the latter. See also Faust, *This Republic of Suffering*.

44 Joan E. Cashin, "Trophies of War: Material Culture in the Civil War Era," *Journal of the Civil War Era* 1, no. 3 (September 2011): 339–367; J. Emory Round, "Relics of the War," *Soldiers' and Sailors' Half Dime Tales of the Late Rebellion* 1, no. 10 (1868): 170–173; Edwin C. Hall, "Whose Coat Was It?" letter to the editor, *National Tribune*, undated clipping in Edwin C. Hall Papers, Box 1, Folder 25, Vermont Historical Society, Barre, Vermont. On trees and vegetation as prized commodities in the relic trade, see Nelson, *Ruin Nation*, 154–157, 229–232. On collecting relics from slavery, see Alexander Neil, letter to his family, 5 May 1865, in Alexander Neil Letter, MSS 6120, ASSpCL. For just one example of a soldier who picked a human skull from a battlefield, see Samuel J. B. V. Gilpin, diary entry, 30 January 1864, in Samuel J. B. V. Gilpin Diary, Manuscript Division, LoC.

45 Marten, *Sing Not War*, 138; Samuel Bloomer Biographical File, in Samuel Bloomer Papers, Box 2, MinnHS; George F. Sparrow, Scrapbook 3, in Captain George F. Sparrow Collection, Coll. 2293, MaineHS; Hall, "Whose Coat Was It?"; Round, "Relics of the War," 170–173.

46 *Loan Exhibition of War Relics in Aid of R. O. Tyler Post, G.A.R., Hartford, December 15–22, 1886* (Hartford: Press of the Case, Lockwood & Brainard Co., 1886), copy at Connecticut Historical Society. See also "The Veteran to His Cloak," *Soldiers' and Sailors' Half Dime Tales* 1, no. 8 (1868); " 'An Empty Sleeve' Takes Down His Old Blue Coat and Expresses an Opinion," *Daily Inter Ocean*, 19 September 1874; and Stewart Bruce Terry, diary fragment, dated 1886, in Stewart Bruce Terry Papers, Box 1, KaHS; *Our Country*, 11 July 1868, copy at American Antiquarian Society; for a similar case, see also William Lyon to Augustus Gordon Weissert, 18 June 1870, in Augustus Gordon Weissert Papers, Box 4, Folder 9, WiVMA.

47 See, for example, Sheldon Thorpe Diary, 19–22 September 1892, in Sheldon Thorpe Diary, North Haven Historical Society, and "We've Drunk from the Same Canteen," *Grand Army Journal*, 10 June 1871; *Program of the Twentieth Annual Reunion of the Society of the Army of the Cumberland* (September 1889), copy in William Stanley Mead Collection, Box 2, Folder 1, InHS; for one of many examples of veterans returning to their battlefields to comb for relics, see Earl J. Hess, *The Knoxville Campaign: Burnside and Longstreet in East Tennessee* (Knoxville: University of Tennessee Press, 2012), 275; Jim Weeks, *Gettysburg: Memory, Market, and an American Shrine*, 102; Devil's Den veteran as quoted in Weeks, *Gettysburg*, 102; "On the Old Battlefield: The Great Celebration at Gettysburg," *New York Times*, 30 June 1888.

48 Property Book, Stannard Post No. 2, in Grand Army of the Republic Post No. 2 Records, Vermont Historical Society, Barre, Vermont; for an analysis of the Grand Army post room, see McConnell, *Glorious Contentment*. See also Marten, *Sing Not War*, 140. The Grand Army meeting spaces in Rockville and Peninsula still exist today and operate as local museums; Drew Gilpin Faust, "Equine Relics of the Civil War," *Southern Cultures* (Spring 2000): 23–49; Dane DiFebo, "Old Baldy: A Horse's Tale," *Pennsylvania Magazine of History and Biography* 134, no. 4 (October 2011): 549–552. Today, "Old Baldy" is on display at the Grand Army of the Republic Museum and Library in a quiet corner of northeast Philadelphia. See also Gary B. Nash, *First City: Philadelphia and the Forging of Historical Memory* (Philadelphia: University of Pennsylvania Press, 2006), 239, 241.

49 *Loan Exhibition of War Relics in Aid of R. O. Tyler Post*, copy at Connecticut Historical Society; Cashin, "Trophies of War," 349; Marten, *Sing Not War*, 140;

George Haven Putnam, "An Experience in Virginia Prisons During the Last Winter of the War," paper read before New York Commandery, Military Order of the Loyal Legion of the United States, 7 December 1910, in A. Noel Blakeman, *Personal Recollections of the War of the Rebellion*, 4th series, reprint ed. (Wilmington, North Carolina: Broadfoot Publishing Co., 1992), 218; George Starr, "In and Out of Confederate Prisons," in A. Noel Blakeman, *Personal Recollections of the War of the Rebellion*, 2nd series, reprint ed. (Wilmington, North Carolina: Broadfoot Publishing Co. 1992), 82–83. On the Libby Prison War Museum, see also Marten, *Sing Not War*, 144–146; Benjamin Cloyd, *Haunted by Atrocity: Civil War Prisons in American Memory* (Baton Rouge: Louisiana State University Press, 2010), 76–78; Katharine W. Hannaford, "Culture Versus Commerce: The Libby Prison Museum and the Image of Chicago, 1889–1899," *Ecumene* 8, no. 3 (2001): 284–316; Bruce Klee, "They Paid to Enter Libby Prison," *Civil War Times Illustrated* 37 (February 1999); and Jennifer R. Bridges, "Tourist Attractions, Souvenirs, and Civil War Memory in Chicago, 1861–1915" (Ph.D. diss., Loyola University Chicago, 2009), 150–209; *New York Herald* as quoted in Bridges, "Tourist Attractions, Souvenirs, and Civil War Memory in Chicago," 161.

50 Starr, "In and Out of Confederate Prisons," 82; Bridges, "Tourist Attractions, Souvenirs, and Civil War Memory in Chicago," 169, 170–173, 181–182; see also Marten, *Sing Not War*, 146.

51 On rituals of "sanctification" and the process of memorialization in the wake of great violence, see Kenneth E. Foote, *Shadowed Ground: America's Landscapes of Violence and Tragedy* (Austin: University of Texas Press, 1997), 111–114, 208. When considering veterans and battlefield preservation, previous scholars have emphasized the "tacit forgetfulness" of Union veterans, who, in their estimation, set aside national battlefields as "shrines" of national reconciliation. This analysis overlooks just how controversial establishing a national battlefield park could be—and likewise neglects the reality that battlefield preservation was tangled up with painful and misunderstood personal memories of the war. For examples of the traditional narrative, see Linenthal, *Sacred Ground*; Mary Munsell Abroe, " 'All The Profound Scenes': Federal Preservation of Civil War Battlefields, 1861–1990" (Ph.D. diss., Loyola University Chicago, 1996); Susan W. Trail, "Remembering Antietam: Commemoration and Preservation of a Civil War Battlefield" (Ph.D. diss., University of Maryland, College Park, 2005); Richard West Sellars, "Pilgrim Places: Civil War Battlefields, Historic Preservation, and America's First National Military Parks, 1863–1900," *Cultural Resource Management Journal* (Winter 2005): 23–52; and Timothy B. Smith, *The Golden Age of Battlefield Preservation: The Decade of the 1890s and the Establishment of America's First Five*

Military Parks (Knoxville: University of Tennessee Press, 2008); Timothy B. Smith, *A Chickamauga Memorial: The Establishment of America's First Civil War National Military Park* (Knoxville: University of Tennessee Press, 2009); Caroline E. Janney offers a much-needed corrective to this "reconciliatory" paradigm in " 'I Yield to No Man an Iota of My Convictions': Chickamauga and Chattanooga National Military Park and the Limits of Reconciliation," *Journal of the Civil War Era* 2, no. 3 (September 2012); Gordon Berg, "The Hazen Brigade Monument," *America's Civil War* 17, no. 5 (November 2004): 10, 12, 14, 58; Smith, *The Golden Age of Battlefield Preservation*, 14; Sellars, "Pilgrim Places," 32; Abroe, " 'All the Profound Scenes,' " 88–91; Sean M. Styles, *Stones River National Battlefield Historic Resource Study* (Washington, D.C.: Government Printing Office, 2004), 38–39; monument description in Styles, *Stones River*, 38. For the "murderous shower of shot and shell," see Hazen's report in *OR*, series I, vol. 20, part 1, pp. 544–546. On the battle of Stone's River, see also Peter Cozzens, *No Better Place to Die: The Battle of Stone's River* (Urbana and Chicago: University of Illinois Press, 1990); Smith, *The Golden Age of Battlefield Preservation*, 14–15; Abroe, "All the Profound Scenes," 91; Sellars, "Pilgrim Places," 32; Benson J. Lossing, *Pictorial History of the Civil War in the United States of America*, vol. 1 (Philadelphia: George W. Childs, 1866), 608; John Townsend Trowbridge, *The South: A Tour of Its Battlefields and Ruined Cities* (Hartford: Lucius Stebbins, 1866), 86–88; P. C. Headley, *Massachusetts in the Rebellion* (Boston: Walker, Fuller & Co., 1866), 534–535; Michael W. Panhorst, "Sacred to the Memory," *Civil War Times* 49, no. 2 (April 2010); Joan M. Zenzen, *Battling for Manassas: The Fifty-Year Preservation Struggle at Manassas National Battlefield Park* (University Park: Pennsylvania State University Press, 1998), 2–3; Smith, *The Golden Age of Battlefield Preservation*, 21. On Civil War battlefield monumentation, see also Edward T. O'Connell, "Public Commemoration of the Civil War and Monuments to Memory: The Triumph of Robert E. Lee and the Lost Cause" (Ph.D. diss., Stony Brook University, 2008), and Kirk Savage, *Standing Soldiers, Kneeling Slaves: Race, War, and Monument in Nineteenth-Century America* (Princeton: Princeton University Press, 1997).

52 See Smith, *The Golden Age of Battlefield Preservation*, 21–29; John Mitchell Vanderslice, *Gettysburg, Then and Now: The Field of American Valor* (New York: G. W. Dillingham Co., 1897), 364, 367–368; John Mitchell Vanderslice, *Gettysburg: A History of the Gettysburg Battlefield Memorial Association* (Philadelphia: Gettysburg Battlefield Memorial Association, 1897), 212; John L. Beveridge, "The First Gun at Gettysburg," paper read before the Military Order of the Loyal Legion of the United States, 8 February 1885, in Charles W. Davis, William Eliot Furness, and Alfred T. Andreas, eds., *Military Essays and Recollec-*

tions, vol. 2 (Chicago: A. C. McClurg and Co., 1894), 92; *Constitution and By-Laws of the Grand Encampment of Veteran Brotherhood of the State of Kansas, Adopted at Topeka, Kansas, August 2, 1866* (Atchison, Kansas: Daily Champion Office, 1866), 3, copy at KaHS; Charles Devens et al. to the Gettysburg Battlefield Association, 22 October 1888, 15th Massachusetts Collection, Folder 3, WHM. On the function of Civil War battlefield monuments, especially at Gettysburg, see also Weeks, *Gettysburg*, 61; "Soldier's Monuments," *Grand Army Journal*, 6 August 1870; see also the appeal of another veteran for civilians to "multiply" soldiers' monuments, "to keep in perpetual memory the heroic deeds of citizens who took up arms in the public defense." *Grand Army Journal*, 19 November 1870. Finally, see "Michigan Soldiers Monument," *Soldier's Friend* (October 1865).

53 Smith, *The Golden Age of Battlefield Preservation*; Marten, *Sing Not War*, 135. Massachusetts was the first state to underwrite regimental monuments for its veterans, appropriating funds for Gettysburg markers in 1883. Richard Allen Sauers, "John B. Bachelder: Government Historian of the Battle of Gettysburg," *Gettysburg Magazine* 3 (July 1990): 118.

54 S. H. Hurst, "Memorial Address," 14 September 1887, in *Ohio Memorials at Gettysburg* (Baltimore: Butternut & Blue, 1998), 88; *National Tribune*, 1 June 1881. See also Vanderslice, *Gettysburg: A History of the Gettysburg Battlefield Memorial Association*, 213; "National Park at Gettysburg," *Confederate Veteran* 7 (1899): 23; "Only C.S.A. Monument at Gettysburg," *Confederate Veteran* 9 (1901): 19, Sellars, "Pilgrim Places," 19–20; "The Gettysburg Celebration," *National Tribune*, 14 June 1888; George F. McFarland, address at dedication of monument for the 151st Pennsylvania at Gettysburg, 1 July 1888, in John Page Nicholson, ed., *Pennsylvania at Gettysburg: Ceremonies at the Dedication of the Monuments*, vol. 2 (Harrisburg: William Stanley Ray, State Printer, 1904), 764; see also remarks at dedication of monument for the 13th New Jersey at Gettysburg in James N. Duffy et al., *Final Report of the Gettysburg Battlefield Commission of New Jersey* (Trenton: John L. Murphy Publishing Co., 1891), 30; Orlando B. Potter, address at dedication of 83rd New York monument at Gettysburg, delivered 1 July 1888, in New York Monuments Commission for the Battlefields of Gettysburg and Chattanooga, *Final Report on the Battlefield of Gettysburg*, vol. 2 (Albany: J. B. Lyon Co., Printers, 1900), 672; Hurst, "Memorial Address," 14 September 1887.

55 J. L. Shook to Bachelder, 5 November 1889, as quoted in Sauers, "John B. Bachelder"; Richard Allen Sauers, "John B. Bachelder: Government Historian of the Battle of Gettysburg," *Gettysburg Magazine* 3 (July 1990): 115–127.

56 George W. Grant, "The First Army Corps on the First Day at Gettysburg," paper delivered 10 May 1898, in *Glimpses of the Nation's Struggle: Papers Read Before the Minnesota Commandery of the Military Order of the Loyal Legion of the United*

States, 1897–1902, 5th series (St. Paul, Minnesota: Review Publishing Co., 1903), 56; Charles W. Roberts, "At Gettysburg in 1863 and 1888," in *War Papers Read Before the Commandery of the State of Maine, Military Order of the Loyal Legion of the United States* (Portland: Thurston Print, 1898), 1:56–57; "On Gettysburg Field Four Thousand Veterans Already on the Grounds," *Philadelphia Inquirer,* 10 September 1889; Grant, "The First Army Corps," 57; Hawthorne, *Gettysburg,* 30.

57 See *Guide to Richmond and the Battlefields* (Richmond: J. L. Hill Printing Co., 1894), in Daniel R. Lucas Papers, Box 1, Folder 6, InHS; Charles Kimmel to Pension Bureau, letter, 13 July 1913, in Charles Kimmel Pension File, application no. 199,641, certificate no. 215,804, RG 15, Records of the Veterans Administration, Civil War Pension Files, NARA; Henry H. Baltzell, memoir, in Henry Baltzell Memoir, SC 2717, Abraham Lincoln Presidential Library; Thomas Pressnell to Samuel Bloomer, 23 March 1893, in Samuel Bloomer Papers, Box 2, Folder 6, MinnHS; see, for example, Fred Cross to Uberto Burnham, 8 June 1928, in Uberto Burnham Papers, Box 1, Folder 20, New York State Archives. Burnham, who was active in the 76th New York's survivors' association, made several excursions to South Mountain and Antietam in the early twentieth century. See also Hess, *The Union Soldier in Battle,* 185–190; T. A. Sloan to "Comrades," 23 September 1919, in 44th Indiana Regimental Association Records, Folder 4, InHS; McCook's Brigade Association, reunion announcement, September 1902, in Allen L. Fahnestock Papers, Abraham Lincoln Presidential Library; Charles Dickson to John Edwin Roller, 9 September 1892, in John Edwin Roller Correspondence, ASSpCL.

58 Henry A. Castle as quoted in "Dinner Gang" Scrapbook, Dinner Gang Scrapbook, MinnHS.

59 Unidentified newspaper clipping in "Dinner Gang" Scrapbook, Dinner Gang Scrapbook, MinnHS; Oliver Wendell Holmes, "Memorial Day Address, 30 May 1884, at Keene, New Hampshire," in Ronald K. L. Collins, ed., *The Fundamental Holmes: A Free-Speech Chronicle and Reader* (Cambridge: Cambridge University Press, 2010), 25–26; Marten, *Sing Not War,* and Grant, "Reimagined Communities."

60 Confino, "Collective Memory and Cultural History"; Grant, "Reimagined Communities."

CHAPTER 4: LIVING MONUMENTS

1 *Daily National Intelligencer,* 5 May 1866.

2 The Resaca battle scene is drawn from *OR,* series I, vol. 38, part 3, pp. 92–93, 190–192, and Albert Castel, *Decision in the West: The Atlanta Campaign of 1864* (Lawrence: University Press of Kansas, 1992), 166–167; Jonathan Allison Pension File, RG 15, NA.

3 *New Haven Daily Palladium*, 21 July 1865; "A Chance for the Maimed," *New Haven Daily Palladium*, 20 October 1865.

4 Jonathan McKinley Allison to WOB, letter, 26 December 1865, WOB Papers, Manuscript Division, LoC (emphasis mine). An early version of this chapter was published as " 'Living Monuments': Union Veteran Amputees and the Embodied Memory of the Civil War," *Civil War History* 57, no. 2 (June 2011): 121–152.

5 Neither was the phrase "living monument" exceptional in postwar writings. "The wooden leg was no longer an unsightly object, but a *living memorial* in its self of the brave loyal heart of the one who used it," one federal veterans' periodical noted (emphasis added). See "Pension Day," *Neighbor's Home Mail: Ex Soldiers' Reunion and National Campfire* (January 1875): 7. On "authority" derived from missing limbs, see Frances M. Clarke, "Honorable Scars: Northern Amputees and the Meaning of Civil War Injuries," in Paul A. Cimbala and Randall M. Miller, eds., *Union Soldiers and the Northern Home Front: Wartime Experiences, Postwar Adjustments* (New York: Fordham University Press, 2002), 378. This chapter is deeply indebted to and builds from many of Clarke's arguments. Rossiter Johnson, *The Fight for the Republic* (New York: Knickerbocker Press, 1917), 366; see also James Barber, *The Nation's Defenders. The New Jersey and the National Homes for Disabled Volunteer Soldiers: How They Are Cared For* (Newark, New Jersey: Dennis, 1874), 5. On the "evocative" power and ubiquitous nature of ruins, see Nelson, *Ruin Nation*, 3. Elaine Scarry, *The Body in Pain: The Making and Unmaking of the World* (New York: Oxford University Press, 1985), 130, 114. The Office of the Surgeon General reported that a total of 29,980 amputations were performed on Union soldiers during the war. Nonetheless, these statistics do not reflect the first eighteen months of the conflict, during which "few or no reports were made of the wounded in the various engagements." Moreover, the totals tabulated by the surgeon general "unavoidably omitted" amputations performed after soldiers demobilized; amputations performed by family physicians; and amputations ineluctably omitted from army medical reports. If one were to exercise extreme caution and estimate that surgeons performed amputations only half as frequently as they did during the last thirty months of the war, this would suggest that the extant "official" numbers exclude some 4,996 amputations. Applying the mortality rate after surgery culled from the surgeon general's statistics (26.8 percent) to the "new" aggregate for Union amputations (34,976), this would suggest—again, very conservatively—that some 25,603 Union soldiers returned to their homes as amputees. *Medical and Surgical History of the Civil War*, reprint ed. (Wilmington, North Carolina: Broadfoot, 1991), 12:877;

Thomas J. Brown, "The Neglect and Decadence of Military Vital Science and the Urgent Need for Reviving the Systematic Study of the Civil War Vital Records under the Direction of a Special Commission of Experts," manuscript dated January 1909, Thomas J. Brown Papers, Manuscript Division, LoC; Charles W. Kepler, address to Crocker's Iowa Brigade, in *Proceedings of Crocker's Iowa Brigade at the Ninth Biennial Reunion Held at Jefferson, Iowa, September 21–22, 1898* (Cedar Rapids, Iowa: Record Printing, 1902), 67; biographical sketch in Charles Kepler Papers, SHSIo.

6 Lisa Marie Herschbach, "Fragmentation and Reunion: Medicine, Memory, and Body in the American Civil War (Ph.D. diss., Harvard University, 1997), 124, and Nelson, *Ruin Nation*.

According to the surgeon general, a total of 6,091 artificial limbs and resection apparatus were supplied to Union veterans through May 10, 1866. Working from the "new" aggregate of amputees, these figures would suggest that a mere 23.8 percent of veterans used prosthetic devices (or had a stump that could accommodate a prosthetic). Figures on artificial-limb use among Union veterans can be culled from J. K. Barnes, "Artificial Limbs Furnished to Soldiers," H.R. Exec. Doc. No. 39-108 (1st Session, 1866), in Guy R. Hasegawa, *Mending Broken Soldiers: The Union and Confederate Programs to Supply Artificial Limbs* (Carbondale: Southern Illinois University Press, 2012), 93; Wecter, *When Johnny Comes Marching Home*, 214. According to Wecter, an "unofficial estimate" of requests for prosthetics published in the November 1868 issue of the *Soldier's Friend* demonstrates virtually no increase in demand subsequent to the 1866 surgeon general's report. Wecter, *When Johnny Comes Marching Home*, 14; Douglas Bly to Henry Spencer Parmelee, letters, 24 October 1866 and 17 December 1866, in Civil War Manuscript Collection, Group 619, Box 20, Folder 11, Manuscripts and Archives, Sterling Memorial Library, Yale University; Conrad Dippel Pension File, RG 15, NA. On developments in the artificial-limb industry, see Hasegawa, *Mending Broken Soldiers*. In February 1866, a Massachusetts newspaper noted, "it is not generally known that soldiers who have lost limbs in the service of the United States are entitled to artificial substitutes." See the *Lowell Daily Citizen & News*, 2 February 1866; Pastor A. Gillette to WOB, letter, 3 May 1866, in WOB Papers, Manuscript Division, LoC (emphasis mine).

7 On the fundamental "inexpressibility" of pain, see Scarry, *The Body in Pain*; Henry C. Allen to WOB, left-handed penmanship contest entry, 21 August 1865, in WOB Papers, Manuscript Division, LoC; Scarry, *The Body in Pain*, 13.

8 "Empty Sleeves," *Soldier's Friend*, 19 September 1868; "The Nation's Debt," *Sol-*

diers' Manual, August 1868, American Antiquarian Society; *Veteran's Advocate*, 26 February 1884, NHHS.

9 Henry H. Meacham, *The Empty Sleeve; or, The Life and Hardships of Henry H. Meacham, in the Union Army* (Springfield, Massachusetts: Sold for the Benefit of the Author, 1869), 1–32.

10 Ann Fabian, *The Unvarnished Truth: Personal Narratives in Nineteenth-Century America* (Berkeley: University of California Press, 2000), 152–153; *Only A Private: A Sketch of the Services of a Private Soldier Who Took Part in the Battles of Fort Pulaski, Fort Wagner, Olustee, and Cold Harbor, by Himself* (Boston: Pratt Brothers, n.d.); George M. Reed, *The One Arm and One Leg Soldier: Wounded at the Battle of Shiloh* (n.p.: George M. Reed, 1865); David B. Tanner, *"Our Limbs Are Lost! Our Country Saved!" A Short Sketch of the Service and Sacrifices of David B. Tanner, Late of the 5th Rhode Island Battery, Who Lost His Leg at the Battle of Antietam* (Boston: John D. Flagg, 1870); A. O. Goodrich, "On the Peninsular Campaign," broadside, James V. Campbell Papers, Valeria Campbell Materials, Box 3, Bentley Historical Library, University of Michigan; Fabian, *The Unvarnished Truth*.

11 "Left-Handed Penmanship," *Harper's Weekly*, 29 July 1865; *Zion's Herald and Wesleyan Journal*, 26 July 1865; Official Contest Affidavit and "Report of the Committee of Award," WOB Papers, Manuscript Division, LoC; Charles Cooney, "The Left Armed Corps," *Civil War Times Illustrated* 23, no. 2 (1984): 40–41; Jalynn Olsen Padilla, "Army of 'Cripples': Northern Civil War Amputees, Disability, and Manhood in Victorian America" (Ph.D. diss., University of Delaware, 2007), 20–66; "Left-Hand Penmanship by Disabled Soldiers—Report of the Committee," *New York Times*, 7 March 1866.

12 William S. Hudson, Jr., to WOB, contest entry, 11 December 1865, in Civil War Records, WOB Materials, Box 3, Butler Library, Columbia University; Clarke, "Honorable Scars," 371; Frank Valleraux to WOB, contest entry, 12 September 1865, WOB Papers, Manuscript Division, LoC; Andrew Fries, Jr., to WOB, contest entry, 27 January 1866, WOB Papers, Manuscript Division, LoC; William A. Till to WOB, contest entry, 26 August 1865, WOB Papers, Manuscript Division, LoC; Clarke, "Honorable Scars," 361–394; Phineas Whitehouse to WOB, letter, 27 April 1865, in WOB Collection, New-York Historical Society Library; see also Whitehouse to "Soldier Brothers," 20 May 1865, *Soldier's Friend* (June 1865).

13 "Honor to the Brave! To the Left-Armed Corps of the Union," handbill announcing second left-handed penmanship contest, WOB Papers, LoC. Premiums were named in honor of Generals Grant, Howard (himself an empty sleeve), Hooker, Geary, Logan, Meade, Hancock, Sheridan, and Sherman, and Rear Admiral Far-

ragut. See also "Soldiers' Left Hand Penmanship," *Lowell Daily Citizen and News*, 9 April 1867, and Clarke, "Honorable Scars," 370.

14 Charles Norton to WOB, contest entry, 31 January 1866, WOB Papers, Manuscript Division, LoC; W. Augustus McNutty to WOB, contest entry, 31 January 1866, WOB Papers, Manuscript Division, LoC. For additional examples of veterans desiring to be included in the memorial volume, see Abel Irish to WOB, contest entry, 22 January 1866; Charles Harrington to WOB, contest entry, 30 July 1865; John F. Finley to WOB, contest entry, 28 December 1865; Samuel Carpenter to WOB, contest entry, 26 January 1866; Samuel Blood to WOB, contest entry, 27 January 1866; and H. O. Thomas to WOB contest entry, 27 September 1865, all in WOB Papers, Manuscript Division, LoC.

15 Frank Otis to WOB, contest entry, 28 December 1865, in WOB Papers, Manuscript Division, LoC. Frances Clarke makes precisely this point in "Honorable Scars"; Samuel A. Carpenter to WOB, contest entry, 26 January 1866; Frank H. Evans, "The Empty Coat Sleeve," contest entry, 30 November 1865; and Lewis E. Kline to WOB, contest entry, 15 September 1865, WOB Papers, Manuscript Division, LoC.

16 Margalit, *The Ethics of Memory*, 48–83; Clarke, "Honorable Scars"; Henry Krahl to WOB, contest entry, 18 June 1867, WOB Papers, Manuscript Division, LoC (emphasis mine); Henry Krahl Pension File, RG 15, NA; George Warner to WOB, contest entry, 30 January 1866; James E. Lee to WOB, contest entry, 16 September 1865; and Seth Sutherland to WOB, contest entry, 24 July 1865, all in WOB Papers, Manuscript Division, LoC; for another example of an empty sleeve noting that he felt compelled by "duty" to enter the contest, see Martin Fitzjames to WOB, letter, 24 March 1866, in WOB Papers.

17 Philip K. Faulk, "A Word with Comrades," contest entry, n.d., WOB Papers, Manuscript Division, LoC; Albion Tourgée, "The Hurt Is in the Heart," in *The Veteran and His Pipe* (Chicago: Belford, Clarke & Co., 1886), 153; *Boston Daily Advertiser*, 20 July 1866. Speech of Hugh Judson Kilpatrick at Ninth Annual Reunion of the First Maine Cavalry Regiment in *Record of Proceedings at the Eighth and Ninth Annual Reunions* (Augusta, Maine: Sprague & Son, Printers, 1881), 77; and clipping about Comrade Hugh Lewis in Grand Army of the Republic Memorial Hall Collection Scrapbook, WiVMA. Bourne likewise recognized the "eloquence" of an empty sleeve when he directed his panel of judges to select winners utilizing "good penmanship" as their only rubric; Frank H. Evans, "The Empty Coat Sleeve"; David Barker, "The Empty Sleeve," *Daily Iowa State Register*, 13 February 1866; see also *Veteran's Advocate*, 5 February 1884.

18 Henry C. Allen to WOB, contest entry, 21 August 1865, and John Chase to WOB, contest entry, 3 January 1866, both in WOB Papers, Manuscript Divi-

sion, LoC. Laurann Figg, "Clothing Adaptations of Civil War Amputees" (M.A. thesis, Iowa State University, 1990), demonstrates that most one-armed soldiers pinned up their empty sleeves for proud display in postwar photographs; Allen to WOB, contest entry, 21 August 1865; Benjamin W. Crowinshield, *A History of the First Regiment of Massachusetts Cavalry Volunteers* (Boston and New York: Houghton Mifflin Co., 1891), 374; Lynne S. Brown, *Gulfport: A Definitive History* (Charleston, South Carolina: Arcadia Press, 2004), 92–93; Stephen W. Sears, *Chancellorsville* (New York: Houghton Mifflin Co., 1996), 363; Michael A. Dreese, *The Hospital on Seminary Ridge at the Battle of Gettysburg* (Jefferson, North Carolina: McFarland & Co., 2002), 141; Marten, *Sing Not War*, 93; J. W. Jones, *The Story of American Heroism: Thrilling Narratives of Personal Adventures During the Great Civil War as Told by the Medal Winners and Roll of Honor Men* (Springfield, Ohio: Werner Co., 1897), 220–221. Chase earned the Congressional Medal of Honor and became something of a celebrity for allegedly asking his attending surgeons, "Did we win the battle?" See J. F. Chase, *Souvenir—Our Flag: What It Cost Me and My Comrades* (n.p.: n.d.), copy in Nicholson Collection, Huntington Library; M. Alonzo Andrew to WOB, contest entry, 23 December 1865, WOB Papers, Manuscript Division, LoC; Scarry, *The Body in Pain*. For examples of other entrants who included photographs prominently displaying injuries, see William Connor to WOB, contest entry, 15 August 1865; William Denney to WOB, contest entry, 21 November 1865; and Martin Keller to WOB, contest entry, 10 August 1865, all in WOB Papers, Manuscript Division, LoC. For a brilliant meditation on Civil War photography, see Anthony W. Lee, "The Image of War," in Anthony W. Lee and Elizabeth Young, *On Alexander Gardner's Photographic Sketch Book of the Civil War* (Berkeley: University of California Press, 2007), 9–51.

19 John Bresnahan to WOB, contest entry, 27 June 1867; Faulk, "Reminiscences of Cedar Mountain," contest entry, 21 September 1866; Phineas Whitehouse, "My First Battle," August 1866; William Connor to WOB, contest entry, 15 August 1865; R. J. Dickinson to WOB, contest entry, 22 December 1865, all in WOB Papers, Manuscript Division, LoC; see also Clarke, "Honorable Scars," 371.

20 John Blanchard, "Amputated," contest entry, n.d., and Phineas Whitehouse, "My Crippled Arm," poem dated August 1866, both in WOB Papers, Manuscript Division, LoC; *A Standard History of Lorain County, Ohio*, ed. George Frederick Wright (New York: Lewis Publishing Co., 1916), 1:273. For additional examples of amputee poetry, see Alfred T. Randolph to WOB, poem dated 28 December 1865, and David Lombard, "Kiss Me Mother, and Let Me Go," poem dated 30 December 1865, both in WOB Papers, Manuscript Division, LoC; George Coo-

per, untitled poem, *Soldier's Friend*, 18 July 1868; "The Empty Sleeve," *New Hampshire Sentinel*, 6 August 1890; "The Empty Sleeve," *Daily Iowa State Register*, 13 February 1866; "The Empty Sleeve," *Youth's Companion*, 8 October 1868; "The Empty Sleeve," *Atchison Champion*, June 15, 1890; "My Lost Limb," *National Tribune*, July 1879. See also Carol Reardon, "Writing Battle History: The Challenge of Memory," *Civil War History* 53, no. 3 (September 2007): 252–263.

21 Ezra Hilts to WOB, contest entry, 12 November 1865; John Stewart to WOB, contest entry, 20 September 1865; J. A. Lantz to WOB, contest entry, n.d.; Alfred Whitehouse to WOB, contest entry, 6 October 1865, all in WOB Papers, Manuscript Division, LoC.

22 E. R. Wise to WOB, contest entry, 15 February 1866; James H. Smith to WOB, contest entry, n.d.; Charles Edwin Horne to WOB, contest entry, 29 December 1865; William Compton to WOB, contest entry, 22 January 1866, all in WOB Papers, Manuscript Division, LoC.

23 Lewis Kline to WOB, contest entry, 12 June 1867; John Lawford to WOB, contest entry, 24 August 1865; Henry Krahl to WOB, contest entry, 20 October 1865; Alva John Williams to WOB, contest entry, 30 December 1865, all in WOB Papers, Manuscript Division, LoC. For additional exploration of this process among Union veterans, see Neff, *Honoring the Civil War Dead*, and Gannon, *The Won Cause*.

24 Compare this to Linderman's notion of "hibernation." In "Honorable Scars," Frances Clarke writes about the "moral authority" of an empty sleeve, but suggests that these men were most interested in cleaving to a cultural ideal of "heroic suffering." Her essay largely misses the antireconciliationist sentiments of the left-handed writers, and their coveted desire to shape the course of Reconstruction. T. S. Bailey to WOB, contest entry, 30 September 1865; Alvin Dibble to WOB, contest entry, 30 December 1865; David Yates to WOB, contest entry, 9 March 1866; John Lawford to WOB, contest entry, 24 August 1865, all in WOB Papers, Manuscript Division, LoC.

25 Ezra Hilts to WOB, contest entry, 12 November 1865; *Watertown Daily Times*, 24 November 1908; Ezra Hilts Pension File, RG 15, NA; Norman Vroman to WOB contest entry, 16 September 1865; Rufus L. Robinson to Bourne, WOB entry, 30 September 1865, all in WOB Papers, Manuscript Division, LoC.

26 Thomas Sanborn to WOB, contest entry, 30 September 1865; Thomas Sanborn Pension File, RG 15, NA. My argument here is especially indebted to Seth Koven, "Remembering and Dismemberment: Crippled Children, Wounded Soldiers, and the Great War in Great Britain," *American Historical Review* (October 1994): 1167–1202. See also Nelson, *Ruin Nation*; "The Duty of the Hour," *Zion's Herald and Wesleyan Journal*, 25 October 1865.

27 Paul A. Cimbala, *Under the Guardianship of the Nation: The Freedmen's Bureau and the Reconstruction of Georgia, 1865–1870* (Athens: University of Georgia Press, 1997), 51, 54–55; Lucius Fairchild, "To Fellow Citizens," address delivered circa 1866, in Lucius Fairchild Papers, Box 55, Folder 6, WiHS. On Fairchild, see Sam Ross, *The Empty Sleeve: A Biography of Lucius Fairchild* (Madison: State Historical Society of Wisconsin, 1964); Henry C. Allen, "To the Union Soldiers," poem, 24 February 1866, both in WOB Papers, Manuscript Division, LoC.

28 Will Thomas to WOB, contest entry, 27 September 1865, WOB Papers, Manuscript Division, LoC. Thomas was one of two African-American veterans who entered Bourne's contests. Sergeant Robert A. Pinn, who lost his right arm and won the Medal of Honor at the battle of Chaffin's Farm, near Petersburg, Virginia, also entered a penmanship specimen. See Pinn to WOB, contest entry, 15 September 1865, WOB Papers, Manuscript Division, LoC. On black troops during the Civil War, see Dudley Taylor Cornish, *The Sable Arm: Black Troops in the Union Army, 1861–1865* (Lawrence: University Press of Kansas, 1956); on black veterans, see Shaffer, *After the Glory*.

29 The experience of African-American veterans has been treated in two award-winning books: Donald R. Shaffer, *After the Glory: The Struggles of Black Civil War Veterans* (Lawrence: University Press of Kansas, 2005); and Barbara Gannon, *The Won Cause: White and Black Comradeship in the Grand Army of the Republic* (Chapel Hill: University of North Carolina Press, 2011), and therefore does not receive specific attention here.

30 Henry Krahl to WOB, contest entry, 18 June 1867; Charles A. Edmonds, "The Great Rebellion," contest entry, 25 September 1865; and John W. Reynolds to WOB, contest entry, 22 April 1867, all in WOB Papers, Manuscript Division, LoC.

31 Conrad Dippel to WOB, contest entry, 19 December 1865, WOB Papers, Manuscript Division, LoC. The historians Andre Fleche and Barbara Gannon have argued that white and black Union veterans fashioned "a joint vision of the war," celebrating their common cause and the common toil with which they suppressed the southern rebellion. These amputees confirm their conclusions. See Fleche, " 'Shoulder to Shoulder as Comrades Tried': Black and White Union Veterans and Civil War Memory," *Civil War History* 51 (June 2005): 175–201, and Gannon, *The Won Cause*.

32 "A Man Knows a Man," *Harper's Weekly*, 22 April 1865.

33 "Sanderson's Minstrels," *Evening Star*, 30 November 1864; Edward Thomas Devine, *Disabled Soldiers and Sailors: Pensions and Training* (New York: Oxford University Press, 1919), 48; "Invitation of the Soldiers' and Sailors' Union of Washington, D.C., to the Exhibition of Left Hand Penmanship," copy of orig-

inal in WOB Papers, Manuscript Division, LoC; *Daily Constitutional Union*, May 4, 1866; "Exhibition of Left Hand Penmanship," *Washington Star*, May 1, 1866; "Left-Hand Writing," *Harper's Weekly*, May 26, 1866; *Daily National Intelligencer*, May 2, 1866; "Exhibition of Left-Hand Writing," *Philadelphia Inquirer*, May 2, 1866; Thomas Townsend to WOB, letter, June 23, 1866, Bourne Papers, Manuscript Division, LoC; Cooney, "Left-Armed Corps," 44; Clarke, "Northern Amputees," 389; *Daily Constitutional Union*, 4 May 1866; "Exhibition of Left Hand Penmanship," *Washington Star*, 1 May 1866; "Left-Hand Writing," Harper's Weekly, 26 May 1866; *Daily National Intelligencer*, 2 May 1866; "Exhibition of Left-Hand Writing," *Philadelphia Inquirer*, 2 May 1866; Cooney, "Left-Armed Corps," 44; unidentified writer to WOB, letter, 3 May 1866, and M. J. Fitzjames to WOB, letter, n.d., both in WOB Papers, Manuscript Division, LoC.

34 "Invitation of the Soldiers' and Sailors' Union of Washington, D.C., to the Exhibition of Left Hand Penmanship"; *Daily Constitutional Union*, 4 May 1866; "Exhibition of Left Hand Penmanship," *Washington Star*, 1 May 1866; *Daily National Intelligencer*, 2 May 1866; "Exhibition of Left-Hand Writing," *Philadelphia Inquirer*, 2 May 1866.

35 "Letter from Washington," *Macon Weekly Telegraph*, 16 May 1866; "Exhibition of Left Hand Penmanship This Evening," *Washington Evening Union*, 1 May 1866.

36 "Washington News," *New York Times*, 5 May 1866; George F. Magoun to WOB, letter, 4 May 1866, WOB Papers, Manuscript Division, LoC; Fanny Fern, "Left-Hand Manuscripts of Disabled Soldiers," *New York Ledger* column reproduced on broadside, copy of original in WOB Papers, Manuscript Division, LoC. On Fern's remarkable life, see Joyce W. Warren, *Fanny Fern: An Independent Woman* (New Brunswick, New Jersey: Rutgers University Press, 1994).

37 Here, my argument has been informed by Scarry, "The Structure of War: The Juxtaposition of Injured Bodies and Unanchored Issues," in *The Body in Pain*, 60–125; Colyer, *Report of Vincent Colyer*, 35–38.

38 *Washington Republican* editorial as quoted in the *Daily Inter Ocean*, 18 September 1875; Wallace Moore to WOB, 27 April 1868, WOB Papers, Manuscript Division, LoC; *Soldier's Friend*, February 1867; *New Orleans Times*, 4 September 1868.

39 *Daily Inter Ocean*, 18 September 1875; " 'An Empty Sleeve' Takes Down His Old Blue Coat and Expresses an Opinion," *Daily Inter Ocean*, 19 September 1874.

40 *St. Louis Daily Globe-Democrat*, 25 June 1877; *St. Albans Messenger*, 19 January 1872; [New York] *Commercial Advertiser*, 26 May 1869; for additional evidence of amputees returning to less than satisfying domestic arrangements, see also "Brutal

Assault," *Albany Argus*, 24 December 1869, and *Indianapolis Sentinel*, 15 February 1877.

41 David Merrill to Arthur Wright, letter, 2 July 1865, Committee on Commemorating the Service of Yale Men Records, Manuscripts and Archives, Sterling Memorial Library, Yale University.

42 Andrew McIlwaine Bell, *Mosquito Soldiers: Malaria, Yellow Fever, and the Course of the American Civil War* (Baton Rouge: Louisiana State University Press, 2010); quote from James Barber, *The Nation's Defenders*, 20, in Nicholson Collection, Huntington Library. See also John D. Blaisdell, "The Wounded, the Sick, and the Scared: An Examination of Disabled Maine Veterans from the Civil War," *Maine History* 42, no. 2 (2005): 67–92; Eugene Payne Pension File, application no. 534,098, certificate no. 311,839, RG 15, Civil War Pension Files, NARA; Pamphlet dated 17 April 1882 in Aurestus Perham Papers, Box 10, Folder 5, MaineHS; letter from George Chase, 17 November 1882, in Joseph Duso Case File, Box 5, Sample Case Files of the Milwaukee Branch, National Home for Disabled Volunteer Soldiers, National Archives and Records Administration, Great Lakes Region.

43 John Shaw Billings, "The Health of the Survivors of the War," *The Forum* (January 1892): 652–658. On Billings, see Silas Weir Mitchell, *Biographical Memoir of John Shaw Billings, 1838–1913* (Washington, D.C.: National Academy of Sciences, 1917). Practically confirming Billings's suspicions, Carol Reardon has recently argued that "the art of war, as senior commanders understood it, paid little attention to the welfare of the common soldier and did not consider the consequences to the army if the physical and mental needs of its soldiers went unmet." Reardon, *With a Sword in One Hand and Jomini in the Other: The Problem of Military Thought in the Civil War North* (Chapel Hill: University of North Carolina Press, 2012), 93; Billings, "The Health of the Survivors of the War," 656; see also Mary C. Gillett, *The Army Medical Department, 1818–1865* (Washington, D.C.: Center of Military History, United States Army, 1987), 279.

44 Mental illness among Civil War soldiers has attracted remarkably little scholarly attention. See Eric T. Dean, Jr., *Shook over Hell: Posttraumatic Stress, Vietnam, and the Civil War* (Cambridge: Harvard University Press, 1997); Dennis W. Brandt, *Pathway to Hell: A Tragedy of the American Civil War* (Lincoln, Nebraska: Bison Books, 2010); and Judith Pizarro et al., "Physical and Mental Health Costs of Traumatic War Experiences Among Civil War Veterans," *Archives of General Psychiatry* 63 (2006): 193–200; Judith Anderson, " 'Haunted Minds': The Impact of Combat Exposure on the Mental and Physical Health of Civil War Veterans," in James M. Schmidt and Guy R. Hasegawa, eds., *Years of Change and Suffering: Modern Perspectives on Civil War Medicine* (Roseville, Minnesota: Edinborough

Press, 2009), 143–158. Horace Porter, address to the Northern Kansas Medical Society, clipping in Sparrow Scrapbook, Captain G. F. Sparrow Collection, MaineHS; Porter, "The Common Nervous Trouble of Old Soldiers," *Western Veteran*, 15 May 1889; Henry Wilson, "Medical Director's Report," in *Journal of the Annual Session of the Department and Encampment, Grand Army of the Republic, Minnesota* (Minneapolis: Co-Operative Printing, 1885), 69–74.

45 Porter, "The Common Nervous Trouble of Old Soldiers," *Western Veteran*, 15 May 1889. In his landmark history of mental health care in the United States, historian Gerald N. Grob argues that in the mid-nineteenth century, "etiological speculation [about insanity] tended to emphasize the moral more than the physical causes of insanity, if only because the latter were not only obscure but generally not preventable. . . . [D]eviations from acceptable lifestyles," it was thought, "could lead to insanity." Grob, *The Mad Among Us: A History of the Care of America's Mentally Ill* (New York: Free Press, 1994), 60; *Relief Guard*, 30 August 1890.

46 "County Care of Insane," *Milwaukee Sentinel*, 6 March 1896. On Wright, see *Minutes of the Sixty-Sixth Annual Meeting of the Congregational Convention of Wisconsin Held at Eau Claire, October 4–6, 1904* (Madison: Tracy, Gibbs & Co., Printers, 1904), 59–60; List of "Insane Soldiers," A. O. Wright Papers, Box 3, WiHS; miscellaneous notes relating to insane soldiers, Wright Papers, Box 2; *Report of the Class of 1867, Union Theological Seminary* (New York: E. Winton, 1882), 40–44. On the Northern Hospital for the Insane, see J. A. Truesdell, comp., *The Blue Book of the State of Wisconsin* (Madison: Hans B. Warner, Secretary of State, 1880), 367–368; Miscellaneous notes relating to insane soldiers in A. O. Wright Papers, Box 2, WiHS.

CHAPTER 5: CAPTIVE MEMORIES

1 Joseph O'Neall as quoted in *Constitution and By-Laws of the Ohio Association of Union Ex-Prisoners of War, Together With Register of Members and Proceedings at the Reunion Held at Dayton, June 14 and 15, 1882* (Columbus: Ohio State Journal Printing Establishment, 1883), 6–7; "Great Preparations for Forthcoming Reunion of Ex-Prisoners," *Cincinnati Daily Gazette*, 6 June 1882; Edwin Beach, "To Ex-Prisoners of War," *Cincinnati Commercial Tribune*, 12 June 1882; "The Ex-Prisoners Reunion," *Cincinnati Daily Gazette*, 15 June 1882; *Daily Inter Ocean*, 15 June 1882. An early version of this chapter was published as "Captive Memories: Union Ex-Prisoners of War and the Work of Remembrance," *Civil War Monitor* 1, no. 1 (2011): 52–61, 77–78.

2 Edwin Beach as quoted in *Constitution and By-Laws of the Ohio Association*, 8; Winter, *Sites of Memory, Sites of Mourning*; Thomas Sturgis, *Prisoners of War, 1861–1865* (New York and London: G. P. Putnam's Sons, 1912), 267.

3 "Bloodhounds at Andersonville," *Daily Inter Ocean*, 20 January 1876; Whitman, "The Real War Will Never Get in the Books"; Gessner, notes for address at Ohio Union Ex-Prisoners-of-War Reunion [circa 1890], Gustavus A. Gessner Papers, Box 1, Folder 4, RHPC; Henry M. Davidson, *Fourteen Months in Southern Prisons* (Milwaukee: Daily Wisconsin Printing House, 1865), vii; Joseph Ferguson, *Life Struggles in Rebel Prisons: A Record of the Sufferings, Escapes, Adventures, and Starvation of the Union Prisoners* (Philadelphia: Joseph Ferguson, 1866), 13–14; Robert Hale Kellogg, *Life and Death in Rebel Prisons* (Hartford, Connecticut: Lucius Stebbins, 1865), v; Warren Lee Goss, *The Soldier's Story of His Captivity at Andersonville, Belle Isle, and Other Rebel Prisons* (Boston: Lee & Shepard, 1866), 3–4. On the publication of Kellogg's book, see also Kellogg to George Whitney, 15 October 1909, in Robert Kellogg Papers, Connecticut Historical Society; "Life and Death in Rebel Prisons," *Summit County Beacon*, 13 April 1865.

4 Civil War historians still await a synthetic work on perceptions of and hatred for the enemy. For examples of this scholarship with respect to other military conflagrations, see especially John Dower, *War Without Mercy: Race and Power in the Pacific War* (New York: Pantheon Books, 1986); Lesley J. Gordon, " 'Surely They Remember Me: The 16th Connecticut in War, Captivity, and Public Memory," in Paul A. Cimbala and Randall M. Miller, eds., *Union Soldiers and the Northern Home Front: Wartime Experiences, Postwar Adjustments* (New York: Fordham University Press, 2002), 327–329; Jonathan Shay, *Achilles in Vietnam: Combat Trauma and the Undoing of Character* (New York: Scribner, 1994), 39–43. On the challenges of homecoming, see also Jonathan Shay, *Odysseus in America: Combat Trauma and the Trials of Homecoming* (New York: Simon & Schuster, 2003).

5 Gessner, notes for address at Ohio Union Ex–Prisoner-of-War Reunion [circa 1890], Gessner Papers, Box 1, Folder 4, RHPC; H. B. Hoffman, unpublished manuscript, H. B. Hoffman Papers, Andersonville National Historic Site Archives. The historian Earl J. Hess, in *The Union Soldier in Battle*, has explored the "gulf of experience," though he neglected to navigate the chasm between ex-prisoners of war and the home front. Historian Lesley J. Gordon begins this task in her essay " 'Surely They Remember Me': The 16th Connecticut in War, Captivity, and Public Memory," in Paul A. Cimbala and Randall M. Miller, eds., *Union Soldiers and the Northern Home Front* (New York: Fordham University Press, 2002), 327–360, upon which this chapter builds. See also Reid Mitchell, *The Vacant Chair: The Northern Soldier Leaves Home* (New York: Oxford University Press, 1993).

6 Ole Steensland, address at reunion of the 15th Wisconsin Infantry, Chicago, Illinois, 29 August 1900, in Civil War Papers, Local History Manuscripts Collection, Milwaukee Public Library; see also Samuel Preston, "Personal Narrative of

Samuel Preston's War Experience," in Samuel Preston Papers, New York State Library; Alson H. Blake, "Speech About Andersonville Imprisonment," Alson H. Blake Papers, Box 1, Folder 10, Vermont Historical Society; Robert Kellogg to George Q. Whitney, 28 December 1907, in George Q. Whitney Papers, RG 69:23, Box 5, Whitney-Kellogg Correspondence, Connecticut State Library.

7 The work of the committee was published as *House Special Committee on the Treatment of Prisoners of War and Union Citizens, Report on the Treatment of Prisoners of War Kept by the Rebel Authorities During the War of the Rebellion*, 40th Congress, 3rd Session, 1869, H. Rept. 45. On the committee structure, see Kenneth White Munden and Henry Putney Beers, *The Union: A Guide to Federal Archives Relating to the Civil War* (Washington, D.C.: National Archives Trust Fund, 1986), 75; on the popularity of ex-prisoner narratives, see Fabian, *The Unvarnished Truth*. N[orton] P. Chipman, "Charges and Specifications Preferred Against Henry Wirz," in Henry Wirz Papers, Manuscript Division, LoC; and Leonard, *Lincoln's Forgotten Ally*, 226–227. On Wirz, see also Samuel A. Creelman, *Collections of a Coffee Cooler* (Pittsburgh: Press of the Pittsburgh Photo Engraving Co., 1890), 33, copy in Samuel A. Creelman Papers, Special Collections, Carol Newman Library, Virginia Polytechnic Institute.

8 Blight, *Race and Reunion*, 152. Scholarship on Civil War prisons has exploded in recent years. In addition to two classic works, Ovid Futch, *History of Andersonville Prison* (Gainesville: University Press of Florida, 1968), and William Best Hesseltine, *Civil War Prisons: A Study in War Psychology* (Columbus, Ohio: Ohio State University Press, 1930), see Charles Sanders, *While in the Hands of the Enemy: Military Prisons of the Civil War* (Baton Rouge: Louisiana State University Press, 2005); Michael P. Gray, *The Business of Captivity: Elmira and Its Civil War Prison* (Kent, Ohio: Kent State University Press, 2001); and Roger Pickenpaugh, *Captives in Blue: The Civil War Prisons of the Confederacy* (Tuscaloosa: University of Alabama Press, 2013). Nonetheless, these works scarcely consider the lives of ex-prisoners of war. Even more surprisingly, two recent studies of Civil War prisons and memory, Benjamin Cloyd, *Haunted By Atrocity: Civil War Prisons in American Memory* (Baton Rouge: Louisiana State University Press, 2010), and Douglas Gibson Gardner, "Andersonville and American Memory" (Ph.D. diss., Miami [Ohio] University, 1998), offer no sustained analysis of the lives of ex-inmates; Sanders, *While in the Hands of the Enemy*, 2.

9 George Hitchcock, diary entries, 26 August 1864 and 16 June 1864, both in George Hitchcock Diary, Massachusetts Historical Society; James M. McPherson, *The Battle Cry of Freedom: The Civil War Era* (New York: Oxford University Press, 1988), 796; Augustus Choate Hamlin, research notes for *Martyria; or, Andersonville Prison*, in Augustus Choate Hamlin Papers, Military Order of the

Loyal Legion of the United States Collection, Houghton Library, Harvard University; see also Futch, *History of Andersonville Prison*, and Fabian, *The Unvarnished Truth*, passim; E. A. Nattinger, "Andersonville Prison Pen," undated newspaper clipping in J. H. Glover Scrapbook—1865, in Bruce Catton Papers, Box 49, The Citadel Archives and Museum; McPherson, *The Battle Cry of Freedom*, 796–797; for the "gates of Death," see Oliver Gates, diary entry, 3 May 1864, in Oliver Gates Diary, Connecticut Historical Society. See also George Edward Kelsey, "Memories of Charles Edgar Smith," typescript dated February 1980, in Civil War Miscellaneous Collection, Box 95, USAMHI; Ole Steensland speech in Civil War Papers, Local History Manuscripts Collection, Milwaukee Public Library, and George H. Luther, "Prison Experiences of George H. Luther," handwritten manuscript in George H. Luther Papers, Miscellaneous Manuscripts Collection, Rhode Island Historical Society. For a tabular comparison of the death rates in Union and Confederate prison camps, see Jordan, "Captive Memories."

10 Norman Hope, "The Story of Andersonville," lecture notes, Norman Hope Papers, Connecticut State Library, Ira Emory Forbes, diary entry, 3 May 1864, in Ira Emory Forbes Diary, Manuscripts and Archives, Sterling Memorial Library, Yale University. For a recent treatment of Forbes, see Lesley J. Gordon, "Ira Forbes's War," in Stephen Berry, ed., *Weirding the War: Stories from the Civil War's Ragged Edges* (Athens: University of Georgia Press, 2011), 340–366. See also Isaac Seeley, narrative of Andersonville, n.d., in Grand Army of the Republic Collection, Minnesota Ex-Prisoner of War Association Personal Narratives, MinnHS; George Edward Kelsey, "Memories of Charles Edgar Smith," typescript dated February 1980, in Civil War Miscellaneous Collection, Box 95, USAMHI; Lessel Long, *Twelve Months in Andersonville: On the March—In the Battle—In The Rebel Prison Pens, and At Last in God's Country* (Huntington, Indiana: Thad and Mark Butler, 1886), 102; Charles Richardson, address at Josiah Weiser Post No. 9, GAR [Valley City, North Dakota], n.d., in Grand Army of the Republic Papers, Box 1, State Historical Society of North Dakota; George Hitchcock, diary entries, 17 June 1864 and 26 August 1864, in George Hitchcock Diary, Massachusetts Historical Society; Daniel Bond, typescript of extracts from Andersonville diary, in Civil War Miscellany Collection, Box 2, Folder 9, InHS.

11 Forbes, diary entry, 24 August 1864, in Ira Emory Forbes Diary, Manuscripts and Archives, Sterling Memorial Library, Yale University; Creelman, *Collections of a Coffee Cooler*, 33, copy in Samuel A. Creelman Papers, Carol Newman Library, Virginia Polytechnic Institute; George Hitchcock, "An Army Diary in the War for Freedom," in George Hitchcock Diary, Massachusetts Historical Society; Isaac Seeley, narrative of Andersonville, n.d., in Grand Army of the Republic

Collection, Minnesota Ex-Prisoner of War Association Personal Narratives, MinnHS; Solon Hyde, *A Captive of War* (New York: McClure, Phillips & Co., 1900), 228; for "shattered" minds, see John Ebenezer Warren, recollections of Andersonville, in John Ebenezer Warren Collection, WiHS; for "dethroned" minds, see typescript of address on Andersonville in Grand Army of the Republic Collection, Series One: General Correspondence, Box 1, Folder 7, NHS; Creelman, *Collections of a Coffee Cooler*, 33.

12 Joseph Waters, reunion address, Kansas Union Ex-Prisoners of War, 5 March 1898, *Topeka Weekly Capital*, 8 March 1898; Long, *Twelve Months in Andersonville*, 5; Albert Hyde, "Life of a Connecticut Soldier in Confederate Prison During the Stormy Days of the War," n.d., Hyde Papers, Connecticut State Library; for similar sentiments, see also W. W. Hensley, "What a Soldier Never Forgets," *National Tribune*, 10 May 1883; Richard Thatcher to Boston Corbett, letter, 7 September 1882, Boston Corbett Papers, KaHS; Ezra Ripple, *Dancing Across the Deadline: The Andersonville Memoir of a Prisoner of the Confederacy*, ed. Mark Snell (Novato, California: Presidio Press, 1996), 148; Gilbert E. Sabre, *Nineteen Months a Prisoner of War: Narrative of Lieutenant G. E. Sabre, Second Rhode Island Cavalry, of His Experience in the War Prisons and Stockades of Morton, Mobile, Atlanta, Libby, Belle Isle, Andersonville, Macon, Charleston, and Columbia and His Escape to the Union Lines* (New York: American News Company, 1865), 9; Ripple, *Dancing Across the Deadline*, 148. For two additional accounts of ex-prisoners who found it "impossible to sleep" upon their return, see John W. Urban, *My Experiences Mid Shot and Shell and in Rebel Den* (Lancaster, Pennsylvania: Hubbard Bros., 1882), 623, and George Bliss, letter to "dear Gerald," 6 April 1865, in George Bliss Papers, Box 1, Folder B1 F39 MSS 298, Rhode Island Historical Society; George Hitchcock, "An Army Diary in the War for Freedom," in George Hitchcock Diary, Massachusetts Historical Society; Elizabeth Maher, letter to "Violet," 6 February 1967, in ANDE 284, Andersonville National Historic Site Archives; John Gunther, narrative of Andersonville, in Grand Army of the Republic Collection, Minnesota Ex-Prisoner of War Association Personal Narratives, MinnHS.

13 "The Starvation of Prisoners," *Chicago Medical Examiner* (June 1865); see also "John Mason's Return," *New York Observer and Chronicle*, 27 July 1865; for such a description, see William Stanley Mead, pension affidavit, in William Stanley Mead Collection, Box 1, Folder 7, InHS; Eric Paul as quoted in Hosea Rood's "Grand Army Corner" column, undated clipping in Grand Army of the Republic Memorial Hall Collection, Box 2, Folder 2, WiVMA; pension affidavits in Thomas Lorimor Papers, KSRL.

14 Nineteen memoirs appeared in 1865, followed by seven in 1866, three in 1867, and five in 1868. This count is from Fabian, *The Unvarnished Truth*, 226n13.

15 United States Sanitary Commission, *Narrative of Privations and Sufferings of United States Officers and Soldiers* (Philadelphia: King & Baird, Printers, 1864), 19–20; "New Publications," *Flag of Our Union*, 2 March 1867; Lee and Shepard to Augustus Choate Hamlin, letter, 21 May 1869, in Augustus Choate Hamlin Papers, Military Order of the Loyal Legion of the United States Collection, Houghton Library, Harvard University. Robert Hale Kellogg's Hartford-based publisher, Lucius Stebbins, complained about his profit margins in an appendix to the second printing of *Life and Death in Rebel Prisons*. See Kellogg, *Life and Death*, 424, and Gordon, " 'Surely They Remember Me' "; on the publication history of ex-prisoner memoirs, my argument is indebted to and derived from Fabian, *The Unvarnished Truth*. For an example of a self-published narrative, see John Worrell Northrop, *Chronicles from the Diary of a War Prisoner in Andersonville and Other Military Prisons of the South in 1864* (Wichita, Kansas: John Worrell Northrop, 1904). For two examples of unpublished manuscripts, see Ripple, *Dancing Across the Deadline*, and Iowa cavalryman Stuart Bruce Terry's account of Cahaba, Alabama, "A Prisoner of War," in Stewart Bruce Terry Papers, Box 1, KaHS. Historians often point to the triumph of John McElroy's *Andersonville: A Story of Rebel Military Prisons* (Toledo, Ohio: D. R. Locke, 1879), to make the argument that the market was flooded with ex-prisoner memoirs. McElroy's book did enjoy success, but only because of McElroy's literary talent (he was a long-time editor of the *Toledo Blade*) and his celebrity among veterans as president of the National Association of Ex-Union Prisoners of War. For one example of the book's popularity, see A. R. Hill to C. C. Buel, letter, 21 September 1890, in *Century* Collection, Civil War Letters, Box 122, New York Public Library. On McElroy more generally, see Andersonville Prison Subject File, RHPC; McElroy, *Andersonville*, xv. "Where hundreds have written of the battles on land and sea for the Union," Ezra Hoyt Ripple echoed in his own autobiography, "not more than a score or two have written of the horrors of Southern prisons." The subject, he explained, was "not a pleasant or attractive one," but rather "revolting, sickening, and sorrowful." Ripple, *Dancing Across the Deadline*, 5–6.

16 *Springfield Republican*, 11 August 1886; George Ford as quoted in "Defense of Slavery," *The Independent*, 10 August 1865; *National Tribune*, 25 January 1883; J. T. Gist to Boston Corbett, letter, 16 March 1882, Boston Corbett Papers, KaHS; Warren Lee Goss to Augustus Choate Hamlin, letter, 6 August 1885, in Augustus Choate Hamlin Papers, Military Order of the Loyal Legion of the United States Collection, Houghton Library, Harvard University; see also *Fourth Annual Reunion, Illinois Association Ex-Prisoners of War*,

Decatur, Illinois, October 17–18, 1883, pp. 35–37, copy in Nicholson Collection, Huntington Library; "An Andersonville Column," *New Orleans Times Picayune*, 9 June 1869; Francis Roy to Editor, *The Veteran's Advocate*, letter, 21 May 1884, in *Veterans' Advocate*, 27 May 1884.

17 George Bliss as quoted in "Survived Horrors," *Worcester Daily Spy*, 19 October 1895. On the networks that developed within various rebel prison camps, see Dora Costa and Matthew Kahn, "Surviving Andersonville: The Benefits of Social Networks in POW Camps," *American Economic Review* 97, no. 4 (September 2007): 1467–1487. See also Jay Winter and Emmanuel Sivan, eds., *War and Remembrance in the Twentieth Century*; Lester Phelps to George Whitney, letter, 12 March 1905, in Connecticut Andersonville Monument Commission Records, Connecticut State Library.

18 The "fictive kin" concept is fully developed in Winter and Sivan, eds., *War and Remembrance in the Twentieth Century*; see, for example, John Vaughter, *Prison Life in Dixie* (Chicago: Central Book Concern, 1880), 5; Richard Thatcher to Boston Corbett, 17 September 1882, Boston Corbett Papers, KaHS; D. L. Jewell to Robert Kellogg, 9 March 1908, in George Whitney Papers, RG 69:23, Box 5, Connecticut State Library; and *National Tribune*, 10 May 1883; Robert Kellogg to Frank Van Dorn, 26 January 1920, and Robert Kellogg to George Goddard, letter, 1 March 1922, in George Whitney Papers, RG 69:23, Box 5, Connecticut State Library; see also Kellogg to Norman Hope, letter, 19 July 1922, in Norman Hope Papers, Connecticut State Library; for examples, see Charles Johnson to Ira Forbes, 23 April 1907, in Connecticut Andersonville Monument Commission Records, Connecticut State Library, and William Nott to George Whitney, letter, 31 March 1909, in George Whitney Papers, RG 69:23, Box 4, Connecticut State Library. On McElroy, see John McElroy to Clara Barton, 3 May 1879, Clara Barton Papers, reel 63, Manuscript Division, LoC.

19 Robert Hale Kellogg to George Q. Whitney, letter, 3 March 1910, in George Whitney Papers, RG 69:23, Box 5, Connecticut State Library; *Dedication of the Monument at Andersonville, Georgia, October 23, 1907, in Memory of the Men of Connecticut Who Suffered in Southern Military Prisons, 1861–1865* (Hartford: Published by the State, 1908), 12; *Memorial Volume of Denison University* (Granville, Ohio: Denison University, 1907), 274.

20 *Constitution of the National Union Survivors of Andersonville and Other Southern Military Prisons* (New York: National Union Survivors of Andersonville and Other Southern Military Prisons, 1882), 1–2. State and local ex-prisoner-of-war associations existed in every Union state, in addition to the border state of Maryland and in Tennessee, North Carolina, and Washington, D.C. See Robert Beath, *History of the Grand Army of the Republic* (New York: Press of Willis, McDonald

& Co., 1888), 680; J. E. Wilkins, remarks of 5 September 1883 as quoted in *Proceedings of the Annual Reunion Iowa Prisoners of War Association*, copy in Petitions and Memorials Referred to Committees (HR 48A-H34.4), Committee on Invalid Pensions, 48th Congress, Records of the House of Representatives, RG 233, NARA; "Union Ex-Prisoners of War Association of Kansas," broadside dated 16 October 1883, copy in Boston Corbett Papers, KaHS.

21 *Constitution of the National Union Survivors*, 2; see also membership blank in Boston Corbett Papers, KaHS; "Andersonville Survivors," *Wilkes Barre Times*, 4 July 1878; *Constitution and By-Laws of the Ohio Association*; "Roster of New York City Association of Union Ex-Prisoners of War," in William Ackerson Papers, Collection 109, Folder 4, Monmouth County Historical Association Library. In 1888, the *New York Times* reported that membership in ex-prisoner associations "flourished" throughout the 1870s and 1880s. "Ex Prisoners of War," *New York Times*, 12 January 1888.

22 Certificate of Membership in the New York State Union Ex-Prisoners of War Association for William T. Ackerson, dated 19 April 1884, in William T. Ackerson Papers, Folder 4, Monmouth County Historical Association Library; Certificate of Membership in the Andersonville Survivors' Association for David Daub, in Miscellaneous Manuscripts Collection, RHPC; "Meeting of Ohio Ex-Prisoners of War," *Cincinnati Commercial Tribune*, 15 May 1884, "The Andersonville Survivors," *Boston Daily Globe*, 10 April 1875; "Union Ex-Prisoners Dine," *New York Tribune*, 22 December 1091, *Constitution of the National Union Survivors of Andersonville and Other Southern Military Prisons*, 12; Ralph Bates, *Billy and Dick from Andersonville to the White House* (Santa Cruz, California: Sentinel Publishing Co., 1910), frontispiece.

23 "War Veterans," *Worcester Daily Spy*, 14 November 1894; "Survived Horrors," *Worcester Daily Spy*, 19 October 1895; "Prisoners of War," *Daily Inter Ocean*, 21 October 1880; "Andersonville," *Daily Inter Ocean*, 9 October 1879.

24 Illinois Prisoners of War Association handbill, dated 1 November 1881, copy in Boston Corbett Papers, KaHS; A. D. Streight as quoted in *Constitution and By-Laws of the Ohio Association*, 18; Western Andersonville Survivors Association, *Report of the Second Reunion of Rebel Prison Survivors in the West*, copy in PA Box 271.3, Ohio Historical Society, Columbus, Ohio; "The Andersonville Survivors," *Daily Inter Ocean*, 20 October 1880; "Dixie's Hideous Dens," *Daily Inter Ocean*, 29 October 1886; "[Iowa] Ex-Prisoners of War," *National Tribune*, 23 November 1882; "Union Ex-Prisoners of War," *Hartford Courant*, 23 February 1894; "Former War Prisoners Meet," *Chicago Daily Tribune*, 17 October 1900; "The Andersonville Survivors," *Daily Inter Ocean*, 7 October 1880; "Days Recalled of Prison Life," *Boston Journal*, 16 August 1904; "Survivors of Prison Pens," *Daily Inter*

Ocean, 28 October 1886; Amos E. Stearns, *Narrative of Amos E. Stearns, A Prisoner at Andersonville* (Worcester, Massachusetts: Franklin P. Rice, 1887), dedication page. On Stearns, see also Reunion Record Book of Company A, 25th Massachusetts Association, WHM.

25 Washington, D.C. Union Ex-Prisoner of War Association, minutes of 4 April 1887 meeting, in Associated Survivors of the Sixth Army Corps Papers, Manuscript Division, LoC; "Union Ex-Prisoners of War," *Washington Post*, 5 April 1887; "The Ex-Prisoners of War," *Washington Post*, 9 April 1887; Thomas O'Dea, *History of O'Dea's Famous Picture of Andersonville Prison* (Cohoes, New York: Clark & Fister, 1887).

26 "Survivors of Prison Pens," *Daily Inter Ocean*, 28 October 1886; "Annual Reunion of Ex-Prisoners," *San Francisco Chronicle*, 19 August 1903; Robert Kellogg to Richard Atwater, 4 January 1909, in Dorence Atwater Papers, Connecticut State Library; "Andersonville Relics," undated newspaper clipping in Ira Emory Forbes Papers, Connecticut State Library; "Michigan Ex-Prisoners of War," *National Tribune*, 21 December 1882; "Frank Smith's Visit to Andersonville," *National Tribune*, 20 September 1883; "War Veterans," *Worcester Daily Spy*, 14 November 1894.

27 "A Genuine Relic of Andersonville Prison," broadside in Boston Corbett Papers, KaHS.

28 *Fourth Annual Reunion, Illinois Association Ex-Prisoners of War, Decatur, Illinois, October 17–18, 1883*, pp. 18–19, copy in Nicholson Collection, Huntington Library; "Prisoners of War," *National Tribune*, 16 November 1882; *Constitution and By-Laws of the Ohio Association*, 17; *Daily Inter Ocean*, 21 October 1880.

29 "Prison Memories," *New York Herald*, 14 May 1879; "Prisoners of War," *Hartford Daily Times* clipping in Robert Kellogg Vertical File, Ohio Historical Society; Illinois State Association of Union Prisoners of War broadside, dated 17 October 1883, copy in Gustavus Gessner Papers, RHPC; "Reply to Jefferson Davis," *New York Times*, 8 February 1876; Gustavus Gessner to Robert Todd Lincoln, n.d., Gustavus Gessner Papers, Box 1, Folder 4, RHPC. Phisterer used postwar figures reported by the Adjutant General. Gessner maintained that this formulation included "14,000 graves at Andersonville" and "12,000 at Salisbury" without "any account of the thousands that are buried at other places in the South." Indeed, no reliable data for the prison camps at Charleston, Cahaba, and Millen was ever compiled. Frederick Phisterer, *Statistical Record of the Armies of the United States*, 70; C. C. Shanklin et al., "Memorial of the National Association of Ex-Union Prisoners of War," 3 April 1884, in Petitions and Memorials Referred to Committees (HR 48A-H11.4), Committee on Invalid Pensions, 48th Congress, Records of the House of Representatives, RG 233, National Archives Building.

30 Gordon, " 'Surely They Remember Me,' " 329. Gordon argues that ex-prisoners "sought to redefine their helpless and dehumanizing incarceration into something courageous and necessary to northern victory."

31 William Franklin Lyon, *In and Out of Andersonville Prison* (Detroit: George Harland Co., 1905), 106–109; Homer Sprague, *Lights and Shadows in Confederate Prisons: A Personal Experience, 1864–1865* (New York: G. P. Putnam's Sons, 1915), 134; Glenn M. Robins, "Race, Repatriation, and Galvanized Rebels: Union Prisoners and the Exchange Question in Deep South Prison Camps," *Civil War History* 53, no. 2 (June 2007): 118, 140; Joseph Twichell, untitled manuscript in Joseph Twichell Papers, Box 12, Beinecke Rare Book and Manuscript Library, Yale University.

32 John Read quoted in *Boston Daily Globe*, 16 August 1904; Gordon, "Surely They Remember Me"; Amos E. Stearns, *Narrative of Amos E. Stearns*, 57; Gessner, manuscript for reunion address, n.d., in Gustavus Gessner Papers, Box 1, Folder 4, RHPC; Augustus Choate Hamlin, *Martyria* (Boston: Lee & Shepard, 1866), 33; see also William Stanley Mead, manuscript on Andersonville, n.d., in William Stanley Mead Collection, Box 2, Folder 4, InHS; Clarke, "Honorable Scars"; Lieutenant A. C. Roach, *The Prisoner of War and How Treated: Containing a History of Colonel Streight's Expedition to the Rear of Bragg's Army, in the Spring of 1863, and a Correct Account of the Treatment and Condition of the Union Prisoners of War in the Rebel Prisons of the South in 1863–1864, Being the Actual Experience of a Union Officer During Twenty-Two Months' Imprisonment in Rebeldom With Personal Adventures, Biographical Sketches, and History of Andersonville Prison* (Indianapolis: Railroad City Publishing House, 1865), 209.

33 "Prison Memories," *New York Herald*, 14 May 1879; "The Andersonville Survivors," *Daily Inter Ocean*, 14 October 1880; "Andersonville Survivors," *Daily Inter Ocean*, 15 October 1881; "Proposed Prisoners' Pension Bill," *National Tribune*, 23 September 1882; "Ex-Prisoners of War," *Philadelphia Inquirer*, 20 August 1885; "More Pensions Wanted," *New York Times*, 20 August 1886; "Reviving Bitter Memories," *Chicago Daily Tribune*, 23 September 1887; "Union Ex-Prisoners of War," *Washington Post*, 24 September 1887; Lyle Adair to Committee on Invalid Pensions, petition dated 7 April 1884, in Petitions and Memorials Referred to Committees (HR 48A-H11.4), Committee on Invalid Pensions, 48th Congress, Records of the House of Representatives, RG 233, National Archives Building; New York State Association of Union Prisoners of War, "Appeal in Behalf of the Union Ex-Prisoners of War," 1 February 1882, in Petitions and Memorials Referred to Committees (HR 47A-H10.2), Committee on Invalid Pensions, 47th Congress, Records of the House of Representatives, RG 233, NARA; "Petition to the Honorable Senators and Representatives of New York at Washington," in

Petitions and Memorials Referred to Committees (HR 47A-H10.2), Committee on Invalid Pensions, 48th Congress, Records of the House of Representatives, RG 233, NARA; Gustavus Gessner, manuscript of reunion address, n.d., Gustavus Gessner Papers, Box 1, Folder 4, RHPC; on the demands of pension claims, see Dean, *Shook over Hell*, 147, and William Best Hesseltine, "The Propaganda Literature of Confederate Prisons," *Journal of Southern History* 1, no. 1 (February 1935): 65; Nathan Goff to Committee on Invalid Pensions, petition dated 2 February 1886, in Petitions and Memorials Referred to Committees (HR 49A-10.5), Committee on Invalid Pensions, 49th Congress, Records of the House of Representatives, RG 233, National Archives; "Resolutions of Toledo [Ohio] Association Union Ex-Prisoners of War, Relative to Pensions," in Petitions and Memorials Referred to Committees (HR 51A-10.1), Committee on Invalid Pensions, 51st Congress, Records of the House of Representatives, RG 233, NARA; J. J. Stuckey, "Memorial of Iowa Prisoner of War Association," in Petitions and Memorials Referred to Committees (HR 51.A-10.1), Committee on Invalid Pensions, 51st Congress, Records of the House of Representatives, RG 233, NARA.

34 *Atlantic Telegraph*, 21 May 1890; "Our Washington Letter," *Friendship Weekly Register*, 17 July 1890. Failed attempts to provide pensions to Union ex–prisoners of war include the Keifer Bill, H.R. 4495 (1880); the Bliss Bill, H.R. 3386 (1881); and the Robinson Bill, H.R. 5968 (1882), which was reintroduced in 1883. On the history of Civil War pensions, see U.S. Bureau of Pensions, *Laws of the United States Governing the Granting of Army and Navy Pensions* (Washington, D.C.: Government Printing Office, 1916); "Gen. Hawley on Pensions," *Argus and Patriot*, 16 April 1890; Hays Post No. 3 to Committee on Invalid Pensions, 27 March 1882, and J. W. Patterson Post No. 15 to Committee on Invalid Pensions, 28 March 1882, both in Petitions and Memorials Referred to Committees (HR 47A-H10.2), Committee on Invalid Pensions, 47th Congress, Records of the House of Representatives, RG 233, NARA; Theda Skocpol, *Protecting Soldiers and Mothers: The Political Origins of Social Policy in the United States* (Cambridge: Harvard University Press, 1992), 122, 128; Linker, *War's Waste*, 18.

35 Robert Hale Kellogg to George Q. Whitney, letter, 21 March 1922, in George Q. Whitney Papers, RG 69:23, Box 5, Connecticut State Library; "Union Ex-Prisoners of War," *Boston Daily Globe*, 17 October 1901; "Men Who Were in Prison," *Washington Post*, 22 September 1892.

CHAPTER 6: A DEBT OF HONOR

1 Leo G. Mazow and Kevin M. Murphy, *Taxing Visions: Financial Episodes in Late Nineteenth-Century American Art* (University Park: Pennsylvania State University Press, 2010), 22; "The Pension Agent," in Thomas Ellis Kirby, *Catalogue of the*

Private Art Collection of Thomas B. Clarke (New York: American Art Association, 1899), 258.

2 See *Weekly Knight and Soldier*, 14 December 1887; Joseph T. Solomon Pension File, application no. 513,731, certificate no. 465,367, RG 15, Civil War Pension Files, National Archives. On the "problem of the pensioner," see Linker, *War's Waste*, 10, 33; *Kansas Knight and Soldier*, 1 July 1886; these insights draw on Peter David Blanck and Michael Millender, "Before Disability Civil Rights: Civil War Pensions and the Politics of Disability in America," *Alabama Law Review* 52 (Fall 2000), especially their observation that "veterans themselves played a role in articulating the meaning of disability in late nineteenth-century America," "aggressively exploit[ing]" the Pension Bureau to recognize their conditions, as well as McConnell, *Glorious Contentment*; Ell Torrance, undated speech extract, in Ell Torrance Papers, Box 34, MinnHS.

3 See John P. Resch, "Federal Welfare for Revolutionary War Veterans," *Social Service Review* 56, no. 2 (June 1982): 171–195; and John P. Resch, *Suffering Soldiers*; James W. Oberly, *Sixty Million Acres: American Veterans and the Public Lands Before the Civil War* (Kent, Ohio: Kent State University Press, 1990), Resch, "Federal Welfare for Revolutionary War Veterans," 172, 190, 191; see also Linker, *War's Waste*, 14–15; John William Oliver, *History of the Civil War Military Pensions, 1861–1865* (Madison: University of Wisconsin, 1917), 5; William Henry Glasson, *Federal Military Pensions in the United States* (New York: Oxford University Press, 1918), 124.

4 Glasson, *Federal Military Pensions in the United States*, 124. Lemuel Cook, the "last full pay pensioner" of the American Revolution, died in May 1866. On Cook, see Benson J. Lossing, ed., *The American Historical Record and Repertory of Notes and Queries*, vol. 2 (Philadelphia: Samuel P. Town, 1873), 357–359; Glasson, 124–125; Megan Jean McClintock, "Binding up the Nation's Wounds: Civil War Pensions and American Families, 1861–1890" (Ph.D. diss., Rutgers University, 1994), 98. As the endnotes will attest, my discussion of pension legislation throughout this chapter is deeply indebted to the work of Glasson, Oliver, and Skocpol. Usher as quoted in Skocpol, *Protecting Soldiers and Mothers*, 106; Glasson, *Federal Military Pensions*, 125–128, 131; Oliver, *History of the Civil War Military Pensions*, 10; "Army Pensions," *Philadelphia Inquirer*, 13 August 1862; Skocpol, *Protecting Soldiers and Mothers*, 106–107; John Gibbon, "Pensions: A Paper Read Before Oregon Commandery of the Military Order of the Loyal Legion of the United States, October 8, 1890," in *Civil War Papers of the California Commandery of the Military Order of the Loyal Legion of the United States* (Wilmington, North Carolina: Broadfoot Publishing Co., 1995), 418. See also Larry M. Logue and Peter Blanck, *Race, Ethnicity, and Disability: Veterans and*

Benefits in Post-Civil War America (Cambridge: Cambridge University Press, 2010); *OR*, series III, vol. 5, p. 510.

5 "The Pension Bureau," *New York Times*, 9 December 1865; "Report of the Secretary of the Interior," in *Executive Documents Printed by Order of the House of Representatives During the Third Session of the Thirty-Seventh Congress, 1862–1863* (Washington, D.C.: Government Printing Office, 1863), 15; Oliver, *History of Civil War Military Pensions*, 18, 21; Glasson, *Federal Military Pensions*, 129, 133; George Sanger, ed., *The Statutes at Large, Treaties, and Proclamations of the United States of America* (Boston: Little, Brown & Co., 1866), 387–389; *Congressional Globe*, 42nd Congress, 3rd Session, p. 1283; Oliver, *History of Civil War Military Pensions*, 37; Glasson, *Federal Military Pensions*, 134; Dora L. Costa, *The Evolution of Retirement: An American Economic History, 1880–1990* (Chicago: University of Chicago Press, 1998), 199. See also Charles Pelham, *Hints and Helps to Lawyers, Claim Agents, Claimants, Applicants for Position in the Civil Service, and All Others Having Business of Any Kind with the Government at Washington City, Compiled from Official Data* (Washington, D.C.: William G. White, Printer, 1887), 53.

6 *Western Veteran*, 18 December 1889.

7 Ibid.; McConnell, *Glorious Contentment*, 143; Pelham, *Hints and Helps*, 53; *National Tribune* 1, no. 1 (October 1877): 6; "Arrears of Pensions," *National Tribune* 1, no. 2 (November 1877): 1; *Western Veteran*, 18 December 1889, and 6 August 1890; Patrick O'Farrell, "Pension Frauds," Grand Army of the Republic circular, in Grand Army of the Republic Collection, Series VII, Box 9, Folder 2, NHS; *Veterans' Advocate*, 10 June 1884, copy at NHHS; *Western Veteran*, 18 December 1889; *National Tribune* 1, no. 1 (October 1877): 6; *Veterans' Advocate*, 4 March 1884, copy at NHHS.

8 Ole Steensland, address at reunion of the 15th Wisconsin Infantry, Chicago, Illinois, 29 August 1900, in Civil War Papers, Local History Manuscripts Collection, Milwaukee Public Library. Steensland sued for a pension on the basis that he could not "stand much walking" since returning from Andersonville. "I know that the majority of those who receive pensions can do more manual labor than I can," he wrote. In 1901, Steensland's congressman pushed through and secured a private pension bill for the former prisoner, which he refused—so enraged by his treatment at the hands of the government that had "left" him at Andersonville "to die"; Skocpol, *Protecting Soldiers and Mothers*, 121–122; Louis Wagner as quoted in "Hearing Before the Committee on Pensions of the Senate of the United States of the Committee on Pensions of the Grand Army of the Republic," 8 March 1884, copy in Benjamin Harrison Papers, Box 18:2, Manuscript Division, LoC; Affidavit of Daniel Eldredge, circa 1873, in Daniel Eldredge Pension File, application no. 119,073, certificate no. 80,269, in RG 15, Civil War Pension Files,

NARA; "Soldier-Hating Examining Boards," *Western Veteran*, 26 June 1889, copy at KaHS.

9 William E. Clark, *Our Debt of Honor: Justice, Humanity, Reason, and Policy Demand Its Payment* (Boston: William E. Clark, 1866), copy at Massachusetts Historical Society. Bounty equalization was an equally divisive issue in the aftermath of the war. Unlike subsequent volunteers, men who enlisted in 1861 and 1862 did not receive enlistment bonuses. As a result, in 1866, veterans crowded into meeting halls throughout the North to demand "equalization" and "equality of compensation"—and, on at least one occasion, the hanging of Jefferson Davis. See *New York Herald*, 6 February 1866, 18 April 1866; *Philadelphia Inquirer*, 26 July 1866; *Macon Telegraph*, 23 September 1866; "Soldier's Meeting on the Bounty Question," *New Orleans Times*, 24 September 1866; and Dearing, *Veterans in Politics*, 57–58; *National Tribune* 1, no. 1 (October 1877): 6; George A. Wilson as quoted in *Fourth Annual Reunion, Illinois Association Ex-Prisoners of War, Decatur, Illinois, October 17–18, 1883*, 30–31, copy in Nicholson Collection, Huntington Library; *Grand Army Journal*, 29 October 1870; see also "The Nation's Debt," *Soldier's Manual* (August 1868); *Grand Army Journal*, 16 July 1870, *Journal of the Twenty-First Session, National Encampment, Grand Army of the Republic, St. Louis, Missouri* (Milwaukee: Burdick & Armitage, Printers, 1887), 217; P. C. Johnson, "To the Soldiers of the Grand Army of the Republic," circular in Grand Army of the Republic Collection, Series I, Box 2, Folder 10, NHS; and *Journal of the Sixteenth Annual Session of the National Encampment, Grand Army of the Republic, Held at Baltimore, Md., June 21, 22, 23, 1882* (Lawrence: George S. Merrill, Printer, 1882), 55.

10 Traditionally, scholars have understood the Grand Army's pension advocacy as an effort to revive a "moribund" organization—slighting the real need of sick and destitute veterans. Dearing, *Veterans in Politics*; McConnell, *Glorious Contentment*; McMurry, "The Pension Question"; *Veterans' Advocate*, 4 March 1884; *Grand Army Journal*, 29 October 1870; I. N. Carr, Decoration Day address, circa 1899, I. N. Carr Papers, Box 6, Folder 3, SHSIo; *Veterans' Advocate*, 4 March 1884; *Grand Army Journal*, 29 October 1870; circulars from Adjutant John E. Myers Post, No. 386, Sligo, Pennsylvania (dated 4 January 1888), George Hill Post, No. 540, Moosic, Pennsylvania (dated 21 November 1887), and Watson Brothers Post, No. 432, Portersville, Pennsylvania (20 March 1888), all in J. K. Taylor Post, No. 182, Box 11, General Scrapbook and Files, GARMA; *Kansas Knight and Soldier* (August 1885); Scrapbook of the 44th Regimental Association, 44th Regimental Association Records, InHS; *Journal of the Twenty-Seventh Annual Session of the Encampment of the Department of the Potomac, Grand Army of the Republic, Washington, D.C., February 21, 23, 25, 27, 29, and March 6, 1895* (Washington, D.C.: Gib-

son Bros., Printers and Bookbinders, 1895), 58; account of Charles Mooney in *Veterans' Advocate*, 18 March 1884; Frank Bell, "The Question of Pensions," *Century* 42 (1891): 790–792; meeting minutes of 7 March 1898 in Minute Book of Reynolds Post, No. 5, Grand Army of the Republic, John F. Reynolds Post No. 5 Records, Folder 2, Institute for Regional Studies, NDSU; GAR Surgeon General quoted in *Journal of the Twenty-Second Annual Session of the National Encampment, Grand Army of the Republic, Columbus, Ohio, September 12th, 13th, and 14th, 1888* (Minneapolis: Harrison & Smith, Printers, 1888), 53; Beath quoted in *Journal of the Twenty-Third Annual Session of the National Encampment, Grand Army of the Republic, Milwaukee, Wisconsin, August 28th, 29th, and 30th, 1889* (St. Louis: A. Whipple, Printer, 1889), 179; George Fitzclarence to J. A. Martin, 26 July 1885, Records of the Governor's Office—Governor J. A. Martin, Box 30, Folder 1, KaHS; John J. Rogner, 19 November 1884, John Denzler Case File, Sample Case Files of the NHDVS, Milwaukee Branch, Box 5, NARA, Great Lakes Division; "Soldier's Home Bazaar, to Be Held at Boston in the Autumn of 1881," broadside in Civil War Pamphlets Collection, USAMHI; A. O. Wright, 30 December 1895, A. O. Wright Papers, Box 2, WiHS; Orlando B. Willcox to William Buel Franklin, 25 June 1889, National Home for the Disabled Volunteer Soldier Collection, Box 1, Folder 2, Milwaukee Public Library; "Ex-Soldiers in the Poor House," *Public Opinion* 2, no. 44 (February 12, 1887): 369; and Joshua Ricketts, 12 March 1887, Jerry Rourke Case File, No. 343, RG 259.002, Case Files of the Illinois State Soldiers' and Sailors' Home, Illinois State Archives. For the 30,000 figure, see *Western Veteran*, 18 December 1889; "Burial of Indigent Deceased Ex-Union Soldiers, Sailors, or Marines," form provided by Wisconsin Chapter 385, passed 8 April 1887, Sauk County, Wisconsin, Soldiers' Funeral Expenses Records, 1891–1902, WiHS; Corporal G. A. Lord, *A Short Narrative and Military Experience of Corp. G. A. Lord* (n.p., n.d.), copy in George Johnston Scrapbook, 1868–1887, Series I, George and William Johnston Papers, InHS; J. S. Anderson, 7 January 1897, Gustav Mueller Case File, Sample Case Files of the NHDVS, Milwaukee Branch, Box 6, NARA, Great Lakes Division; Case Descriptions of William F. Irving, Phillip McGuire, and John McNamara in Charlestown Overseer of the Poor Records, Massachusetts Historical Society; and A. Symonds to Gorman Post No. 13, letter, 3 December 1895, in GAR, Gorman Post No. 13 Records, NeMinnHC; *Albert Lea Enterprise*, 24 January 1895, clipping in Henry House Diary, MinnHS.

11 Minutes of the Veterans Rights Union of Kansas, 13 September 1886, Patrick Coney Papers, Box 4, KaHS. Some, of course, grew restless and cynical about veterans' prospects. One New Hampshire ex-soldier, for instance, thought it "almost a waste of time to agitate" on the matter of pensions, for politicians con-

veniently forgot their promises to veterans once in Washington. "Whether civilian or soldier, all are alike when the veterans ask for justice," he wrote. See L. W. Cogswell, letter to the editor, 10 December 1884, in *Veterans' Advocate*, 16 December 1884; *Relief Guard*, 2 August 1890; Lucius Fairchild, speech, 26 September 1887, Lucius Fairchild Papers, Box 56, Folder 15, WiHS; James Tanner as quoted in "Hearing Before the Committee on Pensions of the Senate of the United States of the Committee on Pensions of the Grand Army of the Republic," 8 March 1884, copy in Benjamin Harrison Papers, Box 18:2, Manuscript Division, LoC; Charles Henry Wilson, letter, 1 September 1885, Charles Henry Wilson Papers, Box 6, Folder 3, NHS; *Journal of the Senate of the State of New York at Their One Hundred and Eighth Session* (Albany: Weed, Parsons & Co., Printers, 1885), 307; J. Worth Carnahan, *Manual of the Civil War and Key to the Grand Army of the Republic and Kindred Societies* (Washington, D.C.: U.S. Army and Navy Historical Association, 1899), 63–64; O. H. Coulter to Patrick Coney, 18 March 1886 and 4 May 1886, both in Patrick Coney Papers, Box 2, KaHS; *Journal of the Nineteenth Annual Session of the National Encampment, Grand Army of the Republic, Portland, Maine, June 24th and 25th, 1885* (Toledo, Ohio: Montgomery & Vrooman, Printers, 1885), 31; "Veterans' Rights Union," *Kansas Knight and Soldier*, 15 April 1886, copy at KaHS. Davies, *Patriotism on Parade*, 151; *Constitution and By Laws of the Union Veteran Army* (New York: Globe Stationery & Printing Co., 1884); "Soldiers and Sailors Land Bounty Bill" [1872], copy in Ramsey Pamphlets Collection, MinnHS; "Attention, Ex-Union Soldiers!," *Weekly Knight and Soldier*, 31 October 1888; William E. W. Ross to Grover Cleveland, letter, 10 December 1885, Grover Cleveland Papers, reel 26, Manuscript Division, LoC; *Western Knight and Soldier*, 30 January 1889, copies at KaHS; and *Philadelphia Inquirer*, 23 July 1885. McConnell, *Glorious Contentment*, 157.

12 Marten, *Sing Not War*, and McConnell, *Glorious Contentment*. In the early twentieth century, these sentiments percolated into historical scholarship, as well. See, for example, Donald L. McMurry, "The Political Significance of the Pension Question, 1885–1897," *Mississippi Valley Historical Review* 9, no. 1 (June 1922): 19–36; "Reconciliation," Minnesota veteran Eliakim Torrance explained, "insults ninety nine out of every one hundred of our soldiers . . . we hate traitors and despise all who stoop to do them honor." Though uttered immediately after the war, this sentiment lingered. Eliakim Torrance, manuscript for speech, 4 July 1866, Ell Torrance Papers, Box 34, MinnHS. "The Blue and the Gray," *Kansas Knight and Soldier* (May 1885); Tourgée, *The Veteran and His Pipe*, 3. For background on the book, see Blight, *Race and Reunion*, 96–97. "R.B.L." to WOB, 31 December 1867, in *Soldier's Friend* (February 1868); *Daily Veteran*, 2 September 1889, NHS; minutes of the Vet-

erans Rights Union of Kansas, 9 August 1886, Patrick Coney Papers, Box 4, KaHS; "Attention, Ex-Union Soldiers," *Weekly Knight and Soldier*, 31 October 1888; *New York Tribune* as quoted in Blight, *Race and Reunion*, 94. See also "That Soldier Racket," *Weekly Knight and Soldier*, 23 November 1887; Milton Carmichael, "Memorial Day Address" [circa 1886], in Milton Carmichael Collection, KSRL; and Tourgée, "Memorial Day," in *The Veteran and His Pipe*. For "shared valor," see Blight, *Race and Reunion*; Dearing, *Veterans in Politics*, 319.

13 Donald McMurry notes that Republican and Democratic campaign "textbooks" in 1884 and 1885 "devoted more pages to pensions and the soldiers than to any other subject except the tariff." McMurry, "The Political Significance of the Pension Question," 20. See also "Old Patriots Protest," *Western Veteran*, 30 September 1891; McMurry, "The Political Significance of the Pension Question," 19. On pensions as "cultural symbols" and "massive redistribution," Jeffrey E. Vogel, "Redefining Reconciliation: Confederate Veterans and the Southern Responses to Federal Civil War Pensions," *Civil War History* 51, no. 1 (2005): 69, 68. Vogel offers telling evidence of the searing southern opposition to Union pensions. See also Thomas Rosser to Editor, *New York Times*, letter dated 14 April 1894, in MSS 6354, ASS-pCL; *Veteran's Advocate*, 29 April 1884; and "Confederate Brigadiers Attack Pensions," *Bucks County Gazette*, 24 March 1892, copy in Grand Army of the Republic Miscellaneous Records, GARMA; Patrick O'Farrell, "Pension Frauds," pamphlet in Grand Army of the Republic Collection, Series VII—Pension Records, Box 9, Folder 2, NHS. On pension fraud and corruption, see also Charles Francis Adams, *The Civil War Lack-of-System, a Four-Thousand-Million Record of Legislative Incompetence Tending to General Political Corruption* (Washington, D.C.: n.p., 1912), and Logue and Blanck, *Race, Ethnicity, and Disability*, 111–127.

14 Robert McElroy, *Grover Cleveland: The Man and the Statesman* (New York: Harper & Bros., 1923), 1:203; on Benninsky, see Alyn Brodsky, *Grover Cleveland: A Study in Character* (New York: St. Martin's Press, 2000), 97, and Grover Cleveland to John E. Hall, letter, 13 September 1887, in Allan Nevins, ed., *Letters of Grover Cleveland, 1850–1908* (Boston and New York: Houghton Mifflin Co., 1933), 152–154. On Cleveland's first election to the presidency, see Mark Wahlgren Summers, *Rum, Romanism, and Rebellion: The Making of a President, 1884* (Chapel Hill: University of North Carolina Press, 2000); Grover Cleveland to John W. Frazier, letter, 24 June 1887, in Nevins, ed., *Letters of Grover Cleveland*, 143; Milton Garrigus, manuscript of address delivered at Third Annual Reunion, 39th Indiana Volunteers, September 1886, in Civil War Miscellany Collection, Box 3, Folder 25, InHS. Garrigus paraphrased remarks made by Andrew Johnson during his military governorship of Tennessee; on Garland, see

Farrar Newberry, *A Life of Mr. Garland of Arkansas* (n.p.: Farrar Newberry, 1908); Brodsky, *Grover Cleveland*, 115–116; and *Grand Forks Herald*, 13 February 1885.

15 McMurry, "The Political Significance of the Pension Question," 28–29, 28n22; on private pension legislation, see Skocpol, *Protesting Soldiers and Mothers*, 121; for the lone veto of a private-pension bill prior to Cleveland's administration, see McElroy, *Grover Cleveland*, 200. For a treatment of Cleveland and the pension vetoes that is sympathetic to the president, see McElroy, *Grover Cleveland*, 189–217. Charles W. Calhoun, *Minority Victory: Gilded Age Politics and the Front Porch Campaign of 1888* (Lawrence: University Press of Kansas, 2008), 37–38; Grover Cleveland, veto message, 16 April 1888, in James Richardson, ed., *A Compilation of the Messages and Papers of the Presidents*, vol. 11 (New York: Bureau of National Literature, 1897), 5223–5224; Milton Garrigus, manuscript of address delivered at Third Annual Reunion, 39th Indiana Volunteers, September 1886, in Civil War Miscellany Collection, Box 3, Folder 25, InHS.

16 McElroy, *Grover Cleveland*, 199; George Kilmer, "Union Veterans and Their Pensions," *Century* 38 (1889): 636–638; for Cleveland's veto message, see "Another Veto," *National Tribune*, 17 February 1887, see also McElroy, *Grover Cleveland*, 199–200, and newspaper clipping dated 24 June 1887 in Grover Cleveland Papers, reel 50, Manuscript Division, LoC; *Weekly Knight and Soldier*, 31 October 1888; McConnell, *Glorious Contentment*, 150–151; "Veto of the Dependent Bill"; *National Tribune*, 17 February 1887; Grover Cleveland to David R. Francis, letter, 4 July 1887, in Nevins, ed., *Letters of Grover Cleveland*, 143–146; *Journal of the Senate of the United States, Being the Second Session of the Forty-Ninth Congress, Begun and Held at the City of Washington, December 6, 1886* (Washington, D.C.: Government Printing Office, 1887), 483; and *Proceedings of the Twentieth Annual Encampment of the Department of California, Grand Army of the Republic, Held at Los Angeles, February 21st, 23rd, and 24th, 1887* (San Francisco: George Spaulding & Co., Steam Book and Job Printers, 1887), 93–94.

17 Drum as quoted in McElroy, *Grover Cleveland*, 202–203. On the battle-flag dispute, see also Blight, *Race and Reunion*, 203, and Silber, *The Romance of Reunion*, 97–98. For "indignant protest," and "his sympathy with the rebellion," see, respectively, John A. Martin to Grover Cleveland, letter, 16 June 1887, and Mitchell Post. No. 45, Department of Ohio, Grand Army of the Republic to Grover Cleveland, letter, 16 June 1887, both in Grover Cleveland Papers, reel 49, Manuscript Division, LoC. See also "Captured Rebel Flags," *Philadelphia Inquirer*, 16 June 1887; Lucius Fairchild as quoted in newspaper clipping dated 16 June 1887, in Grover Cleveland Papers, reel 49, Manuscript Division, LoC; "Wild and Intemperate Language," *Kansas City Star*, 16 June 1887; George H. Thomas Post No. 6, Grand Army of the Republic, to Grover Cleveland, letter, 16 June 1887, in

Grover Cleveland Papers, reel 49, Manuscript Division, LoC; Department of Vermont, Grand Army of the Republic, to Grover Cleveland, 17 June 1887, Grover Cleveland Papers, reel 49, Manuscript Division, LoC.

18 Miran Judy Post No. 480, Department of Ohio, Grand Army of the Republic to Grover Cleveland, 16 June 1887; Phillip Sheridan Post No. 4, Department of Michigan, Grand Army of the Republic, to Grover Cleveland, 17 June 1887; Lee County, Iowa, Soldiers' Association to Grover Cleveland, 16 June 1887; William Larrabee to Grover Cleveland, letter, 15 June 1887; and A. C. Sweetzer to Grover Cleveland, 16 June 1887; and Alva Adams to Grover Cleveland, 17 June 1887, all in Grover Cleveland Papers, reel 49, Manuscript Division, LoC; James Lysle Post No. 128, Grand Army of the Republic, to Grover Cleveland, 17 June 1887; George Gordon Meade Post No. 38, Grand Army of the Republic, to Grover Cleveland, 18 June 1887; and "Monkeying with the Buzz Saw," undated newspaper clipping, all in Grover Cleveland Papers, reel 49, Manuscript Division, LoC; James Lysle Post No. 128, Grand Army of the Republic, to Grover Cleveland, 17 June 1887, in Grover Cleveland Papers, reel 49, Manuscript Division, LoC; newspaper clipping dated 24 June 1887, in Grover Cleveland Papers, reel 50, Manuscript Division, LoC; Grover Cleveland to David R. Francis, 4 July 1887, in Nevins, ed., *Letters of Grover Cleveland*, 145; Nina Silber argues that the hostility behind the battle-flag dispute was not directed at the Confederates, but instead at the "machinations of the Cleveland administration." Yet Silber, who argues that Union veterans generally embraced the "culture of conciliation," does not consider the genuine sense of betrayal felt by these veterans—nor the possibility that veterans could forgive but never forget. Silber, *Romance of Reunion*, 98. See also McMurry, "The Political Significance of the Pension Question," 30.

19 Grover Cleveland to William Endicott, letter, 16 June 1887, in Nevins, ed., *Letters of Grover Cleveland*, 142; Grover Cleveland to John W. Frazier, 24 June 1887, in ibid., 142–143; on the 1887 reunion at Gettysburg, see D. Scott Hartwig, " 'The Most Notable Event at Gettysburg Since the War': The Reunion of the Philadelphia Brigade and Pickett's Division, July 1887," *Civil War Regiments* 6, no. 3 (1999).

20 *Journal of the Twenty-Second Annual Session of the National Encampment Grand Army of the Republic*, 214; "Service Pension," *Weekly Knight and Soldier*, 11 January 1888; Harry J. Sievers, *Benjamin Harrison: Hoosier Statesman* (New York: University Publishers, 1959), 209–210, 284; Calhoun, *Minority Victory*, 89–91.

21 Dearing, *Veterans in Politics*, 392–393. On Tanner, see James Tanner Reminiscences, Abraham Lincoln Presidential Library; "Commissioner James Tanner," *Washington Bee*, 20 April 1889; James Marten, "Union Veterans and Manhood: Corporal James Tanner and Gilded Age Values," paper presented at the Society

of Civil War Historians Biennial Meeting, Lexington, Kentucky, June 15, 2012; Sievers, *Benjamin Harrison: Hoosier President*, 117–118; Donald L. McMurry, "The Bureau of Pensions During the Administration of President Harrison," *Mississippi Valley Historical Review* 13, no. 3 (December 1926): 344, 346; "Corporal Tanner," *Grand Forks Herald*, 14 May 1889; "Political Comments," *Cleveland Gazette*, 4 May 1889; Tanner as quoted in Dearing, *Veterans in Politics*, 393; James E. Smith, *A Famous Battery and Its Campaigns, 1861–1865: The Career of Corporal James Tanner in War and Peace* (Washington, D.C.: W. H. Lowdermilk & Co., 1892), 209, 212; McMurry, "The Bureau of Pensions During the Administration of President Harrison," 350.

22 Dearing, *Veterans in Politics*, 394; "Tanner Is Sustained," *Philadelphia Inquirer*, 30 August 1889; "Corporal Tanner," *Kansas City Star*, 24 April 1889; *Weekly Journal Miner* [Prescott, Arizona Territory], 3 July 1889; McMurry, "The Bureau of Pensions During the Administration of President Harrison," 347, 347n15; *Journal of the Twenty-Third Annual Session of the National Encampment, Grand Army of the Republic*, 163; "Tanner as a Surplus Destroyer," *Milwaukee Journal*, 5 August 1889, quoted by Ellaklin Torrance in speech extract, n.d., in Ell Torrance Papers, Box 34, MinnHS.

23 Tanner as quoted in "Corporal Tanner's Policy," *Philadelphia Inquirer*, 11 May 1889.

24 Harry J. Sievers, *Benjamin Harrison: Hoosier President* (Indianapolis: Bobbs Merrill Co., 1968), 119, 124 126; Dearing, *Veterans in Politics*, 394–396; McMurry, "The Bureau of Pensions During the Administration of President Harrison," 349–351; "Charges Against Tanner," *Philadelphia Inquirer*, 16 August 1889; "Tanner Resigns," *Grand Forks Herald*, 12 September 1889; William Barlow, "U.S. Commissioner of Pensions Green B. Raum of Illinois," *Journal of the Illinois State Historical Society* 60, no. 3 (Autumn 1967): 297–312.

25 Dearing, *Veterans in Politics*, 398–399; Illinois veteran as quoted in *Journal of the Twenty Third Annual Session of the National Encampment, Grand Army of the Republic*, 245–246; Richardson, *West from Appomattox*, 267–268.

26 Sievers, *Benjamin Harrison: Hoosier President*, 128; Homer E. Socolofsky and Allan B. Spetter, *The Presidency of Benjamin Harrison* (Lawrence: University Press of Kansas, 1987), 37; William Henry Glasson, "A Costly Pension Law—Act of June 27, 1890," *South Atlantic Quarterly* 3, no. 4 (October 1904): 363; McMurry, "The Bureau of Pensions During the Administration of President Harrison," 355–356; Wecter, *When Johnny Comes Marching Home*, 252; Linker, *War's Waste*, 18–21; quotes from Glasson, "A Costly Pension Law—Act of June 27, 1890," 369. For a close analysis of this rhetoric, see McConnell, *Glorious Contentment*, and Marten, *Sing Not War*; Bell, "The Question of Pensions," 791–792.

27 "The Remoteness of the War," *World's Work* 7 (1904): 4508; Linker, *War's Waste*, 20, 33–34, 120–147.

28 William H. Glasson, "Federal and Confederate Pensions in the South," *South Atlantic Quarterly* 9, no. 3 (July 1910): 280; Linker, *War's Waste*, 95–96, 144–147; see also Marten, *Sing Not War*.

CHAPTER 7: THIS DEGRADATION OF SOULS

1 Leander Stillwell, "In the Ranks at Shiloh," in *War Talks in Kansas: A Series of Papers Read Before the Kansas Commandery of the Military Order of the Loyal Legion of the United States* (Kansas City, Missouri: Press of the Franklin Hudson Publishing Co., 1906), 110–112.

2 Ibid., 110–112, 114–115; William T. Shaw, "The Battle of Shiloh," in *War Sketches and Incidents as Related by Companions of the Iowa Commandery, Military Order of the Loyal Legion of the United States* (Des Moines: Press of P. C. Kenyon, 1893), 1:185; *OR*, series I, vol. 10, part 1, pp. 104, 277; Historical Register of National Homes for Disabled Volunteer Soldiers, 1866–1938 (National Archives Microfilm Publication M1749, 282 rolls), entry 307.

3 Historical Register of National Homes for Disabled Volunteer Soldiers, 1866–1938 (National Archives Microfilm Publication M1749, 282 rolls), entry 307; Paul James Lindberg, daybook entry [circa 1872], in Paul James Lindberg Papers, Box 1, Folder 1, Huntington Library; see also Lindberg to S. Salverda, letter, 24 June 1878, and Lindberg to "Honored Doctor," 7 October 1878, both in Paul James Lindberg Papers, Box 2, Huntington Library; Lindberg to "Honored Doctor," 7 October 1878, Paul James Lindberg Papers, Box 2, Huntington Library.

4 Paul James Lindberg, daybook entries [circa 1872–1876], in Paul James Lindberg Papers, Box 1, Huntington Library; on the quality of food at the National Home for Disabled Volunteer Soldiers, see letter to the editor dated 2 March 1884, as printed in the *Veteran's Advocate*, 6 May 1884.

5 Paul James Lindberg, daybook entry [circa 1872], in Paul James Lindberg Papers, Box 1, Huntington Library; Paul James Lindberg, daybook entry [circa 1877], ibid.; J. C. Gobrecht, *History of the National Home for Disabled Volunteer Soldiers* (Dayton, Ohio: United Brethren Printing Establishment, 1875), 17. Local officials were often determined to remove needy veterans from their towns. P. V. Carey, the mayor of Des Moines, Iowa, wrote a letter to the Milwaukee home on behalf of one veteran, pleading for his admission. Michael Mattimore Case File, Sample Case Files of Members, National Home for Disabled Volunteer Soldiers, Northwestern Branch, Box 6, in RG 15: Records of the Veterans' Administration, NARA, Great Lakes Region; Anna Dickinson as quoted in A. W. Drury, *History of the City of Dayton and Montgomery County, Ohio* (Chicago: S. J. Clarke, 1909), 1:765.

6 Linus Pierpont Brockett and Mary C. Vaughan, *Woman's Work in the Civil War: A Record of Heroism, Patriotism, and Patience* (Philadelphia: Zeigler, McCurdy & Co., 1867), 756–757; Judith Gladys Cetina, "A History of Veterans' Homes in the United States: 1811–1930" (Ph.D. diss., Case Western Reserve University, 1977), 84–85; *Congressional Globe*, 38th Congress, 2nd Session, p. 1237; *Congressional Globe*, 39th Congress, 1st Session, p. 581; Kelly, *Creating a National Home*, 47, 77–78; Bremner, *The Public Good*, 145–146; Brockett and Vaughan, *Women's Work*, 757. See also John L. Mitchell, "The National Home," in *War Papers: Being Papers Read Before the Commandery of the State of Wisconsin, Military Order of the Loyal Legion of the United States*, vol. 1, reprint ed. (Wilmington, North Carolina: Broadfoot, 1993), 140–148; Cetina, "A History of Veterans' Homes," 85, 97, 97n1, 103; Bellows as quoted in Bremner, *The Public Good*, 146; Gobrecht, *History of the National Home*, 20; Kelly, *Creating a National Home*, 81–83; *Report of the Board of Managers of the National Asylum for Disabled Volunteer Soldiers, July 18, 1867*, Serial Set vol. 1312, no. 1 (40th Congress, 1st Session); "The National Military and Naval Asylum," *Philadelphia Inquirer*, 23 October 1865; Richard S. West, Jr., *Lincoln's Scapegoat General: A Life of Benjamin F. Butler, 1818–1893* (Boston: Houghton Mifflin Co., 1965), 316–317; Robert S. Holzman, *Stormy Ben Butler* (New York: Collier Books, 1961), 201; *Report of the Board of Managers of the National Asylum for Disabled Volunteer Soldiers, February 26, 1869*, Serial Set vol. 1385, no. 1 (40th Congress, 3rd Session): 4. Not surprisingly, veterans anticipated from the very beginning the need for federal veterans' homes. In 1865, Minnesota veterans began collecting funds for a state soldiers home, and in an 1866 address, Illinois veteran Eugene Payne appealed for "asylums and homes" to care for the wounded and disabled. See First Minnesota Battery to Governor, letter, 26 July 1865, in Governor's Records, MinnHS, and Eugene Payne Speech, SC 2701, Abraham Lincoln Presidential Library.

7 John Younglove, *Hon. Marcus L. Ward, "The Soldier's Friend": A Eulogy Delivered Before Marcus L. Ward Post and Friends, in Music Hall, Newark, N.J., on December 18th, 1884* (Newark, New Jersey: Press of the Newark Daily Advertiser, 1885), 19; Joseph W. Morton, Jr., *Sparks from the Campfire*, 632–633; Barber, *The Nation's Defenders*, 6–7, 10, 21; Beath, *History of the Grand Army*, 462; "Soldier's Home at Newark—Dedication of the Building," *New York Times*, 9 September 1866; "The Dedication of the New Jersey Home for Disabled Soldiers, at Newark, New Jersey," *Frank Leslie's Illustrated Newspaper*, 22 September 1866; "Soldiers Homes," *Western Veteran*, 26 June 1889. For examples of Marcus Ward's tireless work as a "soldiers' friend," see Marcus L. Ward Papers, Box 4, Alexander Library, Rutgers University.

8 Kelly, *Creating a National Home*, 66; Mary Clark Brayton and Ellen F. Terry, *Our Acre and Its Harvest: Historical Sketch of the Soldiers' Aid Society of Northern Ohio*

(Cleveland: Fairbanks, Benedict & Co., Printers, 1869), 259–260; Gobrecht, *History of the National Home*, 38; Robert E. Yott, *From Soldiers' Home to Medical Center: A Glance at the 125 Year History of the Bath Soldiers' Home* (Bath, New York: Robert E. Yott, 2006), 1; Lori D. Ginzberg, *Women and the Work of Benevolence: Morality, Politics, and Class in the Nineteenth-Century United States* (New Haven: Yale University Press, 1990), 169, 170–171; Brockett and Vaughan, *Woman's Work*, 544; Soldiers' Home Fund Appeal Circular, copy in Local History Collection, Milwaukee Public Library; *Wisconsin State Register*, 20 May 1865.

9 Timothy L. Smith, *Togus, Down in Maine: The First National Veterans Home* (Charleston, South Carolina: Arcadia Publishing, 1998), 6; William Edward Seaver Whitman, *History and Description of the Eastern Branch of the National Home for Disabled Volunteer Soldiers, Near Augusta, Maine: A Complete Guide-Book for Visitors* (Augusta, Maine: Sprague, Owen & Nash, 1879), 10; *Farmer's Cabinet*, 22 November 1866; James W. North, *The History of Augusta, from the Earliest Settlement to the Present Time* (Augusta, Maine: Clapp & North, 1870), 771–772; *Report of the Board of Managers of the National Asylum for Disabled Volunteer Soldiers, July 18, 1867*, Serial Set vol. 1312, no. 1 (40th Congress, 1st Session): 10; *Report of the President of the Board of Managers of the National Asylum for Disabled Volunteer Soldiers, March 3, 1868*, Serial Set vol. 1350, no. 2 (40th Congress, 2nd Session): 2; Lewis B. Gunckel as quoted in *Report of the Board of Managers*, Serial Set vol. 1312, no. 1 (40th Congress, 1st Session): 14–15; Augustus Waldo Drury, *History of the City of Dayton and Montgomery County, Ohio*, vol. 1 (Chicago-Dayton: S. J. Clarke Publishing Co., 1909), 756; *Dayton Herald*, 27 October 1870; *Souvenir of Dayton and the Soldiers' Home* (Dayton, Ohio: J. J. Keyes, n.d.), copy at Center for Archival Collections, Jerome Library, Bowling Green State University.

10 *Report of the President of the Board of Managers, March 3, 1868*, Serial Set vol. 1350, no. 2 (40th Congress, 2nd Session): 1; West, *Lincoln's Scapegoat General*, 316–317; Whitman, *History and Description*, 9; R. J. Wolfe as quoted in *Daily Iowa State Register*, 23 June 1867; list of ailments taken from *History of Togus: First 100 Years* (Togus, Maine: Veterans' Administration Center, 1966), 163–165, copy at MaineHS; Whitman, *History and Description*, 64; Sample Case Files of Members, National Home for Disabled Volunteer Soldiers, Eastern Branch, in RG 15: Records of the Veterans' Administration, NARA, Northeast Division, Waltham, Massachusetts; and *Report of the President of the Board of Managers of the National Asylum for Disabled Volunteer Soldiers, March 3, 1868*, Serial Set vol. 1350, no. 2 (40th Congress, 2nd Session): 8. For "entirely helpless," see *Report of the Board of Managers of the National Asylum for Disabled Volunteer Soldiers, July 18, 1867*, Serial Set vol. 1312, no. 1 (40th Congress, 1st Session): 4; "The National

Asylum for Disabled Volunteer Soldiers—Condition of Admission," *Daily Iowa State Register*, 4 May 1867.

11 Circular for the National Asylum for Disabled Volunteer Soldiers in Marcus Ward Papers, Box 5, Alexander Library, Rutgers University; "The National Asylum for Disabled Volunteer Soldiers—Condition of Admission," *Daily Iowa State Register*, 4 May 1867; see also Gobrecht, *History of the National Home*, 47; "The National Asylum—Letter from an Inmate," *Milwaukee Sentinel*, 14 September 1867; and a letter to the editor from "Volunteer," 18 October 1880, reprinted in *National Tribune*, 1 November 1880; see also Kelly, *Creating a National Home*.

12 Elizabeth Corbett, *Out at the Soldiers' Home: A Memory Book*, reprint ed. (Skokie, Illinois: ACTA Publications, 2008), 31; Peter Cassidy, letter to the Board of Managers, 28 September 1873, in Peter Cassidy Case File, in Sample Case Files of Members, National Home for Disabled Volunteer Soldiers, Northwestern Branch, Box 2, RG 15: Records of the Veterans' Administration, NARA, Great Lakes Region; for similar sentiments, see also Henry Clinton Parkhurst Papers, SHSIo; Butler as quoted in *Report of the Board of Managers*, Serial Set vol. 1312, no. 1 (40th Congress, 1st Session): 3; *Report of the President of the Board of Managers of the National Asylum for Disabled Volunteer Soldiers, March 3, 1868*, Serial Set vol. 1350, no. 2 (40th Congress, 2nd Session): 5; Barber, *The Nation's Defenders*, 59; Corbett, *Out at the Soldiers' Home*, 65; see also Hannah E. Patchin, *Notes Taken at the Wisconsin Veterans' Home* (Waupaca, Wisconsin: D. L. Stinchfield, 1891), 5, copy in Nicholson Collection, Huntington Library, San Marino, California; and *Second Biennial Report of the Nebraska Soldiers' and Sailors' Home, Grand Island, Hall County, Nebraska, 1888–1890* (Omaha: Henry Gibson, State Printer, 1890), 319–321. On wives of NHDVS inmates at the poorhouse, see Patchin, *Notes Taken at the Wisconsin Veterans' Home*, 17; Emory Owen Case File, Sample Case Files of Members, National Home for the Disabled Volunteer Soldier, Central Branch, Box 7, RG 15: Records of the Veterans Administration, NARA, Great Lakes Division; and letter of J. S. Anderson, Judge of Manitowoc County [Wisconsin] Court, 7 January 1897, in Gustav Mueller Case File, Sample Case Files of Members, National Home for the Disabled Volunteer Soldier, Northwestern Branch, Box 6, RG 15: Records of the Veterans Administration, NARA, Great Lakes Division.

13 "A Nation's Gratitude to the Soldier," *New York Times* editorial as quoted in *Grand Army Journal*, 14 May 1870, copy at American Antiquarian Society; see, for example, T. J. Potter to J. A. Martin, letter, 8 December 1886, in Records of the Governor's Office—Gov. J. A. Martin, Box 30, Folder 1, KaHS; Gobrecht, *History of the National Home*, 35–36, 53–54, 97–98; Corbett, *Out at the Soldiers' Home*, 49, 50–51, 64; Temple H. Dunn to "Bettie," 16

September 1904, in Temple H. Dunn Papers, Indiana State Library; Henry O. Spalding, "Sketch of the Eastern Branch National Home D.V.S.," as quoted in *History of Togus*, 132–133; John Frankenfield to J. K. Taylor Post, Grand Army of the Republic, letter, 22 July 1888, in J. K. Taylor Post Records, Box 11—Scrapbook and General Files, GARMA. For biographical background on Corbett, see Elizabeth Corbett Papers, Local History Room, Milwaukee Public Library. For descriptive details on the barracks, see, for example, Drury, *History of the City of Dayton and Montgomery County, Ohio*, 1:760; and Mitchell, "The National Home," 142.

14 John Frankenfield to J. K. Taylor Post, Grand Army of the Republic, letter, 22 July 1888, in J. K. Taylor Post Records, Box 11—Scrapbook and General Files, GARMA; See also Thomas Symonds Case File, Sample Case Files of Members, National Home for the Disabled Volunteer Soldier, Eastern Branch, in RG 15: Records of the Veterans Administration, NARA, Northeast Region; Henry Crosby to George Crosby, letter, 30 November 1902, in George Crosby Papers, Box 2, Folder 3, MinnHS.

15 Corbett, *Out at the Soldiers' Home*, 64; Gobrecht, *History of the National Home*, 142; Spalding, "Sketch of the Eastern Branch," as quoted in *History of Togus*, 133; Cetina, "A History of Veterans' Homes," 88. For the "bugle note," see Matthew H. Jamison, *Fort Leavenworth and the Soldiers' Home* (Kansas City, Missouri: Hudson-Kimberly Publishing Co., Printers and Binders, 1895), 70; Spalding, "Sketch of the Eastern Branch," as quoted in *History of Togus*, 134; see also Charles Morehouse, diary entry for 30 March 1912, in Charles Morehouse Diary, MinnHS; Ralph J. Tremain to John Love, letter, 15 June 1880, in John Love Papers, Box 2, Folder 25, InHS; Smith, *Togus, Down in Maine*, 15; Samuel Hynes to Governor of Central Branch, n.d., in Sample Case Files of Members, National Home for Disabled Volunteer Soldiers, Central Branch, in RG 15: Records of the Veterans Administration, National Archives and Records Administration, Great Lakes Division. See also "The National Asylum—Letter from an Inmate," *Milwaukee Sentinel*, 14 September 1867; D. B. Burke, "The National Asylum," in *Milwaukee Sentinel*, 14 September 1867. Less than a year later, the twenty-eight-year-old Burke was expelled from the Northwestern Branch on grounds of "insubordination," a testament to the inertia he felt as an inmate of the asylum. Historical Register of National Homes for Disabled Volunteer Soldiers, 1866–1938 (National Archives Microfilm Publication M1749, 282 rolls), entry 97; Jamison, *Fort Leavenworth and the Soldiers' Home*, 71; Joel Campbell Case File, Sample Case Files of Members, National Home for Disabled Volunteer Soldiers, Central Branch, in RG 15: Records of the Veterans Administration, NARA, Great Lakes Division.

16 *Catalogue of the Putnam Library, National Asylum for Disabled Volunteer Soldiers*
(Dayton, Ohio: National Asylum Printing Office, 1872); *Catalogue of Library
Belonging to the National Home for Disabled Volunteer Soldiers (Northwestern
Branch), Near Milwaukee, Wisconsin* (Milwaukee: National Soldiers' Home Print-
ing Office, 1875); see also Spalding, "Sketch of the Eastern Branch," as quoted in
History of Togus, 135; Temple H. Dunn to "Bettie," letter, 16 September 1904, in
Temple H. Dunn Papers, Box 1, Folder 4, Indiana State Library; Gobrecht, *His-
tory of the National Home*, 144–145; Corbett, *Out at the Soldiers' Home*, 75, 76–77;
"Meeting of Veteran Post," *Soldiers and Sailors Journal*, 20 March 1876, copy at
American Antiquarian Society. On veterans' "diversions" in the NHDVS, see also
Kelly, *Creating a National Home*, 161–164; *History of Togus*, 21. See also *Proceed-
ings of the First to Tenth Meetings, 1866-1876 of the Grand Army of the Republic*
(Philadelphia: Samuel P. Town, Printer, 1877), 341–342; *Guide to the Central
National Soldiers' Home for Visitors and Citizens* (Dayton: Guide Publishing Co.,
1891), 18; "The Dayton Soldiers' Home," *Grand Army Journal*, 27 May 1871,
copy at American Antiquarian Society; Gobrecht, *History of the National Home*,
52, 93; "Driving Guide for Touring the Grounds of the Historic Dayton VA
Medical Center," in National Home for the Disabled Volunteer Soldier Vertical
File, Local History Room, Dayton Metro Public Library. Visitors and veterans
of the Central Branch could also take in a Battle of Gettysburg cyclorama painting. See "V. A. Center has Long, Proud History," *Dayton Downtowner*, 16–23
March 1988; Nancy R. Horlacher to Anne New, letter, 28 July 1995, in National
Home for the Disabled Volunteer Soldier Vertical File, Local History Room,
Dayton Metro Public Library; Corbett, *Out at the Soldiers' Home*, 78, 86–88. On
theatrical performances at the NHDVS, see also program for "An Easy Mark" at
the Northwestern Branch in George Crosby Papers, Box 2, Folder 2, MinnHS;
and Temple H. Dunn "to Bettie," letter, 16 September 1904, in Temple H. Dunn
Papers, Box 1, Folder 4, Indiana State Library; "Driving Guide for Touring the
Grounds of the Historic Dayton VA Medical Center," in National Home for the
Disabled Volunteer Soldier Vertical File, Local History Room, Dayton Metro
Public Library.

17 *Plain Facts in Relation to the Management of the Soldiers' Home, Togus, Maine,
Rascality Is the Rule! No Justice for Old Veterans!* (Boston: Published by the Togus
Syndicate, 1895), 12; see also Marten, "Not a Veteran in a Poorhouse"; Ralph J.
Tremain to John Love, letter, 15 June 1880, in John Love Papers, Box 2, Folder
25, InHS.; Paul James Lindberg, daybook entry [circa 1872], in Paul James
Lindberg Papers, Folder 1, Huntington Library; E. R. Reed to "My Dear Old
Comrade" [Hosea Rood], letter, 21 January 1910, in Grand Army of the Repub-
lic Memorial Hall Collection, Box 1, Folder 2, WiVMA; see also James Baker, as

quoted in "Investigation of the National Home for Disabled Volunteer Soldiers" (48th Congress, 2nd Session, Report No. 2676): 308.

18 Michael Brannon to Benjamin Butler, letter, 21 November 1872, in Michael Brannon Case File, Sample Case Files of Members, National Home for Disabled Volunteer Soldiers, Eastern Branch, RG 15: Records of the Veterans Administration, NARA, Northeast Division; for veterans moving in and out of homes in "desperation," see also Marten, "Exempt from the Ordinary Rules of Life," 68. On the search for relevance and respect, see also Marten, "Not a Veteran in a Poorhouse," and *Sing Not War*; Terence O'Brien to W. S. Tilton, letter, 9 November 1874, in Terence O'Brien Case File, Sample Case Files of Members, National Home for Disabled Volunteer Soldiers, Eastern Branch, RG 15: Records of the Veterans Administration, NARA, Northeast Division; Henry Clinton Parkhurst, "Written in a Soldier's Home," in Henry Clinton Parkhurst Papers, Box 5, SHSIo.

19 Hiram L. Jennings to Benjamin Butler, letter, 8 May 1868, in Hiram Jennings Case File, Sample Case Files of Members, National Home for Disabled Volunteer Soldiers, Northwestern Branch, Box 2, RG 15: Records of the Veterans Administration, NARA, Great Lakes Region; see also Samuel Aldrich to Colonel Brown, application for readmission dated 1879, in John Love Papers, Box 2, Folder 25, InHS; Marten, "Exempt from the Ordinary Rules of Life"; James Ford Case File, Sample Case Files of Members, National Home for Disabled Volunteer Soldiers, Northwestern Branch, Box 4, RG 15: Records of the Veterans Administration, NARA, Great Lakes Region; Daniel S. Arnold Case File, Sample Case Files of Members, National Home for Disabled Volunteer Soldiers, Central Branch, Box 4, RG 15: Records of the Veterans Administration, NARA, Great Lakes Region; "Hero's Sad End," *Boston Journal*, 6 December 1897; Historical Register of National Homes for Disabled Volunteer Soldiers, 1866–1938 (National Archives Microfilm Publication M1749, 282 rolls), entry 10,986; Theodore F. Lang, *Loyal West Virginia from 1861 to 1865* (Baltimore: Deutsch Publishing Co., 1895), 292–293; see also John Collins Case File, Sample Case Files of Members, National Home for Disabled Volunteer Soldiers, Northwestern Branch, RG 15: Records of the Veterans Administration, NARA, Great Lakes Region; "The Soldier Tramp," in *Fifth Annual Meeting of the Society of the 28th Wisconsin Volunteer Infantry, Held at Whitewater, Wisconsin, September 7th and 8th, 1887* (Milwaukee: Burdick & Armitage, 1887), 45–46.

20 John Gaspar to E. F. Brown, letter, 18 October 1870, in John Gaspar Case File, Sample Case Files of Members, National Home for Disabled Volunteer Soldiers, Central Branch, RG 15: Records of the Veterans Administration, NARA,

Great Lakes Region; see also L. E. Crane to W. S. Tilton, letter, 26 June 1882, in Cornelius Connell Case File, and Robert Beatty Case File, both in Sample Case Files of Members, National Home for Disabled Volunteer Soldiers, Eastern Branch, RG 15: Records of the Veterans' Administration, Northeast Region, Waltham, Massachusetts; Thomas Fitzgerald Case File, in Sample Case Files of Members, National Home for Disabled Volunteer Soldiers, Central Branch, RG 15: Records of the Veterans Administration, NARA, Great Lakes Region; see also letter of Prescott Gibbs, dated 8 March 1913, in Prescott Gibbs Case File, Box 8, ibid.; Joel Patten to W. H. Thomas, 24 November 1871, in William Rooney Case File, Sample Case Files of Members, National Home for Disabled Volunteer Soldiers, Central Branch, RG 15: Records of the Veterans Administration, NARA, Great Lakes Division; see also Louis Link Case File and Andrew Foster Case File, ibid.; Henry Gould Case File and Michael Brannon Case File, both in Sample Case Files of Members, National Home for Disabled Volunteer Soldiers, Eastern Branch, RG 15: Records of the Veterans Administration, NARA, Northeast Division.

21 Smith, *Togus, Down in Maine*, 40; Historical Register of National Homes for Disabled Volunteer Soldiers, 1866–1938 (National Archives Microfilm Publication M1749, 282 rolls), entry 4,408; see, for example, circular regarding Michael O'Hearn in Benjamin Jones Case File, Sample Case Files of Members, National Home for Disabled Volunteer Soldiers, Box 6, RG 15: Records of the Veterans' Administration, NARA, Great Lakes Region; see also Patrick Clarey Case File, Sample Case Files of Members, National Home for Disabled Volunteer Soldiers, Northwestern Branch, Box 3, RG 15: Records of the Veterans' Administration, NARA, Great Lakes Region; and account of John Kiggan, an inmate of the Ohio State Soldiers' Home at Sandusky, in *Cincinnati Enquirer* clipping dated 12 March 1899, in Mary Ann Ball Bickerdyke Papers, Box 4, Manuscript Division, LoC.

22 *Report of the Board of Managers of the National Asylum for Disabled Volunteer Soldiers for the Year 1871*, Serial Set no. 1527, vol. 4 (42nd Congress, 2nd Session), 13–14; Historical Register of National Homes for Disabled Volunteer Soldiers, 1866–1938 (National Archives Microfilm Publication M1749, 282 rolls), entry 2,182. In 1872, Congress updated the Homestead Act with a "Soldiers' Homestead Bill," which deducted a veterans' years of army service from the five years a homesteader was required to live on and improve his land. See "The Soldier's Homestead Bill," undated *Boston Journal* clipping in Henry Atherton Claims Book, vol. 2, NHHS; on the westward migration of Union veterans, see Bruce R. Kahler, "John A. Martin, Soldier State Visionary," *Kansas History: A Journal of the Central Plains* 34 (Spring 2011): 50–59; Doane

Robinson, "Early History of Potter County," address delivered 9 April 1923, in *South Dakota Historical Collections* 12 (Pierre: Hipple Printing Co., 1924), 265–266; "Civil War Vets Settle Gettysburg [South Dakota]," *Potter County News*, 28 July 1983; and Stephen T. Morgan, "Fellow Comrades: The Grand Army of the Republic in South Dakota," *South Dakota History* 36, no. 3 (Fall 2006): 229–259; *Gettysburg Herald*, 11 September 1883, in William Combellick Papers, DSMC.

23 Mitchell, "The National Home," 143; Gobrecht, *History of the National Home*, 32; and Matthew H. Jamison, *Fort Leavenworth and the Soldiers' Home, With Sketches of Leavenworth and of the Men and Tragedies That Have Made Her Famous* (Kansas City, Missouri: Hudson-Kimberly Publishing Co., 1895). On overcrowding, see also letters of 5 January 1885 and 25 June 1889 from Orlando B. Willcox to William B. Franklin, Box 1, Folder 2, National Home for the Disabled Volunteer Soldier Collection, Milwaukee Public Library; letter of 3 January 1888 in Henry A. Gardner Case File, Case Files of the Illinois Soldiers' and Sailors' Home, RG 259.002, Illinois State Archives; and letter to "dear cousin Julia," dated 17 January 1888, in Letter Written by Resident of the Southern Branch, NHDVS, MSS 11376, ASSpCL; E. F. Brown to J. A. Martin, 27 August 1885, in Records of the Governor's Office—Governor J. A. Martin, Box 30, Folder 1, KaHS; George Pillsbury to J. Rowland, 20 September 1886, in George Pillsbury Case File, Case Files of the Illinois Soldiers' and Sailors' Home, RG 259.002, Illinois State Archives; Frederick A. Marden as quoted in Wisconsin Veterans' Home Records, reel 1, WiHS; Charles McCally Case File, Case Files of the Illinois Soldiers' and Sailors' Home, RG 259.002, Illinois State Archives; See, for example, Henry Booth to J. A. Martin, letter, 27 January 1885, in Records of the Governor's Office—Gov. J. A. Martin, Box 30, Folder 1, KaHS, and William Darragh Case File, Sample Case Files of Members, Central Branch, National Home for Disabled Volunteer Soldiers, Box 5, RG 15: Records of the Veterans' Administration, NARA, Great Lakes Region; "State Homes," in *Appleton's Annual Cyclopaedia and Register of Important Events* (New York: D. Appleton & Co., 1890), 768–771; Yott, *From Soldiers' Home to Medical Center*, 1; "The New York State Soldiers' Home," *Frank Leslie's Illustrated*, 30 June 1877; *Bulletin of Iowa Institutions*, vol. 3 (Des Moines: Welch Printing Co., 1901), 214; clippings in Post Scrapbook, 1887–1893, in E. W. Kinsley Post No. 113 Papers, Carton 2, Massachusetts Historical Society; "A Soldiers' Home," *Philadelphia Inquirer*, 10 February 1885; Wisconsin Veterans' Home Records, reel 1, WiHS; McCrory, *Grand Army of the Republic: Department of Wisconsin*, 40. First quote from Frederick Marden, as quoted in Patchin, *Notes Taken at the Wisconsin Veterans' Home*, 21; second quote from *First Annual Report, Pennsylvania Soldiers and Sailors*

Home, Report for Year Ending 1886 (Philadelphia: Town Print, 1887), 1, copy in Nicholson Collection, Huntington Library. See also "The Greatest of These Is Charity," *Philadelphia Inquirer,* 19 May 1883; "Homes for the Disabled," *Soldiers' and Sailors' Journal,* 20 March 1876; *Proceedings of the Sixth Annual Encampment, Department of New York, Grand Army of the Republic* (New York: Grand Army of the Republic, 1872), 12; Patchin, *Notes Taken at the Wisconsin Veterans' Home,* 21–22; John Scott to J. A. Martin, 26 December 1888, in Records of the Governor's Office—Gov. J. A. Martin, Box 30, Folder 1, KaHS; see also John White Geary and James Addams Beaver as quoted in Richard C. Saylor, *Soldiers to Governors: Pennsylvania's Civil War Veterans Who Became State Leaders* (Harrisburg: Pennsylvania Historical & Museum Commission, 2010), 31, 99; Beath, *History of the Grand Army,* 401, 416, 451, 482–483, 512, 530, 536, 545, 560, 570, 583; "Soldiers' Homes," *National Tribune,* 12 January 1899.

24 The managers of the Wisconsin home insisted that "the soldier who has served in the field in war should never be required against his will to 'play soldier' in time of peace." *Report of the Visiting Committee of the State Board of Control,* copy in Wisconsin Soldiers' Home Records, Box 1, Folder 1, WiHS; Patchin, *Notes Taken at the Wisconsin Veterans' Home,* 17, 20. Veterans who desired to remain in their native states likewise preferred state soldiers' homes to the NHDVS. See, for example, George Pillsbury to J. Rowland, 20 September 1886, in George Pillsbury Case File, Case Files of the Illinois Soldiers' and Sailors' Home, RG 259.002, Illinois State Archives; and remarks of Corporal James Tanner, as quoted in *Hornell Daily Times,* 24 January 1879; *Second Biennial Report of the Nebraska Soldiers' and Sailors' Home,* 319–321; *Pennsylvania Soldiers' and Sailors' Home Report for May 31, 1887–1888* (Philadelphia: Town Print, 1889), 36, copy in Nicholson Collection, Huntington Library (italics mine); see also *Report of the Board of Trustees [of the Pennsylvania Soldiers' and Sailors' Home], 1891–1892* (Philadelphia: J. B. Lippincott, 1893), 40–41, ibid. There were exceptions. Frederick Sutton, an Ohio cavalryman, was "summarily discharged" from the Central Branch after refusing to comply with NHDVS pension regulations. "That a crippled soldier should have his Pension in the hands of dishonest Congressmen, men the most of whom have never smelt powder, men who are no friend of the disabled soldier, is simply absurd," he wrote. Frederick Sutton to Marsena K. Patrick, 2 December 1880, in Frederick Sutton Case File, Sample Case Files of Members, Central Branch, Box 3, RG 15: Records of the Veterans Administration, NARA, Great Lakes Region. See also Thomas Delaney, dishonorable discharge, in John Love Papers, Box 2, Folder 25, InHS; Hugh Wilson to Governor Jeremiah Rusk, letter, 4 December 1887, in Wisconsin Soldiers' Home Records, Box 1, Folder 1, WiHS; Petition of the Inmates of the Pennsylvania Soldiers'

and Sailors' Home, dated 30 November 1898, in *Description of the Pennsylvania Soldiers' and Sailors' Home*, copy in Nicholson Collection, Huntington Library; Discharge Register, 1895–1915, of the Nebraska Soldiers' and Sailors' Home, Grand Island, Nebraska, in Grand Island Veterans' Home Records, NHS; Isaac Caplinger Case File in Case Files of the Illinois Soldiers' and Sailors' Home, RG 259.002, Illinois Archives; Undated newspaper clipping from Marshalltown, Iowa, in William Woods Averell Papers, Box 17, Folder 14, New York State Archives; for "firecrackers and bombshells," see J. R. Ratekin to William Woods Averell, letter, 16 December 1896, in Averell Papers, Box 18, New York State Archives.

25 Joseph Mouteith to James Davidson, letter, 26 March 1906, in Wisconsin Veterans' Home Records, Box 1, Folder 3, WiHS; on "graft" in soldiers' homes, see also Henry Clinton Parkhurst, "Written in a Soldier's Home," in Henry Clinton Parkhurst Papers, Box 5, SHSIo; *Plain Facts in Relation to the Management of the Soldiers' Home*, 10; *Description of the Pennsylvania Soldiers' and Sailors' Home*, copy in Nicholson Collection, Huntington Library; and George M. Hare, *Mysteries and Miseries of the Soldiers' Home* (Woonsocket, Rhode Island: Patriot Printing House, 1885; Spalding, "Sketch of the Eastern Branch," as quoted in *History of Togus*, 133; Charles Barnes to James Davidson, letter, 14 October 1906, in Wisconsin Veterans' Home Records, Box 1, Folder 6, WiHS; Henry Crosby to George Crosby, letter, 1 March 1903, in George Crosby Papers, Box 2, Folder 2, MinnHS; Marten, "Exempt from the Ordinary Rules of Life," 64, and "Nomads in Blue," in Gerber, ed., *Disabled Veterans in History*; *History of Togus*, 133; Kansas State Soldiers' Home Offenders Docket, entry for Frank Ridenour, 28 August 1893, KaHS; John R. Steere as quoted in "Investigation of the National Home for Disabled Volunteer Soldiers" (48th Congress, 2nd Session, Report No. 2676): 313; Andrew J. Smith to J. A. Martin, letter, 24 May 1887, in Records of the Governor's Office—Gov. J. A. Martin, Box 30, Folder 1, KaHS; "Poison in Their Whisky," *Macon Telegraph*, 27 May 1886; "Bath Items," *Hornell Daily Times*, 24 June 1879.

26 E[lisha] R. Reed to "My Dear Old Comrade" [Hosea Rood], letter, 21 January 1910, in Grand Army of the Republic Memorial Hall Collection, Box 1, Folder 2, WiVMA; D. R. Greenlee, M.D., "Alcohol—Its Use in the Soldiers' Home," in Union Veterans' Union Records, Box 2, MinnHS. See, for example, *Fourth Biennial Report of Nebraska Soldiers' and Sailors' Home, Grand Island, Hall County, Nebraska* (Lincoln, Nebraska: Press of Jacob North & Co., 1894), 411; "Complaints, 1906," in "Report of Investigation of the Wisconsin Veterans' Home," Wisconsin Soldiers' Home Records, Box 1, Folder 5, WiHS; Death Register in Ohio Veterans' Home Records, reel 2, Center for Archival Collections, Jerome

Library, Bowling Green State University; Yott, *From Soldiers' Home to Medical Center*, 59; *Pennsylvania Soldiers' and Sailors' Home Report for May 31, 1887–1888*, p. 32; George Ditzell to L. A. Beltzer, letter, 16 August 1900, in Grand Island Veterans' Home Records, NHS; "Clint Parkhurst," in John C. Parish, ed., *The Palimpsest* (Iowa City, Iowa: State Historical Society of Iowa, 1920), 183–192; Clinton H. Parkhurst Pension File, application no. 984,678, certificate no. 931,226, RG 15: Civil War Pension Files, National Archives Building, Washington, D.C.; Parkhurst Scrapbook in Henry Clinton Parkhurst Papers, Box 5, SHSIo; "Written in a Soldiers' Home," manuscript dated 16 August 1910, ibid.; Gerald N. Grob, *Mental Institutions in America: Social Policy to 1875* (New York: Free Press, 1973), 90; testimony of J. St. John Clarkson, in "Investigation of the National Home for Disabled Volunteer Soldiers" (48th Congress, 2nd Session, Report No. 2676): 146; see also Marten, "Nomads in Blue," and Shay, *Odysseus in America*; Charles Renold Case File, Sample Case Files of Members, National Home for Disabled Volunteer Soldiers, Central Branch, Box 2, in RG 15: Records of the Veterans' Administration, NARA, Great Lakes Division; Historical Register of National Homes for Disabled Volunteer Soldiers, 1866–1938 (National Archives Microfilm Publication M1749, 282 rolls), entry 930.

27 Henry Crosby to George Crosby, letter, 1 March 1903, in George Crosby Papers, Box 2, Folder 3, MinnHS; Corbett, *Out at the Soldiers' Home*, 167; testimony of Dayton Mayor John Bettleton in "Investigation of the National Home for Disabled Volunteer Soldiers" (48th Congress, 2nd Session, Report No. 2676): 118; *History of Togus*, 138. Many of these grogshops hired veterans as barkeeps. See, for example, reference to Thomas D. Riggs in General Orders No. 16, dated 12 May 1893, in John F. Kendrick Case File, Sample Case Files of Members, National Home for Disabled Volunteer Soldiers, Western Branch, Box 2, RG 15: Records of the Veterans' Administration, NARA, Central Plains Region; and record of Nelson Olmstead in Discharge Register, 1895–1915, Grand Island Veterans' Home Records, NHS; Corbett, *Out at the Soldiers' Home*, 166; Letter to "dear cousin Julia," dated 17 January 1888, in Letter Written by Resident of the Southern Branch, NHDVS, MSS 11376, ASSpCL; *Cincinnati Enquirer* clipping dated 12 March 1899, in Mary Ann Ball Bickerdyke Papers, Box 4, Manuscript Division, LoC; Corbett, *Out at the Soldiers' Home*, 165; on canteens, see also Cornelius Wheeler Papers, Box 1, WiHS; Jamison, *Fort Leavenworth and the Soldiers' Home*, 69; George Pillsbury to J. Rowland, 20 September 1886, in George Pillsbury Case File, Case Files of the Illinois Soldiers' and Sailors' Home, RG 259.002, Illinois State Archives; and Kelly, *Creating a National Home*, 164–165; *Kennebec Journal*, 15 December 1869, as quoted in *History of Togus*, 17; on the enduring popularity of the dives, see, for example, Cornelius Wheeler Papers, Box 1, WiHS,

and William Schreider Case File, Sample Case Files of Members, National Home for Disabled Volunteer Soldiers, Eastern Branch, RG 15: Records of the Veterans' Administration, NARA, Northeast Division; "The National Asylum," *Milwaukee Sentinel*, 4 March 1870; James J. Murphy to W. F. Rogers, 29 October 1888, in Henry Atherton Case File, Sample Case Files of Members, National Home for Disabled Volunteer Soldiers, Bath Branch, in RG 15: Records of the Veterans' Administration, NARA, Northeast Division.

28 *Kennebec Journal*, 11 June 1879, as quoted in *History of Togus*, 189; Historical Register of National Homes for Disabled Volunteer Soldiers, 1866–1938 (National Archives Microfilm Publication M1749, 282 rolls), entry 3,200; F. S. Shepherd to Central Branch, NHDVS, 9 October 1894, in James Frazier Case File, Sample Case Files of Members, NHDVS, Central Branch, Box 7, RG 15: Records of the Veterans' Administration, NARA, Great Lakes Region; E. A. Leonhard to Central Branch, NHDVS, letter, 16 March 1910, in Frank Paris Case File, Sample Case Files of Members, NHDVS, Central Branch, Box 7, RG 15: Records of the Veterans' Administration, NARA, Great Lakes Region; testimony of James Applegate and George H. Focht in "Investigation of the National Home for Disabled Volunteer Soldiers" (48th Congress, 2nd Session, Report No. 2676): 191, 139. See also Frank Tusant and Andrew Riley Case Files, Case Files of the Illinois Soldiers' and Sailors' Home, RG 259.002, Illinois State Archives; James Taylor Case File, Sample Case Files of Members, National Home for Disabled Volunteer Soldiers, Western Branch, Box 2, RG 15: Records of the Veterans' Administration, NARA, Central Plains Division; George Ackerly Case File, Sample Case Files of Members, NHDVS, Bath Branch, RG 15: Records of the Veterans' Administration, NARA, Northeast Division; James Farmar Case File, Sample Case Files of Members, NHDVS, Western Branch, Box 1, RG 15: Records of the Veterans' Administration, NARA, Central Plains Division. "Impression of the Waupaca Veterans' Home," manuscript, n.d., in Willis Peck Clarke Papers, Box 1, WiHS.

29 Hosea Rood, "Grand Army Corner" column dated 9 April 1911, in Grand Army of the Republic Memorial Hall Collection, Box 2, Folder 3, WiVMA; Letter to "dear cousin Julia," dated 17 January 1888, in Letter Written by Resident of the Southern Branch, NHDVS, MSS 11376, ASSpCL; Butler as quoted in Gobrecht, *History of the National Home*, 58–59; on pawning stolen goods at "rum shops," see Thomas Calvin Case File in Sample Case Files of Members, National Home for Disabled Volunteer Soldiers, Eastern Branch, Box 3, in RG 15: Records of the Veterans' Administration, NARA; Paul James Lindberg Daybook [circa 1873], in Paul James Lindberg Papers, Folder 2, Huntington Library; Discharge Register, 1895–1915, Grand Island Veterans' Home Records, NHS; see

also Luther Stephenson, General Orders No. 22, dated 13 November 1897, in William Woods Averell Papers, Box 18, New York State Archives, Albany, New York; entry for Samuel Shaw in Descriptive Book of Members, NHDVS, Eastern Branch, in RG 15: Records of the Veterans' Administration, NARA, Northeast Division; Summary Reports of Infractions, Bath Soldiers' and Sailors' Home, in RG 15: Records of the Veterans' Administration, NARA, Northeast Division; for "vulgar and foul language," see John D. Gibson Case File, Sample Case Files of Members, NHDVS, Western Branch, Box 3, RG 15: Records of the Veterans' Administration, NARA, Central Plains Division. For "pocket knives, crutches, and hickory canes," see, for example, records of James Anderson, William Anderson, A. L. Colby, Joseph Donovan, Martin Flammer, David Koon, and George Price, in Discharge Register, 1895–1915, Grand Island Veterans' Home Records, NHS; "Investigation of the National Home for Disabled Volunteer Soldiers" (48th Congress, 2nd Session, Report No. 2676): 407–408, 411; Clint Parkhurst, "The Bug House," manuscript dated 1 September 1910, in Henry Clinton Parkhurst Papers, Box 5, SHSIo; Michael Green Case File, Sample Case Files of Members, NHDVS, Bath Branch, Box 3 (1879–1883), in RG 15: Records of the Veterans' Administration, NARA, Northeast Division; Milton Pickerell Case File, Sample Case Files of Members, NHDVS, Western Branch, RG 15: Records of the Veterans' Administration, NARA, Central Plains Division; *Kennebec Journal*, 13 May 1871, as quoted in *History of Togus*, 183; Yott, *From Soldiers' Home to Medical Center*, 53; Discharge Record for Earl Cranston in Fitch's Home for the Soldier Records, Discharges, 1891–1895, in RG 73: Military Department, Box 174, Connecticut State Library; and Paul James Lindberg Daybook, Folder 1, Paul James Lindberg Papers, Huntington Library; Thomas Kenny Case File, Sample Case Files of Members, NHDVS, Eastern Branch, RG 15: Records of the Veterans' Administration, NARA, Northeast Division; H. C. Parkins to Western Branch, NHDVS, letter, 8 August 1900, in Oran F. Bixler Case File, Sample Case Files of Members, NHDVS, Western Branch, Box 2, in RG 15: Records of the Veterans' Administration, NARA, Central Plains Division; Francis Worth Case File, Sample Case Files of Members, NHDVS, Western Branch, Box 4, in RG 15: Records of the Veterans' Administration, NARA, Central Plains Division; see also William Lundy Case File, Case Files of the Illinois Soldiers' and Sailors' Home, RG 259.002, Illinois State Archives; and Richard Allen Case File, Sample Case Files of Members, NHDVS, Eastern Branch, Box 1, in RG 15: Records of the Veterans' Administration, NARA, Northeast Division; Barber, *The Nation's Defenders*, 60, 63; and reports of Oscar Hitchcock and J. A. J. Smiley, dated 14–15 October 1895, in Pennsylvania Soldiers' and Sailors' Home Offense Book, RG 19, PaSA.

30 S. F. Chapin report, quoted in *Report of the Board of Trustees [of the Pennsylvania Soldiers' and Sailors' Home], 1891–1892*, p. 45, copy in Nicholson Collection, Huntington Library; Peter Mueller Case File, Case Files of the Illinois Soldiers' and Sailors' Home, RG 259.002, Illinois State Archives; see also Corbett, *Out at the Soldiers' Home*, 97; Joseph Lapp Case File, Sample Case Files of Members, NHDVS, Western Branch, Box 7, in RG 15: Records of the Veterans' Administration, NARA, Central Plains Division. For other examples of hallucinations of "persecution," see Thomas Symonds Case File, Sample Case Files of Members, National Home for Disabled Volunteer Soldiers, Eastern Branch, Box 3, in RG 15: Records of the Veterans' Administration, NARA, Northeast Division, and Oscar D. Woodward Case File, Sample Case Files of Members, NHDVS, Western Branch, Box 5, in RG 15: Records of the Veterans' Administration, NARA, Central Plains Division. On insane wards and "weak minded" inmates, see "Investigation of the National Home for Disabled Volunteer Soldiers" (48th Congress, 2nd Session, Report No. 2676): 63, 124; and Secretary of the Interior [Ethan Hitchcock] to the Secretary of War [Elihu Root], 27 January 1900, in National Home for the Disabled Volunteer Soldier Collection, Box 1, Folder 3, Local History Room, Milwaukee Public Library; *History of Togus*, 166; see also M. B. Campbell to Mary Ann Ball Bickerdyke, 19 March 1897, in Mary Ann Ball Bickerdyke Papers, Box 3, Manuscript Division, LoC; *Report of the Board of Managers of the National Home for Disabled Volunteer Soldiers for the Fiscal Year Ending June 30, 1894*, Serial Set vol. 3329, no. 3 (53rd Congress, 3rd Session): 133, 66, 98–100; See, for example, Discharges, 1891–1895, Fitch's Home for the Soldier, in RG 73: Military Department, Box 174, Connecticut State Library; entries for Joseph Riker and Oscar Merrill in Death Register, Grand Island Veterans' Home Records, NHS; Patrick McGowan Case File, Case Files of the Illinois Soldiers' and Sailors' Home, RG 259.002, Illinois State Archives.

31 Ohio Veterans' Home Death Records, Ohio Veterans Home Records, reel 2, Center for Archival Collections, Jerome Library, Bowling Green State University; "Investigation of the National Home for Disabled Volunteer Soldiers" (48th Congress, 2nd Session, Report No. 2676): 149; "Investigation of the National Home for Disabled Volunteer Soldiers" (48th Congress, 2nd Session, Report No. 2676): 243; Emily Lippincott "to the editor of the Times," letter, 14 January 1890, copy in Lippincott Family Papers, SC 3138, Abraham Lincoln Presidential Library.

32 Frank Paris Case File, Sample Case Files of Members, National Home for Disabled Volunteer Soldiers, Central Branch, Box 7, in RG 15: Records of the Veterans' Administration, NARA, Great Lakes Division; Death Register, Grand Island Veterans' Home Records, NHS; *Report of the Board of Trustees [of the Pennsylvania*

Soldiers' and Sailors' Home], 1889–1890 (Philadelphia: J. B. Lippincott, 1891), 48, copy in Nicholson Collection, Huntington Library; Descriptive Book of Members, NHDVS, Eastern Branch, in RG 15: Records of the Veterans' Administration, NARA, Northeast Division; Ohio Veterans' Home Death Records, Ohio Veterans Home Records, reel 2, Center for Archival Collections, Jerome Library, Bowling Green State University; Corbett, *Out at the Soldiers' Home*, 42–43; undated newspaper clipping in Cornelius Wheeler Papers, Box 1, WiHS.

33 *Weekly Knight and Soldier*, 27 March 1889; John Robinson and John Christopher Case Files, Sample Case Files of Members, NHDVS, Northwestern Branch, Box 6 and Box 3, in RG 15: Records of the Veterans' Administration, NARA, Great Lakes Division; Samuel Foreman Case File, Sample Case Files of Members, NHDVS, Western Branch, Box 7, in RG 15: Records of the Veterans' Administration, NARA, Central Plains Division; untitled newspaper clipping, dated 27 September 1905, in Grand Army of the Republic Clippings Collection, KaHS; undated newspaper clipping in Cornelius Wheeler Papers, Box 1, WiHS; Charles Morehouse, diary entry, 21 June 1912, in Charles Morehouse Diary, MinnHS.

34 Gobrecht, *History of the National Home*, 133; "Old Boys in Blue," letter to the editor dated 30 July 1899, in Yott, *From Soldiers' Home to Medical Center*, 73–74; Smith, *Togus, Down in Maine*, 35; Paul James Lindberg, daybook entry [circa 1876], in Paul James Lindberg Papers, Box 2, Huntington Library; Grand Army of the Republic General Order dated 14 April 1884, in General Orders Scrapbook, Grand Army of the Republic Post No. 2 Records, Box 20, GARMA; draft of eulogy, n.d., in William Stanley Mead Collection, Box 1, Folder 8, InHS; Gobrecht, *History of the National Home*, 133; Smith, *Togus, Down in Maine*, 3; Jamison, *Fort Leavenworth and the Soldiers' Home*, 71.

EPILOGUE: PARADE REST

1 O. W. Baldwin to William A. Rand, letter, 22 April 1885, in William A. Rand Papers, Box 1, Folder 1, NHHS; Minutes [circa 1886] of the Veterans Rights Union, Patrick Coney Papers, Box 4, KaHS; *Proceedings of the Twenty-Seventh National Encampment of the Grand Army of the Republic at Indianapolis, Indiana, September 6th and 7th, 1893* (Milwaukee: Swain & Tate, Printers, 1893), 45–46; "Passing of the G.A.R.," undated newspaper clipping, in I. N. Carr Papers, Box 6, Folder 6, SHSIo; Martin Pembleton to Sallie McIntosh, letter, 10 October 1910, in Miscellaneous Grand Army of the Republic Records, GARMA; W. T. Kimsey to "Comrade Cox," letter, 11 September 1917, in 44th Indiana Regimental Association Records, Box 1, Folder 4, InHS; S. N. Fox, "The Veterans Are Passing Away," poem in Isadore H. Burgoon Collection, Box 1, Folder 22, RHPC; Lucius

Fairchild, speech delivered 5 July 1884, in Lucius Fairchild Papers, Box 56, Folder 10, WiHS; Elijah Cavins, draft of speech for Grand Army of the Republic Reunion [circa 1900], in Elijah Cavins Papers, Box 2, Folder 3, InHS; newspaper clipping dated 23 September 1891 in Charles Kepler Papers, Box 19, SHSIo; account of 31st Reunion in 44th Indiana Regimental Association Records, Box 1, Folder 8, InHS; P. H. Bristow, "Another Year to the G.A.R.," typescript in Ell Torrance Papers, Box 34, MinnHS; "Soldiers' Home Near End of Its Long Trail," undated newspaper clipping, in Walter Tully Papers, Box 1, Folder 2, NJHSL; "The 'Grand Army' Goes Down Fighting," *Milwaukee Journal*, 25 February 1953, copy in Albert Woolson Papers, Box 1, Folder 29, NeMinnHC; quote from minutes of the 127th Pennsylvania Survivors Association, 3 May 1916, in Henry Alleman Collection, Folder 6, PaSA; Record of the Funeral Committee, George Gordon Meade Post No. 1, Grand Army of the Republic, in Meade Post No. 1 Records, Box 2, GARMA; *Bristol* [Pennsylvania] *Daily Courier*, clipping dated 20 March 1918, in Miscellaneous Grand Army of the Republic Records, GARMA; Franklin D. Tappan, *The Passing of the Grand Army of the Republic* (Worcester, Massachusetts: Commonwealth Press, 1939), 45, 47; *The Haversack*, 23 September 1885, NHHS; T. G. Kephart, letter dated 6 September 1910, in 104th Pennsylvania Survivors' Association Records, Box 1, GARMA; and 29th Indiana Regiment Reunion Association Records, 1900–1902, Folder 1 (General Orders), InHS; Tappan, *The Passing of the Grand Army*, 133–134. E. F. Dexter manufactured the cast-iron markers in Chicago and sold them to posts for $4.50 per dozen or $35.00 per hundred. Tellingly, "when first introduced," many feared that the markers "would be destroyed or stolen" for scrap metal. See "G.A.R. Memorial Tablets" advertisement in William Combellick Papers, DSMC; *Los Angeles Times*, 30 May 1889.

2 Cornelius S. Munhall, manuscript of address [circa 1928], in Cornelius S. Munhall Papers, NHS; William Hamilton Church, manuscript of reunion address [circa 1900], in William Hamilton Church Papers, WiHS; Milton Carmichael, notes for Memorial Day address dated 30 May 1885, in Milton Carmichael Memoranda Book, KSRL.

3 Bristow, "Another Year to the G.A.R."; Marten, *Sing Not War*; John Palmer as quoted in *Journal of the Twenty-Sixth National Encampment, Grand Army of the Republic, Washington, D.C., September 21st and 22nd, 1892* (Albany, New York: S. H. Wentworth, Printer, 1892), 47; Reunion Record Book of the Co. A, 25th Massachusetts Association, minutes for 30 June 1889, WHM; Aurestus Perham, "Patriotism: Its Peril and Redemption," in Aurestus Perham Papers, Box 5, Folder 15, MaineHS; Charles H. Miller, letter, 18 June 1893, in Civil War Manuscripts, S. C. Pierce Collection, Box 2, Folder 4, State University of New York at Binghamton;

and Daniel R. Lucas, "Appomattox Sunday and Forty Years After," in Daniel R. Lucas Papers, Box 1, Folder 6, InHS. On the 1892 national encampment, see Mrs. John A. Logan, "The G.A.R.," manuscript in John A. Logan Family Papers, Box 42, Manuscript Division, LoC; Albert Barnitz to Mrs. Luman Tenney, letter, 1 March 1880, in Luman Tenney Papers, Institute for Regional Studies, NDSU; P. B. Freeman, letter, 4 May 1894, in Civil War Manuscripts, S. C. Pierce Collection, Box 2, Folder 30, SuoNYB; Hosea Rood, "Don't Belittle the Civil War," newspaper clipping in Grand Army of the Republic Memorial Hall Collection, WiVMA, and "Headquarters, Union Veterans' Union, October 11, 1902," in Union Veterans' Union Records, Box 2, MinnHS; "An Old Veteran" and C. H. Adkins, *When the Boys in Blue Are Gone* (Gardner, Massachusetts: Published by George Ross, 1912); see also Hosea Rood Scrapbook in Grand Army of the Republic Memorial Hall Collection, Box 16, WiVMA.

4 Minutes of the 127th Pennsylvania Volunteers Survivors' Association, 3 May 1910, in Henry C. Alleman Collection, Folder 6, PaSA; see also "Grand Army Post Against General Lee," *Confederate Veteran* 18 (1910): 56; C. A. Meek as quoted in Gerald R. Butters, Jr., "The *Birth of a Nation* and the Kansas Board of Review of Motion Pictures: A Censorship Struggle," *Kansas History* (Spring 1991): 8; S. J. Churchill to J. W. Davis, letter, 20 June 1923, in Records of the Governor's Office—Correspondence File, Gov. J. W. Davis, Box 2, KaHS.

5 Charles C. Paige, memoir [circa 1913], in Participant Accounts—Fiftieth Anniversary Vertical File, GNMPL; George Kilmer, "A Note of Peace: Reunions of the Blue and the Gray," *Century* 36 (1888): 440–442.

6 Historians are beginning to appreciate the "limits" of reconciliation. See Caroline E. Janney, *Remembering the Civil War: Reunion and the Limits of Reconciliation* (Chapel Hill: University of North Carolina Press, 2013); Neff, *Honoring the Civil War Dead*; and Gary W. Gallagher, *Becoming Confederates: Paths to a New National Loyalty* (Athens: University of Georgia Press, 2013). Bordewich, "Remembering Gettysburg: The 1913 and 1938 Reunions," paper delivered at the Cosmos Club Civil War Symposium, Washington, D.C., 13 July 2013; Neff, *Honoring the Civil War Dead*, 214, 216–217, 220–221; Kilmer, "A Note of Peace," 441. The Shields' Division Association, for example, planned an "excursion" from Washington, D.C., to the Kernstown battlefield in the Shenandoah Valley during the fall of 1892. Local organizers elected to invite a few Confederate veterans in nearby Harrisonburg, Virginia, to "meet and greet" them. The former enemies exchanged a cordial correspondence, clearly establishing the parameters of the reunion—something that could not have been achieved on a larger scale. See Charles Dickson to John Edwin Roller, letter, 9 September 1892, in John Edwin Roller Correspondence, ASSpCL. See also "Rebel Gush," *National Tribune*, 26 July 1888; on the 1913

reunion, see Participant Accounts—Fiftieth Anniversary Vertical File, GNMPL, and Evan Preston, " 'All May Visit the Big Camp': Race and the Lessons of the Civil War at the 1913 Gettysburg Reunion," *Gettysburg College Journal of the Civil War Era* 2, no. 1 (2011): 66–85.

7 Fiftieth Anniversary of the Battle of Gettysburg Commission Minute Book [minutes for 16 February 1912], p. 29, in RG 25: Records of the Department of Special Commissions—Fiftieth Anniversary of the Battle of Gettysburg Commission, Box 1, PaSA; James Smith to Louis Wagoner, n.d., Fiftieth Anniversary of the Battle of Gettysburg Commission Scrapbook, vol. 2, p. 12, in RG 25: Records of the Department of Special Commissions—Fiftieth Anniversary of the Battle of Gettysburg Commission, Box 1, PaSA. These sentiments may also do much to explain the disparity in attendance—while 44,713 Union veterans attended the reunion, only 8,694 Confederates trekked to Gettysburg. See Participant Accounts—Fiftieth Anniversary Vertical File, GNMPL; Andrew Cowan to Louis Wagoner, letter, 28 June 1911, Fiftieth Anniversary of the Battle of Gettysburg Commission Scrapbook, vol. 2, p. 83, ibid.; "At Gettysburg in July," *New York World*, undated newspaper clipping in Fiftieth Anniversary of the Battle of Gettysburg Commission Scrapbook, vol. 2, p. 65, ibid.

8 The scorching temperatures resulted in over two hundred cases of heat exhaustion. See "Report of the Commissioner of Health" and "Final Commission Report," both in RG 25: Records of the Department of Special Commissions—Fiftieth Anniversary of the Battle of Gettysburg Commission, Box 1. On shared heroism, see Blight, *Race and Reunion*; Bennett H. Young, address at Gettysburg, 1 July 1913, in Autographed Addresses Delivered at Fiftieth Anniversary Reunion, RG 25: Records of the Department of Special Commissions—Fiftieth Anniversary of the Battle of Gettysburg Commission, Box 1, PaSA; John Brooke, address at Gettysburg, 2 July 1913, ibid.; *Raleigh News and Observer*, 3 July 1913, clipping in Participant Accounts—Fiftieth Anniversary Vertical File, GNMPL. The 1917 Vicksburg National Memorial Celebration offers up yet another example of sectional bitterness lurking beneath national reconciliation. A northern veteran who attended the dedication of the Peace Monument at Vicksburg, Mississippi, refused "to ride on a truck loaded with [Confederates]," opting to "patronize a taxi at his own expense" instead. See "Vicksburg National Memorial Celebration," *Confederate Veteran* 25 (1917): 489.

9 James Bryant Post No. 119, Department of Minnesota, Grand Army of the Republic, to the Governor of Pennsylvania, 10 July 1913, in RG 25: Records of the Department of Special Commissions—Fiftieth Anniversary of the Battle of Gettysburg Commission, Box 3—Scrapbook, p. 97, PaSA. The average age achieved by attendees of the 1913 Gettysburg reunion was seventy-two; RG 25:

Records of the Department of Special Commissions—Fiftieth Anniversary of the Battle of Gettysburg Commission, Box 3—Scrapbook, 91–92, 96, and 97, PaSA; on relic-hunting at the 1913 reunion, see George Duke to "Lizzie and Jay," letter, 6 July 1913, copy in Participant Accounts—Fiftieth Anniversary Vertical File, GNMPL; quotes from Charles C. Paige, memoir [circa 1913], ibid.

10 Henry H. Heckman to Maud E. Middleton, letter, 15 August 1929, in 44th Indiana Regimental Association Records, Box 1, Folder 4, InHS; on urbanization and industrialization, see Robert Wiebe, *The Search for Order, 1877–1920* (New York: Hill & Wang, 1967); and Alan Trachtenberg, *The Incorporation of America: Culture and Society in the Gilded Age* (New York: Hill & Wang, 1982); quote from Clarence Edward Macartney, "To the Survivors of the Grand Army of The Republic," handbill [May 1920], in Memorabilia of Michael Floyd, Grand Army of the Republic Collection, Box 9, PaSA; see also Marten, *Sing Not War*; George Lamphere, manuscript reminiscences of trip to Boston, in George Lamphere Papers, Institute for Regional Studies, NDSU.

11 Bruce Catton, *Waiting for the Morning Train*, 192; on the Bonus March, see Paul Dickson and Thomas B. Allen, *The Bonus Army: An American Epic* (New York: Walker & Co., 2004).

12 "Albert Woolson, last man in G.A.R. dies at 109," circular in Albert Woolson Papers, NeMinnHC; see "Oldest Living Civil War Vet's Birthday," "Deacon Enjoying 102nd Birthday," "Hoover, Coolidge Pay Tribute to Oldest Civil War Veteran," newspaper clippings in Joseph Day Papers, NHHS; Calvin Coolidge to Joseph Day, letter, 2 January 1931, and Herbert Hoover to Joseph Day, letter, 5 January 1931, ibid.; Brian Matthew Jordan, "The Last Reunion and the Light of Peace," *Gettysburg* (Spring 2013): 14–15; for quotations and on separating the opposing camps, see undated, untitled newspaper clippings in Mary Edwards Murray Scrapbook, ASSpCL.

13 "GAR Forms Ranks for What May Become Last Session," *Washington Post*, 28 September 1948; *Terre Haute Star*, 14 September 1950.

14 Newspaper clippings dated 28 August 1949, 29 August 1949, 31 August 1949, 1 September 1949, and 27 May 1951, JGDC.

15 Newspaper clippings dated 29 August 1949, 14 September 1950, 19 September 1950, 14 July 1951, and 15 July 1951, ibid.; *Princeton Leader*, 18 January 1951.

16 "Veteran Hard is Dead at 111," *Trenton Evening Times*, 13 March 1953; newspaper clippings dated 13 March 1953, 1 February 1952, 15 March 1953, in JGDC; *St. Paul Pioneer Press*, 24 May 1953; Duluth Chamber of Commerce circular dated 30 March 1956 in Albert Woolson Vertical File, NeMinnHC; Trudy Kobus as quoted in *Duluth News Tribune and Herald*, 20 February 1986. Tennyson Guyer as quoted in undated clipping, and "Monument with a Voice," undated clipping,

ibid. Significantly, many descendants of Union veterans sought to deposit their ancestor's diaries and letters with Woolson.

17 Woolson as quoted in "Monument with a Voice," undated clipping, Albert Woolson Vertical File, NeMinnHC; Albert Woolson Papers, NeMinnHC; Albert Woolson, "The Last Man," reminiscence [circa 1953], ibid.

18 "Albert Woolson, last man in G.A.R. dies at 109," circular in Albert Woolson Papers, Folder 15, NeMinnHC; Bruce Catton, "Muffled Roll for Grand Army," *Life* 41, no. 8 (August 20, 1956), copy in Albert Woolson Vertical File, NeMinnHC; newspaper clippings in Olaf Hagman Papers, Institute for Regional Studies, NDSU.

BIBLIOGRAPHY

PRIMARY SOURCES

MANUSCRIPTS

Abraham Lincoln Presidential Library, Springfield, Illinois
Henry Baltzell Memoir
Allen L. Fahnestock Papers
52nd Illinois Reunion Association Records
Grand Army of the Republic Post No. 80 Records
Henry Hoskins Diary
Lippincott Family Papers
Eugene Payne Speech
Joshua D. Rilea Diary
James Tanner Reminiscences
34th Illinois Volunteers Veterans Association Records

Adams County Historical Society, Gettysburg, Pennsylvania
Battle of Gettysburg—25th Anniversary (1888) Vertical File
Gettysburg Battlefield Memorial Association Vertical File
Johnston H. Skelly Post No. 9, Grand Army of the Republic Records
Trolley Line Vertical File

Akron–Summit County Pubic Library, Akron, Ohio
Ohio State Penitentiary Records

*Albert and Shirley Small Special Collections Library, University of Virginia,
    Charlottesville, Virginia*
Charles D. Barney Letter
William Cullen Bryant Letter (fragment)
Hervey Eaton Civil War Letters
Irwin C. Fox Diary

William S. Hotchkin Diaries
Adam King Papers
Thomas McMaster Papers
McNeir Family Papers
Mary Edwards Murray Scrapbook
Alexander Neal Letters
D. A. Pierce Letter
John Edwin Roller Correspondence
Thomas Rosser Letter
Southern Branch National Soldiers' Home Letter

Alexander Library, Rutgers University, New Brunswick, New Jersey
Marcus L. Ward Papers

American Antiquarian Society, Worcester, Massachusetts
Charles Edgar Abbey Civil War Papers
American Newspapers and Broadsides
Records of Webster, Massachusetts
The Soldier's Friend

Andersonville National Historic Site Archives, Andersonville, Georgia
Simeon Haun Papers
H. B. Hoffman Papers
Elizabeth Maher Letter

Beinecke Rare Book and Manuscript Library, New Haven, Connecticut
The Soldier's Friend
Joseph Hopkins Twichell Papers

Bentley Historical Library, University of Michigan, Ann Arbor, Michigan
James Valentine Campbell Papers
    Valeria Campbell Materials
Francis Willett Shearman Papers

Binghamton Special Collections, State University of New York, Binghamton, New York
Civil War Manuscripts Collection
S. C. Pierce Papers
Fred Walster Papers

Butler Library, Columbia University, New York City, New York
William Oland Bourne Papers
Civil War Miscellany Collection

Center for Archival Collections, Bowling Green State University,
*   Bowling Green, Ohio*
Fast Family Papers

The Citadel Archives, Charleston, South Carolina
Bruce Catton Papers

Connecticut Historical Society, Hartford, Connecticut
Oliver Gates Diary
Robert Kellogg Papers
Nehemiah Solon Diary

Connecticut State Library, Hartford, Connecticut
Andersonville Monument Commission Records
Dorence Atwater Papers
Fitch Soldiers' Home Records
Ira Emory Forbes Papers
Norman Hope Papers
Albert A. Hyde Papers
George Q. Whitney Collection

Dakota Sunset Museum Archives, Gettysburg, South Dakota
William Combellick Papers
Grand Army of the Republic Papers

Gettysburg National Military Park Library, Gettysburg, Pennsylvania
Fiftieth Anniversary Grand Reunion Participant Accounts
Seventy-Fifth Anniversary Grand Reunion Participant Accounts

Grand Army of the Republic Museum Archives, Philadelphia, Pennsylvania
George Gordon Meade Post No. 1 Collection
Grand Army of the Republic Miscellaneous Records
104th Pennsylvania Survivors' Association Records
J. K. Taylor Post No. 182 Collection

Greg Taylor Collection, Van Nuys, California
William Beynon Phillips Letters

Harold Lee Library, Brigham Young University,
Provo, Utah
Weir Family Papers

Henry E. Huntington Library, San Marino, California
Paul James Lindberg Papers
John Page Nicholson Collection

Hiram College Archives, Hiram, Ohio
Wakefield Family Collection

Houghton Library, Harvard University, Cambridge, Massachusetts
Military Order of the Loyal Legion Collection
    Augustus Choate Hamlin Papers

Illinois State Archives, Springfield, Illinois
Illinois Soldiers' and Sailors' Home Case Files
Richard Oglesby Correspondence

Indiana Historical Society, Indianapolis, Indiana
Elijah Cavins Papers
Civil War Miscellany Collection
44th Indiana Regimental Association Records
John Love Papers
Daniel R. Lucas Papers
William Stanley Mead Collection
29th Indiana Regiment Reunion Association Records, 1900–1902

Indiana State Library, Indianapolis, Indiana
Clark County Pension Claim Book
Temple H. Dunn Papers

Institute for Regional Studies, North Dakota State University,
    Fargo, North Dakota
Grand Army of the Republic, John F. Reynolds Post No. 5 Records
Olaf Hagman Papers

George Nathan Lamphere Papers
Luman Tenney Papers

John Gary Dillon Private Collection, Akron, Ohio
John Gary Dillon Scrapbook

Kansas Historical Society, Topeka, Kansas
Patrick Henry Coney Papers
Boston Corbett Papers
Governor's Office Records
    Governor J. W. Davis—Correspondence Files
    Governor J. A. Martin—Correspondence Files
Grand Army of the Republic Papers
    Administrative Records
        Post Court Martial Records
        State Soldiers' Home Investigations
    Clippings Collection
Kansas Soldiers' Home Records
    Offenders' Docket, 1893–1906
Miscellaneous Manuscripts Collection
    Asa Wickizer Letters
Stewart Bruce Terry Papers
Asbury Thornhill Letter
Veteran Brotherhood Collection

Kenneth Spencer Research Library, University of Kansas, Lawrence, Kansas
Milton Carmichael Collection
Henry and Lucy Fike Papers
Thomas Lorimor Papers
Perry O. C. Nixon Papers
J. B. Whitaker Collection

Kent State University Special Collections, Kent, Ohio
American Historical Manuscripts Collection
    William Henry Jones Papers

Local History Room, Dayton and Montgomery County Public Library, Dayton, Ohio
Howard Burba Scrapbooks
Central Branch, NHDVS Clipping Files

Maine Historical Society, Portland, Maine
John Mead Gould Diary
John Mead Gould Papers
Aurestus Perham Papers
G. F. Sparrow Collection

Manuscript Division, Library of Congress, Washington
Associated Survivors of the Sixth Army Corps Papers
Clara Barton Papers
Mary Ann Ball Bickerdyke Papers
William Oland Bourne Papers
Thomas Brown Papers
Benjamin Franklin Butler Papers
Ezra Carman Papers
Grover Cleveland Papers
S. J. Gibson Diary and Notes
Samuel J. B. V. Gilpin Diary
Benjamin Harrison Papers
John Alexander Logan Family Papers
Lyman Trumbull Papers
Henry Wirz Papers

Massachusetts Historical Society, Boston, Massachusetts
Charlestown Overseer of the Poor Records
Civil War Papers Microfilm
Grand Army of the Republic, E. W. Kinsley Post No. 113 Records
George Hitchcock Diaries
William Milo Olin Papers and Letterbooks

Milwaukee Public Library, Milwaukee, Wisconsin
Milwaukee Soldiers' Home Fund Circular
National Home for the Disabled Volunteer Soldier Collection
Ole Steensland Collection

Minnesota Historical Society, St. Paul, Minnesota
Samuel Bloomer Papers
George Crosby Papers
Dinner Gang Scrapbook
Robert C. Eagles Papers

Grand Army of the Republic Collection
    Minnesota Union Ex-Prisoner-of-War Narratives
David Greenlee Pamphlet
Henry A. House Diary
Charles Morehouse Diary
Ramsey Pamphlet Collection
Records of the Governor's Office
Thomas Rice Stewart Memoirs
Eliakim (Ell) Torrance Papers
Union Veterans' Union Records

Monmouth County Historical Association Library, Monmouth, New Jersey
William T. Ackerson Papers

Montana Historical Society, Helena, Montana
Grand Army of the Republic, Montana Department Records

National Archives, Central Plains Division, Kansas City, Missouri
Record Group 15: Records of the Veterans' Administration
    Correspondence Relating to Use of Railroad Tracks at Western Branch, NHDVS
    Western Branch, NHDVS Sample Case Files of Members

National Archives, Great Lakes Division, Chicago, Illinois
Record Group 15: Records of the Veterans' Administration
    Central Branch, NHDVS Sample Case Files of Members
    Northwestern Branch, NHDVS Sample Case Files of Members

National Archives, Northeast Division, New York City, New York
Record Group 15: Records of the Veterans' Administration
    Bath Soldiers' Home Offense Dockets
    Bath Soldiers' Home Sample Case Files of Members

National Archives, Northeast Division, Waltham, Massachusetts
Record Group 15: Records of the Veterans' Administration
    Togus Branch, NHDVS Sample Case Files of Members

National Archives Building, Washington, D.C.
Record Group 15: Records of the Veterans' Administration
    Civil War Veteran Pension Files

Record Group 94: Records of the Adjutant General's Office
Civil War Military Service Records
Record Group 233: Records of the U.S. House of Representatives
    Petitions and Memorials Referred to Committee on Invalid Pensions
Record Group 418: Records of the St. Elizabeth's Hospital (Government Hospital for
    the Insane)
    Registers of Cases

Nebraska State Historical Society, Lincoln, Nebraska
Grand Army of the Republic Collection
    Court Martial Records
    Encampments and Reunions
    General Correspondence and Records
    Pension Records and Miscellany
Grand Island Veterans' Home Records (formerly the Nebraska Soldiers'
    and Sailors' Home)
    Death Register
    Discharge Register
    Inmate Case Files
Abner James Hill Diaries
Joseph Wright Johnson Papers
Cornelius S. Munhall Papers
Charles Henry Wilson Papers

Newberry Library, Chicago, Illinois
John C. Fleming Papers
Edgar McLean Papers
Oliver Perry Newberry Papers

New Hampshire Historical Society, Concord, New Hampshire
Arlon S. Atherton Papers
Asa Bartlett Papers
Joseph Day Papers
Daniel Eldredge Papers
Lyman Jackman Papers
William Rand Papers

New Jersey Historical Society Library, Newark, New Jersey
James A. Garfield Post No. 4 Collection

Grand Army of the Republic Collection
Walter Tully Papers
Marcus L. Ward Papers

New Jersey State Archives, Trenton, New Jersey
New Jersey Home for Disabled Soldiers Case Files

Newman Library, Virginia Polytechnic Institute, Blacksburg, Virginia
William H. Barron Letter
Ansil Bartlett Letter
Henry T. Bartlett Letter
William S. Burns Reminiscences
Civil War Small Manuscripts Collection
      Henry Weldo Hart Letters
Samuel Creelman Papers
Otis Dean Diary
Herbert Deuel Civil War Collection
Georgetown, D.C., Letter, 1865
Wright Gilbert Papers
William Wallace Hensley Autobiography
John Holliday Diary
Joseph Horr Papers
Stephen Kelsey Papers
Letters from a Civil War Union Soldier, MS 96-005
Charles F. McKenna Diary
Stearns Family Papers

New-York Historical Society, New York City, New York
William Oland Bourne Papers

New York Public Library, New York City, New York
Century Collection
Robert Underwood Johnson Letterbooks

New York State Archives, Albany, New York
William Woods Averell Papers
Henry B. Bradt Family Papers
Uberto S. Burnham Papers
Chester Hoke Family Papers

George Howland Papers
John Logan Post No. 477, GAR Papers
Samuel E. Preston Papers
Sydney Post No. 41, GAR Papers

North Haven Historical Society, North Haven, Connecticut:
Sheldon Thorpe Collection

Northeast Minnesota Historical Center, University of Minnesota, Duluth, Minnesota
Grand Army of the Republic Collection
Albert Woolson Papers
Albert Woolson Vertical File

Ohio Historical Society, Columbus, Ohio
Robert Kellogg Vertical File

Pennsylvania State Archives, Harrisburg, Pennsylvania
Henry Alleman Collection
Hiram Alleman Collection
Jacob Gobrecht Diary
Grand Army of the Republic Collection
Records of the Department of Special Commissions
    Fiftieth Anniversary of the Battle of Gettysburg Commission
Records of the Pennsylvania Soldiers' and Sailors' Home
    Discharge and Offense Book

Potter County Free Public Library, Gettysburg, South Dakota
Potter County Civil War Veterans' Censuses and Obituaries

Rhode Island Historical Society, Providence, Rhode Island
George Bliss Papers
Grand Army of the Republic Collection
Soldiers' and Sailors' Historical Society Papers

Rutherford B. Hayes Presidential Center, Fremont, Ohio
Isadore H. Burgoon Papers
Gustavus A. Gessner Papers
Rutherford B. Hayes Papers

Special Collections Department, University of Iowa Library, Iowa City, Iowa
Lot Abraham Papers
Jacob H. Allspaugh Diary
Civil War Collection
Lewis Crater Diary
W. B. Emmons Diary
George Kepner Papers
John W. Pratt Diary
George M. Shearer Diary

Special Collections, Musselman Library, Gettysburg College, Gettysburg, Pennsylvania
Adams County Alms House Register
George Leo Frankenstein Vertical File
Gettysburgiana Collection
James Tanner Letter

State Historical Society of Iowa, Iowa City, Iowa
Isaac N. Carr Papers
George Fisher Diary
Charles Kepler Papers
Henry Clinton Parkhurst Papers

State Historical Society of North Dakota, Bismarck, North Dakota
Grand Army of the Republic Collection

Sterling Memorial Library, Yale University, New Haven, Connecticut
Civil War Manuscripts Collection
    Hiram Blaisdell Family Papers
    Ira Emory Forbes Diary
    George Jarvis Papers
    Henry Parmelee Papers
    William Warren Papers
Committee on Commemorating the Service of Yale Men Records

United States Army Military History Institute, Carlisle, Pennsylvania
Civil War Document Collection
Civil War Miscellaneous Collection
Civil War Pamphlets Collection

Civil War Times Illustrated Collection
    Stephen P. Chase Diary
Grand Army of the Republic Collection—Sedgwick Post No. 17
Harrisburg Civil War Roundtable Collection
    Boyer Family Papers
    George Shuman Papers

Vermont Historical Society Library, Barre, Vermont
Walter Bailey Pension File
Alson H. Blake Papers
Chester W. Dodge Diary
Civil War Pension Claim Files
Hamilton S. Gilbert Papers
Edwin C. Hall Papers
Lyman Knapp Papers
Eugene Rolfe Diary
Stannard Post No. 2 Collection
    Grand Army of the Republic Scrapbook

Wilson Library, University of North Carolina, Chapel Hill, North Carolina
Southern Historical Collection
    Joseph Heft Diary

Wisconsin Historical Society, Madison, Wisconsin
William Hamilton Church Papers
William Henry Church Civil War Papers
Willis Peck Clarke Papers
Henry Dillon Papers
Lucius Fairchild Papers
John A. Johnson Collection
Conrad Kuoni Reminiscences
Edmund Spencer Packard Diary
Guy C. Pierce Letter
Sauk County Clerk's Records
John Ebenezer Warren Collection
Cornelius Wheeler Papers
Wisconsin Soldiers' Home Records
A. O. Wright Papers

Wisconsin Veterans' Museum Archives, Madison, Wisconsin
Grand Army of the Republic Memorial Hall Records
Peter Schaus Collection
John Siggleko Collection
Augustus Gordon Weissert Papers
Wisconsin Veterans' Home Records

Worcester Historical Museum, Worcester, Massachusetts
Company A, 25th Massachusetts Reunion Association Records
15th Massachusetts Reunion Association Records

GOVERNMENT RECORDS, DOCUMENTS, AND DATABASES

Congressional Globe
Historical Register of National Homes for Disabled Volunteer Soldiers, 1866–1938
(National Archives Microfilm Publication M1749, 282 rolls).
"Investigation of the National Home for Disabled Volunteer Soldiers" (48th Congress,
2nd Session, Report No. 2676).
National Park Service, Civil War Soldiers and Sailors System.
*Report of the Board of Managers of the National Asylum for Disabled Volunteer Soldiers,
February 26, 1869,* Serial Set vol. 1385, no. 1 (40th Congress, 3rd Session).
*Report of the Board of Managers of the National Asylum for Disabled Volunteer Soldiers, July
18, 1867,* Serial Set vol. 1312, no. 1 (40th Congress, 1st Session).
*Report of the Board of Managers of the National Asylum for Disabled Volunteer Soldiers,
March 3, 1868,* Serial Set vol. 1350, no. 2 (40th Congress, 2nd Session).
War of the Rebellion, Official Records of the Union and Confederate Armies. Washington,
D.C., United States Government Printing Office, 1889–1900.

NEWSPAPERS AND PERIODICALS

Adams County Sentinel (Adams County, Pennsylvania)
Albany Argus (Albany, New York)
Albany Evening Journal
Albert Lea Enterprise (Albert Lea, Minnesota)
Argus and Patriot (Montpelier, Vermont)
Army Times
Ashland Times (Ashland, Ohio)
Atchison Champion (Atchison, Kansas)
Atlantic Telegraph (Atlantic, Iowa)
Bismarck Tribune (Bismarck, North Dakota)

Boston Daily Advertiser

Boston Daily Globe

Boston Daily Journal

Boston Herald

Boston Investigator

Boston Journal

Carthage Republican (Carthage, Illinois)

Century Magazine

Chicago Daily Tribune

Chicago Medical Examiner

Cincinnati Commercial Tribune

Cincinnati Daily Gazette

Cincinnati Inquirer

Cleveland Gazette

Cleveland Plain Dealer

Columbian Register (New Haven, Connecticut)

Congressional Globe

Coshocton Democrat (Coshocton, Ohio)

Daily Cleveland Herald

Daily Constitutional Union (Washington, D.C.)

Daily Inter Ocean (Chicago, Illinois)

Daily Iowa State Register (Des Moines, Iowa)

Daily Globe-Democrat (St. Louis, Missouri)

Daily National Intelligencer (Washington, D.C.)

Daily Ohio Statesman (Columbus, Ohio)

Davenport Daily Gazette (Davenport, Iowa)

Dayton Daily Empire (Dayton, Ohio)

Dayton Downtowner

Delmarva Star (Wilmington, Delaware)

Des Moines Register and Leader

Duluth News Tribune and Herald

Evening News (San Jose, California)

Evening Star (Washington, D.C.)

Farmer's Cabinet (Amherst, New Hampshire)

Frank Leslie's Illustrated Newspaper

Friendship Weekly Register (Allegany County, New York)

Gettysburg Republican Compiler (Gettysburg, Pennsylvania)

Grand Forks Herald (Grand Forks, North Dakota)

Harper's Weekly

Hartford Daily Courant

Hartford Daily Times

Haversack, The (Ashland, New Hampshire)

Hornell Daily Times (Hornellsville, New York)

Idaho Statesman (Boise, Idaho)

Illustrated Daily Age (Philadelphia, Pennsylvania)

Independent, The

Indianapolis Daily Journal

Indianapolis Daily State Sentinel

Ithaca Citizen and Democrat (Ithaca, New York)

Ithaca Journal and Advertiser

Jackson Daily Citizen (Jackson, Michigan)

Kansas City Star (Kansas City, Missouri)

Kennebec Journal (Augusta, Maine)

Leavenworth Bulletin

Los Angeles Times

Lowell Daily Citizen and News (Lowell, Massachusetts)

Macon Weekly Telegraph (Macon, Georgia)

McClure's Magazine

Methodist Quarterly Review

Milwaukee Daily Sentinel

Milwaukee Journal

Munsey's Magazine

New Albany Daily Ledger (New Albany, Indiana)

New Hampshire Sentinel (Keene, New Hampshire)

New Haven Palladium (New Haven, Connecticut)

New Orleans Times–Picayune

New York Daily Evening Post

New York Herald

New York Observer and Chronicle

New York Times

New York Tribune

North American (Philadelphia, Pennsylvania)

Ohio Repository (Canton, Ohio)

Oregonian, The

Philadelphia Daily Age

Philadelphia Daily Evening Bulletin

Philadelphia Inquirer

Philadelphia Public Ledger

Philadelphia Press
Portsmouth Journal of Literature and Politics (Portsmouth, New Hampshire)
Potter County News (Gettysburg, South Dakota)
Princeton Leader (Princeton, Kentucky)
Public Opinion
San Francisco Chronicle
School Journal
Springfield Republican (Springfield, Massachusetts)
St. Albans Messenger (St. Albans, Vermont)
St. Paul Pioneer Press
Summit County Beacon (Akron, Ohio)
Terre Haute Star (Terre Haute, Indiana)
Toledo Blade
Topeka Weekly Capital
Trenton Evening Times
Trenton State Gazette
USA Today
Washington Bee
Washington Evening Union
Washington Post
Weekly Journal Miner (Prescott, Arizona Territory)
Wilkes-Barre Times (Wilkes-Barre, Pennsylvania)
Wisconsin Chief (Fort Atkinson, Wisconsin)
Wisconsin State Register
Worcester Daily Spy (Worcester, Massachusetts)
World's Work
Youth's Companion
Zion's Herald and Wesleyan Journal

VETERANS' NEWSPAPERS AND PERIODICALS

American Tribune (Indianapolis, Indiana)
Army and Navy Journal (New York, New York)
Confederate Veteran (Nashville, Tennessee)
Connecticut War Record (New Haven, Connecticut)
Daily Veteran (Grand Island, Nebraska)
Flag of Our Union (Boston, Massachusetts)
Grand Army Gazette and National Guardsmen (New York, New York)
Grand Army Journal (Washington, D.C.)
Grand Army Scout and Soldiers' Mail (Philadelphia, Pennsylvania)

Grand Army Sentinel (Berlin, Wisconsin)

Great Republic (Washington, D.C.)

Kansas Knight and Soldier (Topeka, Kansas)

Mirror, The (Philadelphia, Pennsylvania)

National Tribune (Washington, D.C.)

Neighbor's Home Mail: Ex-Soldiers' Reunion and National Campfire (Phelps, New York)

Our Country (Boston, Massachusetts)

Relief Guard (St. Paul, Minnesota)

Soldiers' and Sailors' Half Dime Tales of the Late Rebellion (New York, New York)

Soldiers and Sailors Journal (Philadelphia, Pennsylvania)

Soldier's Casket (Philadelphia, Pennsylvania)

Soldier's Friend (New York, New York)

Soldiers' Manual (Worcester, Massachusetts)

Soldiers' Record (Hartford, Connecticut)

Soldiers' Record (Madison, Wisconsin)

Veterans' Advocate (Concord, New Hampshire)

Weekly Knight and Soldier (Topeka, Kansas)

Western Veteran (Topeka, Kansas)

PUBLISHED PRIMARY SOURCES

Adkins, C. H., and "An Old Veteran." *When the Boys in Blue Are Gone*. Gardner, Massachusetts: George H. Ross, 1912.

Albert, Allen D., ed. *History of the Forty-Fifth Regiment Pennsylvania Veteran Volunteer Infantry*. Williamsport, Pennsylvania: Grit Publishing Co., 1912.

Aldrich, Thomas M. *The History of Battery A, First Regiment Rhode Island Light Artillery in the War to Preserve the Union, 1861–1865*. Providence: Snow & Farnham, Printers, 1904.

Allen, Stacy Dale, ed. *On the Skirmish Line Behind a Friendly Tree: The Civil War Memoirs of William Royal Oake, 26th Iowa Volunteers*. Helena, Montana: Farcountry Press, 2006.

Anderson, Harry H. "The Civil War Letters of Lieutenant Samuel B. Chase." *Milwaukee History* 14, no. 2 (1991): 38–62.

Annual Report of the Adjutant General of the State of New York—Register of the Fifteenth and Sixteenth Artillery in the War of the Rebellion. New York and Albany: Wynkoop Hallenbeck Crawford Co., 1898.

Anonymous. *Opium Eating: An Autobiographical Sketch, by an Habituate*. Philadelphia: Claxton, Remsen & Haffelfinger, 1876.

Bahde, Thomas, ed. *The Story of My Campaign: The Civil War Memoir of Captain Francis T. Moore, Second Illinois Cavalry*. DeKalb: Northern Illinois University Press, 2011.

Barber, James. *The Nation's Defenders: The New Jersey and the National Homes for Disabled Volunteer Soldiers: How They Are Cared For*. Newark, New Jersey: Dennis, 1874.

Barrett, Faith, and Cristanne Miller, eds. *"Words for the Hour": A New Anthology of American Civil War Poetry.* Amherst: University of Massachusetts Press, 2005.

Basler, Roy P. *The Collected Works of Abraham Lincoln.* New Brunswick, New Jersey: Rutgers University Press, 1953–1955.

Bassett, Samuel Clay. *Buffalo County, Nebraska, and Its People: A Record of Settlement, Organization, Progress, and Achievement.* Vol. 1. Chicago: S. J. Clarke Publishing Co., 1916.

Bassett, Wayne R., ed. *From Bull Run to Bristow Station.* St. Paul: North Central Publishing Co., 1962.

Bates, Ralph O. *Billy and Dick: From Andersonville Prison to the White House.* Santa Cruz, California: Sentinel Publishing Co., 1910.

Bauer, K. Jack, ed. *Soldiering: The Civil War Diary of Rice C. Bull, 123rd New York Volunteer Infantry.* San Rafael, California: Presidio Press, 1977.

Beath, Robert. *History of the Grand Army of the Republic.* New York: Press of Willis, McDonald & Co., 1888.

Beecham, Robert K. *Gettysburg, The Pivotal Battle of the Civil War.* Chicago: A. C. McClurg & Co., 1911.

Belknap, W. W., ed. *History of the Fifteenth Regiment, Iowa Veteran Volunteer Infantry.* Keokuk, Iowa: R. B. Ogden & Son, Printer, 1887.

Berry, Chester D., ed. *Loss of the* Sultana *and Reminiscences of Survivors.* Knoxville: University of Tennessee Press, 2005.

Beyer, Walter F., and Oscar F. Keydel. *Deeds of Valor: How America's Heroes Won the Medal of Honor.* Detroit: Perrien-Keydel, 1901.

Billings, John Shaw. "The Health of the Survivors of the War." *The Forum* (January 1892): 652–658.

Bircher, William. *A Drummer Boy's Diary: Comprising Four Years of Service with the Second Regiment Minnesota Volunteers, 1861–1865.* St. Paul: St. Paul Book & Stationary Co., 1889.

Blaisdell, Albert Franklin. *Stories of the Civil War.* Boston: Lee & Shepard, 1890.

Blakeman, A. Noel. *Personal Recollections of the War of the Rebellion.* 2nd series. Wilmington, North Carolina: Broadfoot Publishing Co., 1992.

Blight, David W., ed. *When This Cruel War Is Over: The Civil War Letters of Charles Harvey Brewster.* Amherst: University of Massachusetts Press, 1992.

Boney, F. N., ed. *A Union Soldier in the Land of the Vanquished: The Diary of Sergeant Matthew Woodruff, June–December 1865.* University: University of Alabama Press, 1969.

Bosbyshell, Oliver C., ed. *Pennsylvania at Antietam: Report of the Antietam Battlefield Memorial Commission.* Harrisburg, Pennsylvania: Harrisburg Publishing Co., 1906.

Boston Almanac and Business Directory. Vol. 59. Boston: Sampson, Murdock & Co., 1894.

Botkin, Alex C. *Legislative Manual of the State of Montana*. Helena, Montana: James B. Walker & Co., 1895.

Bowen, James Lorenzo. *History of the Thirty-Seventh Regiment, Massachusetts Volunteers, in the Civil War of 1861–1865*. Holyoke, Massachusetts, and New York: Clark W. Bryan, 1884.

Brayton, Mary Clark, and Ellen F. Terry. *Our Acre and Its Harvest: Historical Sketch of the Soldiers' Aid Society of Northern Ohio*. Cleveland: Fairbanks, Benedict & Co., Printers, 1869.

Brown, Alonzo Leighton. *History of the Fourth Regiment of Minnesota Volunteers*. St. Paul: Pioneer Press, 1982.

Bryant, Edwin Eustace. *History of the Third Regiment of Wisconsin Veteran Volunteer Infantry*. Madison: Veteran Association of the Regiment, 1891.

Buel, Clarence Clough, and Robert Underwood Johnson, eds. *Battles and Leaders of the Civil War*, 4 vols. New York: Thomas Yoseloff, 1956.

Burkhardt, George S., ed. *Double Duty in the Civil War: The Letters of Sailor and Soldier Edward W. Bacon*. Carbondale: Southern Illinois University Press, 2009.

Caba, G. Craig, ed. "Incidents of the Grand Review at Washington, by Professor J. Howard Wert." *Lincoln Herald* 82 (Spring 1980): 337–340.

Carman, Ezra A. *The Maryland Campaign of September 1862, Vol. 1: South Mountain*. Edited by Thomas G. Clemens. New York: Savas Beatie, 2010.

Carnahan, J. Worth. *Manual of the Civil War and Key to the Grand Army of the Republic and Kindred Societies*. Washington, D.C.: U.S. Army & Navy Historical Association, 1899.

The Carnegie Foundation for the Advancement of Teaching—Sixteenth Annual Report of the President and of the Treasurer. Boston: Merrymount Press, 1921.

Carter, Gari, ed. *Troubled State: The Civil War Journals of Franklin Archibald Dick*. Kirksville, Missouri: Truman State University Press, 2008.

Catalogue of Library, Belonging to the National Home for Disabled Volunteer Soldiers (Northwestern Branch), Near Milwaukee, Wisconsin. Milwaukee: National Soldiers' Home Printing Office, 1875.

Catalogue of the Putnam Library, National Asylum for Disabled Volunteer Soldiers. Dayton, Ohio: National Asylum Printing Office, 1872.

Catton, Bruce. *Waiting for the Morning Train: An American Boyhood*. Detroit: Wayne State University Press, 1987.

Clark, Olynthus B., ed. *Downing's Civil War Diary*. Des Moines: Historical Department of Iowa, 1916.

Clark, William E. *Our Dead of Honor: Justice, Humanity, Reason, and Policy Demand Its Payment*. Boston: William E. Clark, 1866.

Cole, Donald B., and John J. McDonough, eds., *Witness to the Young Republic: A Yankee's Journal, 1828–1870.* Hanover, New Hampshire, and London: University Press of New England, 1989.

Collins, Ronald K. L., ed. *The Fundamental Holmes: A Free Speech Chronicle and Reader.* Cambridge: Cambridge University Press, 2010.

Constitution and By-Laws of the Grand Encampment of Veteran Brotherhood of the State of Kansas, Adopted at Topeka, Kansas, August 2, 1866. Atchison, Kansas: Daily Champion Office, 1866.

Constitution and By-Laws of the Ohio Association of Union Ex-Prisoners of War, Together with Register of Members and Proceedings at the Reunion Held at Dayton, June 14 and 15, 1882. Columbus: Ohio State Journal Printing Establishment, 1883.

Constitution and By-Laws of Topeka Encampment No. 1, Veteran Brotherhood. Topeka, Kansas: n.p., 1866.

Constitution and By-Laws of the Union Veteran Army. New York: Globe Stationery & Printing Co., 1884.

Constitution of the Grand Veteran League of New Hampshire. Concord, New Hampshire: McFarland & Jenks, 1865.

Constitution of the National Union Survivors of Andersonville and Other Southern Military Prisons. New York: National Union Survivors of Andersonville and Other Southern Military Prisons, 1882.

Corbett, Elizabeth. *Out at the Soldiers' Home: A Memory Book.* Reprint ed. Skokie, Illinois: ACTA Publications, 2008.

Crapsey, Edward. *The Nether Side of New York; or the Vice, Crime, and Poverty of the Great Metropolis.* New York: Sheldon & Co., 1872.

Creelman, Samuel A. *Collections of a Coffee Cooler.* Pittsburgh: Press of the Pittsburgh Photo Engraving Co., 1890.

Creigh, James J. *Oration and Poem Delivered Before Right Honorable Legion of Veterans of Chester and Delaware Counties, Pennsylvania.* Westchester, Pennsylvania: W. W. Miller, Bookseller, 1866.

Crooker, Lucien B., Henry Stedman Nourse, and John G. Brown. *The Story of the Fifty-Fifth Regiment, Illinois Volunteer Infantry in the Civil War.* N.p.: W. J. Coulter, 1887.

Crotty, D. G. *Four Years Campaigning in the Army of the Potomac.* Grand Rapids, Michigan: Dygert Bros. & Co., Printers and Binders, 1874.

Crowninshield, Benjamin W. *A History of the First Regiment of Massachusetts Cavalry Volunteers.* Boston & New York: Houghton Mifflin Co., 1891.

Davidson, Henry M. *Fourteen Months in Southern Prisons.* Milwaukee: Daily Wisconsin Printing House, 1865.

Davis, Charles W., William Elliot Furness, and Alfred T. Andreas, eds. *Military Essays and Recollections.* Vol 2. Chicago: A. C. McClurg & Co., 1894.

Davis, William G., and Janet B. Davis, eds. *The Diaries of William T. Clark*. Lancaster, Pennsylvania: Lancaster County Historical Society, 1988.

Dedication of the Monument at Andersonville, Georgia, October 23, 1907, in Memory of the Men of Connecticut Who Suffered in Southern Military Prisons, 1861–1865. Hartford: Published by the State, 1908.

Denny, Joseph Waldo. *Wearing the Blue in the Twenty-Fifth Mass. Volunteer Infantry*. Worcester, Massachusetts: Putnam & Davis, 1879.

Documents of the Senate of the State of New York. Albany: Comstock & Cassidy, Printers, 1864.

Documents of the U.S. Sanitary Commission, vol. 2. New York: United States Sanitary Commission, 1866.

Drury, Augustus Waldo. *History of the City of Dayton and Montgomery County, Ohio*. Vol. 1. Chicago & Dayton: S. J. Clarke Publishing Co., 1909.

Duffy, James N., et al. *Final Report of the Gettysburg Battlefield Commission of New Jersey*. Trenton: John L. Murphy Publishing Co., 1891.

Dyer, Frederick H. *A Compendium of the War of the Rebellion*. Reprint ed. New York and London: Thomas Yoseloff, 1959.

Empson, W. H. *Let Us Forgive But Not Forget: Or What I Saw and Suffered*. Lockport, New York: Press of Roberts Brothers, 1895.

Engs, Robert F., and Corey M. Brooks, eds. *Their Patriotic Duty: The Civil War Letters of the Evans Family of Brown County, Ohio*. New York: Fordham University Press, 2007.

Evans, Henry. *Grand Army of the Republic Almanac for 1879*. Worcester, Massachusetts: Noyes, Snow & Co., 1878.

Ewer, James Kendall. *The Third Massachusetts Cavalry in the War for the Union*. Maplewood, Massachusetts: William Perry Press, 1903.

Executive Documents Printed by Order of the House of Representatives During the Third Session of the Thirty-Seventh Congress, 1862–1863. Washington, D.C.: Government Printing Office, 1863.

"Federal Soldiers' and Sailors' Societies," in *The Detroit Journal Year-Book*. Detroit: Detroit Journal Co., 1890.

Ferguson, Joseph. *Life Struggles in Rebel Prisons: A Record of the Sufferings, Escapes, Adventures, and Starvation of the Union Prisoners*. Philadelphia: Joseph Ferguson, 1866.

Fifth Annual Meeting of the Society of the 28th Wisconsin Volunteer Infantry, Held at Whitewater, Wisconsin, September 7th and 8th, 1887. Milwaukee: Burdick & Armitage, 1887.

Fitch, Michael Hendrick. *Echoes of the Civil War as I Hear Them*. New York: R. F. Fenno, 1905.

Floyd, David Bittle. *History of the Seventy-Fifth Regiment of Indiana Infantry Volunteers*. Philadelphia: Lutheran Publication Society, 1893.

Ford, Andrew Elmer. *The Story of the Fifteenth Massachusetts Volunteer Infantry in the Civil War, 1861–1864.* Clinton, Massachusetts: Press of W. J. Coulter, 1898.

Foroughi, Andrea R., ed. *Go If You Think It Your Duty: A Minnesota Couple's Civil War Letters.* St. Paul: Minnesota Historical Society Press, 2008.

Foulke, William Dudley. *Life of Oliver P. Morton, Including His Important Speeches.* Vol. 1. Indianapolis: Bowen-Merrill Co., 1899.

Fox, William F. *Regimental Losses in the American Civil War, 1861–1865.* Reprint ed. Dayton: Morningside Books, 1985.

Fry, Charles "Bud," ed. *The Life and Confession of Thomas Carr: One Notorious Belmont County Resident, 1846–1870.* Reprint ed. Wheeling, West Virginia: Ohio Valley Civil War Roundtable, 1996.

Furney, L. A. *Reminiscences of the War of the Rebellion, 1861–1865.* Flushing, New York: For the Estate of Jacob Roemer, 1897.

George P. Rowell & Co.'s American Newspaper Directory. New York: George P. Rowell & Co., 1869.

Gerry, H. E. *Camp Fire Entertainment and True History of Robert Henry Hendershot, the Drummer Boy of the Rappahannock.* Chicago: Hack & Anderson, 1900.

Gibbon, John. "Pensions: A Paper Read Before Oregon Commandery of the Military Order of the Loyal Legion of the United States, October 8, 1890." In *Civil War Papers of the California Commandery of the Military Order of the Loyal Legion of the United States.* Wilmington, North Carolina: Broadfoot Publishing Co., 1995.

Gobrecht, J. C. *History of the National Home for Disabled Volunteer Soldiers.* Dayton: United Brethren Printing Establishment, 1875.

Goss, Warren Lee. *The Soldier's Story of His Captivity at Andersonville, Belle Isle, and Other Rebel Prisons.* Boston: Lee & Shepard, 1866.

Gould, John Mead. *History of the First—Tenth—Twenty-Ninth Maine Regiment.* Portland, Maine: Stephen Berry, 1871.

Grand Army of the Republic Price List of Uniforms—Caps, Swords, Belts, Banners, and Flags, Manufactured by the M. C. Lilley & Co. Columbus, Ohio: M.C. Lilley & Co., 1886.

Grant, George W. "The First Army Corps on the First Day at Gettysburg," in *Glimpses of the Nation's Struggle: Papers Read Before the Minnesota Commandery of the Military Order of the Loyal Legion of the United States, 1897–1902,* Fifth Series. St. Paul: Review Publishing Co., 1903.

Grant, Ulysses S. *Personal Memoirs of U. S. Grant.* New York: Charles Webster & Co., 1885.

Grebner, Constantine. *We Were the Ninth: A History of the Ninth Regiment Ohio Volunteer Infantry, April 17, 1861–June 7, 1864.* 2nd ed. Translated and edited by Frederic Trautmann. Kent, Ohio: Kent State University Press, 1987.

Gue, Benjamin F. *History of Iowa: From the Earliest Times to the Beginning of the Twentieth Century*. New York: Century History Co., 1903.

Guide to the Central National Soldiers' Home for Visitors and Citizens. Dayton: Guide Publishing Co., 1891.

Hamlin, Augustus. *Martyria; or, Andersonville Prison*. Boston: Lee & Shepherd, 1866.

Hare, George M. *Mysteries and Miseries of the Soldiers' Home*. Woonsocket, Rhode Island: Patriot Printing House, 1885.

Harris, Lee O. *The Man Who Tramps: A Story of Today*. Indianapolis: Douglass & Carlon, Printers, 1878.

Headley, P. C. *Massachusetts in the Rebellion*. Boston: Walker, Fuller & Company, 1866.

Herbert, George B. *The Popular History of the Civil War in America*. New York: F. M. Lupton, 1885.

A History of the City of Chicago: Its Men and Institutions. Chicago: Published by the InterOcean, 1900.

The History of Iowa County, Iowa. Des Moines: Union Historical Co.; Birdsall, Williams & Co., 1881.

History of the Thirty-Sixth Regiment Massachusetts Volunteers. Boston: Rockwell & Churchill, 1884.

Holmes, Oliver Wendell. *Dead, Yet Living: An Address*. Boston: Ginn, Heath & Co., 1884.

Hough, Franklin B. *History of Lewis County in the State of New York*. Albany: Munsell & Rowland, 1860.

Howard, Samuel Meek. *The Illustrated Comprehensive History of the Great Battle of Shiloh*. Kansas City, Missouri: Franklin Hudson Publishing Co., 1921.

Hurst, S. H., "Memorial Address," delivered September 14, 1887, in *Ohio Memorials at Gettysburg*. Baltimore: Butternut & Blue, 1998.

Husby, Karen Jean, and Eric J. Wittenberg, eds. *Under Custer's Command: The Civil War Journal of James Henry Avery*. Washington, D.C.: Brassey's, 2000.

Hyde, Solon. *A Captive of War*. New York: McClure, Philips & Co., 1900.

Jackman, Lyman. *History of the Sixth New Hampshire Regiment in the War for the Union*. Concord, New Hampshire: Republican Press Association, 1891.

Jackson, Oscar Lawrence. *The Colonel's Diary*. Sharon, Pennsylvania: privately published, 1922.

Jamison, Matthew H. *Fort Leavenworth and the Soldiers' Home: With Sketches of Leavenworth and of the Men and Tragedies That Have Made Her Famous*. Kansas City, Missouri: Hudson-Kimberly Publishing Co., 1895.

Johnson, Rossiter. *The Fight for the Republic*. New York: Knickerbocker Press, 1917.

———. *The Story of a Great Conflict: A History of the War of Secession*. New York: Bryan, Taylor & Co., 1894.

Jones, J. W. *The Story of American Heroism: Thrilling Narratives of Personal Adventures During the Great Civil War as Told by the Medal Winners and Roll of Honor Men.* Springfield, Ohio: Werner Co., 1897.

Journal of the Annual Session of the Department and Encampment, Grand Army of the Republic, Minnesota. Minneapolis: Co-Operative Printing, 1885.

Journal of the Nineteenth Annual Session of the National Encampment, Grand Army of the Republic, Portland, Maine, June 24th and 25th, 1885. Toledo: Montgomery & Vrooman, Printers, 1885.

Journal of the Senate of the Forty-Second General Assembly. Des Moines: State of Iowa, 1927.

Journal of the Twenty-First Session, National Encampment, Grand Army of the Republic, St. Louis, Missouri. Milwaukee: Burdick & Armitage, Printers, 1887.

Journal of the Twenty-Second Annual Session of the National Encampment, Grand Army of the Republic, Columbus, Ohio, September 12th, 13th, and 14th, 1888. Minneapolis: Harrison & Smith, Printers, 1888.

Journal of the Twenty-Seventh Annual Session of the Encampment of the Department of the Potomac, Grand Army of the Republic, Washington, D.C., February 21, 23, 25, 27, 29, and March 6, 1895. Washington, D.C.: Gibson Bros., Printers and Bookbinders, 1895.

Journal of the Twenty-Sixth National Encampment, Grand Army of the Republic, Washington, D.C., September 21st and 22nd, 1892. Albany, New York: S. H. Wentworth, Printer, 1892.

Journal of the Twenty-Third Annual Session of the National Encampment, Grand Army of the Republic, Milwaukee, Wisconsin, August 28th, 29th, and 30th, 1889. St. Louis: A. Whipple, Printer, 1889.

Joyce, John A. *Jewels of Memory.* Washington, D.C.: Gibson Bros., Publishers, 1895.

Kellogg, Mary E., ed. *Army Life of an Illinois Soldier: Including a Day by Day Record of Sherman's March to the Sea.* Washington, D.C.: Globe Printing Co., 1906.

Kellogg, Robert H. *Life and Death in Rebel Prisons.* Hartford: Lucius Stebbins, 1865.

Kent, Arthur, ed. *Three Years with Company K.* London: Associated University Presses, 1976.

King, Moses. *Handbook of New York City.* Boston: Moses King, 1893.

Kinnear, John R. *History of the Eighty-Sixth Regiment, Illinois Volunteer Infantry.* Chicago: Tribune Company's Book and Job Printing Office, 1866.

Kiper, Richard L., ed. *Dear Catharine, Dear Taylor: The Civil War Letters of a Union Soldier to His Wife.* Lawrence: University Press of Kansas, 2002.

Kirby, Thomas Ellis. *Catalogue of the Private Art Collection of Thomas B. Clarke.* New York: American Art Association, 1899.

Krug, Mark M., ed. *Mrs. Hill's Journal—Civil War Reminiscences.* Chicago: R. R. Donnelly & Sons Co., Lakeside Press, 1980.

Ladd, David L., and Audrey Ladd, eds. *The Bachelder Papers: Gettysburg in Their Own Words*. Dayton: Morningside Books, 1995.

Lang, Theodore F. *Loyal West Virginia from 1861 to 1865*. Baltimore: Deutsch Publishing Co., 1895.

Laws of the United States Governing the Granting of Army and Navy Pensions. Washington, D.C.: Government Printing Office, 1916.

Leasher, Evelyn, ed. *Letter from Washington, 1863–1865*. Detroit: Wayne State University Press, 1999.

Livermore, Thomas. *Days and Events, 1860–1866*. Boston and New York: Houghton Mifflin Co., 1920.

———. *Numbers and Losses in the Civil War in America, 1861–1865*. Boston and New York: Houghton Mifflin Co., 1900.

Loan Exhibition of War Relics in Aid of R. O. Tyler Post, G.A.R., Hartford, December 15–22, 1886. Hartford: Press of the Case, Lockwood & Brainard Co., 1886.

Logan, Mary. *Reminiscences of the Civil War and the Reconstruction*. Carbondale: Southern Illinois University Press, 1970.

Long, Lessel. *Twelve Months in Andersonville*. Huntington, Indiana: Thad and Mark Butler, 1886.

Longacre, Glenn V., and John E. Haas. *To Battle for God and the Right: The Civil War Letterbooks of Emerson Opdyke*. Urbana and Chicago: University of Illinois Press, 2003.

Lord, Edward Oliver. *History of the Ninth Regiment New Hampshire Volunteers in the War of the Rebellion*. Concord, New Hampshire: Republican Press Association, 1895.

Lossing, Benson J. *The American Historical Record and Repertory of Notes and Queries*. Vol. 2. Philadelphia: Samuel P. Town, 1873.

———. *Pictorial History of the Civil War in the United States of America*. Vol. 1. Philadelphia: George W. Childs, 1866.

Lowe, David W., ed. *Meade's Army: The Private Notebooks of Lt. Col. Theodore Lyman*. Kent, Ohio: Kent State University Press, 2007.

Luebke, Peter C., ed. *The Story of a Thousand: A History of the 105th Ohio Volunteer Infantry*. Kent, Ohio: Kent State University Press, 2011.

Lynch, Charles H. *The Civil War Diary 1862–1865 of Charles H. Lynch*. Hartford: Privately Published, 1915.

Lyon, William Franklin. *In and Out of Andersonville Prison*. Detroit: George Harland, Co., 1905.

Maharay, George S., ed. *Lights and Shadows of Army Life: From Bull Run to Bentonville*. Shippensburg, Pennsylvania: Burd Street Press, 1998.

Marsh, John. *Temperance Recollections: Labors, Defeats, Triumphs*. New York: Charles Scribner & Co., 1866.

Marshall, Benjamin Tinkham. *A Modern History of New London County, Connecticut.* Vol. 1. New York: Louis Historical Publishing Co., 1922.

McElroy, John. *Andersonville: A Story of Rebel Military Prisons.* Toledo: D. R. Locke, 1879.

McWatters, George S. *Knots Untied; or, Ways and By-Ways in the Hidden Life of American Detectives.* Hartford: J. B. Burr & Hyde, 1872.

Memorial Volume of Denison University. Granville, Ohio: Denison University, 1907.

Miller, Charles Dana. *Report of the Great Reunion of the Veteran Soldiers and Sailors of Ohio.* Newark, Ohio: Clark & Underwood, 1879.

Miller, Delavan S. *A Drum's Story and Other Tales.* Watertown, New York: Hugerford-Holbrook Co., 1909.

Minutes of the Sixty-Sixth Annual Meeting of the Congregational Convention of Wisconsin Held at Eau Claire, October 4–6, 1904. Madison: Tracy, Gibbs & Co., Printers, 1904.

Mitchell, Silas Weir. *Biographical Memoir of John Shaw Billings, 1838–1913.* Washington, D.C.: National Academy of the Sciences, 1917.

Mohr, James C., ed. *The Cormany Diaries: A Northern Family in the Civil War.* Pittsburgh: University of Pittsburgh Press, 1982.

Morris, W. S., L. D. Hartwell, and J. B. Kuykendall. *History of the 31st Regiment Illinois Volunteers, Organized by John A. Logan.* Carbondale: Southern Illinois University Press, 1998.

Morton, Joseph W., ed. *Sparks from the Campfire; or, Tales of the Old Veterans.* Philadelphia: Keeler & Kirkpatrick, 1899.

The National Cyclopaedia of American Biography. New York: James T. White & Co., 1897.

N. W. Ayer & Sons American Newspaper Annual. Philadelphia: N. W. Ayer & Sons, 1884.

Nevins, Allan, ed. *A Diary of Battle: The Personal Journals of Colonel Charles S. Wainwright, 1861–1865.* 2nd ed. New York: Da Capo Press, 1998.

———, ed. *Letters of Grover Cleveland, 1850–1908.* Boston & New York: Houghton Mifflin Co., 1933.

New York Monuments Commission for the Battlefields of Gettysburg and Chattanooga. *Final Report on the Battlefield of Gettysburg.* Vol. 2. Albany, New York: J. B. Lyon Co., Printers, 1900.

Nicholson, John Page. *Catalog of Library of Brevet Lieutenant-Colonel John Page Nicholson Relating to the War of the Rebellion, 1861–1866.* Philadelphia: privately printed, 1914.

———. *Pennsylvania at Gettysburg: Ceremonies at the Dedication of the Monuments.* Vol. 2. Harrisburg, Pennsylvania: William Stanley Ray, State Printer, 1904.

North, James W. *The History of Augusta, From the Earliest Settlement to the Present Time.* Augusta, Maine: Clapp & North, 1870.

Northrop, John Worrell. *Chronicles from the Diary of a War Prisoner in Andersonville and*

Other Military Prisons of the South in 1864. Wichita, Kansas: John Worrell Northrop, 1904.

O'Dea, Thomas. *History of O'Dea's Famous Picture of Andersonville Prison.* Cohoes, New York: Clark & Foster, 1887.

Official Souvenir Program of the Twenty-Fourth Annual Encampment. Boston: George H. Richards, Jr., and Co., 1890.

Only a Private: A Sketch of the Services of a Private Soldier Who Took Part in the Battles of Fort Pulaski, Fort Wagner, Olustee, and Cold Harbor, by Himself. Boston: Pratt Brothers, n.d.

Parish, John C., ed. *The Palimpsest.* Iowa City, Iowa: State Historical Society of Iowa, 1920.

Partridge, Charles Addison. *History of the Ninety-Sixth Regiment, Illinois Volunteer Infantry.* Chicago: Brown, Pettibone & Co., Printers, 1887.

Patchin, Hannah E. *Notes Taken at the Wisconsin Veterans' Home.* Waupaca, Wisconsin: D. L. Stichfield, 1891.

Pelham, Charles. *Hints and Helps to Lawyers, Claim Agents, Claimants, Applicants for Position in the Civil Service, and All Others Having Business of Any Kind with the Government at Washington City, Compiled from Official Data.* Washington, D.C.: William G. White, Printer, 1887.

Pepper, George Whitfield. *Personal Recollections of Sherman's Campaigns in Georgia and the Carolinas.* Zanesville, Ohio: Hugh Dunne, 1866.

Personal Narratives of Events in the War of the Rebellion. Providence: Rhode Island Soldiers' and Sailors' Historical Society, 1884.

Phisterer, Frederick. *Statistical Record of the Armies of the United States.* New York: Charles Scribner's Sons, 1883.

Pierce, Solon. *Battlefields and Campfires of the Thirty-Eighth.* Milwaukee: Daily Wisconsin Printing House, 1866.

Plain Facts in Relation to the Management of the Soldiers' Home, Togus, Maine: Rascality Is the Rule! No Justice for Old Veterans! Boston: Published by the Togus Syndicate, 1895.

Popchock, Barry, ed. *Soldier Boy: The Civil War Letters of Charles O. Musser, 29th Iowa.* Iowa City: University of Iowa Press, 1995.

Porter, Horace. "The Common Nervous Trouble of Old Soldiers." *Western Veteran,* May 15, 1889.

Proceedings of Crocker's Iowa Brigade at the Ninth Biennial Reunion Held at Jefferson, Iowa, September 21–22, 1898. Cedar Rapids, Iowa: Record Printing, 1902.

Proceedings of the First to Tenth Meetings, 1866–1876, of the National Encampment, Grand Army of the Republic. Philadelphia: Samuel P. Town, Printer, 1877.

Proceedings of the Sixth Annual Encampment, Department of New York, Grand Army of the Republic. New York: Grand Army of the Republic, 1872.

Proceedings of the Twenty-Seventh National Encampment of the Grand Army of the Republic at Indianapolis, Indiana, September 6th and 7th, 1893. Milwaukee: Swain & Tate, Printers, 1893.

Record of Proceedings at the Eighth and Ninth Annual Reunions [of the First Maine Cavalry Regiment]. Augusta, Maine: Sprague & Son, Printers, 1881.

Reed, George M. *The One Arm and One Leg Soldier, Wounded at the Battle of Shiloh.* N.p.: George M. Reed, 1865.

Reid, Thomas Wemyss, ed. *The Life, Letters, and Friendships of Richard Monckton Milnes, First Lord Houghton.* Vol. II. London, Paris, and Melbourne: Cassell & Co., 1891.

Report of the Fourteenth Annual Reunion. New York: MacGowan & Slipper, Printers, 1888.

Report of the Thirty-Ninth Annual Reunion of the Fifty-Second Illinois Veteran Volunteer Association. Chicago: Binner-Wells Co., 1906.

Report of the Twentieth Annual Reunion, Society of the Army of the Potomac, at Orange, New Jersey, June 12–13, 1889. New York: Macgowan & Slipper, Printers, 1889.

Report of Vincent Colyer on the Reception and Care of the Soldiers Returning from the War, Presented September 14, 1865. New York: Union League Club of New York: G. A. Whitehorne, Printer, 1865.

"Rev. William White Williams' Appeal for the Fourth of July." *Journal of the American Temperance Union and New York Prohibitionist* 29, no. 7 (July 1865).

Richardson, James, ed. *A Compilation of the Messages and Papers of the Presidents.* Vol. 11. New York: Bureau of National Literature, 1897.

Ridpath, John Clark. *The Citizen Soldier: His Part in War and Peace.* Cincinnati: Jones Brothers Publishing Co., 1891.

Ripple, Ezra Hoyt. *Dancing Along the Deadline.* Edited by Mark A. Snell. Novato, California: Presidio Press, 1997.

Roach, Alva C. *The Prisoner of War, and How Treated.* Indianapolis: Railroad City Publishing House, 1865.

Roberts, Charles W. "At Gettysburg in 1863 and 1888," in *War Papers Read Before the Commandery of the State of Maine, Military Order of the Loyal Legion of the United States.* Portland, Maine: Thurston Print, 1898.

Roe, Alfred Seelye. *The Thirty-Ninth Regiment Massachusetts Volunteers, 1862–1865.* Worcester, Massachusetts: Regimental Veteran Association, 1914.

Rood, Hosea Whitford. *Story of the Service of Company E, and of the Twelfth Wisconsin Regiment of Veteran Volunteer Infantry in the War of the Rebellion.* Milwaukee: Swain & Tate, 1893.

Roscoe, William E. *History of Schoharie County, New York, 1713–1882.* Vol. 2. Syracuse: Truair, Smith & Bruce, Printers and Binders, 1882.

Rosenberger, H. E. "Ohiowa Soldier." *Annals of Iowa* 36, no. 2 (Fall 1961): 110–148.

Rosenblatt, Emil, and Ruth Rosenblatt, eds. *Hard Marching Every Day: The Civil War Letters of Private Wilbur Fisk, 1861–1865.* Lawrence: University Press of Kansas, 1992.

Sabre, Gilbert E. *Nineteen Months a Prisoner of War: Narrative of Lieutenant G. E. Sabre, Second Rhode Island Cavalry, of His Experience in the War Prisons and Stockades of Morton, Mobile, Atlanta, Libby, Belle Isle, Andersonville, Macon, Charleston, and Columbia, and His Escape to the Union Lines.* New York: American News Co., 1865.

Sanger, George. *The Statutes at Large, Treaties, and Proclamations of the United States of America.* Boston: Little, Brown & Co., 1866.

Schofield, John M. *Forty-Six Years in the Army.* New York: Century Co., 1897.

Second Biennial Report of the Nebraska Soldiers' and Sailors' Home, Grand Island, Hall County, Nebraska, 1888–1890. Omaha: Henry Gibson, State Printer, 1890.

Sherman, William Tecumseh. *Memoirs of General William T. Sherman.* 2nd ed. New York: D. Appleton & Company, 1904.

Silliker, Ruth L. *The Rebel Yell and the Yankee Hurrah: The Civil War Journal of a Maine Volunteer.* Camden, Maine: Down East Books, 1985.

Simons, Ezra de Freest. *A Regimental History: The One Hundred Twenty-Fifth New York State Volunteers.* New York: E. D. Simons, 1888.

Smith, Jacob. *Camps and Campaigns of the 107th Regiment Ohio Volunteer Infantry.* Edited by Mark L. Gaynor. Navarre, Ohio: Indian River Graphics, 2000.

Smith, James E. *A Famous Battery and Its Campaigns, 1861–1865: The Career of Corporal James Tanner in War and Peace.* Washington, D.C.: W. H. Lowdermilk & Co., 1892.

Smith's Handbook and Guide in Philadelphia. Philadelphia: G. Delp, 1871.

Soldier's and Sailor's Almanac for 1865. New York: Protestant Episcopal Society for the Promotion of Evangelical Knowledge, 1865.

Spear, Ellis. *The Civil War Recollections of General Ellis Spear.* Edited by Abbott Spear, Andrea C. Hawkes, Marie H. McCosh, Craig L. Symonds, and Michael H. Alpert. Orono, Maine: University of Maine Press, 1997.

Spencer, Ambrose. *A Narrative of Andersonville.* New York: Harper & Brothers, 1866.

Sperry, Andrew F. *History of the Thirty-Third Iowa Infantry Volunteer Regiment, 1863–1866.* Des Moines: Mills & Co., 1866.

Sprague, Homer B. *Lights and Shadows in Confederate Prisons: A Personal Experience, 1864–1865.* New York: G. P. Putnam's Sons, 1915.

Stearns, Amos E. *Narrative of Amos E. Stearns, A Prisoner at Andersonville.* Worcester, Massachusetts: Franklin P. Rice, 1887.

Stevens, Michael E., ed. *As if It Were Glory: Robert Beecham's Civil War from the Iron Brigade to the Black Regiments.* Lanham, Maryland: Rowman & Littlefield, 1998.

Stillwell, Leander. *The Story of a Common Soldier of Army Life in the Civil War, 1861–1865.* Kansas City, Missouri: Franklin Hudson Publishing Co., 1920.

Storrs, John Whiting. *The Twentieth Connecticut: A Regimental History.* Ansonia, Connecticut: Press of the Naugatuck Valley Sentinel, 1886.

Stowits, George H. *History of the One-Hundredth Regiment, New York State Volunteers.* Buffalo: Matthews & Warren, 1870.

Sturgis, Thomas. *Prisoners of War, 1861–1865: A Record of Personal Experiences, and a Study of the Condition and Treatment of Prisoners on Both Sides During the War of the Rebellion.* New York and London: G. P. Putnam's Sons, 1912.

Styple, William B., ed. *Writing and Fighting the Civil War: Soldier Letters from the Battlefront.* 2nd ed. Kearny, New Jersey: Belle Grove Publishing Co., 2004.

Tanner, David B. *Our Limbs Are Lost! Our Country Saved!* Boston: John Flagg, 1870.

Thirty-Eighth Annual Report of the Inspectors of the State Penitentiary of the Eastern District of Pennsylvania to the Senate and House of Representatives of the Commonwealth of Pennsylvania. Philadelphia: McLaughlin Bros., Printers, 1867.

Thompson, W. Fletcher. *The Image of War: The Pictorial Reporting of the American Civil War.* New York: Thomas Yoseloff, 1960.

Thoron, Ward, ed. *First of Hearts: Selected Letters of Mrs. Henry Adams.* Bloomington, Indiana: Author House, 2011.

Tourgée, Albion Winegar. *The Veteran and His Pipe.* Chicago: Belford, Clarke & Co., 1886.

Trimble, Richard M, ed. *Brothers 'til Death: The Civil War Letters of William, Thomas, and Maggie Jones, 1861–1865: Irish Soldiers in the 48th New York Volunteer Regiment.* Macon, Georgia: Mercer University Press, 2000.

Trowbridge, John Townsend. *The South: A Tour of its Battlefields and Ruined Cities.* Hartford: Lucius Stebbens, 1866.

Truesdell, J. A. *The Blue Book of the State of Wisconsin.* Madison: Hans B. Warner, Secretary of State, 1880.

Twenty-First Annual Report of the Board of Trustees of the Public Schools of the City of Washington. Washington, D.C.: McGill & Witherow, Printers, 1866.

Urban, John W. *My Experiences Mid Shot and Shell and in Rebel Den.* Lancaster, Pennsylvania: Hubbard Bros., 1882.

U.S. House of Representatives Committee on Military Affairs. *Investigation of the Management of the National Home for Disabled Volunteer Soldiers.* Washington, D.C.: Government Printing Office, 1885.

United States Sanitary Commission. *Narrative of Privations and Sufferings of United States Officers and Soldiers While Prisoners of War in the Hands of Rebel Authorities.* Philadelphia: King & Baird, Printers, 1864.

United States Sanitary Commission. *Supplement to Document No. 90: Bureau of Information and Employment, June 14, 1865.* Washington, D.C.: McGill & Witherow, Printers and Stereotypers, 1865.

Vanderslice, John Mitchell. *Gettysburg: A History of the Gettysburg Battlefield Association*. Philadelphia: Gettysburg Battlefield Memorial Association, 1897.

———. *Gettysburg, Then and Now: The Field of American Valor*. New York: G. W. Dillingham Co., 1897.

Vaughter, John B. *Prison Life in Dixie*. Chicago: Central Book Concern, 1880.

Veterans of the War Whom All Should Assist: Almanac and History of the Late Rebellion, 1860–1865. New York: Soldiers' and Sailors' Publishing Co., 1869.

Wells, James Monroe. *With Touch of Elbow; or, Death Before Dishonor: A Thrilling Narrative of Adventure on Land and Sea*. Philadelphia and Chicago: John C. Winston Co., 1909.

Wharton, Edith. *A Backward Glance: An Autobiography*. New York: Charles Scribner's Sons, 1933.

White, William Allen. *The Autobiography of William Allen White*. New York: Macmillan, 1946.

Whitman, Walt. *The Complete Prose Works of Walt Whitman*. Vol. 1. New York and London: G. P. Putnam's Sons, 1902.

———. *Leaves of Grass*. Philadelphia: Rees Welsh & Co., 1882.

Winther, Oscar Osburn, ed. *With Sherman to the Sea: The Civil War Letters, Diaries and Reminiscences of Theodore F. Upson*. Bloomington: Indiana University Press, 1958.

Woodward, Evan Morrison. *Our Campaigns: The Second Regiment Pennsylvania Reserve Volunteers, 1861–1864*. Edited by Stanley W. Zamonski. Shippensburg, Pennsylvania: Burd Street Press, 1995.

Wright, George Frederick, ed. *A Standard History of Lorain County, Ohio*. New York: Lewis Publishing Co., 1916.

Younglove, John. *Hon. Marcus L. Ward, "The Soldier's Friend": A Eulogy Delivered Before Marcus L. Ward Post and Friends, in Music Hall, Newark, N.J., on December 18, 1884*. Newark, New Jersey: Press of the Newark Daily Advertiser, 1885.

Zon, Calvin Goddard. *The Good Fight That Didn't End: Henry P. Goddard's Accounts of Civil War and Peace*. Columbia: University of South Carolina Press, 2008.

SECONDARY SOURCES

Aaron, Daniel. *The Unwritten War: American Writers and the Civil War*. New York: Alfred A. Knopf, 1973.

Abbott, Edith. "The Civil War and the Crime Wave of 1865–1870." *Journal of the American Institute of Criminal Law and Criminology* 9, no. 1 (May 1918).

Abroe, Mary Munsell. " 'All the Profound Scenes': Federal Preservation of Civil War Battlefields, 1861–1990." Ph.D. diss., Loyola University of Chicago, 1996.

Adelman, Garry E., and Timothy H. Smith. *Devil's Den: A History & Guide*. Gettysburg: Thomas Publications, 1997.

Alderson, Kevin, and Patsy Alderson, eds. *Letters Home to Sarah: The Civil War Letters of Guy C. Taylor, 36th Wisconsin Volunteers.* Madison: University of Wisconsin Press, 2012.

Alexander, Ted, and W. P. Conrad. *When War Passed This Way.* Greencastle, Pennsylvania: Lilian Besore Memorial Library, 1982.

American Psychiatric Association. *Diagnostic and Statistical Manual of Mental Disorders.* 4th ed. Arlington, Virginia: American Psychiatric Association, 2000.

Anderson, Judith. "Haunted Minds: The Impact of Combat Exposure on the Mental and Physical Health of Civil War Veterans," in James M. Schmidt and Guy R. Hasegawa, eds., *Years of Change and Suffering: Modern Perspectives in Civil War Medicine.* Roseville, Minnesota: Edinborough Press, 2009. Pp. 143–158.

Aron, Cindy S. *Working at Play: A History of Vacations in the United States.* New York: Oxford University Press, 1999.

Ash, Stephen V. *Middle Tennessee Society Transformed, 1860–1870: War and Peace in the Upper South.* Knoxville: University of Tennessee Press, 2006.

Attie, Geanie. *Patriotic Toil: Northern Women in the American Civil War.* Ithaca: Cornell University Press, 1998.

Ayers, Edward. *What Caused the Civil War? Reflections on the South and Southern History.* New York: W. W. Norton & Co., 2005.

Bailyn, Bernard. *The Ideological Origins of the American Revolution.* Cambridge and London: Belknap Press, 1992.

Barlow, William. "U.S. Commissioner of Pensions Green B. Raum of Illinois. *Journal of the Illinois State Historical Society* 60, no. 3 (Autumn 1967): 297–312.

Barton, Michael. *Goodmen: The Character of Civil War Soldiers.* University Park: Pennsylvania State University Press, 1981.

Bauer, K. Jack. *The Mexican War, 1846–1848.* Reprint ed. Lincoln: University of Nebraska Press, 1992.

Bell, Andrew McIlwaine. *Mosquito Soldiers: Malaria, Yellow Fever, and the Course of the American Civil War.* Baton Rouge: Louisiana State University Press, 2010.

Bensel, Richard Franklin. *Yankee Leviathan: The Origins of Central Authority in America, 1859–1877.* Cambridge: Cambridge University Press, 1990.

Berg, Gordon. "The Hazen Brigade Monument." *America's Civil War* 17, no. 5 (November 2004): 10, 12, 14, 58.

Berry, Stephen, ed. *Weirding the War: Stories from the Civil War's Ragged Edges.* Athens: University of Georgia Press, 2011.

Biess, Frank. *Homecomings: Returning POWs and the Legacies of Defeat in Postwar Germany.* Princeton: Princeton University Press, 2005.

Blair, William A. *Cities of the Dead: Contesting the Memory of the Civil War in the South, 1865–1914.* Chapel Hill: University of North Carolina Press, 2004.

Blaisdell, John D. "The Wounded, the Sick, and the Scared: An Examination of Disabled Maine Veterans from the Civil War." *Maine History* 42, no. 2 (2005): 67–92.

Blanck, Peter David, and Michael Millender. "Before Disability Civil Rights: Civil War Pensions and the Politics of Disability in America." *Alabama Law Review* 52 (Fall 2000): 1–50.

Blight, David W. *American Oracle: The Civil War in the Civil Rights Era.* Cambridge: Harvard University Press, 2011.

———. "The Memory Boom: Why and Why Now?" in Pascal Boyer and James V. Wertsch, eds., *Memory in Mind and Culture.* Cambridge: Cambridge University Press, 2009.

———. *Race and Reunion: The Civil War in American Memory.* Cambridge: Harvard University Press, 2001.

Boritt, Gabor S. *The Gettysburg Gospel: The Lincoln Speech That Nobody Knows.* New York: Simon & Schuster, 2006.

Boyce, Annabel S. *The Artists Frankenstein.* Bryn Mawr, Pennsylvania: Annabel Boyce, 1981.

Brady, Lisa. *War Upon the Land: Military Strategy and the Transformation of Southern Landscapes.* Athens: University of Georgia Press, 2012.

Brandt, Dennis W. *Pathway to Hell: A Tragedy of the American Civil War.* Lincoln, Nebraska: Bison Books, 2010.

Bremner, Robert H. *The Public Good: Philanthropy and Welfare in the Civil War Era.* New York: Alfred A. Knopf, 1980.

Bridges, Jennifer R. "Tourist Attractions, Souvenirs, and Civil War Memory in Chicago, 1861–1915." Ph.D. diss., Loyola University of Chicago, 2009.

Brodsky, Alyn. *Grover Cleveland: A Study in Character.* New York: St. Martin's Press, 2000.

Brown, Lynne S. *Gulfport: A Definitive History.* Charleston, South Carolina: Arcadia Press, 2004.

Brown, Thomas J. *The Public Art of Civil War Commemoration.* Boston and New York: Bedford/St. Martins, 2004.

———, ed. *Remixing the Civil War: Meditations on the Sesquicentennial.* Baltimore: Johns Hopkins University Press, 2011.

Buck, Paul. *The Road to Reunion, 1865–1900.* Boston: Little, Brown & Co., 1937.

Burton, Crompton B. " 'The Dear Old Regiment': Maine's Regimental Associations and the Memory of the American Civil War." *New England Quarterly* 84, no. 1 (March 2011): 104–122.

Burton, William L. *Melting Pot Soldiers: The Union's Ethnic Regiments.* New York: Fordham University Press, 1998.

Butters, Jr., Gerald R. "*The Birth of a Nation* and the Kansas Board of Review Motion Pictures: A Censorship Struggle." *Kansas History* 14, no. 1 (Spring 1991): 2–14.

Calhoun, Charles W. *Minority Victory: Gilded Age Politics and the Front Porch Campaign of 1888.* Lawrence: University Press of Kansas, 2008.

Carnes, Mark C. *Secret Ritual and Manhood in Victorian America.* New Haven: Yale University Press, 1989.

Carroon, Robert Girard, and Dana B. Shoaf. *Union Blue: The History of the Military Order of the Loyal Legion of the United States.* Shippensburg, Pennsylvania: White Mane Publishing, 2001.

Cashin, Joan E. "Trophies of War: Material Culture in the Civil War Era." *Journal of the Civil War Era* 1, No. 3 (September 2011): 339–367.

Castel, Albert. *Decision in the West: The Atlanta Campaign of 1864.* Lawrence: University Press of Kansas, 1992.

Cetina, Judith Gladys. "A History of Veterans' Homes in the United States, 1811–1930." Ph.D. diss., Case Western Reserve University, 1977.

Cilella, Jr., Salvatore G. *Upton's Regulars: The 121st New York Infantry in the Civil War.* Lawrence: University of Kansas Press, 2009.

Cimbala, Paul. *Under the Guardianship of the Nation: The Freedmen's Bureau and the Reconstruction of Georgia, 1865–1870.* Athens: University of Georgia Press, 1997.

———. *An Uncommon Time: The Civil War and the Northern Home Front.* New York: Fordham University Press, 2002.

———, and Randall M. Miller, eds. *Union Soldiers and the Northern Homefront: Wartime Experiences, Postwar Adjustments.* New York: Fordham University Press, 2002.

———. *The Freedmen's Bureau and Reconstruction: Reconsiderations.* New York: Fordham University Press, 1999.

Clarke, Frances. *War Stories: Suffering and Sacrifice in the Civil War North.* Baltimore: Johns Hopkins University Press, 2011.

Click, Patricia Catherine. *Time Full of Trial: The Roanoke Island Freedmen's Colony, 1862–1867.* Chapel Hill: University of North Carolina Press, 2001.

Cloyd, Benjamin. *Haunted by Atrocity: Civil War Prisons in American Memory.* Baton Rouge: Louisiana State University Press, 2010.

Cole, Garold L. *Civil War Eyewitnesses: An Annotated Bibliography of Books and Articles, 1955–1986.* Columbia: University of South Carolina Press, 1988.

Confino, Alon, and Peter Fritzsche. "Collective Memory and Cultural History: Problems of Method." *American Historical Review* 102, no. 5 (December 1997): 1386–1403.

———. *The Work of Memory: New Directions in the Study of German Culture and Society.* Urbana: University of Illinois Press, 2002.

Cooney, Charles F. "The Left Armed Corps: Rehabilitation for the Veteran." *Civil War Times Illustrated* 23 (1984): 40–44.

Cornish, Dudley Taylor. *The Sable Arm: Black Troops in the Union Army, 1861–1865.* Lawrence: University Press of Kansas, 1956.

Costa, Dora L. *The Evolution of Retirement: An American Economic History, 1880–1990.* Chicago: University of Chicago Press, 1998.

———, and Matthew Kahn. "Surviving Andersonville: The Benefits of Social Networks in POW Camps." *American Economic Review* 97, no. 4 (September 2007): 1467–1487.

Courtwright, David T. *Violent Land: Single Men and Social Disorder from the Frontier to the Inner City.* Cambridge: Harvard University Press, 1996.

Coyle, William. *The Frankenstein Family in Springfield.* Springfield, Ohio: Clark County Historical Society, 1967

Cozzens, Peter. *No Better Place to Die: The Battle of Stone's River.* Urbana and Chicago: University of Illinois Press, 1990.

Cunliffe, Marcus. *Soldiers and Civilians: The Martial Spirit in America, 1775–1865.* Boston: Little, Brown & Co., 1968.

Daly, John Edward, and Allen Weinberg. *Genealogy of Philadelphia County Subdivisions.* 2nd ed. Philadelphia: Department of Records, 1966.

Davies, Wallace Evan. *Patriotism on Parade: The Story of Veterans' and Hereditary Organizations in America, 1783–1900.* Cambridge: Harvard University Press, 1955.

Dean, Eric T. *Shook over Hell: Posttraumatic Stress, Vietnam, and the Civil War.* Cambridge: Harvard University Press, 1997.

Dearing, Mary. *Veterans in Politics.* Baton Rouge: Louisiana State University Press, 1952.

DePastino, Todd. *Citizen Hobo: How a Century of Homelessness Shaped America.* Chicago: University of Chicago Press, 2003.

Desjardin, Thomas. *These Honored Dead: How the Story of Gettysburg Shaped American Memory.* New York: Da Capo Press, 2003.

Devine, Edward Thomas. *Disabled Soldiers and Sailors: Pensions and Training.* New York: Oxford University Press, 1919.

DiFebo, Dane. "Old Baldy: A Horse's Tale." *Pennsylvania Magazine of History and Biography* 134, no. 4 (October 2011): 549–552.

Dluger, Mark A. "A Regimental Community: The Men of the 82nd Illinois Infantry Before, During, and After the American Civil War." Ph.D. diss., Loyola University of Chicago, 2009.

Dower, John. *War Without Mercy: Race and Power in the Pacific War.* New York: Pantheon Books, 1986.

Downs, Jim. *Sick from Freedom: African-American Illness and Suffering During the Civil War and Reconstruction.* New York: Oxford University Press, 2012.

Dreese, Michael A. *The Hospital on Seminary Ridge at the Battle of Gettysburg.* Jefferson, North Carolina: McFarland & Co., 2002.

Dunkelman, Mark H. *Brothers One and All: Esprit de Corps in a Civil War Regiment.* Baton Rouge: Louisiana State University Press, 2004.

———. *Marching with Sherman: Through Georgia and the Carolinas with the 154th New York.* Baton Rouge: Louisiana State University Press, 2012.

———. *War's Relentless Hand: Twelve Tales of Civil War Soldiers.* Baton Rouge: Louisiana State University Press, 2006.

———. " 'We Were Compelled to Cut Our Way Through Them, and in Doing So Our Losses Were Heavy': Gettysburg Casualties of the 154th New York Volunteers." *Gettysburg Magazine* 18 (1998): 34–56.

Edkins, Jenny. *Trauma and the Memory of Politics.* Cambridge: Cambridge University Press, 2003.

Ellis, Allen. "Yankee Captain Daniel Ellis, the Old Red Fox of East Tennessee." *Blue and Gray Magazine* 9, no. 4 (April 1992): 28–34.

Etcheson, Nicole. *A Generation at War: The Civil War Era in a Northern Community.* Lawrence: University Press of Kansas, 2011.

Fabian, Ann. *The Unvarnished Truth: Personal Narratives in Nineteenth Century America.* Berkley: University of California Press, 2000.

Fahs, Alice. *The Imagined Civil War: Popular Literature of the North and South, 1861–1865.* Chapel Hill: University of North Carolina Press, 2003.

Faust, Drew Gilpin. "Equine Relics of the Civil War." *Southern Cultures* (Spring 2000): 23–49.

———. *This Republic of Suffering: Death and the American Civil War.* New York: Alfred A. Knopf, 2008.

———. "We Should Grow Too Fond of It: Why We Love the Civil War." *Civil War History* 50, no. 4 (2004): 368–383.

Fawcett, Winifred, and Thelma Hepper. *Veterans of the Civil War Who Settled in Potter County, Dakota Territory.* Gettysburg, South Dakota: n.p., 1993.

Figg, Laurann. "Clothing Adaptations of Civil War Amputees." M.A. thesis, Iowa State University, 1990.

Figley, Charles R., and Seymour Leventman, eds. *Strangers at Home: Vietnam Veterans Since the War.* New York: Brunner/Mazel Publishers, 1980.

Filler, Louis B. *The Crusade Against Slavery, 1830–1860.* New York: Harper & Row, 1960.

Fish, Carl Russell. "Back to Peace in 1865." *American Historical Review* 24, no. 3 (April 1919): 435–443.

Fisher, Noel C. *War at Every Door: Partisan Politics and Guerrilla Violence in East Tennessee, 1860–1869.* Chapel Hill: University of North Carolina Press, 2001.

Fleche, Andre. " 'Shoulder to Shoulder as Comrades Tried': Black and White Union Veterans and Civil War Memory." *Civil War History* 51 (June 2005):175–201.

Foner, Eric. *Who Owns History? Rethinking the Past in a Changing World*. New York: Hill & Wang, 2002.

Foote, Kenneth E. *Shadowed Ground: America's Landscapes of Violence and Tragedy*. Austin: University of Texas Press, 1997.

Foote, Lorien. *The Gentlemen and the Roughs: Violence, Honor, and Manhood in the Union Army*. New York: New York University Press, 2010.

Foroughi, Andrea R. "Ephemeral Town, Enduring Community: Space, Gender, and Power in Nininger, Minnesota, 1851–1870." Ph.D. diss., University of Minnesota, 1999.

Foster, Gaines. *Ghosts of the Confederacy: Defeat, The Lost Cause, and the Emergence of the New South, 1865–1913*. New York: Oxford University Press, 1987.

Fredrickson, George M. *The Inner Civil War: Northern Intellectuals and the Crisis of the Union*. Urbana and Chicago: University of Illinois Press, 1965.

French, Harry Willard. *Art and Artists in Connecticut*. Boston: Lee & Shepard, 1878.

Futch, Ovid. *History of Andersonville Prison*. Gainesville, Florida: University Press of Florida, 1968.

Gallagher, Gary W. *Becoming Confederates: Paths to a New National Loyalty*. Athens: University of Georgia Press, 2013.

———. *Causes Won, Lost, and Forgotten: How Hollywood and Popular Art Shape What We Know About the Civil War*. Chapel Hill: University of North Carolina Press, 2008.

———. *The Union War*. Cambridge: Harvard University Press, 2011.

Gallman, J. Matthew. *Mastering Wartime: A Social History of Philadelphia During the Civil War*. Cambridge: Cambridge University Press, 1990.

———. *The North Fights the Civil War: The Home Front*. Chicago: Ivan R. Dee, 1994.

Gannon, Barbara A. "Sites of Memory, Sites of Glory: African-American Grand Army of the Republic Posts in Pennsylvania," in William A. Blair and William Pencak, eds., *Making and Remaking Pennsylvania's Civil War*. University Park: Pennsylvania State University Press, 2001.

———. *The Won Cause: White and Black Comradeship in the Grand Army of the Republic*. Chapel Hill: University of North Carolina Press, 2011.

Gardner, Douglas Gibson. "Andersonville and American Memory." Ph.D. diss., Miami [Ohio] University, 1998.

Gerber, David A. *Disabled Veterans in History*. Ann Arbor: University of Michigan Press, 2000.

Giesberg, Judith Ann. *Civil War Sisterhood: The U.S. Sanitary Commission and Women's Politics In Transition*. Boston: Northeastern University Press, 2000.

Gillett, Mary C. *The Army Medical Department, 1818–1865*. Washington, D.C.: Center of Military History, United States Army, 1987.

Gillette, William. *Jersey Blue: Civil War Politics in New Jersey, 1854–1865*. New Brunswick, New Jersey: Rutgers University Press, 1995.

Glasson, William Henry. "A Costly Pension Law—Act of June 27, 1890." *South Atlantic Quarterly* 3 no. 4 (October 1904).

———. "Federal and Confederate Pensions in the South." *South Atlantic Quarterly* 9, no. 3 (July 1910).

———. *Federal Military Pensions in the United States.* New York: Oxford University Press, 1918.

Gordon, Lesley J. "I Never Was a Coward": Questions of Bravery in a Civil War Regiment," in James Marten and A. Kristen Foster, eds., *More Than a Contest Between Armies: Essays on the Civil War Era.* Kent, Ohio: Kent State University Press, 2008.

———. " 'Surely They Remember Me': The 16th Connecticut in War, Captivity, and Public Memory," in Paul A. Cimbala and Randall M. Miller, eds., *Union Soldiers and the Northern Home Front.* New York: Fordham University Press, 2002.

Grant, Susan-Mary. "Reimagined Communities: Union Veterans and the Reconstruction of American Nationalism." *Nations and Nationalism* 14, no. 3 (July 2008): 498–519.

Grimsley, Mark. *The Hard Hand of War: Union Military Policy Toward Southern Civilians, 1861–1865.* Cambridge: Cambridge University Press, 1995.

Gray, Edward G., and Jane Kamensky, eds. *The Oxford Handbook of the American Revolution.* New York: Oxford University Press, 2013.

Gray, Michael P. *The Business of Captivity: Elmira and Its Civil War Prison.* Kent, Ohio: Kent State University Press, 2001.

Grob, Gerald N. *The Mad Among Us: A History of the Care of America's Mentally Ill.* New York: Free Press, 1994.

———. *Mental Institutions in America: Social Policy to 1875.* New York: Free Press, 1973.

Grossman, Dave. *On Killing: The Psychological Cost of Learning to Kill in War and Society.* New York: Little, Brown & Co., 1995.

Halsey, Ashley, ed. *A Yankee Private's Civil War.* Chicago: Henry Regnery Co., 1961.

Hannaford, Katharine W. "Culture Versus Commerce: The Libby Prison Museum and the Image of Chicago, 1889–1899." *Ecumene* 8, no. 3 (2001).

Hansen, J. T., A. Susan Owen, and Michael Patrick Madden, eds. *Parallels: The Soldiers' Knowledge and the Oral History of Contemporary Warfare.* New York: Aldine de Gruyter, 1992.

Harris, M. Keith. "Across the Bloody Chasm: Reconciliation in the Wake of Civil War." Ph.D. diss., University of Virginia, 2009.

———. "Slavery, Emancipation, and Veterans of the Union Cause: Commemorating Freedom in the Age of Reconciliation, 1885–1915." *Civil War History* 53, no. 3 (September 2007): 264–290.

Hartwig, D. Scott. " 'The Most Notable Event at Gettysburg Since the War': The Reunion of the Philadelphia Brigade and Pickett's Division, July 1887." *Civil War Regiments* 6, no. 3 (1999).

Hasegawa, Guy R. *Mending Broken Soldiers: The Union and Confederate Programs to Supply Artificial Limbs.* Carbondale: Southern Illinois University Press, 2012.

Haverstock, Mary Sayre, Jeannette Mahoney Vance, and Brian L. Meggitt, eds. *Artists in Ohio, 1787–1900: A Biographical Dictionary.* Kent, Ohio: Kent State University Press, 2000.

Hawthorne, Frederick W. *Gettysburg: Stories of Men and Monuments.* Gettysburg, Pennsylvania: Association of Licensed Battlefield Guides, 1988.

Heck, Frank H. "The Civil War Veteran in Minnesota Politics." Ph.D. diss., University of Minnesota, 1938.

Herdegen, Lance. *The Iron Brigade in Civil War and Memory: The Black Hats From Bull Run to Appomattox and Thereafter.* El Dorado Hills, California: Savas Beatie, 2011.

Herschbach, Lisa Marie. "Fragmentation and Reunion: Medicine, Memory, and Body in the American Civil War." Ph.D. diss., Harvard University, 1997.

Hess, Earl J. *The Knoxville Campaign: Burnside and Longstreet in East Tennessee.* Knoxville: University of Tennessee Press, 2012.

———. *Liberty, Virtue, and Progress: Northerners and Their War for the Union.* New York: New York University Press, 1998.

———. *Pickett's Charge—The Last Attack at Gettysburg.* Chapel Hill: University of North Carolina Press, 2001.

———. *The Union Soldier in Battle: Enduring the Ordeal of Combat.* Lawrence: University Press of Kansas, 1997.

Hesseltine, William Best. *Civil War Prisons: A Study in War Psychology.* Columbus: Ohio State University Press, 1930.

Hessler, James A. *Sickles at Gettysburg: The Controversial Civil War General Who Committed Murder, Abandoned Little Round Top, and Declared Himself the Hero of Gettysburg.* New York: Savas Beatie, 2009.

Hoganson, Kristin. *Fighting for American Manhood: How Gender Politics Shaped the Spanish-American and Philippine-American Wars.* New Haven: Yale University Press, 1998.

Hogue, James K. *Uncivil War: Five New Orleans Street Battles and the Rise and Fall of Radical Reconstruction.* Baton Rouge: Louisiana State University Press, 2006.

Holberton, William B. *Homeward Bound: The Demobilization of the Union and Confederate Armies, 1865–1866.* Mechanicsburg: Stackpole Books, 2001.

Hollandsworth, James G. *An Absolute Massacre: The New Orleans Race Riot of July 30, 1866.* Baton Rouge: Louisiana State University Press, 2001.

Homer. *The Odyssey.* Translated by Robert Fagles. New York: Penguin Books, 1996.

Hunt, Robert. *The Good Men Who Won the War: Army of the Cumberland Veterans and Emancipation Memory.* Tuscaloosa: University of Alabama Press, 2010.

Hynes, Samuel Lynn. *The Soldier's Tale: Bearing Witness to Modern War.* New York: Penguin Press, 1998.

Jacob, Kathryn Allamong. *Testament to Union: Civil War Monuments in Washington, D.C.* Baltimore: Johns Hopkins University Press, 1998.

Janney, Caroline. " 'I Yield to No Man an Iota of My Convictions': Chickamauga and Chattanooga National Military Park and the Limits of Reconciliation." *Journal of the Civil War Era* 2, no. 3 (September 2012).

———. *Remembering the Civil War: Reunion and the Limits of Reconciliation.* Chapel Hill: University of North Carolina Press, 2013.

———. "The Root of Sectional Bitterness: Slavery, Emancipation, and Civil War Memory." Lecture at the Civil War Institute at Gettysburg College, Gettysburg, Pennsylvania, June 24, 2012.

Jones, James Pickett. *Black Jack: John A. Logan and Southern Illinois in the Civil War Era.* Tallahassee: Florida State University Press, 1967.

Jordan, Brian Matthew. "Captive Memories: Union Ex-Prisoners of War and the Work of Remembrance." *Civil War Monitor* 1, no. 1 (September 2011): 58–67, 77–78.

———. "Fighting for South Mountain: How the Army of the Potomac Won a Crucial Battle but Lost Control of Its Legacy." *Civil War Monitor* 2, no. 2 (Summer 2012): 52–59, 77–79.

———. "The Last Reunion and the Light of Peace." *Gettysburg* (Spring 2013): 14–15.

———. "Living Monuments: Union Veteran Amputees and the Embodied Memory of the Civil War." *Civil War History* 57, no. 2 (June 2011): 121–152.

———. Review of James Marten, *Sing Not War: The Lives of Union and Confederate Veterans in Gilded Age America*, in Matthew Hulbert, ed., *The Civil War Monitor Bookshelf* (October 2011).

Kahler, Bruce R. "John A. Martin, Soldier State Visionary." *Kansas History* 34 (2011): 50–59.

Karamanski, Theodore J. *Rally 'Round the Flag: Chicago and the Civil War.* Lanham, Maryland: Rowman & Littlefield, 2006.

Katz, Michael B. *In the Shadow of the Poorhouse: A Social History of Welfare in America.* Revised ed. New York: Basic Books, 1996.

Kelly, Patrick J. *Creating a National Home: Building the Veterans' Welfare State, 1865–1900.* Cambridge: Harvard University Press, 1997.

Klee, Bruce. "They Paid to Enter Libby Prison." *Civil War Times Illustrated* 37 (February 1999).

Koven, Seth. "Remembering and Dismemberment: Crippled Children, Wounded Soldiers, and the Great War in Great Britain." *American Historical Review* (October 1994): 1167–1202.

Kreiser, Lawrence A., Jr. "A Socio-Economic Study of Veterans of the 103rd Ohio Volunteer Infantry Regiment After the Civil War." *Ohio History* 107 (Summer/Autumn 1998): 171–184.

Krick, Robert K. " 'Lee to the Rear,' the Texans Cried," in Gary W. Gallagher, ed. *The Wilderness Campaign*. Chapel Hill: University of North Carolina Press, 1997.

Lande, R. Gregory. *Madness, Malingering, and Malfeasance: The Transformation of Psychiatry and Law in the Civil War Era*. Washington, D.C.: Brassey's, 2003.

Lawson, Melinda. *Patriot Fires: Forging a New American Nationalism in the Civil War North*. Lawrence: University Press of Kansas, 2002.

Lears, Jackson. *Something for Nothing: Luck in America*. New York: Vintage, 2003.

Lears, T. J. Jackson. *Rebirth of a Nation: The Making of Modern America, 1877–1920*. New York: HarperCollins, 2009.

Lee, Anthony W., and Elizabeth Young. *On Alexander Gardner's Photographic Sketch Book of the Civil War*. Berkley: University of California Press, 2007.

Leed, Eric J. *No Man's Land: Combat and Identity in World War I*. New York: Cambridge University Press, 1979.

Leonard, Elizabeth. *Lincoln's Avengers: Justice, Revenge, and Reunion After the Civil War*. New York: W. W. Norton, 2004.

———. *Lincoln's Forgotten Ally: Judge Advocate General Joseph Holt of Kentucky*. Chapel Hill: University of North Carolina Press, 2011.

Leonard, Thomas C. *Above the Battle: War-Making in America from Appomattox to Versailles*. New York: Oxford University Press, 1978.

Lewis, Lloyd. *The Assassination of Abraham Lincoln: History and Myth*. Lincoln: University of Nebraska Press, 1994.

Linderman, Gerald F. *Embattled Courage: The Experience of Combat in the American Civil War*. New York: Free Press, 1987.

Linenthal, Edward Tabor. *Sacred Ground: Americans and Their Battlefields*. Urbana: University of Illinois Press, 1991.

Linker, Beth. *War's Waste: Rehabilitation in World War I America*. Chicago: University of Chicago Press, 2011.

Litwack, Leon. *North of Slavery: The Negro in the Free States, 1790–1860*. Chicago: University of Chicago Press, 1965.

Logue, Larry M. *To Appomattox and Beyond: The Civil War Soldier in War and Peace*. Chicago: Ivan R. Dee, 1996.

———, and Peter Blanck. *Race, Ethnicity, and Disability: Veterans and Benefits in Post–Civil War America*. Cambridge: Cambridge University Press, 2011.

Long, Clarence D. *Wages and Earnings in the United States, 1860–1890*. Princeton: Princeton University Press, 1960.

Longacre, Edward G. *To Gettysburg and Beyond: The Twelfth New Jersey Volunteer Infantry, II Corps, Army of the Potomac, 1862–1865*. Hightstown, New Jersey: Longstreet House, 1988.

Lord, Francis A. *They Fought for the Union*. New York: Bonanza Books, 1960.

Lossing, Benjamin J. *Our Country: A Household History for All Readers*. Vol. 3. New York: Johnson & Miles, 1878.

Lowry, Thomas P. *The Story the Soldiers Wouldn't Tell: Sex in the Civil War*. Mechanicsburg, Pennsylvania: Stackpole Books, 1994.

Madison, James H. "Civil War Memories and 'Pardnership Forgittin,' 1865–1913." *Indiana Magazine of History* 99, no. 3 (September 2003).

Manning, Chandra. *What This Cruel War Was Over: Soldiers, Slavery, and the Civil War*. New York: Alfred A. Knopf, 2007.

Margalit, Avishai. *The Ethics of Memory*. Cambridge: Harvard University Press, 2004.

Marten, James. "Exempt from the Ordinary Rules of Life: Researching the Postwar Adjustment Problems of Union Veterans." *Civil War History* 47, no. 1 (2001): 57–71.

———. "Not a Veteran in a Poorhouse," in Gary W. Gallagher and Joan Waugh, eds., *Wars Within a War: Controversy and Conflict over the American Civil War*. Chapel Hill: University of North Carolina Press, 2009.

———. *Sing Not War: The Lives of Union and Confederate Veterans in Gilded Age America*. Chapel Hill: University of North Carolina Press, 2011.

Marvel, William. "Introduction and History of the Military Order of the Loyal Legion of the United States," in *Biographical Sketches of the Contributors to the Military Order of the Loyal Legion of the United States*. Wilmington, North Carolina: Broadfoot Publishing Co., 1995.

———. *Race of the Soil: The Ninth New Hampshire Regiment in the Civil War*. Wilmington, North Carolina: Broadfoot Publishing Co., 1988.

Maxwell, William Quentin. *Lincoln's Fifth Wheel: The Political History of the United States Sanitary Commission*. New York: Longmans, Green & Co., 1956.

Mazow, Leo G., and Kevin M. Murphy. *Taxing Visions: Financial Episodes in Late Nineteenth-Century American Art*. San Marino, California: Huntington Library, 2010.

McClintock, Megan Jean. "Binding Up the Nation's Wounds: Civil War Pensions in American Families, 1861–1890." Ph.D. diss., Rutgers University, 1994.

McClurken, Jeffrey. *Take Care of the Living: Reconstructing Confederate Veteran Families in Virginia*. Charlottesville: University of Virginia Press, 2009.

McConnell, Stuart. *Glorious Contentment: The Grand Army of the Republic, 1865–1900*. Chapel Hill: University of North Carolina Press, 1992.

McCrory, Thomas J. *Grand Army of the Republic, Department of Wisconsin*. Black Earth, Wisconsin: Trails Books, 2005.

McElroy, Robert. *Grover Cleveland: The Man and the Statesman*. New York: Harper & Bros., 1923.

McMurry, Donald L. "The Bureau of Pensions During the Administration of President Harrison." *Mississippi Valley Historical Review* 13, no. 3 (December 1926).

———. "The Political Significance of the Pension Question, 1885–1897." *Mississippi Valley Historical Review* 9, no. 1 (June 1922).

McNamara, Brooks. *Day of Jubilee: The Great Age of Public Celebrations in New York, 1788–1909*. New Brunswick, New Jersey: Rutgers University Press, 1997.

McPherson, James M. *Abraham Lincoln and the Second American Revolution*. New York: Oxford University Press, 1995.

———. *Battle Cry of Freedom: The Civil War Era*. New York: Oxford University Press, 1988.

———. *For Cause and Comrades: Why Men Fought in the Civil War*. New York: Oxford University Press, 1997.

———. *Writing the Civil War: The Quest to Understand*. Columbia: University of South Carolina Press, 2000.

Melish, Joanne Pope. *Disowning Slavery: Gradual Emancipation and Race in New England, 1780–1860*. Ithaca: Cornell University Press, 2000.

Merrill, Peter C. *German Immigrant Artists in America: A Biographical Dictionary*. Lanham, Maryland: Scarecrow Press, 1997.

Miller, William J. *Civil War City: Harrisburg, Pennsylvania, 1861–1865*. Shippensburg, Pennsylvania: White Man, 1990.

Mitchell, Reid. *Civil War Soldiers: Their Expectations and Experiences*. New York: Viking Press, 1988.

———. *The Vacant Chair: The Northern Soldier Leaves Home*. New York: Oxford University Press, 1993.

Montgomery, David. *Beyond Equality: Labor and the Radical Republicans, 1862–1872*. New York: Alfred A. Knopf, 1967.

Munden, Kenneth White, and Henry Putney Beers. *The Union: A Guide to Federal Archives Relating to the Civil War*. Washington, D.C.: National Archives Trust Fund, 1986.

Nash, Gary B. *First City: Philadelphia and the Forging of Historical Memory*. Philadelphia: University of Pennsylvania Press, 2006.

Neely, Mark E., Jr. *The Civil War and the Limits of Destruction*. Cambridge: Harvard University Press, 2007.

———. *The Union Divided: Party Conflict in the Civil War North*. Cambridge: Harvard University Press, 2002.

———, and Harold Holzer. *The Union Image: Popular Prints of the Civil War North*. Chapel Hill: University of North Carolina Press, 2000.

Neff, John. *Honoring the Civil War Dead: Commemoration and the Problem of Reconciliation*. Lawrence: University Press of Kansas, 2005.

Nelson, Megan Kate. *Ruin Nation: Destruction and the American Civil War*. Athens: University of Georgia, 2012.

Neu, Jonathan D. " 'No Falser Finding Was Ever Made Since Courts Began': The 72nd Pennsylvania Monument Controversy." *Gettysburg Magazine* 40 (2009): 79–93.

Nevins, Allan, and Milton Halsey Thomas, eds. *The Diary of George Templeton Strong*. New York: Macmillan Co., 1952.

Nietzsche, Friedrich Wilhelm. *The Use and Abuse of History*. New York: Liberal Arts Press, 1949.

Niven, John. *Connecticut for the Union: The Role of the State in the Civil War*. New Haven: Yale University Press, 1965.

Noonan, Mark J. *Reading* The Century Illustrated Monthly Magazine: *American Literature and Culture, 1870–1893*. Kent, Ohio: Kent State University Press, 2010.

Nora, Pierre. *Realms of Memory: Rethinking the French Past*. New York: Columbia University Press, 1996.

Oberly, James W. *Sixty Million Acres: American Veterans and the Public Lands Before the Civil War*. Kent, Ohio: Kent State University Press, 1990.

O'Connell, Edward T. "Public Commemoration of the Civil War and Monuments to Memory: The Triumph of Robert E. Lee and the Lost Cause." Ph.D. diss., Stony Brook University, 2008.

Oliver, John William. *History of the Civil War Military Pensions, 1861–1865*. Madison: University of Wisconsin, 1917.

Padilla, Jalynn Olsen. "Army of 'Cripples': Northern Civil War Amputees, Disability, and Manhood in Victorian America." Ph.D. diss., University of Delaware, 2007.

Panhorst, Michael W. "Sacred to the Memory." *Civil War Times* 49, no. 2 (April 2010).

Patterson, John S. "From Battle Ground to Pleasure Ground: Gettysburg as a Historic Site," in Warren Leon and Roy Rosenzweig, eds. *History Museums in the United States: A Critical Assessment*. Champaign: University of Illinois Press, 1989.

Petruzzi, J. David. "Opening the Ball at Gettysburg: The Shot That Rang for Fifty Years." *America's Civil War* 19, no. 3 (2006): 30–36.

Phillippi, Laura, and Nolan Sunderman. *Lansing*. Charleston, South Carolina: Arcadia Publishing, 2008.

Phillips, Jason. "Battling Stereotypes: A Taxonomy of Common Civil War Soldiers." *History Compass* 6, no. 6 (2008): 1407–1425.

Pickenpaugh, Roger. *Captives in Blue: The Civil War Prisons of the Confederacy*. Tuscaloosa: University of Alabama Press, 2013.

Piehler, G. Kurt. *Remembering War the American Way*. Washington, D.C.: Smithsonian Institution Press, 1995.

Potter, Jerry O. *The* Sultana *Tragedy: America's Greatest Maritime Disaster*. Gretna, Louisiana: Pelican, 1992.

Preston, Evan. " 'All May Visit the Big Camp': Race and the Lessons of the Civil War at the 1913 Gettysburg Reunion," *Gettysburg College Journal of the Civil War Era* 2, no. 1 (2011).

Pride, Mike. *Our War: Days and Events in the Fight for the Union.* Concord, New Hampshire: Monitor Publishing, 2012.

———, and Mark Travis. *My Brave Boys: To War with Colonel Cross and the Fighting Fifth.* Hanover, New Hampshire: University Press of New England, 2001.

Rable, George C. *But There Was No Peace: The Role of Violence in the Politics of Reconstruction.* Athens: University of Georgia Press, 1984.

———. *God's Almost Chosen Peoples: A Religious History of the American Civil War.* Chapel Hill: University of North Carolina Press, 2010.

Ramold, Steven J. *Baring the Iron Hand. Discipline in the Union Army.* DeKalb: Northern Illinois University Press, 2010.

———. " 'We Should Have Killed Them All': The Violent Reaction of Union Soldiers to the Assassination of Abraham Lincoln." *Journal of Illinois History* 10 (Spring 2007): 27–48.

Randall, James Garfield. "The Blundering Generation." *Mississippi Valley Historical Review* 27 (1940): 3–28.

Reardon, Carol. *Pickett's Charge in History and Memory.* Chapel Hill: University of North Carolina Press, 1997.

———. *With a Sword in One Hand and Jomini in the Other: The Problem of Military Thought in the Civil War North.* Chapel Hill: University of North Carolina Press, 2012.

———. "Writing Battle History: The Challenge of Memory." *Civil War History* 53, no. 3 (September 2007): 252–263.

Resch, John P. "Federal Welfare for Revolutionary War Veterans." *Social Service Review* 56, no. 2 (June 1982): 171–195.

———. *Suffering Soldiers: Revolutionary War Veterans, Moral Sentiment, and Political Culture in the Early Republic.* Amherst: University of Massachusetts Press, 1999.

Richardson, Heather Cox. *The Greatest Nation of the Earth.* Cambridge: Harvard University Press, 1997.

Robertson, James I. *Soldiers Blue and Gray.* Columbia: University of South Carolina Press, 1988.

Robins, Glenn M. "Race, Repatriation, and Galvanized Rebels: Union Prisoners and the Exchange Question in Deep South Prison Camps." *Civil War History* 53, no. 2 (June 2007).

Robinson, Doane. "Early Days in Potter County." Address in Gettysburg, South Dakota, 9 April 1923, in *South Dakota Historical Collections* 12 (1924): 265–266.

Rohrbaugh, W. J. *The Alcoholic Republic: An American Tradition.* New York: Oxford University Press, 1979.

———. "Who Fought for the North?" *Journal of American History* 73, no. 3 (December 1986): 695–701.

Rosenbaum, Betty B. "The Relationship Between War and Crime in the United States." *Journal of Criminal Law and Criminology* 30, no. 5 (January-February 1940): 722–740.

Rosenberg, Charles. *The Cholera Years: The United States in 1832, 1849, and 1866.* Chicago: University of Chicago Press, 1962.

Ross, Sam. *The Empty Sleeve: A Biography of Lucius Fairchild.* Madison: State Historical Society of Wisconsin, 1964.

Rotblat, Cameron. "Last in the Hearts of Their Countrymen: Union Naval Veterans and the Struggle for Naval Memory." Unpublished seminar paper, Yale University, 2012.

Royster, Charles. *The Destructive War: William Tecumseh Sherman, Stonewall Jackson, and the Americans.* New York: Alfred A. Knopf, 1991.

———. *A Revolutionary People at War: The Continental Army and American Character, 1775–1783.* Chapel Hill: University of North Carolina Press, 1979.

Salecker, Gene Eric. *Disaster on the Mississippi: The Sultana Explosion, April 27, 1865.* Annapolis, Maryland: Naval Institute Press, 1996.

Sanders, Charles. *While in the Hands of the Enemy: Military Prisons of the Civil War.* Baton Rouge: Louisiana State University Press, 2005.

Sandow, Robert M. *Deserter Country: Civil War Opposition in the Pennsylvania Appalachians.* New York: Fordham University Press, 2009.

Sauers, Richard Allen. *Fighting Them Over: How the Veterans Remembered Gettysburg in the Pages of the* National Tribune. Baltimore: Butternut & Blue, 1998.

———. "John B. Bachelder: Government Historian of the Battle of Gettysburg." *Gettysburg Magazine* 3 (July 1990): 115–127.

———. *"To Care for Him Who Has Borne the Battle": A Research Guide to Civil War Material in the* National Tribune. Jackson, Kentucky: History Shop Press, 1995.

Savage, Kirk. *Standing Soldiers, Kneeling Slaves: Race, War, and Monument in Nineteenth-Century America.* Princeton: Princeton University Press, 1997.

Scarry, Elaine. *The Body in Pain: The Making and Unmaking of the World.* New York: Oxford University Press 1985.

Schildt, John. *Roads to Antietam.* Chewsville, Maryland: Antietam Publications, 1985.

Schivelbusch, Wolfgang. *The Culture of Defeat: On National Trauma, Mourning, and Recovery.* New York: Metropolitan Books, 2003.

Scott, Sean A. *A Visitation of God: Northern Civilians Interpret the Civil War.* New York: Oxford University Press, 2011.

Sears, Stephen W. *Chancellorsville.* New York: Houghton Mifflin Co., 1996.

Sellars, Richard West. "Pilgrim Places: Civil War Battlefields, Historic Preservation, and

America's First National Military Parks, 1863–1900." *Cultural Resource Management Journal* (Winter 2005): 23–52.

Severo, Richard, and Lewis Milford. *The Wages of War: When America's Soldiers Came Home, From Valley Forge to Vietnam.* New York: Simon & Schuster, 1989.

Sewall, Richard B. *The Vision of Tragedy.* New Haven: Yale University Press, 1959.

Shaffer, Donald R. *After the Glory: The Struggles of Black Civil War Veterans.* Lawrence: University Press of Kansas, 2004.

Shay, Jonathan. *Achilles in Vietnam: Combat Trauma and the Undoing of Character.* New York: Scribner, 1994.

———. *Odysseus in America: Combat Trauma and the Trials of Homecoming.* New York: Simon & Schuster, 2003.

Sheehan-Dean, Aaron. "The Long Civil War: A Historiography of the Consequences of the Civil War." *Virginia Magazine of History and Biography* 119, no. 2 (2011): 107–153.

Sheets, Georg R. *The Grand Review: The Civil War Continues to Shape America.* York, Pennsylvania: Bold Print, 2000.

Shultz, David. "Gulian V. Weir's 5th U.S. Artillery, Battery C." *Gettysburg Magazine* 18 (1998): 77–95.

Sievers, Harry J. *Benjamin Harrison: Hoosier President.* Indianapolis: Bobbs-Merrill Co., 1968.

———. *Benjamin Harrison: Hoosier Statesman.* New York: University Publishers, 1959.

Silber, Nina. *Daughters of the Union: Northern Women Fight the Civil War.* Cambridge: Harvard University Press, 2005.

———. *Gender and the Sectional Conflict.* Chapel Hill: University of North Carolina Press, 2008.

———. *The Romance of Reunion: Northerners and the South, 1865–1900.* Chapel Hill: University of North Carolina Press, 1993.

Silkenat, David. *Moments of Despair: Suicide, Divorce, and Debt in Civil War Era North Carolina.* Chapel Hill: University of North Carolina Press, 2011.

Simpson, John A. *S. A. Cunningham and the Confederate Heritage.* Athens: University of Georgia Press, 1994.

Simpson, Marc, ed. *Winslow Homer: Paintings of the Civil War.* San Francisco: Fine Arts Museum of San Francisco, 1988.

Skocpol, Theda. *Protecting Soldiers and Mothers.* Cambridge: Harvard University Press, 1992.

Smith, Michael Thomas. *The Enemy Within: Fears of Corruption in the Civil War North.* Charlottesville: University of Virginia Press, 2011.

Smith, Timothy B. *A Chickamauga Memorial: The Establishment of America's First Civil War National Military Park.* Knoxville: University of Tennessee Press, 2009.

————. *The Golden Age of Battlefield Preservation: The Decade of the 1890s and the Establishment of America's First Five Military Parks*. Knoxville: University of Tennessee Press, 2008.

Smith, Timothy L. *Togus, Down in Maine: The First National Veterans Home*. Charleston, South Carolina: Arcadia Publishing, 1998.

Socolofsky, Homer E., and Allan B. Spetter. *The Presidency of Benjamin Harrison*. Lawrence: University Press of Kansas, 1987.

Starr, Stephen Z. "The Grand Old Regiment." *Wisconsin Magazine of History* 48, no. 1 (1964): 21–31.

Stellhorn, Paul A., and Michael J. Birkner, eds. *The Governors of New Jersey, 1664–1974*. Trenton: New Jersey Historical Commission, 1982.

Sternhell, Yael A. *Routes of War: The World of Movement in the Confederate South*. Cambridge: Harvard University Press, 2012.

Stilgebour, Cece, and Ruth Stilgebour, comps. *Gettysburg, South Dakota—75th Anniversary, July 11–12, 1958*. Pierre, South Dakota: State Publisher, 1958.

Styles, Sean M. *Stones River National Battlefield Historic Resource Study*. Washington, D.C.: Government Printing Office, 2004.

Summers, Mark Wahlgren. *A Dangerous Stir: Fear, Paranoia, and the Making of Reconstruction*. Chapel Hill: University of North Carolina Press, 2009.

Sutherland, Daniel E. *A Savage Conflict: The Decisive Role of Guerrillas in the American Civil War*. Chapel Hill: University of North Carolina Press, 2009.

Swan, James B. *Chicago's Irish Legion: The 90th Illinois Volunteers in the Civil War*. Carbondale: Southern Illinois University Press, 2009.

————. *Rum, Romanism, and Rebellion: The Making of a President, 1884*. Chapel Hill: University of North Carolina Press, 2000.

Tappan, Franklin D. *The Passing of the Grand Army of the Republic*. Worcester, Massachusetts: Commonwealth Press, 1939.

Taylor, Kate. "Veterans of Iraq War, Some Argue, Also Deserve a Parade." *New York Times*, 7 February 2012.

Thackery, David T. *A Light and Uncertain Hold: A History of the Sixty-Sixth Ohio Volunteer Infantry*. Kent, Ohio: Kent State University Press, 1999.

Trail, Susan W. "Remembering Antietam: Commemoration and Preservation of a Civil War Battlefield." Ph.D. diss., University of Maryland, College Park, 2005.

Trenerry, Walter N. "Last Campaign of the Civil War: Aged Minnesota Veteran Takes on the GAR." *Minnesota History* (Winter 1980): 133–140.

————. "When the Boys Came Home." *Minnesota History* (June 1963): 287–297.

Vinovskis, Maris. *Toward a Social History of the American Civil War: Exploratory Essays*. Cambridge: Cambridge University Press, 1990.

Vogel, Jeffrey E. "Redefining Reconciliation: Confederate Veterans and the Southern Responses to Federal Civil War Pensions." *Civil War History* 51, no. 1 (2005).

Walters, Ronald G. *American Reformers, 1815–1860*. New York: Hill & Wang, 1978.

Warren, Craig A. *Scars to Prove It: The Civil War Soldier and American Fiction*. Kent, Ohio: Kent State University Press, 2009.

Warren, Joyce W. *Fanny Fern: An Independent Woman*. New Brunswick, New Jersey: Rutgers University Press, 1994.

Warren, Robert Penn. *The Legacy of the Civil War*. New York: Random House, 1961.

Waskie, Anthony. *Philadelphia and the Civil War: Arsenal of the Union*. Charleston, South Carolina: History Press, 2011.

Waugh, Joan. *US Grant: American Hero, American Myth*. Chapel Hill: University of North Carolina Press, 2009.

Weber, Jennifer L. *Copperheads: The Rise and Fall of Lincoln's Opponents in the North*. New York: Oxford University Press, 2006.

Wecter, Dixon. *When Johnny Comes Marching Home*. Boston: Houghton Mifflin Co., 1944.

Weeks, Jim. *Gettysburg: Memory, Market, and an American Shrine*. Princeton: Princeton University Press, 2004.

Weigley, Russell F. *Quartermaster General of the Union Army: A Biography of M. C. Meigs*. New York: Columbia University Press, 1958.

Wei-Siang Hsieh, Wayne. *West Pointers and the Civil War: The Old Army in War and Peace*. Chapel Hill: University of North Carolina Press, 2009.

Wells, Cheryl A. *Civil War Time: Temporality and Identity in America, 1861–1865*. Athens: University of Georgia Press, 2005.

Wiebe, Robert. *The Search for Order, 1877–1920*. New York: Hill & Wang, 1967.

Wiley, Bell Irvin. *The Life of Billy Yank: The Common Soldier of the Union*. Indianapolis: Bobbs-Merrill Co., 1952.

———. *The Life of Johnny Reb: The Common Soldier of the Confederacy*. Indianapolis: Bobbs-Merrill Co., 1943.

Wilkinson, Warren. *Mother, May You Never See the Sights I Have Seen: The Fifty-Seventh Massachusetts Veteran Volunteers in the Last Year of the Civil War*. New York: Harper & Row, 1990.

Wilson, Charles Reagan. *Baptized in Blood: The Religion of the Lost Cause, 1865–1920*. Athens: University of Georgia Press, 1987.

Wilson, Christopher Kent. "Winslow Homer's *The Veteran in a New Field*: A Study of the Harvest Metaphor and Popular Culture." *American Art Journal* 17 (1985).

Winter, Jay. *Remembering War: The Great War and Historical Memory in the Twentieth Century*. New Haven: Yale University Press, 2006.

———. *Sites of Memory, Sites of Mourning: The Great War in European Cultural History.* Cambridge: Cambridge University Press, 1998.

Winter, Jay, and Emmanuel Sivan, eds. *War and Remembrance in the Twentieth Century.* Cambridge: Cambridge University Press, 2001.

Witt, John Fabian. *Lincoln's Code: The Laws of War in American History.* New York: Free Press, 2012.

Wood, Gordon S. *The Creation of the American Republic, 1776–1787.* Chapel Hill: University of North Carolina Press, 1998.

Wood, Peter H. *Near Andersonville: Winslow Homer's Civil War.* Cambridge: Harvard University Press, 2010.

Woodworth, Steven E. *While God Is Marching On: The Religious World of Civil War Soldiers.* Lawrence: University Press of Kansas, 2001.

Writers Program of the Works Progress Administration in New Jersey. *New Jersey: A Guide to Its Past and Present.* New York: Stratford Press, 1939.

Yott, Robert E. *From Soldiers' Home to Medical Center: A Glance at the 125 Year History of the Bath Soldiers' Home.* Bath, New York: Robert E. Yott, 2006.

Young, Alfred. *The Shoemaker and the Tea Party: Memory and the American Revolution.* Boston: Beacon Press, 1999.

Zenzen, Joan M. *Battling for Manassas: The Fifty-Year Preservation Struggle at Manassas National Battlefield Park.* University Park: Pennsylvania State University Press, 1998.

Zinn, John G. *The Mutinous Regiment: The Thirty-Third New Jersey in the Civil War.* Jefferson, North Carolina: McFarland & Company, 2005.

IMAGE CREDITS

———❦———

Frontispiece: Library of Congress, 1865.

Plate 1: Library of Congress, 1865.

Plate 2: Adams County Historical Society, Gettysburg, Pennsylvania, 1930.

Plate 3: Going Home, Julian Scott, Private Collection, Photo © Christie's Images/ Bridgeman Images, 1887.

Plate 4: R. Newell, Library of Congress, 1865.

Plate 5: Vincent Colyer, *National Cyclopaedia of American Biography* (New York: James T. White & Co., 1897), 7:541.

Plate 6: William Sargent, Bundy & Williams, Library of Congress, 1861–1865.

Plate 7: Calvin Bates, Library of Congress, 1864–1865.

Plate 8: Library of Congress, 1884.

Plate 9: The Pension Claim Agent, Eastman Johnson, Mildred Anna Williams Collection, Museum of Fine Arts, San Francisco, 1867.

Plate 10: [J. C. Gobrecht], *History of the National Home for Disabled Volunteer Soldiers: With a Complete Guide Book to the Central Home at Dayton, Ohio* (Dayton, Ohio: United Brethren Printing Establishment, 1875), 170.

Plate 11: Adams County Historical Society, Gettysburg, Pennsylvania, 1913.

Plate 12: Harris & Ewing, Library of Congress, 1931.

Plate 13: H. N. (Bert) Woolson Collection on Albert Woolson, WCMss12, Whitman College and Northwest Archives.

INDEX